HARVARD HISTORICAL STUDIES · 169

Published under the auspices
of the Department of History
from the income of the
Paul Revere Frothingham Bequest
Robert Louis Stroock Fund
Henry Warren Torrey Fund

YOUTH IN THE FATHERLESS LAND

War Pedagogy, Nationalism, and Authority in Germany, 1914–1918

ANDREW DONSON

HARVARD UNIVERSITY PRESS

Cambridge, Massachusetts, and London, England

2010

Library of Congress Cataloging-in-Publication Data

Donson, Andrew.
   Youth in the fatherless land : war pedagogy, nationalism, and authority in Germany, 1914–1918 / Andrew Donson.
      p. cm.   —   (Harvard historical studies ; 169)
   Includes bibliographical references and index.
   ISBN 978-0-674-04983-3
   1. World War, 1914–1918—Social aspects—Germany.   2. Youth—Germany—Social conditions—20th century.   3. Youth—Germany—History—20th century.   4. War and society—Germany—History—20th century.   5. Nationalism—Germany—History—20th century.   I. Title.
   D524.7.G8D66 2010
   940.3'430835—dc22   2009041244

To my parents,
Gail Grollman
Theodore Donson

Contents

Illustrations, Figures, and Tables

Tables

Acknowledgments

The joy of writing history is being part of a collective project, and I am grateful to have had colleagues, family, and friends who tenderly supported this endeavor. Geoff Eley and Kathleen Canning advised me steadily through its revisions. Giving me encouragement at the University of Michigan were also Scott Spector, H. D. Cameron, Daniel Saferstein, Holde Borcherts, and Sonya Rose. Jeffrey Wilson remained a most loyal friend and intellectual companion while he extended his encyclopedic knowledge of German history. Ian McNeely, Katherine Pence, Ellen Willow, Jordan Shapiro, Jeffrey Rothstein, Andy Evans, Mia Lee, and Mary Wheeler challenged me to take my subject but not myself seriously. My arguments were cultivated by colleagues in seminars and writing groups: Robin Judd, Timothy Kaiser, Edward Mathieu, Julie Stubbs, Isaac Land, K. O. Chong, and Amanda Bailey at the University of Michigan; Timothy McMahon, Mary Conley, Sean Field, Alan Singer, Barbara Fox, Jim Marten, and Rebecca Wittmann at Marquette University; and Brian Bunk, José Hernández, Tobias Nagl, Maureen Gallagher, Chris Appy, and Catherine Epstein in the Five-College Faculty Seminar in History in Amherst, Massachusetts. My interpretations were also helped by colleagues who reviewed sections of this book at various stages: Reinhard Rürup, Jürgen Kocka, Dirk Schumann, Bradley Naranch, Frank Trommler, Stefan Goebel, James Albisetti, Maureen Healy, Bryan Ganaway, Till van Rhaden, Harold Ross, Charles Maier, Ute Frevert, M. J. Maynes, Belinda Davis, Ari Sammartino, Ann Taylor Allen, Christina Benninghaus, and the reviewer for Harvard University Press. A long and thoughtful commentary by an anonymous reviewer at the *Journal of Modern History* fundamentally changed how I thought about youth in the First World War. I am especially indebted to both Derek Linton, who generously read the entire manuscript, and the anonymous reviewer for the Harvard Historical Studies for their sharp criticisms and suggestions that led to the final structure of this book. My colleagues in German and Scandinavian Studies and the Department of History at the University of Massachusetts Amherst created a supportive and inspiring environment, more wonderful than I ever expected.

Sections of this book were first published in the following articles and appear with the permission of the publishers: "Why Did German Youth Become Fascists? Nationalist Males Born 1900 to 1908 in War and Revolution," *Social History* 31 (2006): 337–358 (http://www.informaworld.com); "Models for Young Nationalists and Militarists: Youth Literature in the First World War," *German Studies Review* 27 (2004): 575–594; and "From War Pedagogy to Reform Pedagogy: Education and Youth Reform before 1914 and the Mobilization for War in Germany," in *Raising Citizens in the "Century of the Child": Child-Rearing and Education in the United States and Central Europe in the Twentieth Century,* ed. Dirk Schumann (New York: Berghahn Books, forthcoming).

I was fortunate to receive financial support from the German Academic Exchange Service (DAAD), the Spencer Foundation, the Mellon Foundation, the Centre de Recherche of the Historial de la Grande Guerre, the College of Humanities and Fine Arts at the University of Massachusetts Amherst, and the Department of History and the Rackham School of Graduate Studies at the University of Michigan (Ann Arbor).

Above all, I wish to thank my family—Erin, Nicole, Emma, Oliver, Marvel, Keith, Carol, Jon, my mother, my father, and, in memoriam, Bill—for their unconditional support. Among other things, my father taught me to value clarity and omit needless words; my mother, the schoolteacher extraordinaire, gave me her pedagogical wisdom. Nicole extended her generous heart, and her good humor made me laugh and see the positive even when things were the worst. Erin patiently answered my questions on style, and her eyes brightened and filled me with joy whenever I talked about this book. When she wasn't there, thoughts of her made me smile and get back to work.

YOUTH IN THE FATHERLESS LAND

Introduction

Just as [the Russians] destroyed everything in East Prussia, so should our troops in Russia destroy and kill everything. . . . Just as the Russians treat our prisoners and lead them into icy fields where they get nothing to eat or drink, so I'd like the Russians to get it still much worse. . . . I would like to demolish all ships and destroy the weak English army and thereby win the despotism of the English. . . . Then we will be the rulers of the world.

—*Original composition by an anonymous elementary school boy, 1915*

I began the research for this book naïvely assuming that adults during the First World War shielded youths and schoolchildren from crass jingoism, violence, and radical politics. I discovered quite the opposite: educational curricula and popular youth literature during the war regularly glorified military violence; and in schools, recreational groups, and military youth companies, teachers and other mentors encouraged a chauvinism that was on occasion shockingly bellicose. Most youths would remain firmly committed to the war until its end. But after 1915 growing ranks of these young people refused to dignify German military power and the monarchical political order. They too would endorse violence, though against the German regime and its war rather than enemy nations. Some illegally distributed propaganda to overthrow the state in a proletarian revolution. Many more snubbed the strident calls for patriotic sacrifice and resorted to crime in order to survive the terrible deprivation after 1915.

After 1918 most German youths went on to lead uneventful lives, but hundreds of thousands grew up inured to violence and, in their bitterness over the disastrous defeat, turned to fascist groups. In early 1919 middle-class male teenagers who had never fired a weapon during the war rushed to join counterrevolutionary paramilitary groups. Within a decade males in the birth cohort never conscripted during the war would make up nearly half the members of the Nazi Party, the SA, the Stahlhelm, and other right-wing paramilitary organizations. Others equally deprived during the war embraced radical-left organizations after 1918 because they believed that the leaders of the Social Democratic Party had sold out the working class to the war for their own political gain and then accepted reforms during the revolution that were incomplete. These youths increasingly carried out the left's extreme campaigns, such as the Spartacist uprising in 1919 and the acts of sabotage by the Communist Party in the 1920s. Most accounts of the violence and radicalism in postwar German politics have addressed the motivations of these youths only tangentially, emphasizing mostly the inability of the angry, disaffected soldiers to assimilate into civilian society. But close to half of the male agents in right- and left-wing paramilitary groups after 1918 were in fact too young to have been conscripted during the war. This book, a comprehensive history of German youths and schoolchildren during the war, tells the story of their radicalization, which crystallized during the revolution of November 1918.[1]

This book also shows how the First World War ushered in the great era of mobilizing youths and schoolchildren for extreme political movements and experiments in state building. Long before 1914, young people had of course been targets of reformers and revolutionaries. Hoping to raise pious, compliant, and diligent subjects who feared God as well as their sovereign, German monarchs during the Enlightenment had been among the first to found free and compulsory elementary schools for the masses. Over the course of the nineteenth century, reformers throughout the Western world established a host of other institutions, from sports clubs to reformatories, to turn out reliable young citizens or nationalists. But none of these projects integrated female or male youths under 20 years of age (the age of conscription in Germany before 1914) into the violence of war. Furthermore, none before 1914 expected them to endure such awful deprivation in the name of patriotism. The mass mobilization of youths, the demise of the family due to conscription, and the observation that millions of children willingly went hungry for a military victory radicalized how politicians on the extremes approached youths after 1918. For example, the Hitler Youth, founded in 1926, had the mission of mobilizing along the model of autonomous groups such as the Wandervögel (Wandering Birds), which had devoted themselves assiduously to supporting the war. Armed with rhetoric that glorified war and generational conflict, including the legend that pacifist parents on the home front had lost the war, the Hitler Youth helped carry out the National Socialist revolution after 1933 by rivaling and in some cases triumphing over families as the supreme institution shaping the younger generation. On the other end of the political spectrum, Lenin came to recognize the power of marshalling youths through his close association in 1916 and 1917 with the exiled Willi Münzenberg, who led oppositional Socialist youths in Germany in their spirited attack on the war, the government, and the Majority Social Democratic Party. The Komosomol, the mass Bolshevik youth organization founded in November 1918 with the goal of carrying out social revolution, proved to be the key institution providing an ideologically reliable cohort that revolutionized Soviet culture after 1928.[2]

This comprehensive approach to forming youths and children politically, a hallmark of dictatorships in the early twentieth century, became radicalized during the mobilization for war. However, it had its origins in institutions and practices pioneered before 1914 and in Germany before all other nations and states. By the mid-nineteenth century, the German states were among the first to achieve near-universal literacy in their drive to use elementary schools to create loyal subjects. Although progressive reformers maligned the Prussian elementary school for its rigid drill methods and its exclusion of the working class from access to secondary education, it was supremely successful in teaching millions on the cheap. Its model was adopted around the world. Germany was also the nation that, after the traditional apprenticeship system unraveled during industrialization, most vigorously addressed the problem of young wage workers. Fearing that autonomous teenagers were susceptible to Socialism and delinquency, reformers created free and compulsory continuation schools *(Fortbildungsschulen)* for working male youths in skilled trades in almost all major cities. This was the first comprehensive, post-elementary schooling for urban teenage boys in any major European nation, and reformers believed it successfully reinserted paternalism into job training. Although authorities and reformers had particular concerns about boys because they would be soldiers and the citizens who could vote for the Social Democratic Party, in the years immediately before the war they began to devote their energy to molding girls as well. Hoping to create healthy, competent, and patriotic wives and mothers, the Prussian state at the turn of the century began offering funds for training in home economics and, in 1913, for physical recreation. Germany also had far more research institutes and pedagogical and psychological journals devoted to youths and children than any other country, and despite the war, its continuation and elementary school systems were the model for the educational reforms England instituted in 1916 and 1918. The abundance of literature on pedagogy and adolescent psychology attested to the German reformers' remarkable zeal to create modern institutions that complemented and in some cases competed with families in raising productive, responsible, and patriotic citizens.[3]

Germany also led the world in founding mass youth organizations whose aims were implicitly political. The sheer number of sport, confessional, patriotic, and Socialist recreation groups in 1914 was unparalleled: whereas in many large German cities over half of all teenage boys were members of a youth association, in no British city did more than 12 percent join clubs, and in France and the United States the percentages were even lower. The high participation in associations sponsored by bitter rivals—the army, the radical right, the Catholic Church, the Protestant churches, the liberal middle class, and the Social Democratic Party—spurred divisive competition for unripe hearts and minds. The rivalry polarized the politics of youth to a degree unseen elsewhere. Before 1914, Germany's Socialist youth organization was by far the largest and best organized by any political party in the world. To combat its growing influence, in 1911 Prussia became the first major state worldwide to subsidize patriotic, sport, and confessional youth associations. Myriad so-called autonomous youth organizations, such as the Socialist Association of Young Workers and the middle-class hiking groups calling themselves Wandervögel, anticipated the Communist and fascist mass youth organizations by establishing the principle that modern society could be rejuvenated only when youths led youths. Nowhere else before 1914 were these autonomous youth associations as widespread as in Germany.[4]

Germany's prewar schools, recreational associations, and youth cultures attracted attention from post-1945 scholars who claimed that they cultivated the gross militarism and nationalism that led to National Socialism. This charge needs to be qualified, however. Before 1914 the military had enormous prestige, and the officials who ran the schools were moderately militarist in their goal of inculcating veneration for the army and the navy. Teachers and school administrators were also nationalist in choosing curricula that celebrated Germany. Excitement about Germany's growing world power was also piqued by the increasingly popular stories written for youths about the colonial and unification wars. Because of the high esteem for the military, tens of thousands of male youths joined recreational associations that taught shooting and organized war games. However, before 1914 almost no teachers or youth workers were militarists in the sense that they glorified war as a virtue in itself or viewed it as the primary means to solve international disputes.

Though arguably most of the middle class supported the arms race and the country's assertion of world economic power, these policies almost never entered school curricula or youth literature. Youths played war games in only a handful of recreational organizations, and even these were arguably benign amusements. Youth war literature made up just a fraction of the book market, and it faced intense criticism from Social Democrats and liberal middle-class reformers alike. It was the outbreak of the war, not prewar imperialism, that exposed youths widely to a militarism and nationalism that exalted war and expected citizens to die for the sake of Germany's territorial expansion and status as a great power.

Many post-1945 scholars also charged that prewar schools and recreational associations reinforced the authoritarianism that was allegedly endemic in German society. This imputation—that elites both subjugated the working class and dominated youths to maintain an unequal class structure—was in many ways true but should not be exaggerated. Germany had one of the world's most spirited educational reform movements, whose champions sought to introduce softer, child-centered teaching methods and to create a school system that gave poor but talented schoolchildren the opportunity for educational advancement. Because the mainstream youth recreational associations competed for members, youths shunned clubs that imposed severe discipline and chose those with activities to their liking. Germany's autonomous youth associations pitted themselves against a putatively corrupt, adult-led society. Still, the numbers in the autonomous associations made up just a fraction of the total in recreational organizations. The evidence overwhelmingly shows that teachers in all levels of schooling could be tyrants who treated their pupils like *Untertanen*—like worthless, obedient subalterns. They used monotonous drill methods that smothered schoolchildren's individuality and thwarted independent, critical thinking. Although the new continuation schools taught useful skills, they extended social controls over youths past age 14. On the eve of the war, the education system fortified the elites' domination by blocking access to full-time schooling past age 14 for all but the wealthiest 5 percent or so of the population. On balance, there was considerable potential for breaking the authoritarianism in schools, but it did not happen to any marked extent until 1914.

The Patriotic Mobilization, 1914–1915

Authoritarian practices waned, and nationalist and militarist content intensified in schools after 1914, because teachers and education officials selectively remembered the joy they felt about the extraordinary political unity when the war broke out. On 4 August 1914, all the political parties agreed to put Germany's interests ahead of their own particular agendas and voted unanimously in the Reichstag in favor of funding the war through bonds. The settlement, called the *Burgfrieden* (literally "fortress peace" but more exactly "party truce"), was also an agreement among the parties to refrain from publicly criticizing the government, the war, and each other. Few in the middle class had expected this cooperation. Until August 1914, the Social Democratic Party, which won over a third of the popular vote in the 1912 Reichstag elections, was vehemently opposed to war. Its leaders argued that the government inequitably taxed the working class to pay for the monstrous arms buildup. They also recognized that workers around the world had common interests, and so they refused to sanction the workers killing each other for the profit of imperialists and arms manufacturers. In the weeks following the assassination in Sarajevo, the Social Democratic Party denounced the "war provokers" and organized antiwar protests that drew hundreds of thousands in the major cities. Most members of the party agreed with the centrist theorist Karl Kautsky that they should work ardently to prevent war. But they also agreed quietly with his principle that in the event of war, particularly one of defense against an autocratic nation like Czarist Russia, they would support the government and hope, resignedly, for a quick and painless victory. Before 1914, however, the Social Democratic Party's support for a defensive war was not well known. More conspicuous was its brash antimilitarist rhetoric, which ended abruptly in August 1914. By supporting the *Burgfrieden,* the Social Democratic Party sanctioned martial law and a gag rule that overnight expunged almost all dissent from the public sphere. Instead, for months political tracts extolled the achievement of unity.[5]

The *Burgfrieden* astonished the public, producing an ebullience comparable in modern German history only to the victory over France in 1870. Thousands of middle-class patriots wrote books, pamphlets, poems, and articles claiming that the new political cooperation was akin to what had happened in France in 1789—that is, a truly popular nationalist mobilization, a liberation of national spirit, had taken place. They were enthusiastic because the war had apparently led politicians to overcome decades of bitter conflicts, united by the simple fact that they were German. Although the Social Democrats were more cautious about claiming the war was positive, they too thought the moment was auspicious. Most supported repelling what in their view were the Russian "half-barbaric hordes" who wanted to impose the "rule of Czarism in Europe." By supporting the war credits, the Social Democrats came out of the political ghetto: government ministers who had earlier ostracized Social Democratic leaders now consulted them and made them optimistic that substantial reforms were soon coming. Reich Interior Minister Clemens von Delbrück's August 1914 meeting with the Social Democrat Eduard David, the future president of the Weimar National Assembly, was the first of the government's many gestures of reconciliation toward a party whose propaganda and membership drives had been illegal only twenty-five years earlier. The good feeling about the political unity grew after the string of military victories in August 1914. At the Belgian fortress city of Liège on 16 August and then at Tannenberg in East Prussia on 30 August, the army repelled its enemies and ensured the war would not be fought on German soil. These victories led to mass parades and celebrations on Sedan Day, the national holiday on 2 September, including flag waving by youths from all milieus, even in staunchly Socialist neighborhoods in Berlin. The expressions of unity and cooperation during these first months of the war produced the legend that would become known as the Spirit of 1914. Preserving this good feeling and the populace's willingness to make fantastic sacrifices in turn became the military and government's conscious strategy to win the war.[6]

The reality in August 1914 was more complex. Authors remembered the elation felt at the announcement of *Burgfrieden* and the large celebrations that took place after the victories. They wrote less about the other days when the mood was gloomy. The declaration of war (on 1 August) provoked zeal among some, particularly middle-class radical nationalists, but apprehension among most. Germans sang patriotic songs and cheered departing soldiers, but they also wept and fretted as they waved good-bye. The public was no longer celebratory after the bloody battle of the Marne in September 1914 and the start of the stalemate on the Western Front. Although most Germans wanted the benefits of victory, few were enthusiastic about fighting a war in which loved ones were going to die. When the Battle of the Marne dispelled the illusion of a short conflict, rural Bavarians and thousands of Socialist youths began to speak out against the war, and the number of silent critics grew.[7]

Still, the apprehension coexisted with resolute support. The war in the West was stalemated, but the army occupied Belgium and strategic regions in France. Furthermore, the campaigns on the Eastern Front in the spring and summer of 1915 were successful. With vast swaths of territory conquered, all but the most cautious military experts believed that victory over Russia was imminent, freeing the army in the East to conquer France. In this situation, few could accept the demands, issued by only a small group of radical Socialists and middle-class peace activists, for an immediate peace without annexations and reparations. Even after 1915, civilians more generally had to ask themselves, why agree to a negotiated peace and give up all Germany had gained when hundreds of thousands of men had already died? Given their sacrifices, why not hold out a little longer for the territorial and financial benefits that would come from a victorious peace?

Because of this persistent hope for victory and the abundant literature referencing the Spirit of 1914 and the *Burgfrieden,* school officials and teachers believed in 1914 and 1915 that almost all Germans were cooperative and enthusiastic and that the appropriate response was to diminish the authoritarian practices in schools and introduce new nationalist and militarist content. When school began after the summer holiday in 1914, administrators encouraged teachers to introduce *war pedagogy (Kriegspädagogik).* This was an improvised curriculum that aimed to make pupils enthusiastic about the war by using child-centered methods from the educational reform movement. Because the populism in the Spirit of 1914 undermined any justification for exacting obedience and combating Social Democracy, severe acts of discipline in schools—liberal use of corporal punishment, slurs by haughty teachers against their pupils, and drill teaching methods that obstructed personal expression—abated. Teachers replaced instruction-by-repetition with free discussion of politics, reading of newspapers, writing of personal essays, recitations of nationalist poetry, celebrations of victories, excursions to war exhibitions, and widespread dismissal of pupils for voluntary patriotic projects. These new activities ended much of the monotony and severity of the old school regime and introduced more variable rhythms. At the same time, they infused the classroom with nationalism and militarism; in all these activities the war and Germany's certain victory were at the forefront. Pupils regularly studied the narratives of the battles and read the heroic letters of soldiers. They adorned their classrooms with maps of the fronts and photographs of generals and celebrated victories by reciting war poems and singing victory songs. On occasion, they calculated the tons of ammunition needed to destroy French divisions at Verdun. They wrote enthusiastically about not only their pretend war games but also the mass killing on the front. Teachers who were previously quiet about patriotism now saw it as their duty to nurture it in their pupils. Those who had earlier kept their radical nationalist ideas out of the classroom now immersed their pupils in the glory of war and German territorial acquisition. Under the *Burgfrieden*, no one could publicly criticize this jingoism. Evidence from over twelve hundred original compositions by schoolchildren in 1915 shows how these practices transmitted militarist and nationalist ideas to youths and reinforced their support for the war and its violence.

The flood of youth war literature into the book market fed the jingoism further. In my survey of over eighty war novels and six hundred war stories that dominated Germany's magazines for youths, ideas of a "holy" war combined with notions of martyrdom to justify the brutality and fearlessness of soldiers. Youth war literature portrayed an exciting war of movement and a home front of celebrations and national harmony—a gross distortion of the ugly war of attrition that increasingly divided the populace. Though written by middle-class adults, these stories represented the war fantasies of a wide spectrum of young readers, both schoolchildren and working youths. Despite bans that were supported across the political spectrum, war penny dreadfuls *(Kriegsschundschriften)*—the excessively nationalist, cheap paperbacks, with lurid descriptions of the front—remained immensely popular even after 1918.

Several factors particular to Germany—the country's vast network of youth associations, its district youth workers *(Kreisjugendpfleger)* with salaries paid by the Prussian state, and its elementary school teachers eager to demonstrate their national loyalty and make education more immediate for their pupils—mobilized millions of youths and schoolchildren for voluntary patriotic labor especially well. Whatever the original motivations of the youths and schoolchildren who sold war bonds, collected recyclables, knit socks, marched in military companies, or worked in agriculture, offices, and hospitals, their activities placed them in a difficult position to oppose the war. State youth workers heeded the insistence of psychologists such as Aloys Fischer, the director of the Pedagogical-Psychological Institute in Munich, that volunteering to work for Germany's belligerent policy reinforced commitment. Beyond providing the essential labor to recycle goods, the schoolchildren advertised the war's legitimacy. Because voluntary activities often went unsupervised, the schoolchildren also found new opportunities to act independently while earning public admiration for their patriotism.

Social Breakdown and Political Radicalization, 1916–1918

This last effect—the increasing autonomy of youths—was a countervailing and paradoxical development in an era of mass mobilization. While teachers, youth workers, and state officials took innovative steps to get youths to aid the war effort and conform to government policy, the conscription by 1916 of approximately 13 million men—two-thirds of Germany's male adults age 18 to 45—increasingly undermined social controls. Fewer and fewer qualified teachers and social workers supervised young people. After 1915 most schools held instruction for just a half-day and in many cases only a third of a day. During the harsh winters of 1916/17 and 1917/18, schools closed for weeks at a time. Even worse for officials trying to maintain the social order, paternal authority was increasingly absent at work; on the street; and in schools, families, and voluntary associations. Depending on the region, 30 to 65 percent of fathers, teachers, policemen, judges, and youth workers were conscripted by 1916. In addition, youths had the inordinate burden of searching for food and coal for as many as twenty hours weekly. Like Germans of all ages, youths worried about loved ones on the front and were distressed by the millions of dead and wounded. Exhausted and lacking adequate footwear, clothing, and nutrition, most young people could no longer participate in voluntary patriotic activities. Quadrupling truancy and crime rates and the first widespread incidence in modern Germany of theft by pubescent gangs were just some of the persistent reminders that the mobilization had faltered by 1916 and that tens of thousands of youths were becoming dangerously independent.[8]

This breakdown in the country's vaunted institutions of social control undermined the war's popular legitimacy and edged Germany toward the precipice of revolution and civil war. Many working youths dismissed the shrill calls to make patriotic sacrifices and hold out for victory. Empowered by absent fathers, closed continuation schools, and high nominal wages in the war industries, male working youths disregarded the calls for thrift and displayed their new status by splurging on consumer pleasures such as the cinema, the pub, and tobacco. In addition, a horrifying realization that hundreds of thousands were dying for the ambitions of imperialists emboldened a group of male and female working teenagers to try to end the war completely. Alienated by the Social Democratic Party's betrayal of antimilitarism and its cooperation with the government in the war, these young people organized illegal grassroots movements for peace and worldwide proletarian revolution and played a major role in fomenting the mass antiwar strikes of April 1917 and January 1918. These teenagers in turn ensured that the future German Communist Party would become a radical protest movement whose dynamism came from involving and representing disenfranchised youths. They stood in stark contrast to the hundreds of thousands of upper-middle-class youths and schoolchildren in the big cities and lower-middle-class ones in the Protestant small cities and countryside who vigorously affirmed the war until its end. These youths continued to march in military companies, knit socks and sweaters for soldiers, recite nationalist war poems in school, and volunteer for patriotic projects such as harvests and recycling drives. Slackening adult supervision and a new sense of their own importance moved boys to stage ever more elaborate war games on the streets, sometimes simulating combat with firearms and guns. Many flaunted the armbands and regalia of their military companies and cultivated an addiction for soldiering, comradeship, and public displays of aggression.

By the end of the war, German politics had become not only polarized and violent but also, on both the left and the right, dependent on the extremism and militancy of male and even some female youths. On the one hand, Germans in this cohort who became Communists—mostly children of left-wing Socialists—believed that the moderate Social Democrats had sold the workers out to the war and had thereby lost their credibility. On the other hand, early Nazis born after 1899 variously recalled the key experiences in their political development as being their stint in a military youth company, their great enthusiasm for military victories and war games, or their feelings of humiliation when the army rejected their attempted enlistment on (often arbitrary) grounds that they were physically or mentally weak. Their attraction to violent right-wing politics after 1918 was a result of their frustration in having trained to defend Germany but never having demonstrated their manhood on the front. For these youths, the mobilization for war invalidated the Victorian masculinity of caution, self-control, and paternal steadiness and legitimized a new manliness of fearlessness, risk-taking, and youthful vigor.[9]

The mobilization for war both challenged and reinforced pre-1914 notions of femininity, creating contradictory models of gender for girls in the war youth generation. Teachers, administrators, youth workers, and authors of youth literature suggested that because boys, as adults, would soon kill and brave death while girls would cope with shortages and nurse wounded men, the war accentuated gender roles. Germany needed more than ever to cultivate in female youths virtues such as selflessness, loyalty, and tenderness. School curricula and youth war literature for girls were accordingly replete with stories about women who withheld all complaints and made extraordinary sacrifice for their country and families. Furthermore, a consequence of increased work burdens during the war and the discrepancy between men's and women's wages was that girls spent less time on the street and in school and more at home, the traditional women's sphere. In families in which a mother took care of the household full time before 1914 but saw her breadwinner husband conscripted during the war, a rational survival strategy was for her to take on wage work outside the home and leave her daughter at home to oversee domestic chores. Both a mother's and her son's earning potentials were twice or more than that of her teenage daughter. This strategy explains why the official number of male teenagers under 17 employed in wage work increased while the number of females the same age decreased and why annual school reports claimed that, because they were supervising younger siblings, more female than male schoolchildren were truant.[10]

However, the education of girls under war pedagogy was similar to and in many cases the same as that of boys. Two-thirds of classrooms were coed, and female teachers who led all-girl classrooms were generally staunch supporters of war pedagogy and, like their male colleagues, exposed their pupils to graphic images of the combat. Surveys, diaries, and school compositions indicate that some girls' knowledge and fascination with the war was as deep as the boys'. Furthermore, the war could paradoxically expand equality and independence for female youths. As in the national and popular wars of the long nineteenth century more generally, women gained more agency and respect, even as the calls for gender differences grew. In their wartime civic activism, adult women founded and expanded recreational associations with such fervor that in many regions membership of girls for the first time exceeded that of boys. All-female spaces like knitting circles and hiking groups sprang up, and girls stepped in to do men's chores, like shoveling snow and hauling coal. Tens of thousands of female teenagers spurned positions in domestic service for higher-wage jobs in the munitions industries, gaining freedom as they escaped from the authority of their mistresses. Above all, girls gained political experience in informal street protest over food and in both the mainstream and oppositional Socialist organizations, which preached and practiced radical equality between the sexes. These trends countered those that accentuated gender differences and domestic roles. The new equality and independence of female youths also contributed to the emerging model of the so-called new woman who both flourished after 1918 and became an object of derision.[11]

The omission of the younger generation from most narratives of the First World War has left the false impression that Germans determined the course of the war in the trenches, General Staff meetings, strike committees, party conferences, and bread lines, but not in schoolhouses, families, or military youth companies. On the basis of numbers alone, however, youths and children mattered profoundly in this first total war in history. In 1916, close to half of the civilians living in Germany were under 18. This was the highest proportion in the history of modern Germany, an effect of mass conscription of adult males in 1914 and two preceding decades of extraordinarily brisk population growth, which skewed the demographics toward a preponderance of youths. In addition, youths and schoolchildren were the civilians who had the most regular contact with a state official (usually a teacher) and the greatest amount of free time to work voluntarily. Facing belligerents who outnumbered them, state officials and patriotic citizens recognized that a demographic group this large and malleable was both an untapped source of labor for the war effort and a potential burden that could divert scarce resources from the army. Indeed, in 1914 and 1915 the German states maintained support for the war in no small part because teachers, reformers, state officials, and social workers were successful in getting youths and schoolchildren to advertise the war, work for it without compensation, and endure its deprivations and hardships. And when adults were increasingly unsuccessful after 1915 in selling the war to the younger generation and providing for their needs, they speeded the erosion of the social order and provoked thousands of youths to agitate for peace and revolution.[12]

Sources and Methods

A claim that the war initiated an ideological and social mobilization of youths unprecedented in history may seem to imply that it also undermined youths' freedom of action and expression. More generally, the history of youth institutions is about how adults shape a younger generation, and if a pedagogical program is successful—I argue that indeed was the case in Germany in 1914 and 1915—then the policy constrains youths' independence. However, the war in many ways *widened* youths' agency. Officials felt it was inappropriate to be severe to youths and schoolchildren when so many happily volunteered for patriotic projects. For their part, teachers under war pedagogy were successful because they recognized and nurtured pupils' active learning, merging the popular nationalism in the Spirit of 1914 with child-centered methods that loosened discipline and rigid hierarchies. The compositions by schoolchildren accordingly showed a broad range of attitudes toward the war, from outright rejection to enthusiastic endorsement of the violence and territorial acquisition. War pedagogy was effective because it reinforced militarism and nationalism and legitimized war in a process that opened, however paradoxically, new opportunities for expression and in some cases even permitted dissent.

Youth agency widened further because conscription reduced surveillance by police and supervision by fathers and teachers, while teenagers who became soldiers or high-wage-earning munitions workers enjoyed higher status. Particularly toward the end of the war, when parents recognized the impending disaster, intergenerational quarrels regularly broke out in middle-class families over the choice of 16- and 17-year-old boys to volunteer for the army. The boys took the more extreme position that fighting for Germany's victory was worth risking death for, and, enabled by teachers, youth workers, and authors of youth literature, they often prevailed. As teenage soldiers, they then enjoyed a status that shielded them from adult criticism over behaviors such as strolling and kissing girls in public. On the other side of the political spectrum, youths were empowered by the high wages and the lack of men in factories. During the strike against the compulsory savings plan in Lower Saxony in April 1916, for example, working boys and girls forced the deputy commanding general to rescind his decree. The absence of men empowered female youths too, such as those who replaced enlisted male teenagers as editors of the middle-class youth movements' journals.

Demonstrating the agency of youths in history is fraught with problems, however. Documents written by youths themselves have the potential to show youths' independent thinking and action, but the number of these sources is small. Youths also produced them under constraints imposed by adults. When writing the allegedly "free" compositions, pupils wanted to please their teachers and doubtlessly concealed opinions. Just two wartime diaries by youths exist of any notable length and detail, and both show a tension between what the young authors believed and what their parents and teachers wanted them to write. All other extant journals exhibited what the adults generally expected from so-called war diaries by youths: chronicles of the war victories and descriptions of weapons like 42-cm howitzers, not catalogs of personal suffering and ambivalence about the war. Only a few hundred youths wrote articles for the journals of the middle-class youth movement, and those who turned against the war in this group alarmed authorities and provoked vigilant censorship. The recollections in memoirs and oral histories, potentially useful sources for understanding agency, are highly selective. For example, in the memoirs written by early Nazi Party members and collected by Theodore Abel in 1934, authors born from 1900 to 1908 emphasized memories of war pedagogy, military youth companies, and voluntary patriotic labor in large part because they lived in a culture of defeat that vilified peacemakers and glorified war.[13]

Since sources written by youths are in such short supply, most claims in this book are, in the end, less about the agency of youths than about the processes that made them appear to be chauvinist, pacifist, quiescent, cooperative, independent, enthusiastic, annoying, haughty, or dangerous. This book is as much about schoolchildren and youths as about the fears and aspirations of teachers, policemen, youth workers, newspaper reporters, government officials, military officers, and authors of youth literature. The words of adults—whether they were about the Spirit of 1914, annexations and a military victory, or the call for mass strikes and a negotiated peace—circumscribed how youths understood the war. The arguments about why youths volunteered for the war, actively protested against it, or resigned themselves to hardship are inductions based on the mass of evidence about the policies, practices, institutions, and observations of adults. Some may object that this approach yields some arguments that are suggestive and not definitive. Leaving them out, however, would have not only effaced whole realms of experience but also left out a key set of likely reasons for the political radicalism of the war youth generation.

Like youths, adults faced constraints on their agency, particularly on what they wrote under the wartime regime of censorship, but the restrictions were less severe than one might expect. The German states explicitly requested sober assessments from the police, school directors, and district youth workers. These reports grew briefer during the years of the deprivation, though no less revealing of the social breakdown and political radicalization. Furthermore, although martial law curbed freedom of the press, military and government censors could not review even a fraction of the 3,600 daily newspapers and the tens of thousands of books and journals, let alone the estimated 28 billion letters sent to and from the front. Military intelligence, not politics, was the censors' primary concern. In general, officials expected the press to support the *Burgfrieden* and to censor itself on political matters. Almost all editors cooperated. From August 1914 to March 1916, only four liberal or left-liberal newspapers were censored. Except for the Social Democratic newspapers, twenty-three of which were censored just 149 times, almost all of the sources used in this book were simply not on the examiners' radar screen. Oppositional Socialist youth newspapers were under surveillance but also underground, and the authors did not care what the censors thought. What was said and not said in the sources had more to do with what schoolchildren, teachers, youth workers, authors of youth literature, and other adults expected of each other during wartime. Loyalty to loved ones on the front or fear of being ostracized by peers undoubtedly restrained antiwar views. But evidence of a broad commitment to mobilizing youths through literature, war pedagogy, and voluntary patriotic labor was not an artifice of government censorship.[14]

In addition to showing constraints on behavior and constructions of meaning, this study uses ideal types—that is, categories or typical cases that permit evaluation and comparison, even though they never correspond to an immeasurably more various reality. Though based on objective measures of age, employment, and education and not some reductive Marxist or other class theory, these classifications of people were malleable, and their meanings during the early twentieth century changed depending on the teachers, politicians, youth workers, and state officials who used them. In some usages, *youths (Jugend)* consisted of an amorphous group that included schoolchildren, teenagers, and university students. In other usages, youths were specifically boys age 14 to 20 (18 during the war because the army lowered the conscription age), or girls age 14 to their early 20s (girls passed no state institutional marker like conscription, and the age of marriage was various).

This study is primarily about the *war youth generation,* a term coined in the early 1930s. In this book it designates those born from 1900 to 1908—that is, boys and girls who were schoolchildren or working youths at the outbreak of the war but (for boys) did not attend university by 1918 and with some exceptions were never conscripted. (The handful of boys born in 1900, 1901, and

1902 who volunteered needed permission from their parents. Boys born in 1900 began to be conscripted in the summer of 1918, but few ever saw combat.) The war youth generation has also been understood more broadly to include those born as early as 1897, some of whom were still in secondary school in 1914, and as late as 1912, who began elementary school in 1918. In early-twentieth-century usage, *elementary school children* designated the 93 percent of working- and middle-class pupils age 6 to 14 who attended the public schools (*Volksschulen, Gemeindeschulen*, etc.) and the 7 percent who attended the private ones *(Vorschulen). Secondary school children* (for boys, *Gymnasiasten, Oberrealschüler*, etc., and for girls, *Schülerinnen* in the *Lyzeen* or their equivalent) designated the elite and overwhelmingly male 2 to 7 percent of each age cohort who had the privilege of continuing their education full time from age 14 until graduation at age 19 or 20. Most secondary school children were *middle-class (bürgerlich)*, the children of clergy, state officials, industrialists, wealthy merchants, or professionals like doctors, or, if they could afford the tuition (which most could not), *lower-middle-class (mittelständisch, kleinbürgerlich*, etc.), the children of artisans, small shopkeepers, small landowning farmers, and lower-level bureaucrats like elementary school teachers.

Working youths (arbeitende Jugend) referred to boys and girls who had ended their education, usually at age 14, and entered the commercial, artisanal, industrial, or service trades as apprentices or wage earners. The category of *working-class youths (Arbeiterjugend)* referred to a subset of working youths, the children of parents who worked in factories and were the primary constituency for membership in the Social Democratic youth organizations. The category excluded lower-middle-class working youths, such as boys and girls who worked in the commercial and service trades. This last group had an ambiguous position. They sometimes earned less than factory workers, but their jobs required them to dress well, speak foreign languages, master the art of politeness, and in general function in the social, political, and cultural world of the middle class. While young industrial workers drank in the pub, these youths took dates to cafés, restaurants, racetracks, cabarets, and theater. Active in sport and patriotic associations, they became the most spirited members of military youth companies among working teenagers in the fall of 1914.

These ideal types do not capture the reality that a handful of working-class youths received scholarships to attend secondary schools; that many members of the Social Democratic youth organizations were the children of middle-class intellectuals; and that some working-class youths were in the military companies, even after 1915. Still, such cases were the exceptions to the rule, and the ideal types make it possible to generalize about youths' experiences.[15]

This book is about German youths in the federal states of Prussia, Saxony, and Bavaria, the Hanseatic city of Hamburg, and, to some a extent, the smaller states of Württemberg, Baden, and Thuringia. It excludes the German-speaking regions of Austria-Hungary, even though elementary and secondary school teachers there read German-language literature on reform pedagogy and used similar methods and curricula. In Linz, Vienna, and other cities, recreational organizations like the Wandervögel had affiliates, and youths read books published in Germany. However, nationalism and its influence on youths had a wholly different set of meanings and developments in the supranational Austro-Hungarian Empire. In Germany, nationalists worked with the state to create youth institutions, like continuation schools that would raise an ideologically reliable cohort, one prepared, if necessary, to fight a European war. By contrast, German-speaking nationalists in Austria, Moravia, and Bohemia worked *against* the state, seeking to carve out their own nation-state from the supranational state by "reclaiming" youths—that is, by turning those youths whose nationality was ambiguous into Germans, both linguistically and culturally, through schooling and other practices. That was not the case in Germany, where even youths in Alsace-Lorraine who had descended from French speakers had become linguistically German and generally identified themselves as citizens of Germany. The contestations over youths in Germany were more related to disagreements about imperialism, social justice, economic efficiency, law and order, political equality, and the degree to which a citizen would accept war as a means of resolving international conflict and death as a worthwhile sacrifice for German world power. State support for nationalism at the outbreak of the war intensified in Germany as it related to youths, and the war satisfied the long-standing hopes of nationalists who wanted everyone to support their conception of an imperialist nation-state free of political conflict. However, after 1915 in Germany, rising antiwar sentiment and then defeat and revolution crushed the hopes of nationalists and polarized the politics of youth. Austria-Hungary had nearly the opposite development. At the outbreak of the war, the supranational state temporarily quelled nationalist agitation and promoted the image of an imperial child without nationality. Defeat and revolution led to a German-speaking nation-state in Austria, fulfilling the goals of the Habsburg nationalists and beginning a new era there of making youths German.[16]

Because research on youths in the other belligerents is still limited, arguments about German particularity can be only provisional. The scholarship suggests, however, that although all the belligerents introduced a school curriculum that focused on the war to various extents, German teachers were especially enthusiastic because they held the army in particularly high esteem, wanted colonies that the other nations already had, and, if they taught in an elementary school, saw war pedagogy as a way to improve their lowly status. Germany was also remarkable because the war eroded the previously authoritarian relationship between pupils and teachers. Youth war literature could be graphically violent everywhere, but whereas French books claimed the war was necessary to defend the rights of man, destroy German militarism, and maintain peace, German books claimed the war was justified by France's and Great Britain's refusal to recognize Germany's right to be a world power. In all the belligerents with the exception of the United States, mass conscription reduced male authority enormously, and the absence, mutilation, and death of men took an immeasurable emotional toll. However, youths in Germany but not in France (the occupied zone aside), Great Britain, and the United States were traumatized by starvation, cold, physical exhaustion, and, worst of all, defeat and revolution. Autobiographies attest that these last two conditions were in particular necessary for the rise of fascism and radical communism. It was always possible that things would have been different if Germany had won the war and the Kaiser remained in power, but the war ended in a defeat and a revolution, both of which crystallized the political radicalism nurtured during the war.

Still, most youths did not become fascists or radical communists. In fact, most in the war youth generation eschewed violence, bellicose nationalism, and extreme political ideologies both during and after the war. They were simply concerned with getting enough to eat and staying warm and hoped desperately for a good peace. Like the vast majority of German adults in 1919, they supported a moderate, nonviolent Republican regime. The following chapters tell their war story as well.

1

The Pedagogy of Obedience
and Its Critics

Autobiographers, novelists, and British and American observers before 1914 as well as scholars after 1945 regularly disparaged adults in imperial Germany for treating youths like delinquents in cruel reformatories. They denounced the numerous institutions that aimed not only to mold schoolchildren into obedient, uncritical subjects but also to raise youths, particularly working-class teenagers, to accept the class structure and, in Prussia and Saxony, the constitutions that disenfranchised them. Teachers punished pupils physically, overwhelmed them with homework, spit invective, and taught through methods that aped military drills, stifled creativity, and undermined critical thinking. Secondary school teachers in particular terrorized boys, and in a few highly publicized cases, they allegedly moved some to commit suicide. The entire school system preserved the power of Germany's elites by obstructing social mobility; secondary schools, which opened graduates to the universities and the key positions of power, were available mostly to boys and some girls from the wealthiest 5 percent or so of families. An explicit goal of the reformers who founded the compulsory, post-elementary continuation schools was to put young workers under an official with the right to punish transgressions in the hope of diverting them from Socialism and its trenchant criticisms of the regime. The rigidity was in social realms beyond schooling as well. With assistance from state officials who wanted reliable soldiers, Prussia supported recreational associations that exercised male youths in military drills. The leadership of the Social Democratic Party, which purported to defend equality and fairness for the working classes, opposed giving autonomy to its youth associations. In a few cases where the youths asserted their political independence, it even denounced them to the police. According to some scholars, this treatment of youths supplemented inequitable taxation, political repression, a large standing army, courts biased toward elites, and disenfranchisement by the three-class voting system in ruling elite's project of quashing dissent and maintaining power. As portrayed in Heinrich Mann's satirical novel *Der Untertan (The Loyal Subject)*, which he completed in 1914, youth institutions reinforced the allegedly endemic authoritarianism in imperial Germany.[1]

However, despite the accusations, German press and association laws were liberal and enabled spirited reformers to found movements to break the rigidity and inequity. Jurists overhauled laws relating to minors, setting up juvenile courts and a foster care system that aimed to rehabilitate young offenders rather than punish them. An increasing number of elementary school teachers and self-professed pedagogues rejected drill teaching methods and thought that unyielding teacher-pupil relationships were repulsive. The new continuation schools might have been strict, but they did teach working teenagers skills that brought higher wages and, to a few, social mobility. The policies in all levels of schooling that aimed to undermine the Social Democratic Party arguably had the exact opposite effect: in the 1912 elections the party won more than a third of the popular vote, its greatest electoral victory to that time. Youths could take advantage of the myriad unsupervised commercial leisure venues in the growing cities, where they developed a culture distinct from the adult world. Recreational associations, whose founders hoped would keep youths from partaking in commercial pleasures, in the end exerted little social controls because, as voluntary organizations, youths quit them if they were not to their liking. Notable academics and politicians supported autonomous youth associations such as the Wandervögel, which in an explicit rejection of higher authority excluded adults and ran their organizations on the principle that only youths should lead youths. On balance, recreational organizations imposed less discipline than some scholars have suggested.

Still, the demand to respect authority ran deeply through families and schools. Memoirs and oral histories indicate that, except in progressive families, after work fathers typically socialized with male peers, took time to be alone undisturbed, and generally ignored their children. This absence did not, however, undermine the authority they wielded in their role as disciplinarians. Across social classes, corporal punishment of children by fathers was the norm in 1914. For working-class fathers who felt emasculated by their low status and monotonous work, the beatings could be especially brutal forms of asserting their masculinity and compensating for their lack of authority and control at the workplace. Fathers of all social classes had a reputation for being aloof, uncaring, sometimes tyrannical, and regularly willing to act on their legal right under paragraph 1631 of the *Bürgerliches Gesetzbuch*, the German law code, to beat their children.[2]

Teachers' harsh treatment of pupils was also undoubtedly real. Before 1914 the pedagogical reform movement, though vibrant, brought about few changes in practice, and teachers had little leeway to make changes themselves because in Prussia and other states, the clerical school inspectors ensured that they followed the curriculum and rigid methods almost to the letter. The school inspectors also expelled them for joining the Social Democratic Party or, in some cases, even the left-liberal Progressive Party, the only parties that favored school reform. The secondary schools remained the single institution in prewar Germany that most strongly blocked social mobility. The continuation schools, which were supposed to give young workers skills, often impoverished families who needed their children's wages, and teenagers hated them for the discipline and control they exacted. On the eve of the war, teachers and fathers were by our standards imperious disciplinarians even if their authoritarianism increasingly came under attack.

The Severity of Schooling and the Proponents of Reform

Elites fortified the authoritarianism in prewar Germany through the state education systems and their preferred teaching methods. Aristocrats and middle-class university graduates ran the school bureaucracies, and, in Prussia and Saxony, the school inspectors who exerted state authority over elementary school teachers were almost exclusively politically conservative Protestant ministers who had no training in education. In Saxony and Prussia, the legislatures and the municipal school boards were controlled by representatives of the first two classes—the aristocracy and the middle class—in the inequitable three-class voting system. These elites ensured that education served their own constituencies by making it prohibitively expensive for any but the very wealthiest to attend a secondary school. Although the secondary schools received state and municipal financing, close to 50 percent of their operating revenue came from tuition. Because most parents lacked the money or needed the wages that their teenagers could earn, less than 7 percent of male Germans in a birth cohort had parents who could afford the fees or won the few available scholarships to continue their schooling full-time in the first year after they graduated elementary school at age 14. Less than 2 percent of Germans had the money to finish with an *Abitur,* the prerequisite for admission into universities, which opened the doors to the professions, the upper echelons of the civil service, and other key institutions of power. Middle-class parents secured special access to secondary schools for their children by paying high tuition for a private elementary school, which better prepared pupils for the entrance exams than the public elementary schools and had relationships with an affiliated secondary school that guaranteed admission for most of their pupils.[3]

Middle schools *(Mittelschulen)* offered an extra year or two of instruction beyond the elementary-school-leaving age, but in 1914 Germany had only a handful. Most industrial cities required male graduates from the elementary schools to attend continuation schools, which offered 14- to 18-year-olds eight to twelve hours of instruction per week in connection with apprenticeships in a variety of trades. Graduation from a middle or continuation school did not offer the privilege of attending university or serving *einjährig-freiwillig* (one year as an unpaid volunteer) in the army, which enabled recruits to become reserve officers, a position that bestowed enormous prestige. After they graduated from special preparation schools *(Präparandenanstalten),* which they attended from age 14 to 17, prospective elementary school teachers were trained for three years in teacher-training colleges *(Seminare)* that were unaffiliated with either the universities or the elite secondary schools. Graduation from these colleges did confer the *einjährig-freiwillig* privilege in Prussia after 1895, but only a few could afford it and even fewer ever became reserve officers. Before 1918 the universities in Prussia and other states did not admit elementary school teachers.[4]

Reflecting the general patriarchal character of imperial German society, the educational opportunities for female youths were even fewer. Working-class mothers regularly discouraged their daughters from getting an education and, in violation of state law, regularly kept them from attending elementary school to do housework while they worked in factories. Although pressure from the middle-class women's movement increasingly led to more opportunities for female youths, until 1908 the lyceum in Prussia did not confer the *Abitur* and the right to attend university. Many believed that taking exams and competing for grades was, in the words of one critic, "repugnant to the essence of femininity." Placating these detractors, directors of the lyceum established curricula that cultivated allegedly feminine skills, such as speaking French or playing piano, which middle-class wives could use when hosting in their salons. With the exception of becoming a schoolteacher, which required that they remain unmarried, girls were not prepared for careers in other professions, such as law, medicine, or engineering. Above all, unless female youths had no brothers or came from considerably wealthy families, they gave up getting a secondary education so that their brothers could. In 1911, 1 percent of female Germans graduated from a secondary school.[5]

In sum, the educational system used taxes paid by all Germans to subsidize the education of male elites and advance pupils based on wealth rather than merit. It was arguably the key feature in imperial Germany that reinforced a patriarchal society, blocked social mobility, and maintained the power of the aristocracy and the middle class.

A second quality reinforcing the authoritarianism was the methods that aimed to prevent critical thinking and raise Germans to be submissive. In secondary schools, this severity stemmed in part from the almost unassailable authority that the teacher had in his position as a state official. Because parents had no recourse if the teacher sullied their child's record, they dreaded approaching him about disciplinary problems or other issues. By contrast, though the lessons in secondary schools in Great Britain were as dreary and monotonous as those in Germany, the teachers were usually privately paid and answerable to parents. In Germany parents socialized their children at an early age to accept the teacher's authority unconditionally and become conscious of state authority and law. One influential textbook on pedagogy in fact argued that school was "for little humans a state in miniature."[6]

In Prussia and the other large states, the training of elementary school teachers reproduced and reinforced these hierarchies and authoritarian qualities. With few exceptions, the directors of the teacher training colleges were elites who had attended the university but neither studied pedagogy nor had experience teaching elementary school children. About one-third of the instructors had the same background as the directors, and they regularly sneered at the rest of their colleagues who did not have their privileged education. These riffraff instructors had to endure directors who disciplined them for having romantic affairs, demanded that they vote for the conservative parties, and on occasion expelled them arbitrarily, ending their careers. Below these ordinary instructors were the teenage prospective teachers, who had to accept this elitism and severity. Directors of the teacher-training colleges frowned on spontaneity and discouraged self-directed learning about general subjects or pedagogies beyond the strict drill methods in which the students were diligently trained. About half of the colleges were purposely erected in rural places to prevent access to large libraries and cosmopolitan life. Prussia and many of the other states never accorded elementary school teachers the full status of civil servants. Often referred to as the "step-siblings" of secondary school teachers, they were quintessential *Untertanen*, the servile underlings of the imperious state. When they became teachers, some broke with this authoritarian culture, but many took out their resentment about their low status by asserting their prerogatives to abuse and control their schoolchildren. Though they rarely said so explicitly, state officials supported this practice because they feared that elementary schooling empowered the working class if teachers did not raise pupils to be obedient. Not surprisingly given this system, British and American observers characterized both elementary and secondary school teachers as strict drill sergeants, overzealous in demanding respect for their authority and usually indifferent to the curiosity and personal development of their pupils.[7]

These practices were of course far from universal. On the eve of the war, they were growing out of favor among male and female elementary school teachers in intellectually vibrant cities such as Hamburg, Berlin, and Leipzig. Female elementary school teachers experienced less tension over social class. Until 1908, prospective female elementary school teachers in Prussia could be trained in the lyceum. Even after they had to attend separate, sometimes humiliating female teacher-training colleges, they still enjoyed a more extensive and prestigious education than all other women in Germany except the graduates from the lyceum. Far more female than male elementary school teachers came from the middle-class milieu, the daughters of lawyers, doctors, professors, upper-level bureaucrats, and industrialists, as well as some shopkeepers, merchants, and other lower middle-class families who could afford the opportunity costs and substantial fees. Because women were shut out of most professions in imperial Germany, female teachers enjoyed one of the most distinguished careers available to them. Able to support themselves financially in a middle-class lifestyle without depending on a husband, they enjoyed an independence that enabled many, such as Gertrud Bäumer and Helene Lange, to become leaders of the women's movement. Female schoolteachers accordingly harbored less resentment about their status than their male counterparts and had less reason to take out any anger on their pupils. The belief that women had a propensity toward nurturing translated into softer relationships with their schoolgirls.[8]

Still, because officials feared that mothers and pregnant women could not be good teachers and vice versa, the German states forbade women from teaching once they married. The teaching profession in Germany was overwhelmingly male: whereas women composed 60 percent of schoolteachers in France and 75 percent in both Great Britain and the United States, they made up just 20 percent in Germany, and schooling bore the general imprint of a male culture that valued giving orders and having them obeyed. Male elementary school teachers followed the strict clerical school inspectors, who like most secondary school teachers gave priority to rote memorization in German, history, and foreign languages; they rejected teaching methods that involved free speaking, undirected writing, and other activities that mitigated their authority. Liberal use of sarcasm and corporal punishment, including ear-smacking, hair-pulling, and caning, were the ultimate weapons in making schoolteachers, according to one strident assessment, one of "the primary instruments of social control" that got pupils to accept the authoritarian ways of imperial Germany.[9]

Despite these generalizations, thousands of progressive teachers, university professors, and other reformers reproached this elitism and severity in a movement referred to today as *reform pedagogy (Reformpädagogik)*. The reformers advocated for changes using a vibrant forum—an estimated 440 pedagogical journals, including the weekly newspapers published by the teachers' professional associations, such as secondary school teachers' *Deutsches Philologenblatt* (Leipzig) and the elementary school teachers' *Schulblatt der Provinz Sachsen* (Magdeburg), *Pädagogische Zeitung* (Berlin), and *Leipziger Lehrerzeitung*, each of which had as many as fifty articles per issue. They proposed two general changes. The first was to end the exclusionary structure of the educational system by creating a national (rather than state) education system, the *Einheitsschule* (literally, unity school). The *Einheitsschule*, they envisioned, would advance pupils on merit, not wealth, wrest control from clerical school inspectors, reduce class differences, promote competent leaders, integrate the working class into the nation-state, and allow children of workers and professionals to get to know each other. It would enable poor but talented schoolchildren to reach the university and thereby increase German productivity. Above all, by opening university education to deserving working-class and lower-middle-class pupils, including the elementary school teachers them-selves, it would end a system through which elites passed on their privilege to their children.[10]

The second set of reforms involved reviving the early-nineteenth-century theories of Johann Pestalozzi and other education philosophers. Countless turn-of-the-century schoolteachers, psychologists, academics, and self-professed pedagogues investigated the causes of childhood anxiety and suicide, founded research institutes to advance the psychology of learning and development, and sought to implement a pedagogy that enabled spontaneity, creativity, and hands-on learning. Some set up experimental schools that made art education central in the curriculum. Others introduced curricula and methods that culti-vated practical skills and critical thinking. Although these reformers had par-ticular agendas, they agreed that authoritarianism in schooling needed to end. Influenced by the Swedish reformer Ellen Key's call to inaugurate a "Century of the Child," they argued for a "child-centered" pedagogy *(Pädagogik vom Kinde aus)*. The movement was supremely populist: secondary school teachers who were university graduates generally rejected it, while elementary school teachers, their lower status "step-siblings," enthusiastically embraced it. The 1912 congress of the elementary school teachers' professional organization overwhelmingly endorsed reform pedagogy and the *Einheitsschule*, and in lec-tures, conferences, and their professional journals, elementary school teachers began on their own to discuss and advocate for it.[11]

Two movements within reform pedagogy later shaped education during the war in particular. The first was spearheaded by Friedrich Wilhelm Foerster, a professor of philosophy in Berlin and later Munich, and Georg Kerschen-steiner, the superintendent of Munich's schools and after 1912 a delegate for the Progressive Party in the Reichstag. Both Foerster and Kerschensteiner wanted to redress the overemphasis in German schools on imparting knowl-edge, which they pejoratively labeled the *Lernschule* (literally, "learn school"). They wanted to introduce curricula and methods that instead developed the skills and the character in schoolchildren necessary for them to be citizens in a constitutional state and open society. In a prize-winning essay, Kerschen-steiner suggested that through civic education *(staatsbürgerliche Erziehung)* teachers should not only inform schoolchildren about the German constitu-tional monarchy but give them experiences that developed their self-esteem, conscientiousness, diligence, perseverance, responsibility, self-restraint, religi-osity, and other traits necessary for a civilized and productive country. These

experiences would come from running schools on liberal principles and allowing pupils to participate in school life through self-government. To actu-
alize this philosophy, Kerschensteiner founded a model *Arbeitsschule* (sometimes literally translated as "work school" but more accurately as "activity
school") in a working-class neighborhood in Dortmund in 1909, in which
pupils pursued tasks with minimal direction from their teacher. In the first
months of the first grade, the pupils established a trusting relationship with
their teacher by singing songs, playing games, and listening to stories. Only
after this initiation did they move on to learn arithmetic and reading. In the
highest grades, teachers discarded the prescribed stale reader of German classics and instead chose material based on the pupils' preferences. The Dortmund activity school was successful beyond anyone's expectations: absenteeism was low, and motivation and achievement were high. The independence
in the activity school stimulated the pupils, developed their sense of self-
reliance, exercised their critical thinking skills, and taught them to be cheerful and active participants in learning rather than resentful recipients of authoritarian state education. On the eve of the war, Kerschensteiner, along
with other pedagogues, such as Hugo Gaudig, planned to open several new
activity schools and hoped to make them the model for a thorough reform of
Germany's elementary school system. After substantial pressure from teachers, administrators in Leipzig, one of the centers of the reform pedagogy
movement, agreed in 1911 to open twenty-four experimental classes based on
the model.[12]

A second movement predating 1914 that shaped elementary school education during the war was the "home teaching school" *(Hauslehrerschule),* spearheaded by Berthold Otto. In Otto's model school, teachers were not required
to follow any lesson plans but were instead expected to adapt an elastic curriculum to the interests of the pupils. In the last hour of instruction every
week, all pupils in the school met together for a community meeting during
which they decided the themes of instruction for the following week. The
teachers and pupils also shared personal experiences and discussed technical,
cultural, and sometimes even controversial issues about education. Instruction on a topic ended when pupils tired or had no more interest. The teachers
did not grade pupils, and instead of making attendance mandatory and pun-
ishable with set fines, the pupils themselves decided how to discipline tardi-
ness and absences. Teachers started with the premise that joy was the best
motivation for learning.[13]

Contrary to the claim that schools always pursued a "strategy of permanent indoctrination with the goal of stabilizing and widening state rule," the Prussian state itself occasionally worked with these reformers. A good deal of the reformers' research and experiments, such as Kerschensteiner's and Otto's, received financial support from the Kaiser and the Prussian and Bavarian education ministries.[14]

Still, while imperial Germany was a fertile environment for these ideas, on the eve of the war few elementary school teachers had put the educational reforms into practice. The reforms were popular among younger teachers, particularly in Berlin, Leipzig, Dresden, Hamburg, and the small cities in Thuringia, but the bulk of the profession, especially secondary school teachers, was skeptical. Older teachers and the clerical school inspectors denounced the reform methods for their leniency and unmanliness. Progress was halted in Saxony in 1913 when the education minister reduced the number of experimental activity school classrooms from twenty-four to ten. The reformers' only allies in the Prussian and Saxon state legislatures were the Progressive and Social Democratic parties, both of which lacked support from the others parties that made up the majorities. Though energetic, advocates of reform pedagogy had made little real progress on the eve of the war.[15]

Curbing Commercial Leisure: Continuation Schools and Recreational Associations

The growth of big cities, together with the anonymity and commercial leisure they offered, was another development that, like reform pedagogy, had the potential to undermine the authoritarian relationship between youths and adults. By the turn of the century, the traditional apprenticeship system in which youths worked and lived under the discipline of a master had all but disappeared. Moreover, rising real wages enabled more working youths than ever to enjoy paid commercial leisure such as tobacco, alcohol, penny dreadfuls, films, racetracks, cafes, and variety shows. These leisure activities were on one level simply an escape from the tedium of factory work. On another level they were a way for working youths to assert their independence and status vis-à-vis adults and to reject conforming to the values of middle-class institutions like schools and recreational associations. By taking part in ritualized social drinking in the pub, male youths won entry into the workingman's world of charged politics and masculine displays of bravado, the very antithesis of middle-class respectability. Similarly, by lighting a cigarette and loitering on the street, working youths could reject bourgeois prescriptions for good health and showcase their individuality and independence.[16]

The escape from supervision offered by commercial leisure venues alarmed middle-class parents, teachers, officials, and youth welfare workers. In 1913 a German female elementary school teacher was horrified by the boisterous behavior in a cinema:

> The entire room (500 capacity) is filled to the last seat with children. There is an indescribable din: running, yelling, shrieking, laughing, talking. Boys scuffle. Orange peels and empty bon-bon boxes fly through the air. The ground is studded with candy wrappers. Along the windowsill and radiators young toughs romp around. Girls and boys sit together, densely packed. Fourteen-year-old boys and girls with hot, excited faces tease each other in un-childish ways. . . . Young boys smoke furtively.

The unruly behavior had much to do with the novelty of a large, commercial space being occupied by youths without adult supervision, a gathering un-imaginable before the rise of cinemas just a decade earlier. But Social Democrats and middle-class reformers alike charged that the cause of such antics was not the spaces but the films—usually comedies with buffoons as antiheroes or sensationalist dramas about cowboys, criminals, adulterers, alcoholics, and the unemployed. They were exasperated that few could stop a schoolchild, let alone a wage-earning youth, from buying a ticket to see them. Teachers derided the films for encouraging bad behavior and "apathy for learning, carelessness, and a tendency to daydream." They were frustrated that municipal censorship boards could do little to stanch visits to the cinema: in a two-day period in 1912, for example, a third of the schoolchildren in Elberfeld and Düsseldorf visited the cinema, according to researchers.[17]

Adults were agitated by the opportunities that the commercial leisure venues offered to youths who wanted to play rough and woo the opposite sex unsupervised. With the rise of youth wage labor, boys for the first time had pocket money to "treat" girls regularly. This new form of courtship, which in the 1920s developed into a flourishing dating system, offered youths more independence in their choice of partners than the preindustrial urban form under which master craftsmen disciplined male apprentices and journeymen for consorting with young women whom they disapproved. "Treating" threatened middle-class parents, who feared their daughters could meet young, possibly working-class men outside the preferred calling system, in which mothers oversaw prospective partners by hosting eligible young men in the safety of their homes.[18]

Treating complemented peer-regulated forms of courtship on the street. The street was the place for organized political protest and spontaneous actions like confronting policemen and mocking marching soldiers, the space where working-class Germans of all ages contested the government and middle-class respectability. For youths, games on the street were rough-and-tumble ways to snub adult authority. During the war, male and female working youths also asserted their independence by acting out what the British called "mare street" and the "monkey parade"—rituals in which boys dressed in their best clothes, linked arms, and chased girls. These courtship parades were a tacit rejection of the middle-class value placed on the calling system. Urban parents aspiring to be "respectable" usually forbade their children to play in the street unsupervised, but it was hard to discipline working male youths. Wage-earning sons had more clout vis-à-vis their parents, and employers rarely exercised their right to dock young workers' wages for drinking, smoking, or attending the racetrack, the cinema, or the music hall. Police chased away boys and girls who loitered, but in the big cities it was easy for them simply to go elsewhere and maintain control over the norms regulating their peer interaction.[19]

Middle-class reformers and state officials identified working male youths as a bigger problem than female youths because boys earned on average twice the wages, had more opportunity for commercial leisure, and were the ones who could grow up to be unproductive voting citizens and, more threateningly, undisciplined soldiers. Furthermore, a good portion of female teenagers did not work but stayed at home and helped their mothers run the household. The most common trade for female youths was domestic service, which kept them under the supervision of a mistress and gave them little opportunity for commercial leisure. Reformers saw a problem in particular with the one- to two-fifths of male youths who took "blind alley" jobs—unskilled positions such as errand boy, which often did not require attendance of a continuation school and offered 14- to 18-year-olds as much as five to six times higher compensation than the best paid apprenticeships. Critics worried that boys in these jobs mortgaged higher wages they could earn in the future from the skills they could master in an apprenticeship. They also denounced the blind-alley jobs for rewarding lazy, undisciplined, and impulsive male teenagers with money for commercial pleasures. In truth, the decision to take an unskilled position was rational for teenagers from the poorest urban families. When they took home wages, their families began to emerge from the poverty that having non-earning dependents inflicted for a decade or more. Another incentive was the privileges these boys gained within their families. Evidence suggests that wage-earning male youths escaped corporal punishment from fathers, skipped family meals to socialize with friends, no longer abided by parents' curfews, and, after contributing to family expenses, had money to treat girls at the cafe and the cinema. Unskilled positions such as errand boy allowed a teenager to work independently without suffering the deadening monotony of industrial jobs. Male working youths had ample opportunity to quit blind-alley jobs and find ones more to their liking because youth unemployment in unskilled work on the eve of the First World War was virtually nil.[20]

After the turn of the twentieth century, middle-class reformers in Germany arguably took the most extensive steps in the world to remedy the lack of supervision over these 14- to 18-year-old male youths "between school and the barracks" through founding continuation schools *(Fortbildungsschulen)*. Though financed primarily by municipalities, employers, and state governments, trade associations overseeing apprenticeships contributed money and expertise. The continuation schools had support from liberals who wanted a more competitive economy, artisans who felt industrialization threatened their independence, and Social Democrats who wanted working youths to have better vocational training. Progressive liberals like Kerschensteiner, who oversaw the expansion of municipal continuation schools in Munich, dictated that the curricula have a smattering of patriotic, moral, and religious themes and a focus on civic education and technical skills such as accounting and geometry. By 1910 continuation schools based on Kerschensteiner's model were mandatory for youths going into skilled jobs in all Prussian cities with over one hundred thousand residents. Most Prussian and non-Prussian cities with over ten thousand residents had continuation schools as well. In the years immediately preceding the war, municipalities began to found continuation schools for girls as well as boys. The girls' schools had particular support from manufacturers in the textiles industries, a main employer of working-class women, and from middle-class housewives, who liked the idea that the schools taught cooking, cleaning, child care, and sewing and produced a generation of more capable domestic servants. They also had support from reformers who worried that the street and commercial leisure venues were places where female youths could "fall" into a life of prostitution. Forcing working youths to attend continuation schools fueled their resentment at being obligated to study civics and other nonpractical topics when they could be earning money. Many of their families, particularly those from the poorest strata, also preferred that their children support the family rather than go to school. The worst-performing children in the elementary schools had to attend continuation schools in trades like haircutting that paid miserably and offered little social mobility. Still, though youths often escaped attending them by choosing blind-alley jobs, in 1914 they had become established institutions to create productive, disciplined, and orderly youths.[21]

Another branch of the movement to "save" young workers was the founding of sport, "patriotic" *(vaterländisch)*, and confessional recreational organizations to get youths off the street and away from the alleged dangers of commercial leisure. Youth associations also appealed to increasing numbers of middle-class parents who thought that vigilant attendance to their children's moral and social well-being was a categorical duty. Because home and work became separated during industrialization, and fathers were increasingly absent in child-raising, disciplining children during the day was left to mothers, who were allegedly less strict. By contrast, before industrialization the lives of urban male youths were disciplined not only by fathers but also by master craftsmen acting *in loco parentis*. By the end of the nineteenth century traditional apprenticeship in guilds had all but disappeared, and recreational associations, like continuation schools, were supposed to make up for the lacking parental authority.

Recreational associations played a more significant role in Germany than elsewhere in the world. Their numbers and growth were spectacular: membership in recreational associations grew from an estimated one hundred thousand youths in 1875 to over 4 million in 1920. The figures are a matter of some speculation because the network of associations was diverse and overlapping, and despite all efforts, no one ever succeeded in gathering comprehensive statistics. But contemporaries estimated that Germany in 1914 had some 2 million youths in recreational associations—roughly 25 percent of male and 20 percent of female youths. Because rural youths had fewer opportunities for recreation, the percentages were considerably higher in cities. Many cities had five to six times as many male youths in recreational associations as did the best-organized British cities. The number of American youths who were members of revivalist church groups such as the Epworth League or Christian Endeavor was comparable to the numbers in German associations, but the vast majority of the American organizations were little more than Bible study groups whose members were required to take oaths; they offered little, if any, supervised recreation. The high level of organization was due in part to the long affinity in German-speaking Central Europe (going back to the early nineteenth century) to found associations. The German Gymnasts, with over one-half million youth members in 1914, had an institutional history going back to the 1830s. At the turn of the century, it was easier than ever to found clubs because the long decline in birthrates concentrated family resources, and the prosperity after 1896 allowed more families to forgo their teenage children's wages and give them more leisure. Municipalities and charities also had more money than before to buy equipment, buildings, and playing fields.[22]

Some scholars have argued that the involvement of Prussia and other states in recreational associations was a new intrusion of the state into a hitherto independent realm of civil society. This charge needs to be qualified. The education ministries hoped that recreational organizations, like continuation schools, would create a politically and morally reliable cohort, one prepared to fight a European war, if necessary. The recreational associations did keep many youths off the street and out of trouble. After 1911 the recreational associations, with the help of the state-paid district youth workers *(Kreisjugend-pfleger)*, established a foundation for encouraging youths to be patriotic, devout, and well-behaved. But because they were *voluntary*, youths could avoid authoritarian associations, or they could choose not to participate at all. With the exception of laws that banned politics in the associations and, as for adult all ones, required registration with the police, Prussia never decreed how the associations should operate. Recreational associations thus did not give the imperial German states any power to discipline working-class youths, about whom officials worried the most. Any claim that state involvement in youth recreation represented another arm of the German states' prewar authoritarian tentacles is largely an exaggeration.

Teenagers Leading Teenagers

Germany also stood out in the world in having youth movements whose sine qua non was to challenge adult authority. The middle-class youth movement, which was strictly separate from the Socialist youth movement and had affiliates in the German-speaking areas of Austria-Hungary, began in the decade before the war with the founding at the Steglitz Gymnasium in Berlin of the Wandervogel, a network of hiking groups composed of some Catholic and primarily Protestant secondary school children aged 14 to 20. The boys and girls championed naturalism and German folklore, took oaths to abstain from alcohol and tobacco, repudiated materialism and industrialism as sores of modernity, and dressed in the folkloric German dress of decorated shirtfronts, flamboyant hats, and leather shorts or flowery skirts. They imagined themselves escaping the sordid urban world of their elders by exploring the countryside—that is, their *Heimat* (local geography). During these trips, they cooked their own food and sang traditional folk songs to the accompaniment of lutes. They also met in barns or around campfires for so-called nest evenings. Through these activities they aimed to cultivate simplicity, modesty, and spirituality.[23]

The youth movement's great contribution to modern culture was its pioneering of autonomous organization. German law required that the Wandervogel, like all youth associations, have adult mentors who registered with the police, but the mentors agreed to play a minimal role. By contrast, though the British and American Boy Scouts allowed members to elect older teenage boys to lead their "patrols," the younger members did not elect troop leaders or establish national policy. By contrast, in the Wandervogel youths led youths in all aspects of organization. Some historians have attributed authoritarian tendencies to them because the first groups followed their older youth leader under the so-called *Führerprinzip* (leader principle), but on the eve of the war, the vast majority of groups were in fact organized democratically. Many of the 50,000 members believed their activities—what they called self-education and self-liberation—made the Wandervogel a more important institution in their education than family and school. This idea was implicitly a radical attack on parents and teachers, the two central sources of adult authority. However, most Wandervögel repudiated taking hard positions on national political issues, preferring instead to withdraw into their peer groups. This unwillingness to confront and criticize society directly was the reason the Wandervogel, unlike the working-class youth movement, generated little controversy among state officials, despite some misguided claims by historians otherwise.[24]

The middle-class youth movement underwent an incipient, inchoate politicization in October 1913 at an event later known as the Meißner Festival, a three-day conference held in the open air on the Meißner Mountain outside Cassel. Encouraged by Gustav Wyneken, the iconoclastic school reformer and director of the progressive Wickersdorf School, former Wandervögel, university students favoring abstinence, and secondary school children chose the date to coincide with the centennial of the Battle of Leipzig, an event that symbolically marked German national liberation and renewal. In addition to dancing, singing around campfires, participating in athletic competitions, watching a production of Goethe's *Iphigenia*, and listening to speeches by Wyneken and other youth reformers, the two thousand young participants took the celebrated "Meißner-Oath," which asserted their desire for independence: "The Free German Youth wants to shape their lives on their own terms, taking their own responsibility, according to their own concept of truthfulness." The participants adopted the name "Free German Youth" from a term coined by Johann von Fichte in *Addresses to the German Nation* (1808). Like Fichte, they believed that they stood before a revolution in German culture and society. They imagined themselves not as members of a formal political organization but as participants of a popular mobilization. In practice, they lacked concrete platforms. Still, the Meißner Festival had an important symbolic consequence: it awakened a set of middle-class German youths to the idea that, by "creating their lives themselves" and going beyond the insular Wandervogel organizations, they could solve, not escape from, the problems of modernity. For this progressive spirit, the Free German Youth received support from a variety of prominent social reformers, including Max Weber, Gertrud Bäumer, Friedrich Naumann, Ludwig Gurlitt, Georg Kerschensteiner, and Paul Natrop.[25]

Unlike mainstream Wandervogel groups, the Free German Youth attracted the attention of authorities, who forced them to withdraw from political action on the eve of the war. By 1913 most Wandervögel rejected the recent state financing of youth recreational associations as an unwelcome influence of adults. Most were also critical of imperialism and the "hurrah" patriotism of the German right. A far left wing took inspiration from Wyneken's calls for extensive school reform and his sharp attacks on the chauvinism of the Pan-Germanists and other radical nationalists. In the journal *Der Anfang* secondary school boys, including the future literary critic Walter Benjamin, denounced the rigidity of the school system. They condemned restrictions on sexual expression between unmarried lovers and endorsed a vague form of utopian socialism based on the British settlement movement.

This incendiary content incited Bavarian and Prussian authorities to censor the journal.

In Munich in January 1914, scandal subsequently broke out after a delegate of the Center Party accused the Free German Youth of promoting homosexuality and combating patriotism, religion, and parental authority. The minority chauvinist wing of the Free German Youth that professed the virtues of racial hygiene branded the *Der Anfang* "a Jewish journal." Though facing outbreaks of anti-Semitic violence at the Easter 1914 meeting, where a small cadre of right-wing youths beat Jewish boys and girls who attended, the Free German Youth and the Wandervogel together passed resolutions not to issue any organization-wide ban on Jews, leaving the decision to the local groups. In practice, few groups did. But the rancor forced the Free German Youth to adopt a policy of apoliticism and to reject "endorsement of economic, confessional, and political parties for being a premature restriction on our self-education." Like much of the German middle class, they believed that they were above the alleged sordidness of national politics. Even so, they could not win over those Wandervögel still skeptical of the Free German Youth's "deformed cosmopolitanism" and the "intellectualization" of the youth movement. The Free German Youth agreed to keep Wyneken out of the organization (he had resigned as a mentor during the scandal in Munich). They accordingly lost their most strident advocate of pacifism, and in the months preceding the war, they receded into the safety of civic quietism.[26]

In rejecting the strictures of imperial German society, the middle-class youth movement highlighted both the pervasiveness of authoritarian institutions in youths' lives *and* the increasing will to reform them. The teenagers in the Wandervogel engaged in active protests, including reciting the Meißner Oath and calling for sexual liberation, and passive protests, such as wearing loose clothing and holding "nest evenings" that excluded adults. The right wing of the Wandervogel aimed to create exclusively homosocial communities, but on the eve of the war, a sizable minority of the members were female, and the all-girl and coed branches (boys and girls mixed at the nest evenings but rarely on hikes) fostered independence, self-reliance, and the sense among girls that they played a role equal to boys in rejuvenating Germany through youth culture.[27]

Still, in practice the youth movement posed only a minor challenge to the status quo in Germany. Until the war, few female members wrote, let alone debated, males in the self-published magazines. Even during the war, when female Wandervögel took over hundreds of organizations, most had no intention of challenging dominant conceptions of gender and continued to idealize their future role as wives and mothers. With about fifty thousand members, almost all of whom were reliably middle class, the Wandervogel and Free German Youth constituted just a fraction of the 8 million teenagers in Germany. Although they have been the subjects of dozens of dissertations, master's theses, and lay and local historical studies, with the exception of the Free German Youth, the Wandervogel barely raised an eyebrow among state officials, who were far more concerned with how the millions of Germany's other, less privileged teenagers spent their free time.

The Socialist youth movement, which had almost no relations with its middle-class counterpart, also posed a spirited challenge to adult authority. Unlike the Wandervogel, however, it was viewed by state officials as a dangerous challenge to monarchy, colonialism, and the capitalist order. The Socialist youth movement also met resistance from the Social Democratic Party itself, which, in a policy similar to its attempt to reform rough working-class behaviors like drinking schnapps and tussling with the police, repulsed the youth movements' demands for autonomy. West German historians have explained the secession in the Socialist youth movement as a parallel to the more general split of the Social Democratic Party in 1917. East German historians, in an homage to the young founders of the Communist Party, argued that the secession was because the youths were antiwar and pro-revolution. An overlooked interpretation is that relationships of authority—Communists granting youths autonomy and the long-term stifling of youth independence by the Social Democrats—also played a key role in the eventual split.[28]

The first self-consciously Socialist, working-class youth organization in Germany, the Association of Apprentices and Young Workers, was founded in Berlin in 1904 by male teenagers themselves. Although adults sponsored it, as required by Prussian law, the mentors, like those of the middle-class Wandervogel, granted it autonomy in practice. The principle of youths leading youths proved to be popular. The Berlin group grew rapidly and helped found affiliates that amalgamated in 1906 into the Federation of Free Youth Organizations with 5,400 male members by 1908. In practice, maintaining complete autonomy was quixotic because the Prussian Law of Association forbade youth organizations from engaging in politics. Consequently, activities were officially limited to redressing the abuses of apprentices at the workplace, defending youths' economic interests, sponsoring lectures on history and natural science, informing members about the German constitution, and urging them to refrain from alcohol, tobacco, and penny dreadfuls. But behind the legal façade of apoliticism, the youth organizations became charged. They regularly circumvented the ban on politics by hosting discussions on the social theories of Karl Marx and Charles Fourier. They also turned to the Social Democratic Party for legal advice and money to bankroll their newspaper, *Die arbeitende Jugend.* The police began regular surveillance of lectures, and even though the Law of Association in theory did not prohibit politics in youth publications, *Die arbeitende Jugend* was produced under the constant threat of arbitrary censorship. Making membership more conspiratorial, many employers required their apprentices to sign contracts that forbade joining Socialist organizations, and these youths had to keep their membership secret. The experience confirmed the Marxist doctrine that the bourgeoisie was engaged in a fundamental conflict with the working class and that the state was its apparatus of repression.[29]

Because of the more liberal laws of association in the southern states of Baden and Württemberg, working-class youth organizations could engage more vocally in national and international affairs. The first southern working-class youth organization, the Association of Young Workers, was founded in 1904 in Mannheim at the urging of Ludwig Frank, a 30-year-old Social Democratic lawyer who hoped to enlist youths in the struggle for progressive reform. Although Frank was a revisionist, who unlike revolutionary Socialists wanted the Social Democratic Party to make progressive reforms gradually, he thought that the energy of young people could help with positive social and political change. He also believed that male youths nearing the age of conscription had a keen interest in preventing a world war. The southern groups were quickly led in a more radical direction, however, by the revolutionary Socialist Karl Liebknecht, the president of the Socialist Youth International who was jailed in 1907 for publishing *Militarism and Antimilitarism with Special Significance for the Youth Movement.* Inspired by Liebknecht, they organized a conference where Socialist youths from thirteen countries passed a resolution condemning militarism. In the first years of its publication, their newspaper, *Die Junge Garde (The Young Guard),* which had a circulation of eleven thousand in 1908, called upon male youths to resist conscription.[30]

Centrists in the Social Democratic Party recognized the usefulness of mobilizing teenagers for the Socialist cause, but they and the right wing of the party were leery about the youths' autonomy. August Bebel, the party chairman, endorsed the southern youth organizations at the 1906 Party Congress, but he spoke for most functionaries when he called their activities "dangerous playing around." Other centrists and almost all on the right rejected the independence of the youth associations altogether. Their paternalism stemmed from their desire to make Socialist organizations respectable. It was also a reaction to the problems that the youths' vigorous antimilitarism posed to the need to train working-class men in arms. The Social Democrats of course opposed imperialist wars as more advanced forms of working-class exploitation. In the Reichstag they systematically voted down military spending because the indirect taxes financed arms production that burdened the working class. But most did not oppose military spending per se or accept the categorical antimilitarism of radicals like Liebknecht. They cited passages in Marx's writings that supported defensive wars against attacks by more autocratic states such as Russia. According to historical materialism, wars by politically and economically advanced nations against reactionary and backwards ones were acceptable. The reason, as the Social Democratic Party's leading centrist theorist Karl Kautsky argued, was that war under capitalism was inevitable and such conflicts at least moved history forward toward the Socialist revolution. Bebel cited this theory as an explanation for why in 1870 he abstained in the vote on the war credits bill in the Prussian Parliament on the eve of the war against Napoleon III. After the turn of the century, he and most Social Democrats opposed the Prussian army for abusing working-class recruits, denying them their rights, and carrying out imperialist adventures. But they were not opposed to their constituents getting military training in a national army. Regardless of whether the Socialist revolution was in the near or distant future, a successful one required trained soldiers to serve in citizen militias.[31]

Moreover, after the Social Democratic Party for the first time since the lapse of the anti-Socialist laws lost seats in the Reichstag during the elections of 1907, its leaders realized that antimilitarist rhetoric was a liability that alienated the middle-class voters they needed to gain seats and carry out a gradual reform strategy. It was foolish, they reasoned, to sponsor protest by unruly teenagers against the military when the Social Democratic Party needed working-class men with military training and when the middle classes feared an "encirclement" of Germany by the European nations' alliances, colonial acquisitions, and military buildups.

Fearing political isolation, the Social Democratic Party leadership after 1907 sought to depoliticize the youth organizations and bring them under adult control. In an extraordinary sabotage of a proposal to expand their con-stituents' rights, trade unionists and the right wing in the Social Democratic Party successfully *opposed* the liberal provisions in the draft of the 1908 Reich Law of Association that would have allowed youth membership in political organizations. In its final form, paragraph 17 of the Reich Law of Association extended the Prussian ban on politics in youth associations to the southern states. Consequently, the southern youth organizations disbanded, planning to reconstitute themselves as independent but outwardly apolitical cultural associations like the northern groups. But at the 1908 Social Democratic Party Congress, the trade unionists persuaded the delegates to repudiate the independence of youth associations and to found the Central Office for Working Youth *(Zentralstelle für die arbeitende Jugend)* to coordinate activities and ensure compliance with the new law. Members in both the northern and southern youth organizations were outraged. But denied the Social Demo-cratic Party's legal advice and financial support and unwilling to brook a fragmentation of the working-class youth movement, they reluctantly agreed to be subsumed into the party hierarchy.[32]

Nourished with money and attention from the party, the Socialist youth organizations expanded after 1908, offering ever more concerts, festivals, theater, libraries, museum trips, arts and crafts, and instruction in gymnas-tics, swimming, and business skills such as stenography. Membership rose to 108,000 by 1914, making it the largest Socialist youth organization in the world. The growth alarmed leaders of the middle-class youth associations, who now had to compete vigorously with the Socialists. Fear of losing working-class youths also prompted the Prussian education minister to issue the 1911 *Jugendpflege* Edict. As critics like Liebknecht emphasized, most district So-cialist youth organizations differed little in substance from the middle-class recreational associations. The structure of the Central Office's board ensured the organization was paternalistic: functionaries from the Social Democratic Party and the conservative trade unions, who were hostile to giving young persons control, had twice as many representatives as youths on the board, which was led by Friedrich Ebert, the cautious revisionist party chairman after September 1913. True to its conservative nature, the board had rejected joining the radically antimilitarist Youth International in 1910, spurning the Socialist youth activists in other nations. Furthermore, Social Democratic Reichstag delegate and future Weimar education under-secretary Heinrich Schulz, a contributing editor of *Arbeiter-Jugend,* the weekly newspaper that replaced the publications of the autonomous groups, steadfastly opposed allowing youths to engage in class struggle. (Schulz later insisted with little evidence that the working-class youth organization was "from its beginning never a political movement.") Under the new leadership, the Socialist youth organizations increasingly advertised their respectability. For example, it became the custom to wear one's finest Sunday clothes on hikes; the middle-class Wandervögel by contrast wore loose clothing in protest of bourgeois restrictiveness. Because of police surveillance, including undercover agents who infiltrated and made mass arrests when activities seemed political, the Central Office became increasingly vigilant in preventing youths from violating paragraph 17 of the Reich Law of Association. State authorities and the Socialist leaders accordingly smothered public expressions of radicalism in the youth organizations.[33]

The Socialist youth organizations had highly intelligent and respected female mentors like Rosa Luxemburg and Clara Zetkin and did not separate the sexes in main activities like the Wandervogel and most mainstream recreational associations. All the same, the Socialist youth organizations were 80 percent male and devoted almost no energy to challenging prevailing assumptions about gender. These youth organizations like all Socialist ones were in principle integrated, but in practice few female youths joined because working-class parents tended to be morally conservative and discouraged their teenage daughters from engaging in politics and socializing with boys in groups. Willi Münzenberg, an early member of the Southern Socialist youth organization and an advocate of radical equality between the sexes, was hard-pressed to recruit female youths through lectures on imperialism and capitalism. He succeeded in attracting them only through hosting a talk on how a working girl could find a good husband. The language and political style of the Socialist youths were shaped in good part by male bravado even during the war years, when female youths streamed into the organization.[34]

Antimilitarism and political agitation persisted underground in the Socialist youth organizations that had a history of independence. Youths in Berlin, Hamburg, Düsseldorf, and Stuttgart—cities where Socialist youths organized the antiwar movement after 1914—took their cue from radicals like Liebknecht and even centrists like Kautsky. These men argued that though armies were necessary and certain kinds of war were useful, Socialists everywhere had a duty to work diligently for world peace. In Stuttgart, for example, Socialist youths regularly protested German militarism on the Pentecost holiday. Although the police in 1914 shut down their organization to prevent an imminent rally, 1,500 youths met anyway in an out-of-the-way reception hall in the Heslach Forest. They danced, distributed smuggled copies of Liebknecht's banned *Militarism and Antimilitarism,* and marched back to the city chanting old Socialist fight songs. In Berlin and Düsseldorf, youths who detested the restrictions posed by the Law of Association regularly flaunted their politics, taunted the police, and played games of cat and mouse outwitting the authorities. When the police shut down the organizations, the youths revived them as informal reading groups. During the years 1908 to 1914, protests like these were the exception rather than the rule. But on the eve of the war, a core of Socialist youths, mostly the children of party members, had nonetheless grown accustomed to underground and illegal organization and forged a culture hostile to the authority of the state and the revisionist adult functionaries in the Social Democratic Party.[35]

On the eve of the war, liberal press and association laws gave reformers powerful weapons to challenge the authoritarianism in imperial Germany. In newspapers and professional societies, countless pedagogues urged officials to reform a system that blocked social mobility and to eliminate the harsh teaching methods in schools through a child-centered approach. In pedagogical realms outside of schooling, reformers had significant victories: unlike England, where the horrifying conditions in the youth reformatories made the threat of them "the ultimate weapon" of middle-class social control, the juvenile courts and foster care networks *(Jugendfürsorge)* set up in Germany in the 1890s were comparatively benign and had success rehabilitating troubled children. The liberal association laws of the German Empire made it possible for sympathetic mentors to help found a youth movement that rejected the adult authority through organizations run by youths only. The same laws meant that leaders of other youth recreational associations had to be careful about exerting their authority too much lest the teenagers quit. Ultimately, there was no surefire way to prevent youths from smoking and participating in unsupervised leisure on the street and in the cafes, pubs, music halls, and cinemas.[36]

Nevertheless, even if they had no real authority over youths, the leaders of recreational associations could persuade their members to conform, as they did with remarkable success during the first year of the war. Furthermore, by almost all accounts, the discipline exacted by teachers was severe: most teachers still favored drill methods, and the classroom continued to be a stifling, sometimes cruel place. Many Social Democratic Party leaders, the supposed defenders of freedom of speech and association, happily cooperated with state officials and conservative politicians in suppressing the autonomy of the Socialist youth organizations. Working teenagers faced discipline through the continuation schools, and because they and their middle-class counterparts lived with their nuclear families and rarely left their home cities, they remained under the dominion of their stern fathers. After Germany industrialized, master craftsmen no longer restrained youths, but teachers, politicians, and other officials of the modern state were more than adequate substitutes.

2

The Constraints on Chauvinism

The memoirs, histories, novels, and oral accounts cited in the previous chapter often imputed that youth institutions were not only boot camps for raising uncritical citizens but also pep rallies for making Germany a military power-house. Indeed, reserve officers were legion among the ranks of secondary school teachers, and the curriculum in German and history had a particular emphasis on the monarchical dynasties and their wars. Tens of thousands of boys voluntarily joined uniformed associations where they learned shooting and military tactics, and hundreds of thousands of youths were members of avowedly patriotic recreational associations. In addition, publishers sold youths hundreds of thousands of imperialist adventure stories and even more nation-alist classics like the war poems of Schiller and the speeches of Fichte. Ac-cording to some scholars, threatening youths with the cane while whetting their interest in the greatness of Germany and the battling of soldiers aided the army, the veteran leagues, the conservative parties, and the extraparlia-mentary pressure groups like the Navy League in their goal of suppressing democracy and garnering popular support for world domination. In the 1970s these scholars suggested that the alleged chauvinism in schools, youth litera-ture, and recreational associations moved Germans to embrace war in 1914 and a militarist and nationalist dictatorship in 1933.[1]

Nevertheless, it is a distortion to claim that a militarism and nationalism like that of the Nazis infused German youth culture before 1914. Germans generally supported a colonial policy and navy building, and being an officer in the army brought prestige. Yet official policy ensured that the curriculum in schools almost never glorified war itself or engaged pupils directly in the politics of imperialism. Furthermore, the middle-class peace movement, though small, augmented its organizational capacity in the years before the war, and targeted nationalist secondary schools in particular. The war exercises in the uniformed youth associations were usually just capture-the-flag-like games, and the members did not learn the violent tactics that German expeditionary soldiers followed in the colonial wars. In any case, they made up only a tiny portion of the 2 million boys and girls in sport, confessional, patriotic, and other clubs. Influential middle-class and Socialist critics condemned the nationalist youth war literature, and publishers sold youths far more fairy tales, bildungsromans, and detective and cowboy tales. A few youths from families with members in the Pan-German League and other radical right-wing groups upheld a militarism and a rabid chauvinism that called for territorial expansion within Europe, but the Social Democratic Party and moderates in the middle class arguably succeeded in turning youths away from jingoism. These limits of militarism and nationalism were evidenced in a survey of 222 boys in elementary schools in Munich in 1912/13 in which just 2.6 percent of the respondents claimed they wanted to be professional soldiers. Male youths of all social milieus supported a policy of national defense in the event of an aggressive attack, but before 1914 just a handful wanted to risk death for territorial expansion and German world power.[2]

Teaching Patriotism

Nationalism and militarism certainly *did* become more pervasive in schools after Kaiser Wilhelm II upstaged the 1890 school conference and, in a notorious rebuke of the classical *Gymnasium*, blustered, "We should raise national young Germans, not young Greeks and Romans!" Administrators in Prussia subsequently initiated new militarist and nationalist content in elementary and secondary schools, increasing the weekly hours of German instruction in some places, requiring more emphasis on war in history in others, regularly using poems such as Schiller's that lauded soldiers' heroism, and organizing celebrations of the birthdays of the Hohenzollern monarchs and the defeat of France on Sedan Day. Throughout the Empire, school librarians stocked shelves with memoirs of battles and colonial domination. School music grew more belligerent and nationalist: pupils now sang not just pieces from the classical repertoire but also songs like "Desire for Battle" and "When the

Earth Turns Red with the Blood of Soldiers." Journals for German instructors like the *Zeitschrift für den deutschen Unterricht* increasingly adopted a nationalist tone, railing against everything un-German.[3]

Teachers in secondary schools generally greeted Wilhelm's charge to instill nationalist convictions with enthusiasm. Before the war, they were active in the Conservative and National Liberal parties and made up one-fifth of the local chairmen of the radical nationalist Pan-German League. A great many were reserve officers and unreflectively upheld military prestige and nationalist goals. Most, though far from all, elementary school teachers clamored to become reserve officers through the *einjährig-freiwillig* privilege (they earned it in Prussia in 1900). To prove their worthiness, they willingly carried out the nationalist mission. Those who did not faced discipline from the strict clerical school inspectors. Elementary school teachers in Bavaria were as enthusiastic about the military as in Prussia. Close to 90 percent of them attempted to take the *einjährig-freiwillig* privilege, at considerable personal expense. Their patriotism and loyalty to imperialist policy were rarely questioned.[4]

However, an estimated 70 percent of elementary school teachers voted for the progressive parties; historians, professors, and public figures opposed introducing nationalist and militarist content; and overall the modified school curricula had only a moderate influence on schoolchildren. Most school administrators did not follow the Kaiser's call to give the German language more prominence. The Prussian *Gymnasium* for the most part maintained the old curricula in classical languages; the *Oberrealschulen* never increased the hours of German instruction. Fewer weekly hours were devoted to German in Berlin elementary schools in 1900 than in 1872. The German Historians' Congresses rejected the Kaiser's call in 1890 to "awaken love of the Fatherland and a strong sense of duty to the front" through instruction in history. Consequently, few history books glorified war itself. Most portrayed France, Germany's rival, as a pinnacle of Western civilization, which in the Revolution introduced the principle of equality before the law. Elementary school teachers strongly supported this moderate content.[5]

The forces working against the Kaiser's call were substantial. Social Democrats tried to slow the implementation of militarist and jingoist curricula, as did the mentor to the Free German Youth Gustav Wyneken, who in 1913 wrote that the militarist and nationalist Young Germany League "scorned the striving for international reconciliation." Wilhelm Rein, the influential professor of pedagogy at the University of Jena, argued that the state needed to separate the schooling of boys firmly from their preparation for the military. Custom and the Reich Law of Association prohibited schoolteachers from engaging pupils in politics. This prohibition in most cases prevented more extreme nationalist ideas, such as those of the Pan-Germanists, from entering the curriculum. Despite some misguided claims to the contrary, the radical nationalist of ideas of Julius Langbehn and Paul de Lagarde never entered the mainstream educational discourse, let alone the classroom. The War Ministry had little if any direct influence on educational curricula. Lastly, in the years before the war, many elementary school teachers increasingly held pacifist sentiments and even published antimilitarist verse in their trade journals. In Bavaria, Baden, and Württemberg, Wilhelm's 1890 call led to a curriculum weighted toward a regional and local culture *(Heimat)*, rather than a national one, and administrators reduced the number of topics in international history primarily because the old curriculum had been too crammed with material.[6]

In sum, following the 1890 school conference, militarist and nationalist content was implemented in only piecemeal fashion, and its tone modulated according to the region, school, and individual teacher. One thing is certain: the content did not succeed in getting working-class youths to embrace imperialism and the constitutional monarchy or in turning them away from the antimilitarist and internationalist Social Democratic Party.

Fairy Tales and Far-Flung Wars

Conservatives in the late nineteenth century could target youths with nationalism and militarism in a way never done before because the market for youth literature had ballooned. The thriving business in books and magazines was a result of advances in printing technologies such as the typesetting machine and the rotary press, which lowered costs. In addition, the liberal Reich Press Law of 1874 freed publishers from excessive regulation by the various states. Above all, the prosperity after 1896, the achievement of near-universal literacy, and the substantial increase in leisure gave the first generation of youths from a broad spectrum of regions and social classes the money and time to buy and read printed matter. Even those who could not afford to own many books had access to them in the abundant public and paid lending libraries. On the eve of the war, reading had become the most popular leisure activity for youths. After 1914, it gradually lost ground to the cinema and the radio as the dominant mass media for youths. After the introduction of television, it never again achieved its earlier importance. In 1914 youth reading culture was arguably more vibrant than at any other time in history. Books and magazines in the decades before the war fulfilled the precondition for transmitting popular nationalism because they could reach all youths anywhere in the German-speaking lands. In practice, authors of war and nationalist literature for youths fell short of achieving that goal. Their books made up just a fraction of the book market for youths, and influential critics like the elementary school director Heinrich Wolgast, who edited lists of good books for youths in *Jugendschriften-Warte* (Youth Literature Observer), ensured that few ended up in libraries, bookstores, or the hands of young people. They also faced spirited criticism from Social Democrats.[7]

Youth war and nationalist literature had its origins in books that celebrated the early nineteenth-century wars of liberation. By the mid-nineteenth century, authors like Gustav Nieritz and Franz Hoffmann were selling military histories written for youths. With the onset of German imperialism in the 1890s, military adventure literature grew more profitable, and the authors turned to graphic stories of battles in the colonies. Many of these authors and the publishers who had the money to finance them were staunch supporters of imperialism. For example, the erstwhile elementary school teacher Wilhelm Kotzde and the retired cavalry general Fedor von Zobeltitz made it a priority to promote colonialism and celebrate military power in their stories. Many adopted the lurid adventure story as their model, and the sensationalism brought commercial success. Novels of soldiers fighting for German world power had endorsement and financing from the military and middle-class nationalists, including prominent Pan-Germanists such as Heinrich Claß and August Keim. Though most of the war stories were poorly written, youths found them engaging. In the decades before 1914, they became a popular genre for boys and some girls.[8]

These war stories projected a masculinity modeled on the courageous and merciless young soldier, the warrior fiercely loyal to the nation. They accordingly transmitted the idea that manhood was tied to youthful vigor—what Theodore Roosevelt called "strenuous masculinity" and what in Europe and North America increasingly became a dominant concept of manliness. Youths were receptive to stories exalting strenuous masculinity particularly during the international crises over colonialism after 1900, when Germans increasingly thought that middle-class boys were effeminate and feared that the country lacked virile soldiers. In the years before the outbreak of the war, youth war and imperialist adventure literature inspired middle-class male teenagers like Georg Heym to fantasize in their diaries and letters that a European war would end their alienation and boredom. The promise of adventure and manhood in this patriotic youth literature doubtlessly inspired tens of thousands of other young men to volunteer in August 1914.[9]

Despite its moderate popularity, war and nationalist literature before 1914 competed with a broader set of genres for young German readers. It did not reach most girls. The hundreds of novels modeled on Emmy von Rhoden's *Trotzkopf* (1885) traced the conflicts female youths experienced in balancing the feminine values of passivity and selflessness against the reality that middle-class women, who did not marry on average until age 26, needed to be proactive in learning trades. Novels for girls rarely invoked nationalist and militarist themes. Boys and girls regularly bought or borrowed older children's books like Heinrich Hoffmann's *Struwwelpeter* (1845) and Wilhelm Busch's *Max und Moritz* (1865); classical masterpieces, such as Goethe's *Götz von Berlichingen* (1771), Schiller's *Wilhelm Tell* (1805), Kleist's *Michael Kohlhaas* (1810), and Lessing's *Minna von Barnhelm* (1763); translations of foreign classics like Jules Verne's *Twenty Thousand Leagues under the Sea* (1870), James Fenimore Cooper's *Leatherstocking Tales* (1823–1841), and Daniel Dafoe's *Robinson Crusoe* (1719); and, above all, contemporary newspapers, novels, essays, and literary journals intended for adult audiences. The most popular genre of youth literature before 1914 remained fairy tales; youths had access not only to editions of the Grimm brothers' collection but also to scores of new ones published every year. Finally, becoming wildly popular in the decade before the war were the penny dreadfuls, the cheap, lurid paperbacks for young customers, with adventure tales of American and British characters like Buffalo Bill, Nick Carter, Lord Lister, and Texas Jack. Many penny dreadfuls described military adventures and asserted that white Europeans were superior to native peoples. But because the publishers wanted to increase profits by selling on an international market, the penny dreadfuls were not particularly nationalist; few exalted a particularly *German* superiority. In sum, literature lacking specifically militarist and nationalist themes as they related to imperialism constituted the lion's share of books and stories for youth.[10]

Another limit on war and nationalist literature was the middle-class and Socialist movements that contested the genre's value. Though being a military man was a mark of status in imperial Germany, many in the middle class favored a masculinity based on self-control and fatherhood. By one account, the "sign of dignity" of refined gentlemen in Central Europe was gray hair and a habit of passing "over all reports of war in the newspapers just as they did the sporting pages." This ideal contradicted the masculinity of youthful release and aggression in the imperialist stories. The poor quality of war and nationalist literature also irked parents and teachers. Pedagogically minded reformers like Wolgast and Johannes Tews, the elementary school teacher who edited the monthly review of good literature in *Volksbildung* (Continuing Education), pointed out that stories by Goethe were better for youths than novels of teenagers fighting in far-flung places. Though accused of being an "enemy of the Fatherland" by the Pan-Germanists, Wolgast like Tews had widespread support from liberal parents. Also supporting him was the central professional organization of German elementary school teachers (Tews sat on the executive committee), which condemned the stories of impetuous soldiers battling aboriginals in Africa and Asia. Parents consequently bought the editions of classics published by Dürerbund and the other reputable presses that Wolgast and Tews endorsed. Although the Social Democratic Party did not work directly with Wolgast, its members sympathized with his cause. Their youth organizations prohibited war and nationalist literature in their lending libraries. In 1906 the centrist Karl Kautsky and the revolutionary Clara Zetkin successfully petitioned the Social Democratic Party to create and disseminate a youth literature expressly intended to combat militarism and nationalism. The Social Democratic Party together with Wolgast and Tews ensured that most books published for youths in Germany until 1914 had nothing to do with war. Their efforts also meant that many books for youths were antiwar.[11]

The only broadly recommended nationalist genre that at times glorified military adventure was German classical literature. In celebrating nationalist wars as noble, the works of Fichte, Schiller, and others doubtlessly induced the romantic dreams that war was chivalrous, particularly among secondary school boys who read them widely. But the influence of these romantics' conception of war and nation should not be exaggerated. Written before the unification of Germany, they dealt with national identity, not support for the arms race, colonialism, and the assertion of German world power. These works were valued for their aesthetic beauty in the tradition of the *Iliad* and the *Aeneid*; men in power read them throughout Europe and North America without wanting to make war. German classical literature likely motivated the tens of thousands of young *Gymnasium* graduates who volunteered for the

colors in August 1914. But they had less influence on youths who did not attend a secondary school. Most male youths rejected the kind of militarism
and nationalism in which dying for your country's world power was cast as an
act of glory.

Exercising Nationalism

Because of the arms race, the scramble for colonies, the growing popularity of
the Social Democratic Party, and the party's preaching of internationalism,
conservatives and state officials hoped that recreational associations would
not only redress the alleged moral degeneracy of urban male youths but also
raise loyal patriots, particularly young workers susceptible to Socialism. They
also wanted to turn weak middle-class boys into manly soldiers; in their view,
boys who no longer did strenuous manual labor were namby-pambies. They
were influenced in particular by G. Stanley Hall, the author of the interna-
tionally acclaimed *Adolescence* (1904), the first comprehensive treatise on youth
psychology, which impugned middle-class parents for a home life that undermined their sons' vigor.

The model for these conservatives was partly "muscular Christianity," the
British movement that claimed church attendance and physical conditioning
would purge male youths of sin and enhance their self-control and diligence.
The most celebrated offshoots of British muscular Christianity, the so-called
uniformed associations, such as the Boys' Brigades (founded in 1884) and the
Church Lads' Brigades (1891), inspired imitations across North America and
Western Europe. As imperialist rivalry grew, the importance of religion receded in the muscular Christian organizations. Reformers in France, Germany, Great Britain, Austria-Hungary, and the United States insisted that
the priority was to cultivate strength, endurance, and virility, what Theodore
Roosevelt called strenuous masculinity. The British Boy Scouts was one of the
first non-Christian uniformed youth associations created along these ideals.
It aimed to redress Britain's failures in the Boer War and the alleged crisis
of masculinity caused by the aggression of suffragettes, the lack of adult supervision in commercial leisure, the homosexuality trial of Oscar Wilde, the
decline in national fertility, and the increasing military and economic competition with Germany, where uniformed youth groups had by then grown ex-
ponentially. In 1914 the Boy Scouts had over 150,000 members in Great
Britain, 100,000 in the United States, 90,000 in Germany, and 11,000 in

France (which lagged behind other nations in founding youth recreational associations).[12]

Unlike nations and states elsewhere, which never became directly involved with recreational associations to any notable extent, Prussia took an active part in financing not just the Boy Scouts but all sorts of sport and patriotic—that is, non-Socialist—groups. Its involvement began in 1891 with a few small programs, but the Prussian ministers felt a new urgency in 1907, when Liebknecht began radicalizing a generation of Socialist youth. One of the ministers' measures was to push the Reichstag to pass paragraph 17 of the 1908 Reich Law of Association, which forbade politics in youth organizations (in practice the law targeted only the Socialist ones). Another was interior minister Bethmann-Hollweg's plan for "positive measures" in youth affairs—that is, financing recreational programs. This task was undertaken by the Central Office for Welfare of the People *(Zentralstelle für Volkswohlfahrt)*. Earlier, this office had been concerned almost exclusively with endangered youths—orphans, young offenders, children from troubled homes, and young workers living independently of their families. Yet the debates over the Law of Association caused a paradigm shift in the German concept of state welfare for youths: instead of overseeing coercive or compulsory welfare for endangered youths *(Jugendfürsorge)*, state officials began to offer *all* male and later female youths opportunities for a recreation *(Jugendpflege)* that would inculcate patriotism and promote physical fitness. Bavaria, Saxony, and other states followed, sponsoring programs similar to the Prussian ones.[13]

The financing increased over tenfold when the Prussian education minister issued the *Jugendpflege* Edict of January 1911. The decree sought to create "joyful, physically capable, ethically proficient youths filled with a sense of community, a fear of God, and a love of *Heimat* and the Fatherland"—that is, the opposite of the secular, internationalist, and antimilitarist youths that the Social Democratic organization cultivated. For this reason the decree initially won warm approval from the Catholic and Protestant churches, which despised the Socialists for denigrating religion. Under the decree, patriotic youth associations—athletic clubs, paramilitary groups, and even confessional organizations—were eligible for discounts on train tickets and accident insurance and could make use of equipment paid for by the state. The decree implied that all youths had a right to recreation, provided it was patriotic. The Social Democratic groups were accordingly not given any money.[14]

The 1911 *Jugendpflege* Edict established a new official, the district youth worker *(Kreisjugendpfleger)*—the only such bureaucrat paid for by a major state in the world—and immediately started training forty thousand of them. The youth workers were mostly full-time teachers but they also included school directors, school inspectors, gymnastics instructors, jurists, pastors, priests, and retired officers. Although states offered them remuneration, they often worked in an honorary capacity. Because the 1911 Edict merely funded already existing youth associations, the youth worker's main chore was to write municipalities and private associations, requesting that they share facilities and equipment such as playing fields and slide projectors. In addition, they founded libraries, intervened in disputes among recreational associations over soliciting young members, organized and publicized large events like athletic competitions, oversaw training seminars for association leaders, lobbied the municipalities and private charities for money, and worked with the elementary and vocational schools to recruit youths. Most youth workers imagined themselves belonging to a community of colleagues who shared social and national goals. In Frankfurt a.M., they held regular meetings, invited guest lecturers, and then ate dinner together in a restaurant. Journals such as *Ratgeber für Jugendvereine* and the numerous regional publications, such as *Achtern Ploog!* (Stade) and *Jugendpflege im Regierungsbezirk Cöln*, forged a professional community.[15]

Prussia and the other states got involved in youth recreation primarily because they worried about the physical and political reliability of male youths in their future role as soldiers and voting citizens. For these reasons, the first programs did not include money for female organizations. But leaders in the women's movement pointed officials to studies showing that working girls suffered from poor health and were increasingly susceptible to becoming Socialists and "falling" into prostitution. Furthermore, Germany's security depended on having healthy, fertile, and patriotic mothers to bear and raise strong and ideologically reliable sons to be soldiers in future armies. Existing recreational associations for girls also offered courses in gardening, knitting, sewing, ironing, and other skills needed by Germany's future housewives and domestic servants, which were increasingly in short supply as rural female youths took good paying jobs in factories rather than go into service with middle-class families. Using these arguments, the leaders of the women's movement convinced the Prussian education minister in 1913 to extend the *Jugendpflege* Edict to associations for female youths. On the eve of the war, Germany accordingly had more advanced financial and administrative structures to mobilize female youths for patriotic purposes than did other countries.[16]

As officials hand-chosen by the Prussian and other state governors, the youth workers were dedicated to their mission. Coordinating youth associations was a complex task, however. For example, in the district of Biedenkopf in Hessen, which had two thousand youths age 14 to 18, a single youth worker had to negotiate the interests of forty-four different sport associations, five business youth associations, and ten other groups. During the war, his district also had fifteen military youth companies, with fifty-five leaders. Furthermore, he had to reckon with the jurisdictions of eight local youth welfare committees. A youth worker in Unterwesterwald near Montabaur in Hessen operated in eighty different communities, coordinating over fifty associations that served five thousand youth. Unlike most youth workers, he had the good fortune of having a telephone line installed in 1917. That was not the case in 1916, when he wrote 1,526 letters himself, all by hand. Some association leaders viewed the youth workers as an official seeking to wrest away local control, representing yet another arm of the state's regulatory apparatus that swelled during the war. All the same, even though youth workers sat on municipal recreational committees that disbursed funds, they lacked any powers beyond persuasion, and a financially independent association could rebuff them. It took a bold character to bring the state into organizations hitherto proudly separate from the Prussian bureaucracy. The annual reports depicted such a talented official: the intrepid and determined Martha Abicht from affluent Charlottenburg (Berlin). She was so self-righteous about her work that she made regular surprise visits to associations—calls that clearly irritated the individual associations' leaders. But even when the youth worker finally met with obstinate leaders, their "contact" often resulted in little more than a conversation. Noble aims and hard work alone were no use without charm, enterprise, and negotiation skills. Less charismatic youth workers reported feelings of alienation from the clubby world of the private youth associations. Others were frustrated that many educated people still had no idea what *Jugendpflege* was.[17]

Although it created state youth workers, the 1911 Edict was "remarkably anemic" in cultivating nationalism and militarism because it financed already existing confessional, sport, and patriotic youth associations indiscriminately. Because there was no compulsion, the decree did not socialize working male or female youths with Socialist leanings, the very ones about which the Prussian cabinet was most concerned. Even worse, the decree brought the inflammatory conflicts of German high politics into youth associations, as political organizations with different agendas competed for young members. Conservatives in the army, the veteran societies, and the middle-class Protestant political parties and organizations at first hailed the 1911 decree. They argued that steering young members into patriotic, athletic, or paramilitary associations was now a key part of their "national work." But within a few months, both Catholic and Protestant confessional youth associations believed that state financing for patriotic secular associations, though small, threatened their own stagnating membership. Furthermore, in places where patriotic youth associations were well established, conservatives decried giving money to Catholic confessional groups. Between 1911 and 1912 many Catholic youth sodalities had been successful in their requests for money to buy gymnastics equipment and to lure members away from the rival secular patriotic associations. These actions led Protestant leaders of secular patriotic associations to call for an end of support for Catholic associations. The decree that was supposed to unify youth associations to cultivate nationalism instead produced new confessional conflicts. A hue and cry over "splintering" became acute. The anxiety in the Rhine provinces was so great that the Prussian authorities there called an emergency conference with the education minister to calm fears of a renewed *Kulturkampf,* a political campaign against Catholics. Youth workers spent a good deal of their time mediating these disputes.[18]

Conservative officials in Prussia had already grown frustrated with the situation in the summer of 1911 because the state was doling out funds to associations even though they did not further military training. Indeed, just a handful of the funded associations marched the boys in drills, organized war games, or taught them shooting and other military skills. For this reason, General Fieldmarshal Colmar Freiherr von der Goltz founded the Young Germany League in November 1911, ten months after the *Jugendpflege* Edict. With the explicit goal of cultivating patriotism and military preparedness, the League sponsored activities similar to those of the Boy Scouts but with greater emphasis on army skills. To participate in a Young Germany League event or workshop, a boy had only to be a member of one of its subsidiary organizations. Many non-Socialist youth associations were members by 1914: by proclaiming, without authority, that belonging to the Young Germany League aided receipt of government funds under the 1911 decree, von der

Goltz was able to browbeat hundreds of youth associations, including some from Bavaria and other states, to become dues-paying members. By 1914 the League ballooned to 750,000 members, making it the single largest secular youth organization in the world. Its budget in 1914, 745,000 marks, constituted over a fifth of state funds earmarked for youth recreation. Enterprising businessmen capitalized on the League's cachet, etching its initials on camping equipment and field watches.[19]

The success of the Young Germany League exasperated the leaders of confessional and Social Democratic youth organizations alike. They had never expected capture-the-flag-like war games to be so popular with male youths. Leaders of both Protestant and Catholic associations resented the League for abandoning religious edification. *Die Wacht*, the main Catholic youth weekly, which had long supported German nationalism and colonialism, denounced the League for aiming to turn "all of Germany into a giant barracks." When the Young Germany League organized working youths in the yellow (company) unions, and boys patrolled in uniforms near factories, leaders of the Christian unions accused the League of "terrorization." For spending workers' tax money on programs that excluded Social Democratic groups and promoted militarism and nationalism, the Social Democrats called the Prussian House "the world's most reactionary parliament."[20]

In their "monocular focus on the military," historians who impugned recreational associations for cultivating German chauvinism overlooked that the overwhelming number of youth associations were nonmilitarist and only moderately nationalist. As in German-speaking regions of Austria-Hungary, uniformed youth associations in Germany made up no more than 10 percent of the total. Beyond the ninety thousand Boy Scouts, which basically taught camping skills, no more than sixty-eight thousand male youths in 1914 were in the paramilitary *Jugendwehren* that taught shooting and marched boys in military drills. The associations in the Young Germany League attracted some working-class male youths; war games *were* popular among middle-class male youths; and the Young Germany League certainly *did* get its members to identify with militarism and nationalism. But the League did not significantly introduce militarism into confessional organizations and had only a moderate effect on sport clubs, which represented by far the most popular recreational associations. Above all, the 1911 *Jugendpflege* decree and the founding of the Young Germany League did not integrate youths of different social classes and confessions or bring them together for a nationalist cause.

On the contrary, they merely intensified the politicization and reviled "splintering" of youth associations.[21]

Schools, youth literature, and recreational associations did contribute to the nationalism and militarism of prewar Germany, and they played a part in motivating the tens of thousands of male teenagers to rush to the recruiting garrisons in August 1914. After 1890 many schools introduced new nationalist and militarist content into the curriculum, and teachers were in general good patriots who respected the prestige of the army. The two decades before the war also saw the growing popularity of military songs in music instruction. War literature that was graphic in its depiction of the colonial wars became popular and was readily available in bookstores and public, school, and paid lending libraries. More recreational organizations in Germany than in other nations drilled male youths in military exercises. Germany also had far more patriotic youth associations than other nations, and unlike anywhere else, the states offered them subsidies.

Yet there were significant limits to this nationalism and militarism. History curricula avoided graphic descriptions of war, and the politics of navy building and acquiring colonies was banned from the classroom. The hours given to instruction in German never changed significantly. The lion's share of youth literature was not militarist or nationalist, and there were well-respected, trenchant critics of war literature. Militarist youth associations were just a fraction of the vast network of recreational clubs. Most of these clubs were patriotic, and many boys adored the activities sponsored by the militarist and nationalist Young Germany League, but gymnastics, hiking, swimming, crafts, religion, and homemaking were far more common. When schools, youth literature, and recreational associations did cultivate patriotism and respect for the military, they did not invoke the crass chauvinism seen later during the war.

3

War Pedagogy in the Era
of the *Burgfrieden*

The German curricula contained some moderate militarism and nationalism before the war, but their tone became radicalized in August 1914, when teachers and educational reformers who had railed against the elitism and authoritarianism in schools proclaimed their patriotism and endorsed the war. In general, the middle class's optimism regarding political and social change in 1914 stoked good feelings about the war and led to a national self-mobilization. That university professors now felt hopeful is well known; less understood is that schoolteachers, administrators, and reformers had similar views and undertook a wholesale revision of German education. Teachers used the war and the perceived universal enthusiasm for it as a topic in all academic subjects, from writing to physical science. The good feelings about war and the cultivation of nationalism and militarism varied, of course, by region, period, and type of school. But in Catholic and Protestant secondary schools, as well as in elementary schools in Protestant small cities, towns, and villages, teachers glorified military heroes and whetted the pupils' interest in weapons and destruction. Because of the *Burgfrieden* and the censorship of pacifists, officials and teachers no longer believed that the topic of German world power was political and violated custom and paragraph 17 of the Reich Law of Association. As a result, teachers now regularly discussed German military might with their pupils.[1]

One might suspect that schools would become militarized with the mobilization for war. After all, in August 1914 the state made an extraordinary intrusion into people's lives with countless new regulations and deep claims on the citizens' bodies and wallets. But historians have erred in claiming that relationships of authority in German schools hardened during the war. In fact, the political opportunities of the *Burgfrieden* and the ad hoc emergency measures to deal with conscription enabled teachers to *reform* the authoritarian classroom in ways never before possible. Provided they used content that firmly supported the war, teachers could forge a more compassionate relationship with pupils and experiment with progressive teaching methods such as having pupils read newspapers and write autobiographies. After the outbreak of the war, German teachers introduced child-centered methods while cultivating nationalism and militarism more energetically than before. Evidence of this change is found in articles in the daily and pedagogical press, decrees of the state and provincial officials, and a set of schoolchildren's original compositions from 1915. Many described this change as war pedagogy, after Theobald Ziegler, the Strasburg professor and member of the left-liberal Progressive Party who in 1917 became an activist in the radical nationalist Fatherland Party, popularized this term in his prescription "The Ten Commandments of a War Pedagogy." His rules were printed at one time or another in almost every professional journal for teachers (see the Appendix).[2]

The progressive nature of war pedagogy suggests that nationalism and militarism intensified in Germany not because state officials under Wilhelm II excluded the progressive middle classes or foisted nationalism on schoolchildren through authoritarian practices, but rather because they encouraged teachers to institute child-centered reforms during an era of national self-mobilization. The narrative of war pedagogy also suggests a revision of the view that the widespread experimentation with pedagogical methods first began with the founding of the Weimar Republic. It points instead to reform achievements that coincided with the popular nationalist exuberance at the outbreak of the war.[3]

The convergence of militarism and nationalism with reform principles produced a variety of reactions in schoolchildren. Because one of the main principles in war pedagogy was to respect schoolchildren's ideas, teachers tolerated a modicum of negative reactions to the war. Yet they were invariably successful in making these pupils connect their grief and discomfort to patriotic virtue. By shunning the old drill system, teachers under war pedagogy refrained from crass indoctrination, but they still practiced a form of inculcation, only more subtle and sophisticated than before. They doubtlessly infused war deeply into the everyday life and sentiments of their pupils. Paradoxically, the success of an ideology that lent the war popular legitimacy and extolled nationalism and militarism depended on using reform methods that tolerated a modicum of dissent. In their accommodation to a variety of voices, teachers nonetheless reinforced an even more intense nationalism and militarism in many male pupils because they no longer prohibited belligerent and chauvinist expressions.

Through its content and particularly the writing of compositions about combat, teachers encouraged boys to fantasize about the power of Germany and the violence of soldiers, furthering the development of strenuous masculinity. Because two-thirds of classrooms were coed, and female teachers of all-girl classes tended to be spirited advocates of war pedagogy, schoolgirls often shared in these fantasies, as shown in their first-person compositions about soldiers' exploits. But the teachers thought that girls would make a particular contribution to the war by developing their feminine capacities through knitting, caring for siblings and wounded soldiers, withholding complaints, making sacrifices, and cultivating the selflessness they would allegedly need to be good German wives and mothers.

The Implementation of War Pedagogy

War pedagogy was implemented with remarkable speed through a set of ad hoc measures. Immediately after the outbreak of the war, the state education ministers gave teachers permission to be flexible with the curriculum. Teachers then experimented with new content and methods, and the ministers responded with affirming decrees. On 7 August 1914, August von Trott zu Solz, the aristocratic Prussian education minister (*Kultusminister,* or *Minister der geistlichen und Unterrichts-Angelegenheiten*) and a Conservative Party member, laid the foundation for the new curricula by issuing a decree asking teachers "to make room everywhere to exploit the great events of the times for education and instruction." The edict recognized that teachers sometimes needed to forgo the standardized curriculum. Although he intended his directive for secondary school teachers, elementary school teachers interpreted it as applying to them as well. The Bavarian education minister's first major decree, issued on 19 October 1914, drew on the language in the Prussian edict and claimed it was necessary to cultivate patriotism and enthusiasm through the school celebrations that teachers were already regularly holding.[4]

Giving more specific instructions than the education ministers were local administrators: the district school inspectors, the provincial school authorities *(Provinzialschulkollegien, Oberpräsidenten)*, and the notables on the local school boards *(Schuldeputation, Schulverwaltung, Schulkommission)*. For example, in October 1914 the district school inspector in Linden-Hanover told continuation and elementary school teachers that they no longer had to adhere strictly to the curriculum. He gave teachers the freedom to focus on the daily events and suggested that war material, such as battle reports in newspapers, be used "wherever it was exciting." Teachers were to discuss their personal experiences in the war freely with pupils. In the other German cities, the school inspectors and regional administrations told elementary school teachers not to worry about the prescribed curriculum and encouraged them to introduce whatever content and methods they considered appropriate for wartime.[5]

The education ministers and school inspectors initiated war pedagogy, but its implementation was ultimately the work of the teachers themselves. Teachers could be brazen in demanding the freedom to nurture enthusiasm through a new approach to schoolchildren, a stance that contrasted to the conservatism of officials, who were more concerned about maintaining order. For example, elementary and secondary school teachers in Prussia denounced the High Command for refusing to release pupils from school to celebrate the seizure of Brussels on 20 August. Following General Hindenburg's victory at Tannenberg on 30 August, they also lambasted the Prussian education minister and local authorities for denying schoolchildren the opportunity to join the exuberant crowds on Sedan Day (2 September). The education minister von Trott zu Solz justified his decision by pointing out how schoolchildren, in the excitement of the first month of the war, were falling behind in their studies. He reiterated the slogan in his decree from 5 August that it was "not in accordance with the times to let youths be idle." But this was no consolation for the *Vossische Zeitung*, the influential liberal Berlin daily. On 31 August its editors called the minister's refusal to release pupils for the celebration "deplorable educational absolutism [*klägliche Schulmeisterei*]," an explicit attack on his authoritarianism. At the last minute the education minister conceded and ordered the Berlin authorities to release pupils for the Sedan Day holiday. But he failed to transmit the order to many school directors in time. Consequently, hundreds of teachers in Berlin had no idea they were permitted to release their pupils. Many had released them anyway, snubbing the central authorities. Those who did not fulminated about the bungle. Analogous disputes over releases for victory celebrations between teachers and administrators unfolded in other cities as well. In a dispute in Stralsund, where the Prussian governor censured the school inspector for issuing a victory holiday, the editors of *Der Volksschullehrer* sneered, "As if the number of hours is the most important aspect of education." In this and other challenges to the authority of the central administrators, no teacher was, to my knowledge, ever disciplined.[6]

In the following months, teachers carried out their wholesale changes in the curriculum and methods, but the Prussian education minister had nothing to say about this transformation until 6 November 1914, when he issued his next decree on methods and content, "Cultivation of Patriotic Enthusiasm in the Secondary Schools."

I have viewed with satisfaction the notices sent to me that many secondary schools have admirably strived during individual lesson hours and other

No school: victory holiday! *Source:* Franz Führen, *Lehrer im Krieg: Ein Ehrenbuch deutscher Volksschullehrer* (Leipzig: Georg Kummer, 1936), plate 22.

appropriate times to place teaching assignments into lively relationship the great events of the war that fill all of our hearts and minds. I approve of these endeavors and am convinced that none of the secondary schools under my auspices will refrain from leading youths to witness this glorious time sympathetically and to ingrain it perpetually in their memories. Every one of us who did not march to the front will give thanks by announcing the heroism of those over there sacrificing their blood for the Fatherland. All teachers will also see it as their most lovely task to plant, through constant reference to the great deeds of our people and the enormous achievement of our brave army, the seeds of patriotic enthusiasm into the souls of youths, who should carry this rich fruit into the future. Such a task in no way hinders the demand for loyal fulfillment of duty to schoolboys and schoolgirls, even if now and then there are small postponements or even gaps in the prescribed teaching material in order to address the daily events.

Because it addressed secondary school teachers only, the edict angered the editors of *Pädagogische Zeitung,* the organ of the Berlin Teachers' Association and central German pedagogical weekly for elementary school teachers. They claimed that they too deserved recognition for being patriotic. As an afterthought, the minister then directed his decree to them as well. Elementary school teachers brushed off the insult and joined secondary school teachers in regularly citing the decree to justify foregoing the old methods and curricula and initiating new kinds of instruction related to the war. The reaction of the elementary school teachers demonstrates how they were already bringing about war pedagogy without any elaborate orders from the central administration. In the November decree the Prussian minister retroactively approved of the patriotic "endeavors" already undertaken by the secondary school teachers.[7]

Throughout 1915, school inspectors continued to ask elementary school teachers to nurture enthusiasm for the war by placing all instruction in relation to the present. The teachers were irritated that they had to tell the inspectors that they were already doing so. For example, in response to an inspector in East Prussia who asked teachers in November 1915 to focus on the war, abridge the prescribed lesson plans, and bring in current material to make the war events lively, the editors of *Leipziger Lehrerzeitung* quipped: "One doesn't know if one should laugh or be angry about this obvious measure that the school inspector presents as pedagogical wisdom." In early 1916 delegates in the Prussian House censured the few remaining school inspectors who were obstinately enforcing the prewar curriculum and lesson plans.[8]

Elementary school teachers were enthusiastic about the war because the political settlement of August 1914 promised reforms of the exclusionary structures and practices in the German educational system. In Prussia they had been smarting from the failure of reforms in 1906 that would have weakened the authority of clerical school inspectors. They had also been humiliated by subsequent judicial rulings that denied them the full status and privileges of civil servants. Lastly, they opposed the continued de facto separation of elementary and secondary education, which made them the lesser "step-siblings" of the better-paid secondary school teachers who attended university *(Oberlehrer)*. In the spring of 1914 their professional organization, the German Teachers' Association, had endorsed the Progressive Party for its support of school reform, risking censure from the school inspectors. Now because of the *Burgfrieden*, they looked forward to a postwar national coalition of the Progressive and the Social Democratic parties, which would implement extensive educational reforms, including their right to attend university. Like the Social Democrats, elementary school teachers knew that to justify future reforms it was now necessary to show their patriotism to help in the mobilization.[9]

The war also offered new opportunities for reforms sought by the so-called academic *Germanisten*, the secondary school teachers and their allies who wanted to replace the *Gymnasium* curriculum of ancient languages and literatures with one focused on German literature and culture. The new imperatives to focus on the present war bolstered their arguments that texts and languages from distant millennia were no longer relevant. They maintained that everyone now recognized that a "deepening of the popular German spirit" was the goal for all schools—even the classical *Gymnasium*. The National-Liberals in the Prussian House agreed. Even many philologists conceded that the time had come to make secondary schools more German.[10]

In response to these attacks, the defenders of the Latin and Greek curricula asserted that the *Gymnasium* had in fact succeeded in raising schoolboys to be enthusiastic patriots. Many pointed out that because ancient literature stressed how war was noble, almost every eligible boy in the upper grades in the *Gymnasien* had joined the army voluntarily. Other secondary school teachers perpetuated the legend of the martyrdom at Langemarck near Ypres: on 10 November 1914, hundreds of schoolboys, volunteers fresh out of the classical *Gymnasien*, allegedly marched into French machine-gun fire to their deaths singing "Deutschland, Deutschland über alles" (which became the

German national anthem in 1922). Scores of *Gymnasium* teachers published articles extolling their efforts to excite schoolboys by connecting the German soldiers' exploits with the brave actions of Greek and Roman soldiers. They also examined the speeches of illustrious generals like Hannibal and Julius Caesar and discussed the military strategies of the Persian, Peloponnesian, and Punic wars. After his pupils read the diaries of Caesar, one Latin teacher "transformed the peaceful classroom into a strategy meeting of the General Staff, driving the army to storm fortifications and surround enemy forces effortlessly."[11]

The single organization most responsible for validating and spreading war pedagogy was the Central Institute for Education and Teaching *(Zentralinstitut für Erziehung und Unterricht)* in Berlin. Though founded under the Prussian education minister von Trott zu Solz with an endorsement by the Kaiser in March 1914, the Central Institute's politics was reform-oriented. Its director, Luigi Pallat, supported the *Einheitsschule* and in 1920 organized the conference that aimed to implement it. But despite a misguided claim by a French propagandist, there is no evidence that he had plans to make the Central Institute a national education bureaucracy. At its inaugural lecture, Pallat envisioned an organization that would distribute critical information on methods, materials, libraries, school hygiene, youth associational life, and youth welfare, preferably through traveling exhibitions. He envisioned a "living workshop."[12]

When it opened its doors in April 1915, the Central Institute devoted most of its energies to disseminating the war pedagogy curriculum. Under Pallat's leadership, the Central Institute's hall in Berlin hosted a variety of lectures, including "The Military Training of Our Schoolchildren," "War Help of German Schools," "War Compositions in Elementary Schools," "War Compositions in Secondary Schools," "Our War Poems," "War Diaries of Pupils," "War Drawings by Pupils," "Pedagogical Questions of Elementary Schools in War Literature," and "Pedagogical Questions for Secondary Schools in War Literature." The Central Institute also organized an exhibition in the spring of 1915 entitled "School and War," which presented visual evidence showing why classical education was now outmoded. It displayed the new teaching materials, such as war albums, postcards, collections of correspondences with soldiers *(Feldpostbriefe)*, and essays and war poems composed by schoolchildren. A major part of the exhibition was dedicated to original art about the war by children. According to the Progressive *Berliner*

Tageblatt, the drawings demonstrated that schoolchildren were enthralled by the war of movement, General Hindenburg, battleships, zeppelins, airplanes, and submarines. Typical of the reviews of the exhibition, the *Berliner Tageblatt* claimed that "schools correctly know how to imprint the essence of the war on children."[13]

Because all pedagogical journals discussed the exhibition, its influence in solidifying the new curriculum was enormous. Newspapers in cities far from Berlin exhorted their readers to attend. "School and War" was so popular that it remained open eight months beyond the originally planned four. Not all reactions were positive. In reaction to what they saw, the editors of the left-wing Social Democratic Party newspaper *Vorwärts* scoffed, "Our work after the war truly won't be an easy one." Nevertheless, they admitted that one could certainly observe the "joy" that the pupils had in making their drawings of battles and other subjects relating to the war: the "war-colored thoughts and feelings penetrate through all the pores of the child." It is not surprising that in October 1917 the Prussian education minister looked back at the exhibition fondly. In his mind, the war had permanently changed how schools taught and managed pupils.[14]

The Jingoism of the Curricula in 1914 and 1915

Most educators at all levels of schooling raved about how the war invigorated education. Perpetuating the legend of the Spirit of 1914, secondary school teachers regularly proclaimed that the war had wiped out all class differences and political conflict and united all Germans in a nationalist mission. This change in society, they believed, allowed them to teach about recent domestic and international events without violating the ban on politics in schools. Despite their quietism about nationalism before 1914, reformers and elementary school teachers were also ecstatic that the apparent universal nationalism in August 1914 purged Germany of internationalists and pacifists, thereby initiating a new era of progressive change, national in scope. For example, Georg Kerschensteiner claimed that the war destroyed "egoists and cowards, ambitious social climbers, and dull Philistines." The elementary schools' chief in Leipzig, the city on the vanguard of elementary school reform, was effusive in his enthusiasm: at the outbreak of war "a great wave of patriotic enthusiasm washed everything impure and dull, and the fire of our love of the Fatherland burned bright and clear." Even Friedrich Wilhelm Foerster, one of the very few who later publicly opposed the war, described his amazement about the patriotism and self-sacrifice he witnessed in Munich's working-class neighborhoods in August 1914. These and similar views were reprinted widely by the schoolteachers' trade and professional journals and created the impression that war had brought social harmony and put the German nation on course toward greatness. Not surprisingly, almost all these journals made reference to Johann Fichte's popular nationalism. In their own compositions, school-children regularly connected the current war to the historic Wars of Liberation in 1813.[15]

Elementary and secondary school teachers agreed with reformers and most administrators that every academic subject, from writing and German to physical science and religion, needed to focus on the war. In the pedagogical press, the most popular slogans to this effect were "let young people experience the greatness of the times" and "war is now the great teacher." Instructors revamped the content of their normal lessons plans under the principle that the present trumped the past. "Who would want to force teachers in these times to address the prescribed material?" asked one elementary school teacher from Baden. "Aren't the daily experiences more important to us?" Among the few who objected to this belief were a handful of secondary school teachers who questioned whether pupils could learn higher-level mathematics, physical and natural sciences, and classical languages only in relation to the war. Instead of changing all their curricula, these teachers introduced voluntary "war lessons" during the last hours of weekly instruction. Another objection was to the growing language of hate and the hanging of "crass" illustrations about the war in the classroom in 1915. But even the negative articles praised teachers for awakening patriotism. Negative articles were also rare. While the extent to which teachers should abandon the old curricula and how they should depict the war were still a matter of debate, the notion that war was the highest educational priority went uncontested in administrative orders and the teachers' journals. Although many teachers harbored secret reservations about war pedagogy, in their public statements, teachers across the social spectrum—male, female, Protestant, rural, urban, elementary, and secondary alike—proclaimed that Germany needed to introduce a nationalist curriculum centered on the war.[16]

Making their task easy were the new patriotic and militarist genres: heroic obituaries, cheerful war reports, prescriptions for good patriots in the illustrated magazines and daily newspapers, as well as the collections of patriotic war sermons, soldiers' letters, and war poems in the bookstores. War pedagogy, unlike the nationalist initiatives before 1914, had the advantage that this patriotic material appeared to well up from the German people themselves. Thus, as one chronicler of schools observed, "never before had schools had so rich and immediately powerful illustrative material for inspiring love of the Fatherland." A contributor to *Frankfurter Schulzeitung* exclaimed, "I could easily produce 500 new instructional materials." Teachers only had to ask their pupils to bring a magazine, poem, newspaper, or recently published books to class to fix attention on the war and the great patriotism it had unleashed. In fact, teachers had no real need for textbooks on the war; none was published until late 1915.[17]

Not surprisingly in an environment that silenced criticisms, the militarism and nationalism of lessons in countless examples became brash and animated. Teachers had their pupils read soldiers' letters in class because this activity supposedly mediated the "thrill" of war. During religious instruction in both Protestant and Catholic regions, teachers reinforced the idea of a purifying "holy war." They suggested that biblical war heroes like Joshua, Samson, David, and the Maccabees cultivated warrior ideals (anti-Semitism was entirely absent from the discourse about war pedagogy). In arithmetic lessons, elementary school children calculated the ammunition necessary to destroy a French division. Schools organized regular celebrations of the war, such as a slide presentation in Moabit-Berlin, praised by the liberal *Vossische Zeitung* for its "infinitely high educational value":

> With no small anticipation, the "boy battalions marched" in under the leadership of their teachers into the hall. The hall was packed up to the last seat; many had to stand, but everyone was filled with a glowing enthusiasm for the great holy task that their fathers, brothers, and relatives in such an incredible way filled on the battlefields in the East and West and South. . . . How the young heroes clearly idolize Hindenburg! . . . With earthy power, the enthusiasm of the boys roared through the hall.

Lively celebrations in schools—assemblies with speeches, poems, songs, and hero's stories, and classrooms adorned with flags, ribbons, and photographs of generals—now marked not only Sedan Day and the birthdays of the Hohenzollerns but, after September 1914, every military victory as well. After the celebrations, pupils were let out from school. In Berlin in October 1915, scores of teachers took their pupils to celebrate "Iron Hindenburg" by hammering nails into a wooden statue of the general on his birthday. In art class, schoolchildren drew trenches and battles. The prewar history curriculum had almost completely ignored the post-1870 period, but teachers now skipped over the pedantic narratives of the Hohenzollern dynasty and instead covered the German Empire and the current war, especially the successes of the military and its heroic soldiers. Especially popular were war poems by both Schiller and the millions of citizen-patriots who published in newspapers and magazines for the first time in 1914. According to one female teacher, the poems returned pupils to the delirium of August 1914, with "the shouting for joy, thirst for action, desire for battle, and blissful feeling of restless self-sacrifice for greatness." Most elementary and secondary schools erected honor boards with photographs or engraved names of teachers and schoolboys who had volunteered, died in battle, or earned the Iron Cross, the army's award for bravery.[18]

The Reform Teaching Methods of War Pedagogy

It is in some ways counterintuitive that war softened the pedagogical approach of German teachers and administrators. After all, German society stood under martial law, and the military regularly appropriated property, regulated prices, censored the press, arrested protestors, and conscripted millions of men. But these changes, together with assumptions about the authoritarianism of schools in imperial Germany, misled historians to claim that "the spirit of absolute authority" and "'the old drill school' experienced a rehabilitation under the leadership of well-known and respected pedagogues." These changes also led them to assume that under war pedagogy the educational bureaucracy raised "future obsequious subjects *(Untertanen)*" who "learned to follow the orders of the authorities" and that the war postponed educational reforms. While the tone of teachers' and educational reformers' proclamations certainly became more belligerent and nationalist, and many teachers called for more discipline to raise reliable soldiers, there is little evidence that war pedagogy bolstered authoritarian approaches to schoolchildren. In fact, articles in the pedagogical press and reports from the state bureaucracies indicated quite the opposite: the practical demands of the war and, more deeply, the political settlement of the *Burgfrieden* resulted in a new willingness to reform the "old drill school."[19]

The changes were possible for many reasons. Conscription required that most schools split the day into two sessions and reduce the number of weekly teaching hours for each pupil by half or more, and releases for victory celebrations further cut into the cumulative hours in the classroom. Consequently, teachers had to revise the curriculum wholesale. Furthermore, because countless officials left their posts for the army, administrators had less oversight over teachers who experimented with new methods and no longer went by the book. The conservative press and administrators were also sympathetic to the burdens on teachers. The agrarian conservative daily *Deutsche Tageszeitung* urged readers, for example, not to "judge the work of schools with the usual severity," a position that freed teachers from scrutiny over their classroom practices.[20]

Aiding those teachers who wished to experiment was the absence of open political dissent and the rhetoric of universal patriotism in magazines and newspapers. These conditions allayed the conservatives' fears that progressive teaching methods would raise schoolchildren to be critical of the government and its policies. The radical nationalist, Pan-Germanist *Tägliche Rundschau* published such a view, for example, in response to complaints that teachers were abandoning the prescribed curriculum:

> Can one avoid such petty nagging in a time when the German people is straining with all its strength to bring about the greatest possible sacrifice, when the profession of teachers and schools have stepped in enthusiastically for the holy and great affairs of the Fatherland? . . . Away with all the petty limitations on schools.

By contrast, teachers and pedagogical theorists who before the war had experimented with progressive methods, such as having pupils write autobiographical essays, had been careful to work with only the least controversial content like themes from everyday life. This caution kept politics out of the classroom, as officials and parents wanted. Yet it raised criticism that the new methods were teaching children about pets and friendship but not about valuable subjects such as national history and literature. However, for the entire war teachers and pupils regularly discussed international politics without breaking the taboo of politics in the classroom and violating the spirit of paragraph 17 of the Reich Law of Association. The justification of progressive methods was that they bolstered support for Germany and its war. Eduard Spranger, professor of pedagogy in Leipzig and a leading voice in school reform, employed this argument: an instructor could now teach as he or she wished because of the new "German consciousness of unity" and the end of "party and class differences."[21]

August 1914 offered a golden opportunity for reform because implicit in the *Burgfrieden* and the Spirit of 1914 was the recognition that public institutions needed to be more inclusive. In terms of high politics, this involved government cooperation with the Social Democratic Party, labor unions, and other organizations previously ostracized. More broadly, the political discourses on unity at least superficially stimulated efforts to minimize social and political conflict. In the first two years of the war, for example, the desire for class reconciliation and the future integration of the Social Democratic Party into the government institutions, such as school boards, led to new hopes for implementing the *Einheitsschule* (unity school). Reformers could tap into the semantic closeness that the word *Einheitsschule* had with the language of the *Burgfrieden* and the Spirit of 1914. For example, the maverick experimental psychologist Max Brahn justified reform by citing the new "feeling of belonging together." Others cited the "spiritual national unity" or the sacrifice of all classes in the war. In February 1916 Wilhelm Rein, the eminent professor of pedagogy in Jena, appealed for the *Einheitsschule* on the front page of the liberal *Vossische Zeitung*. He argued that the participation of everyone in the war effort required a national education system open to all social groups. The tenor of the demands for an *Einheitsschule* mellowed after 1916 when exhaustion set in and the more pressing necessity was the extreme shortages of coal, food, and personnel. But in the last years of the war most proponents simply assumed that the German state would implement an *Einheitsschule* after victory. According to one scholar, the calls for an *Einheitsschule* were an example of how "positions apparently became acceptable that before 1914 had been deemed revolutionary."[22]

In addition to promoting arguments in favor of social mobility, the war also helped another goal of the educational reformers: mitigating the severity and aloofness of German teachers and attending to the curiosity of schoolchildren. A haughty and distant attitude toward pupils did not accord with the populist ideas in the *Burgfrieden* and the Spirit of 1914. Schoolchildren, like all Germans, were making sacrifices—enduring the absences of loved ones and shortages of food and coal—in order to bring about victory. According to teachers, they also showed immense curiosity about the military operations. Secondary school boys showed up for their exams sporting military uniforms, and reporters noted that the most enthusiastic onlookers during the mobilization were schoolchildren. Given the patriotic goals of the curriculum, it seemed natural to make this excitement and self-sacrifice the starting point for lessons. Doing so necessitated abandoning drill methods and implementing activities that engaged schoolchildren more immediately. Teachers embraced free discussions more than before. As an elementary school teacher in the Rhineland claimed, wartime was the wrong time to stay "in the dull land of desolate drills."[23]

Teachers could experiment with activities that eliminated the monotony of the old school regime because administrators almost universally agreed with Ziegler's "Ten Commandments of a War Pedagogy." The fourth and eighth commandments endorsed the abandonment of the official lesson plans *(Lehrpläne)*. Enforced by state school inspectors before the war, lesson plans had been the primary way to regulate what happened in the classroom, stipulating topics and hours to be spent on them. Not surprisingly, the debates over curricula, whether in the pedagogical press or during the school conferences of 1890 and 1900, centered on the efficacy of the lesson plans. The most progressively minded teachers and reformers wanted the lesson plans to be more flexible in order to make pedagogical experimentation possible. But few in the bureaucracy, particularly in the Prussian Ministry of Education under von Trott zu Solz after 1909, were willing to budge on them. Their obstinacy ebbed in August 1914, however. Improvisation resulted in part from the practical difficulties of running schools in wartime and from the shortened schooldays, victory holidays, and acute shortages of teachers that frustrated fulfilling the plans to the letter. The Prussian Education Ministry also recognized the benefits of pedagogical experimentation for a nationalist and militarist mobilization. Elementary school teachers in particular tinkered with the lesson plans and wrested control of curriculum away from the school inspectors and central administrations. "No reasonable teacher now follows the prescribed curriculum strictly," a Catholic elementary school teacher in Prussia asserted. Rather, the priority was now to help pupils understand the current "powerful events" in order to "penetrate deeply into the youths' hearts."[24]

The use of newspapers in classrooms was an integral part of the new reform methods. Before the war, administrators generally banned using newspapers in classrooms because they were believed to expose schoolchildren to the sordidness of German politics. However, censorship, the *Burgfrieden*, and the Spirit of 1914 ended political dissent in newspapers, making patriotism appear universal. In this context, administrators permitted reform-minded teachers to ask pupils to cull articles from newspapers. Teachers wanted to use them in class to develop research skills and direct the curriculum toward their pupils' interests. "The reservations that one justifiably had against newspapers has disappeared," reported the conservative National Liberal daily, *Der Tag.* "Because there is now a *Burgfriede,* we no longer have to fear the danger of a one-sided political or religious opinion." Reading daily newspapers became an accepted method not only in the elementary and secondary schools but in the continuation schools as well. "There is, in fact, no schoolhouse," one advocate of war pedagogy wrote, "where the newspaper reports of the General Staff are not known." Teachers still had their pupils reading them long after the *Burgfrieden* eroded and the war-aims controversies became bitter. In numerous secondary schools, pupils wrote and published their own so-called war newspapers as well.[25]

Under war pedagogy even the physical environment of the classroom changed to match the reformers' goals. Almost all descriptions of classrooms in elementary and secondary schools before 1914 described a gloomy atmosphere. The walls of classrooms were bare and gray, and without decoration, they resembled military barracks. According to American professors who observed schools before 1914—despite its flaws, the German educational system still commanded enormous prestige around the world—the buildings and classrooms "always [had] an impression of cheerlessness and lack of color, life or happiness." Foreign observers maintained that this dullness reinforced the general pedagogical goal of breaking individuality and encouraging conformity. Most reformers before the war wanted to remedy this blandness. Kerschensteiner's model activity schools had gardens, kitchens, aquariums, and lab equipment. Alfred Lichtwark wanted student art on the walls, and Berthold Otto urged adopting a homier environment. Although none of these visions came to dominate the war pedagogy classroom, the physical environment of schools took on a more festive and colorful air. The walls were now adorned with maps of the front with flags marking the battles. Hanging in the classroom were pictures of generals, trenches, machine guns, airplanes, submarines, and pupils on collection drives, all cut from magazines and assembled into posters. Ribbons from victory holidays remained in classrooms after the celebrations. Many schoolchildren's own artwork about the war—architectural drawings of trenches, depictions of dogfights, and the like—also hung in classrooms. Images of war were not exactly what the reformers had in mind when they sought to enliven the classroom before 1914, but teachers under war pedagogy adopted their principle and then innovated by using militarist and nationalist content. In general, the war brought together two movements that had been separate: the introduction of reform teaching methods and the implementation of militarist and nationalist curricula.[26]

School administrators also asked teachers to attend to pupils' emotional needs and to cultivate not only historical or geographical knowledge but also feelings of national togetherness. The result, according to the chief of Leipzig's elementary schools, was that "the teacher's relationship to the pupils became warmer, friendlier, more personal and tender." Although secondary school teachers were in general more hesitant to implement reform teaching methods, Paul Hildebrandt, a former secondary school teacher who covered education for the *Vossische Zeitung* and wrote prolifically in the pedagogical press, made reference to Kerschensteiner's reform suggestions when he claimed that the relationship between pupils and teachers undoubtedly softened:

> In general this war extraordinarily transformed the old learn-school to a life-school and an activity-school. . . . Precisely those who earlier were the most aloof now opened themselves up most easily to the teacher. The attitude of the secondary school toward the pupil [was] very severe, so much so that . . . nobody had a pleasant memory of his school. . . . [But] that old type of rod-wielding senior teacher, the horror of earlier generations, is almost extinct. . . . The shared experience of pupils and teachers of such greater things brought them together and enabled a deep trust.

Corroborating this view was an American scholar who visited Germany both before and after the war. He observed that the greatest change to German education was the end of the "old relationship of authority on the one side and respect on the other side," a relationship replaced by "new bonds of natural comradeship." Scholars have generally claimed that such changes in German state institutions resulted from the 1918/19 Revolution, but they had equally important origins in the reform spirit that prevailed at the outbreak of the war.[27]

Schoolchildren's War Compositions

Evidence on writing lessons under war pedagogy provides the richest and most detailed illustration of how educational reform coalesced with nationalist and militarist goals. Before the war, the dominant way of teaching writing was to use so-called fixed compositions *(gebundene Aufsätze)*. Using this method, the teacher provided, either orally or schematically on the blackboard, the composition's content together with its thesis, style, structure, evidence, development, and conclusion. Not surprisingly, the resulting compositions were highly uniform. As a visiting American scholar observed, "no other activity in the German schools shows so clearly the conscious attempt to cast all the mental activity of the children in the same mold." Defenders countered that fixed compositions were the tried and true way to produce essays that were elegant, logical, orderly, and syntactically correct.[28]

In the decade before the war, however, many wanted to replace fixed compositions with "free" *(frei)* ones consisting of expository essays, autobiographies, personal narratives, or short stories. In these compositions, the pupils independently chose the subject, conceived the form, or developed his or her own line of argument. The most sensational advocates of free compositions, the Hamburg elementary school teachers Adolf Jensen and Wilhelm Lamszus, theorized in 1910 that pupils were motivated by instruction that nurtured individual fantasy and personal opinion. A pupil could not learn to write, they charged, "with the teacher's tongue sticking out and his whip behind him." This advocacy of free compositions was a particularly sharp attack on the authoritarianism of Wilhelmine Germany: the movement demanded that the state raise schoolchildren who could think for themselves rather than follow the orders of their teachers. It was also a populist movement: its proponents were almost exclusively elementary school teachers who did not attend university. Notably, the proponents of free compositions were also pacifists; Lamszus was later dismissed for publishing his terrifying and prophetic *Slaughterhouse of Humans* (1912), a novel about the nature of the coming industrial war.[29]

Opponents of free composition countered that children's ideas were incoherent and dull. To support their case, they could point to published collections of free compositions that addressed only the most mundane themes of everyday life—dogs, rainstorms, furniture, sunsets, and Santa Claus. Implicit in their criticism was also the charge that free compositions were a departure from the comforts of the authoritarian relationship between teacher and pupil. In 1908 a chorus of elementary school teachers was able to convince the Prussian education minister Ludwig Holle to permit occasional lessons plans in which pupils wrote compositions based on personal experience. Although the minister did not include the term *free composition* in his 1908 decree, it did appear in the subsequent overhaul of lesson plans in Berlin, Munich, and the state of Saxony in 1913. From the many contributions to *Pädagogische Zeitung,* it is apparent that most schoolteachers in Berlin occasionally used free compositions. Still, large surveys of teachers indicated that the free compositions were still unpopular outside the progressive cities. Free compositions were permissible but disparaged, particularly by principals and school inspectors. Older schoolteachers resisted them.[30]

The outbreak of the war gave new reasons to champion free compositions. Schoolchildren were witnessing the extraordinary mobilization of German military might, reading about the victories of the army, observing a time of alleged national unity, and seeing common Germans sacrifice for their nation. All these experiences, administrators, reformers, and teachers agreed, were worth putting down on paper and preserving in pupils' memories. With these encouragements and all prohibitions lifted, teachers openly experimented with free compositions. According to Otto Karstädt, an elementary school teacher and a leading advocate of free compositions, the "Great War ended the small pedagogical war over them abruptly." Another indication of their popularity was the Central Institute's success in soliciting thousands of them and displaying them at its inaugural exhibition "School and War." Subsequently, museums and research institutes in other cities followed the Central Institute and solicited free compositions of schoolchildren for display and archiving.[31]

The result of these solicitations was that hundreds of free compositions written primarily in 1915 wound up in the hands of researchers studying the effect of the war on schoolchildren. They also arrived on the desks of editors and publishers who wanted to document the success of schools in mobilizing for the war. I located close to 850 such compositions in six anthologies. The largest of these (with 383 compositions) were compiled by Karstädt, who taught in the small Protestant town of Nordhausen in Thuringia. The second largest (150) came from the predominately Catholic city of Elberfeld (now Wuppertal), Prussia, and the third largest (110) from the small Protestant city of Meerane in Saxony. The three other anthologies included compositions from all over Germany. I found another 258 compositions from elementary schools in and around Breslau. These appeared mostly as excerpts in a published study by researchers at the Institute for Applied Psychology and Psychological Research led by William Stern, the inventor of the intelligence quotient test. Still another 76 compositions by middle school boys were in the municipal archive in Darmstadt, likely intended for publication. An additional 86 were published in various articles in the pedagogical press. The regional and confessional diversity of the sources demonstrated that teachers implemented progressive teaching methods such as free compositions widely beyond the centers of the pedagogical reform movement. These compositions, encompassing a total of 1,286 personal and expository essays, fictional stories, poems, and short autobiographies, provide some of the richest material on children's thoughts available to historians.[32]

Of course, although their authors were of various ages and came from different regions, religions, and social classes, they were not a representative sample. With the exception of the researchers working under William Stern, collectors were biased in their wish to show how the new methods and content of school curricula helped the war effort. The compositions show, however, that teachers widely experimented with free compositions to support the war and the national mobilization. The compositions also reveal the ideology that teachers tried to instill.

The designation "free" needs to be placed in context. These compositions were written in schools under the supervision of teachers and, for those published or about to be published, selected to put schools in a positive light. In addition, pupils never had complete choice in topics. Suggestions of topics for free compositions invariably accorded with the nationalist agenda of war pedagogy, steering pupils toward jingoism and belligerency, as the following selection of the crassest topics shows:

- How I Play War
- Why I Would Like to Enter the War
- Our Volunteers in the Army
- Why Do We Hate England?
- England's Jealousy
- France's Old Hate and Desire for Revenge
- The Apotheosis of Prussia in 1813 and the Mobilization in 1914
- The Pious Cannot Remain in Peace When Evil Neighbors Do Not Fall
- To What Extent Has the World War Produced an Upsurge in National Consciousness?

Many compositions were also free reactions to a photograph or an illustration about the war presented by the teacher. In the end, it is impossible to measure how much pupils really believed what they wrote or to know the topics they would have chosen if they had had complete freedom. But in a free composition, a pupil could write what he or she wished under the available rubrics.

While this may not seem innovative to us today, it was pathbreaking in 1915 in a German educational system that had previously stifled creativity and individuality. Pupils had more opportunity than before to take an original point of view and thereby take ownership of their writing. By having pupils develop a positive perspective on the war using their own words, teachers under war pedagogy avoided engaging in crass indoctrination while still mobilizing their schoolchildren patriotically.[33]

Analysis of the compositions shows that the young authors wrote on a range of personal experiences: the joyous outbreak of the war, the remarkable military mobilization, the tearful departures of loved ones and soldiers, the loneliness of life without fathers, the joy of victory celebrations, the somber atmosphere of Christmas, yearnings for peace, encounters with soldiers, funerals of soldiers, visits to the front, volunteer activities, enforcement of bans on foreign words, everyday life in the classroom, and the war game escapades among peers, to name a few. The fictional accounts touched on a breadth of issues and presented a diversity of details: soldiers on watch ruminating about their homesickness and loneliness; the wounded in hospitals celebrating Christmas; parents receiving news of their sons' death; brave youths volunteering for God and country; Jesus blessing soldiers during artillery fire; a conscripted farmer being reunited with his horse; Santa Claus packing toy German soldiers; hens clucking about patriotic sacrifice; a young soldier dying, blowing victory out of his trumpet. Pupils described what they would do if they were king of Italy (stay out of the war) or if their mother were a witch (destroy all of Germany's enemies and conquer the world). The diversity of topics shows that the teachers were open to a variety of views that marked the reform spirit of war pedagogy.[34]

The compositions also show how pupils regularly divulged their emotions and travails and how teachers sympathized with them and departed from the aloof and authoritarian ways. For this reason, many attitudes in the compositions did not perfectly correspond to the nationalist goals of war pedagogy, with its firm support of the war. In fact, many of the free compositions revealed an inchoate opposition to the war. For example, in a fictional tale, a pupil wrote how a soldier on watch shot an enemy patrol and then was struck by loneliness:

What can he think about now? His loved ones, who now are sleeping sweetly. They are dreaming of their father. When might he come home?

Will he really come back? These are the thoughts that now move our souls. A tear rolls down his beard.

Other fictional accounts portrayed the anxiety that plagued the loved ones of soldiers. For example, grief overcame a woman as she thought about her soldier husband:

> She couldn't think about him at all, because the tears always came to her eyes. . . . She thought: "How wonderful it would be if there was peace. Then we wouldn't all have to have all these worries. We could all live in peace and friendship with the other peoples."

Two months later she received news that her husband had died. A 13-year-old Catholic girl described the departure of her father at his conscription:

> At the farewell he shook our hands and hugged us in his arms. At this moment we shed bitter tears because it was a painful hour. The eyes of my father did not remain dry either. . . . I couldn't look on when my father said goodbye to my mother. It was time that my father had to go. But he continued to hold her tight. Because of the pain she could no longer cry; it was an agonizing farewell. Finally, my father tore himself loose, and he went with a heavy heart. I tried with all my strength to comfort my mother. But it wasn't useful. She was sad and cried a lot.

An anecdote by a secondary school boy—published by the Pan-Germanist Hermann Reich—described an amputation:

> A wounded soldier was placed on the table. A couple of cuts separates the legs of his shredded trousers, a large wound is visible, the doctor takes up the saw, a grating sound of steeled teeth, then a cry—I stand numb and see this frightening scene that is playing out before my eyes. The saw grates, the knife cuts through its bloody work, the male and female attendants stand with pale faces. The wounded soldier is lifted down and a loud monotone reverberates in the room: "Next!"

The graphic description of the operation and its inhuman proportion was remarkable given the patriotic goals of the editors and the usually conservative curricula of the German *Gymnasium.* In these and other selections, the young authors challenged the view of a joyous and patriotic war.[35]

Compositions that took an unambiguously negative perspective on the war were rare and on the extreme end in the spectrum of beliefs that teachers tolerated under war pedagogy, however. In most of the negative compositions, the pupils offered a range of other dispositions: scenes of pity and disdain for the war were juxtaposed against assertions of nationalism, and a modicum of pathos framed a patriotic script. The pupils rejoiced about the unity and purpose of the war while at the same time expressing grief and fear for the safety of loved ones. Contradictions within individual worldviews abounded. For these young writers an antiwar stance on some matters did not preclude a prowar stance on others. For example, a boy wrote that the departure of his father made his family sad at first, but he assured his audience: "We got used to the absence." Another recounted the tears of his relatives after attending a funeral but then justified the loss by writing that the dead soldier won the Iron Cross and was a "hero." In a fictional story, the female protagonist noted "cries of pain" from some of the onlookers when the soldiers departed, but she nevertheless thought soldiers were undertaking a patriotic duty to protect the country and "with God to fight for victory for the Kaiser and the Fatherland." A 9-year-old girl from an elementary school in Nordhausen, whose father was on the front, had mixed emotions: "If only the terrible war would stop. The poor soldiers in the trenches, they freeze. It's great when the Germans capture Russians." The young authors expressed their suffering, but they palliated it or gave meaning and purpose through heroic and patriotic language. In writing war compositions, schoolchildren reinforced their repertoire of language of patriotic self-sacrifice. They raised their expectations about victory's bounty and justified privation in their own terms. Writing war compositions was accordingly a method for fulfilling directives like the one from Cassel in 1915 to get children to hold out for victory by making "lasting friendship with death"—that is, accepting that hundreds of thousands of soldiers were dying.[36]

The teachers who supervised these compositions wanted to encourage their pupils' patriotism. Not surprisingly, in over 17 percent of the compositions (209), the pupils described early victory celebrations (Liège, Tannenburg, Sedan Day 1914, Masurian Lakes) or asserted that a new patriotic spirit among soldiers and the population marked August 1914. An additional 29 percent of the compositions (367) described the front as an exciting war of movement with infantry that stormed trenches, zeppelins that dropped bombs on Paris, and generals like Hindenburg who took tens of thousands of Russians prisoner. Their battle scenes described impersonalized heroism. They detailed victories in blood, boots, and flying shrapnel but avoided the emotions of the war and accordingly anticipated the stylized cold, ruthless soldier later made famous by Ernst Jünger.

In these compositions boys and sometimes even girls fantasized, often graphically, about combat. Yes, there was danger, but the German soldier was almost always successful:

> The faces of the party get tense, the hands start shaking. The command resounds: "Attack!" The soldiers attack forward with roaring "hurrahs." A few minutes later the French trenches are taken.

Often the German troops killed unmercifully and prodigiously but emerged unscathed from the battle. A teenage boy imagined a deed that would earn him the Iron Cross:

> Because they were near the German trenches, we began to shoot fearsomely without stopping. The French fell like hay under the scythe. Not a single one of ours died. Only a few were lightly wounded.

In compositions like these, the authors reproduced the masculinity of war literature that linked manliness to bursts of raw violence and the fierce prowess of youth. The young authors believed that the soldier's death was heroic and glorious and brought joy or guaranteed immortality. For example, after storming the French trenches and securing them, a bleeding soldier wrote his wife his last words: "Don't cry! I gave my life for the Fatherland." A "holy smile" appeared on his face as he slipped into death.[37]

The framing of these fantasies in the first person by the pupils shows that teachers encouraged or tacitly approved their pupils' identification with the destruction of enemy property and life. Of the compositions I located, over one-fifth indulged in a fantasy of meting out brutality, mainly, though not exclusively, authored by boys. A seventh-grade boy from small-town Nordhausen wrote:

> If I were 18 years old, I would join the infantry. . . . I would most like assault attacks. You can call out firm hurrahs during attacks. I would plunge into everything that came in my way with my bayonet.

An eighth-grade boy from Breslau did not spare the gruesome details of combat:

> I only wish that I could be a soldier. Then I would like to stand across from the English, whose skulls I would smash with my rifle butt so that they would lose their hearing and sight.

A fictional account fantasized about catching an enemy patrol:

Two French came near to me; with my sword I split the skull of the first. The other, who was already wounded, begged me for mercy.

Punishment, particularly of the Russians and English, by any means possible was the great wish of these pupils who identified with being merciless, fearless, and invincible.[38]

Remarkably, the editors of these collections were exuberant about the positive effect of the war on schoolchildren. The exception was Alfred Mann, a researcher in Breslau at Stern's Institute, who exclaimed after excerpting a series of extremely violent compositions that they represented a "mental infection." In my research in the pedagogical press, I found only one teacher who stated that the compositions were "excessive in their rage." War pedagogy was not the sole cause of such hateful and violent fantasies, which were also a product of a more general climate of intensified nationalism and militarism. But it certainly encouraged them.[39]

Gender and Schoolgirls

Although teachers and pedagogues agreed in theory that schooling should be different for the genders, the curriculum for boys and girls under war pedagogy was in practice often the same. Over 60 percent of elementary schoolchildren in Prussia learned in coeducational classrooms, particularly in small cities, towns, and the countryside, the places where teachers were most enthusiastic about war pedagogy. Boys and girls sat on opposite sides of the room, but they had the same lessons and read the same material. By law in Prussia until June 1916, they also uniformly had male teachers. There was more possibility to create curriculum specific to gender in the big-city schools that had enough rooms to segregate the sexes, but under war pedagogy the female teachers who taught most of the all-girl classes regularly used the same material and methods as the male teachers in the coed or all-boy classes. They encouraged girls to read the daily reports of the High Command, study maps of the war, and bring both to school for discussion. Girls compared Roman strategy in the Punic Wars to contemporary British naval policy; studied battleships, torpedo boats, and submarines; wrote essays about the siege of Antwerp and the fall of the fortress at Liège; and kept war diaries that chronicled the battles and victories of the German army. Such activities in all-girl classes were in accordance with the Prussian education minister's November 1914 decree, which made no distinction between male and female pupils, and the orders by the Prussian provincial governors, such as the one in Stettin in October 1914 that asked teachers to instruct girls as well as boys in topography and military strategy. In his sixth commandment, Ziegler suggested that pupils read Schiller as much as possible because he was "the manliest of our poets," but female teachers regularly assigned him to schoolgirls. One had her schoolgirls relate each stanza in a Schiller poem to something in the present war, such as "thoughts upon viewing the 42-cm canon."[40]

Teachers condoned and perhaps even encouraged girls to fantasize about being soldiers just like boys. In approximately 14 percent of the free compositions in the published collections (77), girls described combat situations, expressed hate toward Germany's enemies, or celebrated the killing of soldiers and the destruction of property. A 13-year-old girl wrote this fictional account:

> The bayonets of our infantry flash on the guns and will wreak havoc on the enemy. . . . Then the riders storm forward over their fallen comrades. . . . The losses of the enemy are enormous, and he begins gradually to retreat. Many thousand are taken prisoners.

A 14-year-old girl wrote about the violence of combat:

> The flock of cavalry jumps out, the French officer is the first to get impaled with a lance, now there is no stopping it, a few brave [French] soldiers try to defend themselves, but they too are put down.

The approval that teachers lent to such imaginations helps explains why many girls yearned to be soldiers like their brothers, and why in a survey of 248 girls in Munich in 1915, 25 percent said they would like to be a military officer. Not surprisingly, in memoirs and oral histories, even schoolgirls who later opposed the war wrote that they had greeted the militarism and nationalism enthusiastically in 1914 and 1915.[41]

Nevertheless, teachers and pedagogues agreed with spokesmen for the women's movement like Helene Lange that the war accentuated differences in gender roles, because most boys would leave civilian society and become soldiers, while girls would tend the home front. Likewise, in his ninth commandment, Ziegler emphasized the distinction between the heroism of men and women. He also called for less coeducation "because we need masculine men and feminine women." Lessons on writing original compositions and interpreting war poems and stories accordingly encouraged boys to imagine becoming fearless soldiers, prepared to die or endure wounds and privation for Germany's victory. For girls war was the time to show the feminine virtues: selflessness, thriftiness, and steadfast, cheerful support of men and Germany, whatever the hardship. As one female teacher argued, the goal was to cultivate a "sensitivity and deepness of heart" in order "soothe the hardship for men."[42]

For teachers, administrators, and schoolgirls themselves, the most visible expression of this patriotic sacrifice was knitting. The dominance of knitting in handwork instruction was the most explicit difference in the curriculum for boys and girls ordered by the Prussian and Bavarian ministers after the outbreak of the war. Teachers organized after-school knitting clubs, and informal circles proliferated. Some boys learned to knit in coeducational handwork instruction and participated in the circles, but knitting generally happened in all-female spaces. For girls, knitting items for soldiers was an opportunity to converse and socialize in an activity that the public marked as the feminine expression of patriotism, a gesture of generosity to soldiers. The zeal with which schoolgirls in schools assembled "love-packages" *(Liebesgaben)* of knitted items for soldiers in 1914 was so great that the Prussian trade and commerce minister feared it was threatening the already precarious jobs

Voluntary knitting session in a Berlin elementary school. *Source:* Franz Führen, *Lehrer im Krieg: Ein Ehrenbuch deutscher Volksschullehrer* (Leipzig: Georg Kummer, 1936), plate 9.

of female wage workers in the textile, service, and luxury goods industries. As in German-speaking Austria-Hungary, girls knitted to express their love for the nation, soldiers, and the Kaiser. Gifts to soldiers of scarves, mittens, socks, earmuffs, and sweaters became a penultimate expression of steadfast feminine devotion in war. Regular references to the time, joy, and pride girls took in knitting appeared in fiction, poetry, autobiographies, diaries, schoolchildren's compositions, government reports, and articles in newspapers and the pedagogical press. As one teacher observed for the classroom and female associational life more generally, "Wherever one looks and goes, there is knitting!"[43]

Beyond knitting instruction, officials did not order major curricular changes specific to gender, but teachers designed lessons that encouraged girls to achieve the allegedly feminine ideal of selflessness. Sometimes these lessons were practical and to the point, as when a teacher had her schoolgirls calculate the number of wheat-rolls a family could save weekly if everyone had oatmeal for breakfast. Other times they embraced a larger moral imperative of suffering and enduring privation in order to bring about victory. For example, a Catholic schoolteacher read to her pupils the poem "Heroine," about a woman who endured the hardship of the war and ultimately the death of her husband, who "sacrificed his life for freedom! / Died in the Father's name for the Reich and Throne." The teacher elicited as a response from her pupils that the father died in peace because he knew his wife would devote herself to her children. In a revision of Ziegler's prescription, a director of a lyceum changed the seventh commandment to "give up your free time, give up your comforts, offer your service joyfully. . . . First school homework, then visiting military hospitals and knitting socks for soldiers." Teachers were especially concerned about getting girls to do without sweets and luxuries.[44]

Girls sometimes wrote compositions and drew pictures about the war that were indistinguishable from ones by boys, but adults expected girls to produce content consonant with feminine ideals. In the free compositions boys were twice as likely as girls to describe combat situations, express hate toward Germany's enemies, or celebrate the killing of soldiers and the destruction of property. Boys were also 50 percent more likely to describe the war positively and half as likely to describe it negatively, according to my blind ratings. Girls were three times more likely to mention peace and twice as likely to depict a person crying or in grief. According to reporters, the art submitted to the "School and War" exhibition showed an even starker contrast between boys' and girls' depictions of the war. Boys preferred more complicated battle scenes or technical objects like flags, iron crosses, zeppelins, railway cars, and barracks. For boys over 10, the most popular subjects were ships, sea battles, and technical drawings of the trenches. The girls also drew these subjects, but a reviewer wrote that they were "not as good as boys" and accordingly revealed a widely held bias that discouraged girls from imagining and depicting the war in terms of weapons. Girls allegedly substituted feeling and sensitivity for their lack of concrete detail. They tended to draw pictures that demonstrated their sympathy with titles like "The Lonely Sentry," "The Soldiers' Grave," and "Care of the Wounded."[45]

Until 1916, war pedagogy was successful in affirming schoolchildren's enthusiasm for the war and condoning their fascination with its violence and nationalism. Despite some skepticism by teachers in the *Gymnasien* about a curriculum that focused wholly on the present, war infused the culture of secondary schools, as directors attested in their 1914/15 and 1915/16 annual reports. By June 1915, 80 percent of the boys in the highest grade and 40 percent in the second-highest grade had volunteered for the army. In the teacher-training colleges, the figures were similar. Part of their motivation was that volunteering conferred the right to take an easy emergency final exam. But youths eagerly volunteered despite regular opposition from their parents, who feared that their sons would receive inadequate military training and perhaps die on the front. Teachers used their authority to win over the parents and coax the pupils to fight for Germany. Hoping to achieve the status of their older peers, most of those left behind in the lower grades waited impatiently to volunteer. This was the case even for some schoolboys whose parents were pacifists.[46]

Surveys, memoirs, and biographies confirm that both elementary and secondary school children were in general enthusiastic about the war in 1914 and 1915. In a survey of 222 11- to 14-year-old boys and 248 girls in Munich taken in 1912/13, and then followed up in 1915, which asked who they would most like to be, the number of boys answering soldier rose from 3 percent to 14 percent. The number answering military officer or government official like the Kaiser rose from 6 to 32 percent. Most surprisingly, the number of girls answering the same question rose from 3 to 25 percent! Pupils in the Otto-Berthold School, who chose the content of their lessons themselves under the practice of *Gesamtunterricht*, had great interest in the war. "We were all astounded at how closely the pupils followed the events," exclaimed a teacher. The pupils wrote letters to soldiers, sent handmade gifts to them, and participated in the collection drives. Wildly enthusiastic about the events of the war was the 16-year-old Berthold (Eugen) Brecht, the future Communist playwright and author. According to his brother Walther's recollection, Brecht published several patriotic war poems, including one about a brave Junker, and wrote prowar essays, one of which he sent to the Kaiser. Only in the middle of 1915 did his poetry begin to imply skepticism about the war. Gustav Heinemann, who in later years became a peace activist and served in Konrad Adenauer's cabinet, was also immensely patriotic. He wrote a euphoric war poem, "Heroic Death of a Lad"; compositions entitled "Why Our Hate against England Is Justified" and "The Most Beautiful Death Is to Die for the Fatherland"; and a piece about how the victory at Tannenberg constituted revenge for the Prussian loss in 1410. In June 1917, at age 18, he volunteered for service. Numerous other memoirs and biographical studies corroborate that these activities and views were common.[47]

While the new methods of war pedagogy generally sought to get children to internalize nationalism and militarism on their own terms, they paradoxically offered an opportunity to express hardship and grief as well. These opportunities to dissent were integral in producing an ideology necessary to wage the war, as they yoked suffering to patriotism. Far from a one-sided process of indoctrination, the creation of the war's popular legitimacy proceeded in such a way that an individual's support of the war remained consonant with the recognition of privation. Under war pedagogy, teachers permitted a range of reactions to the war while introducing into classrooms the political language of nationalism and militarism.

A curriculum centered on the war was a phenomenon in all the belligerents. German-speaking teachers in Vienna urged that children "experience the iron times" and put the events of the war in the service of academic subjects. They remarked on their pupils' enthusiasm for the war and their "fearless commitment to victory." As in Germany, they introduced reform teaching methods, such as writing free compositions about the war, which teachers exhibited and published. The pupils brought up similar themes like sacrifice for the national cause and imagined participating in violence against their enemies. Italy instituted a system of "war education" in its state elementary schools with the goal of raising patriotic children. The Italian schoolteachers' main organizations served as a major producer of Italian propaganda, done voluntarily, without any order from above. As in Germany, elementary school teachers who supported the professional organizations pushed for expansion and democratic reform. These teachers had their pupils read military bulletins, study war geography, and perform other patriotic activities. French schools also reoriented lessons around the war after the education minister issued a circular at the start of the 1914/15 school year, asking teachers to engage pupils in current events and recognize the heroism of soldiers. In French-occupied areas of Alsace-Lorraine, the curriculum became more extreme in its nationalism. Throughout France, teachers generally cooperated enthusiastically in the mission, and the education minister remarked in January 1915 that he doubted there was a single teacher who ignored the war and stayed with the same old lessons. According to the leading scholar on the subject, this transformation constituted "a veritable revolution in content and methods."[48]

Historians have reached the opposite conclusion for England, where "a revolution of content and methods of learning *did not* take place." English schools did modify their their curriculum somewhat, occasionally placing academic subjects in relation to the war, and they persuaded many of their pupils to contribute to the war effort, such as making shells during physics class and organizing collection drives. But English schools showed more restraint in using graphic images of warfare, and they were relatively lackluster in overhauling the curriculum.[49]

German war pedagogy differed from education in the multinational Austro-Hungarian Empire because the supranational state had to limit jingoism and manage nationalism to preserve its own existence. Austro-Hungarian authorities cracked down on the schools of the Czechs and other non-Germans where nationalist content would challenge the legitimacy of the German state administration. The project of raising children to identify with the supranational state, which ultimately failed, was a goal at odds with the mobilization by German nationalists. Teachers in multilingual regions were reluctant to introduce German-celebratory content lest they provoke conflict with non-Germans. School administrations in Germany did not face such restrictions. The war curriculum in Austria-Hungary was also limited by their elementary school teachers who were more openly sympathetic to the Social Democratic Party and at times voiced opposition to patriotic programs such as military youth training. As a result of this position, in May 1915 the Austrian army leadership charged that there was "high treason" and an "exceedingly alarming agitation among part of the teaching profession." In contrast, German military officers never questioned the patriotism of schoolteachers until later in the war and, even then, they generally had faith in the profession. Their tone was never alarmist.[50]

Current research suggests that war pedagogy in Germany was more jingoist than that in France. French schoolchildren indulged in combat stories assigned under the war curriculum, but the focus of these stories was the German atrocities. French instruction manuals in use before the war urged teachers to "love France and hate war." Whereas in Germany reading material in schools justified the war as necessary for its renewal and realization of world power, in France readings glorified the "soldier of justice" and portrayed the war as the only way to defeat German militarism, maintain world peace, and bring republican values to the world. Furthermore, pacifism was far more common among teachers in France than in Germany. Although most teachers were patriots, more teachers in France than Germany openly opposed the war, and they opposed it sooner, some as early as October 1914. In Germany, not a single teacher criticized war pedagogy as a whole until January 1916.[51]

4

The Content and Popularity of
War Literature

War literature became the most popular genre for youths in the months following the outbreak of the war, eclipsing fairy tales, girls' stories, and
nineteenth-century classics. As in war pedagogy, the tone of the nationalism
and militarism in this war literature intensified and transmitted to a wider audience than before the myths of heroism, patriotism, sacrifice, afterlife, adventure, and manhood. Like teachers and leaders of youth organizations,
most authors of youth literature wanted to mobilize boys and girls in support
of the war, and they reproduced the same patriotic portraits, shibboleths, and
concepts of the Spirit of 1914 that dominated adult literature. They depicted
the German people in August 1914 as transfixed by universal enthusiasm for
the war and committed to forging unity and ending all social and political
conflicts. Their stories portrayed girls and boys whose bravery and sacrifice
ensured Germany's victory. Like priests and ministers, they spread the theo-
logical idea of a "holy war"—the notion that war was willed by God and that
the patriotism of soldiers guaranteed their entry into heaven. Above all, in
casting conditions on the front heroically, the authors distorted the industrial
slaughter. This distortion was perhaps not intentional, as the military censored first-hand knowledge, and many in the middle class found the second-
hand accounts of the horrors too hard to swallow. The authors of youth literature retained ideas about war that had dominated Romanticism, the old
regime, and Western literature since the *Iliad*. Two world wars ultimately
discredited these "myths of the war experience" in Europe. Even late in the
First World War, however, they eased Germans' distress by assuring them

that millions were not dying in vain. The myths of the war experience have perhaps been a necessary part of conducting all wars, whether they were defensive, religious, just, colonial, racial, or revolutionary. But an extended conflict had never happened after Europe had universal literacy, cheap printing methods, mass consumer marketing, and youths with pocket money. The First World War marked the first time in history that the abundance of books infused youths with these concepts, the first time that literature mobilized masses of youths for war.[1]

Helping in the mobilization were both shabby publishing houses such as Mignon and prestigious ones such as Ullstein, Reclam, and Cotta, which quickly realized that war books not only improved their reputation as good patriots but also earned them fat profits in contracts with the army and sales to a young public hungry to read about the war. All the new issues of penny dreadfuls and most of the new hardcovers for youths from 1914 to 1918 were about the war. In youth magazines, too, the war became the overwhelmingly dominant topic. War books occupied the commanding position in advertisements and shop windows. War permeated even girls' novels, which before did not have significant militarist or nationalist content. Although the subject of war became less dominant after 1915, it remained a durable favorite well into the Weimar Republic and the Nazi period.[2]

The nationalism and militarism in youth literature resonated in a brasher key in part because the *Burgfrieden* silenced the Socialist and middle-class critics. Although the political settlement started unraveling in 1915, the mainstream Social Democratic leadership over the course of the war respected the army's request to close their antiwar presses and purge their libraries of pacifist literature. Directly reportable to the chairman Friedrich Ebert, Social Democratic Party youth leaders Karl Korn and Heinrich Schulz reminded readers in the youth yearbooks to cease political struggle. They also published poems that praised the loyalty of soldiers and the victories of the military. This content mirrored the bland patriotism in the Social Democratic Party youth weekly *Arbeiterjugend* and flouted the prewar traditions of antimilitarism among Socialist youths. Youths who wanted antiwar literature had to procure smuggled copies published in Switzerland by Willi Münzenberg and other exiled Socialist internationalists, but government repression of these radicals made finding their publications difficult.[3]

The deluge of patriotic enthusiasm at the outbreak of the war also isolated Heinrich Wolgast and other middle-class critics. After 1914, many of his most ardent supporters encouraged the reading of war literature as a way to mobilize youths patriotically. For example, before 1914 Johannes Tews spat with radical nationalist authors such as Wilhelm Kotzde, but after 1914 Tews endorsed the patriotic war literature. Authors justified their focus on the war by invoking the slogans common in the pedagogical press, such as "let the spirit of the great times influence youths." Wolgast had to halt publication of *Jugendschriften-Warte* for the first year and a half of the war because most of his co-workers had been conscripted. He consequently had to give up his crusade against chauvinist youth literature. In early 1916, Wolgast was able to find help to revive the journal, but by then the corpus of youth literature about the current war was already on the bookshelves. The profits were financing new war books that all sorts of male youths still craved. To maintain its legitimacy in a time when combat stories had become fabulously popular, Wolgast and his colleagues contradicted their earlier policies and began reviewing and recommending war books.[4]

Like teachers under war pedagogy, editors lifted the taboo on nationalist subjects previously deemed political. Early in the war, authors reasoned that the patriotic transformation of Germany invalidated the old rules. For example, the editors of the popular magazine *Der gute Kamerad* argued:

> [We] have up to now avoided politics—that is, talking about any slippery agitation pursued by the government or political parties. . . . But now that the god of war is sweeping through almost all of Europe, it seems appropriate to break the rule and make an exception for purely patriotic reasons.

This practice of engaging youths in politics continued after 1915, even during some of the most controversial political discussions, such as the peace treaty negotiations in Brest-Litovsk and dialogues about the necessity of unrestricted submarine warfare. Oral histories suggested that before 1914 schoolchildren had had little knowledge of bitter political debates like those during the Morocco Crises or the negotiations over the Navy bills. After August 1914, however, they were intimately engaged in international relations.[5]

Authors of youth literature, in league with youth workers and teachers, whetted young readers' appetite for violent, graphic war stories, as evidenced in the market for war penny dreadfuls *(Kriegsschundschriften)*. Adults tried to ban these cheap, lurid paperbacks, but youths, boys in particular, went to great efforts to procure them and satisfy a masculine fantasy that celebrated war and its violence. The war penny dreadfuls not only exposed youths to an extreme militarism but also created a culture of disobeying adults and state authority. The popularity of war themes in the penny dreadfuls after 1914 shows the rise of a distinctive anti-authoritarian male youth culture whose fascination with violence and masculine prowess differed from that of most of the adult population.

Youth literature offered a variety of views about the war, but the positive ones overwhelmed the negative ones. Most youth war literature minimized the horrors of the front. Negative portrayals were almost always accompanied by warm approval for the greatness of the war, and implied that the young readers could become heroes only if they made sacrifices like soldiers and endured the war's privation. Because the *Burgfrieden* silenced authors skeptical of the war, and most authors came from the nationalist middle class that supported it, wholly negative portraits of the war were as rare for youths as they were for adults. Even though youth literature was not on the censor's radar screen, in my survey of over 80 novels and 700 stories in magazines and collected editions I found only a single one published between 1914 and 1918 that could be construed as openly antiwar: the script of a Punch and Judy show printed in 1918 in which a man avoided conscription by murdering a policeman.[6]

Authors of youth literature consistently cultivated strenuous masculinity for their male readers through their portrayal of soldiers but developed contradictory models of femininity for their female audience. Stories for girls emphasized women's special capacity for selflessness and their devotion to family and the domestic ideal. They also highlighted women's independence and equality and even depicted them doing the work of soldiers in fluid combat situations. The stories accordingly offered girls a range of feminine models to which they could aspire. This jumble contributed to the upheaval in gender and the controversy over the new woman after the war.

The Enthusiastic Home Front

Although Germans in August 1914 were as anxious about the war as they were supportive of it, most stories and novels about the home front portrayed Germans from all social classes in enthusiastic and wildly patriotic crowds. The crowds cheered the volunteers; gave out flowers, chocolate, and other gifts *(Liebesgaben)*; and celebrated the early military victories. If the plot and character development of stories for girls and boys did not begin with this depiction of the Spirit of 1914, they revolved around its memory. As in the larger public sphere, national greatness came from the political unity, and the *Burgfrieden* figured centrally. The authors of youth war literature reproduced the slogans of the Kaiser: "I know no parties, I know now only Germans," and the Social Democrats: "We won't abandon the Fatherland in the hour of danger." They also transmitted the myths of a classless society: "All differences among the people ceased; there were no more workers and no more factory owners; everyone knew himself to be internally united in feeling German, fiercely prepared to sacrifice life and property for the protection of the threatened Fatherland!" For youths in places that did not participate in the August 1914 celebration, the literature gave the impression that an absence of effusive patriotism in their towns or neighborhoods was an exception. A young worker had only to consider the story of a Social Democrat, who, irritated at accusations before 1914 that he was not a patriot, celebrated the war and happily fought with young middle-class men who now welcomed him. Whether or not the enthusiasm of August 1914 was a myth, it had a reality in both youth fiction and nonfiction. In my research, not a single story denied the enthusiasm of August 1914.[7]

In their fictions, the authors structured their plots and shaped their characters by spinning the *Burgfrieden* and the Spirit of 1914 into a theme of reconciliation. They followed a simple but effective structure to cast the war positively: the young protagonist had a long-standing conflict or problem, but the war provided the key opportunity for a resolution. There were many variations on this theme. Schoolboys who were arch-nemeses before the war became great friends while on the front. War let two brothers resolve their years-long acrimony. Combat brought together friends whose petty parents had severed their close ties in childhood. Lovers from different social classes demonstrated their patriotism, and each convinced their previously skeptical parents of their beloved's worth. Orphans discovered their foster parents' generosity. War gave outcasts the opportunity to earn the respect from the communities that had ostracized them. In all these plots, the harmony and unity brought by war was the elixir for the most intractable personal problems. The Spirit of 1914 rejuvenated in a most intimate sense, bringing the estranged closer together.[8]

In these patriotic home-front plots, male youths gained not only closeness in relationships but also authority over parents. Most of the young male characters noted that the war initiated them into adulthood unexpectedly. Many plots centered on a family drama in which a young secondary school boy announced his intentions to volunteer. In some cases, his decision earned him his parents' immediate approbation, but other times, the mother cried or the father was reluctant, concerned about the boy's maturity and the future of his studies. The drama of the nation then played out within the German family, and the resolution of the conflict came after the boy convinced his parents that volunteering was a national duty. In all the stories where both parents denied permission, the schoolboy absconded to the front against their will. In pitting the patriotic intentions of male youths against the desires of their parents, these plots reshaped the themes of revolt popular in prewar youth fiction. They also laid the foundation for the legend that Germany lost the war because parents had failed their more patriotic sons.[9]

Girls as Soldiers and Caretakers

The fiction that girls read during the war mirrored the content in war pedagogy as it related to gender. On the one hand, girls read outside school much of the same material as boys. Aiming for a broad readership, authors of war stories suggested that their books were for both sexes; in the title they either claimed that the story was "for youths" or did not indicate the intended audience at all. That girls could describe guerrilla tactics, submarine attacks, and adventures of cruisers in compositions and diaries suggests that they regularly read these war stories. Indeed, one girl wrote how she learned about assault attacks from a favorite war book.[10]

On the other hand, authors of literature specifically for girls (almost all were women from the upper echelons of German society) suggested that in wartime girls more than boys needed to sacrifice, be thrifty, give unconditional support to the war, and offer care to the needy in their capacity as potential mothers. These adolescent-girl novels *(Backfischromane)* and stories in girl magazines such as *Mädchenpost* and *Das Kränzchen* belonged to the profitable genre that before 1914 portrayed female teenagers who aspired to be more than mothers and housewives, but faced parents, siblings, fiancés, employers, and neighbors who believed a woman's primary role was in the home. The female authors suggested that though being motherly was a woman's highest calling, a young woman could marry without giving up her aspirations or, if she remained unwed, integrate her special feminine trait for care and selflessness into an avocation, a career, or a particular talent. In

wartime girl-stories, the protagonists made their lives meaningful by becoming not mothers but selfless patriots willing to sacrifice everything for
victory. Trying to be strong for their fathers and brothers in the army, young
female characters withheld complaint about the deprivation and the death.
They deflected their suffering in reassurances and shibboleths like "no death
is more beautiful than death for the Fatherland." They actualized their
motherly talents in caring for orphans and wounded male soldiers. "What
damage is it if he has a lame leg?" remarked a young woman after her fiancé
was wounded. "Even if he didn't have any legs at all, I would still take him!"
In an extreme version of this narrative about ersatz mothering, a woman
cared for a husband who had lost both arms, both legs, and both eyes; his
loyal wife forever, she promised never to leave him. Lacking a rite of passage like conscription that marked entry into adulthood, the authors suggested that teenage girls became women by serving soldiers' needs and denying their own.[11]

Still, although the wartime girl-stories reinforced and even glorified the
care and selflessness that only women could allegedly give, many stories did
not emphasize the gender of the female characters at all. Magazines depicted
boys and girls playing war without either taking a particular role. In one
story, the girls carried makeshift shotguns, pistols, and sabers. Some female
authors broke out of the old girl-story genre by portraying female youths in
feats of bravery on par with men's. Girls bound the wounds of their male
comrades not only behind the lines but also under enemy fire. Like Rosa Zenoch, the legendary "girl from Rawa Ruska" who provided soldiers water under fire, the female youths in these fictions served as brave assistants to soldiers in combat. They reported on troop movements in Tyrol and stood ground
in East Prussia during the Russian attack, courageously guarding prisoners
of war. Far from sharpening the gender differences, these war stories showed
female youths taking on the roles of male soldiers. They encouraged the fantasy that women could achieve the status of men through their heroism in
combat.[12]

Religion and the Logic of Submission

Although we might be skeptical of the cliché that the First World War destroyed belief in God, after 1914 Europeans doubtlessly found it difficult to
accept that God would allow millions of soldiers and civilians to starve and

die in a stalemate. Marxist antiwar atheists argued that religion had helped cause the war. The historical evidence was in their favor: in 1914 Protestant and Catholic clerics embraced war fully. But while belief in God continued to be abandoned during the war, the majority of Germans still participated in the rites of baptism, confirmation, and religious funerals. Despite the long secular trend, histories of religion in Germany before 1914 confirm that in rural areas and middle-class urban neighborhoods church attendance in both Protestant and Catholic churches was the norm, not the exception. In 1914, German schoolchildren had three to four hours of religion weekly. During the war, participation in religious rites increased because clerics played a critical role in addressing their congregants' grief and fears. Authors of youth war literature accordingly gave religion a prominent place and transmitted the dominant belief that God-fearing Germans endured the sacrifice for victory. Authors of novels and stories developed plots and characters that explained to youths the religious logic for submission to Germany's political goals.[13]

These authors took their beliefs from the war sermons of Protestant and Catholic clergymen. The corpus of war theology written in the decades before 1914 had provided Protestant ministers with well-developed belief systems for dealing with the many contradictions of sacrificing life for nation. Although many ministers were socially progressive, most of them were cozy with the government. A good number served as school inspectors or held other sinecures in Prussia's elitist system of notable politics *(Honoratorienpolitik)* and shared the nationalist goals of the Conservative and the National Liberal parties. Not surprisingly, the vast majority of ministers supported the war in 1914 and 1915. Their war sermons showed a genuine belief that the war was just. Most also believed that the war was a "holy war" because it allegedly purged Germany morally and religiously. Their sermons described a war that cleansed the nation of selfishness, materialism, atheism, socialism, and other alleged sores of modernity. During the years of deprivation, after millions were dead and wounded, a good many like Otto Baumgarten turned against the war and supported the July 1917 Reichstag Peace Resolution. But from 1914 to 1916, when most of the youth war literature was written, Protestant ministers still supported the war. The same was true of the Catholic clergy, who drew on their own corpus of war theology. Moreover, although priests in Prussia were skeptical of the government—the memory of the persecutions during the *Kulturkampf* of the 1870s was still alive, and persecutions of the Polish Catholic minorities were still common— they wanted to demonstrate that they were good nationalists like the Protestants. Their war sermons, too, therefore depicted war as both just and cleansing.[14]

War theology shaped the content of the youth literature published by the Protestant and Catholic youth associations as well as the commercial presses. In the cheap church broadsides and newspapers, stories regularly asserted that the soul of the dead soldier always entered a peaceful and glorious afterlife in heaven. The implication was that those not soldiering or making an equivalent patriotic contribution were not guaranteed such good fortune. Secular magazines reproduced the same idea: soldiers died the "beautiful death; God ensures that it is not in vain." Trust in God and the ultimate benefits of patriotic sacrifice allowed characters to endure and even enjoy emotional and physical torment like amputations. Stories and poems depicted characters who felt God joined them in battle or roused them to fight ferociously. The general religious theme was that the unity and self-sacrifice in August 1914 made this war a "holy war" that purified Germany.[15]

Adventures and Violence on the Front

A remarkable feature of youth war literature was that character development ended entirely once the male protagonist arrived at the front. Lacking intimate knowledge of conditions on the front, or perhaps fearful that the truth would make youths reject the war, some authors digressed to chronicle Germany's military victories, without any reference to their protagonists. In other novels, technical depictions of soldiers doing their duty in combat replaced characterization. This literature, like adult war literature, portrayed action devoid of human feeling, and few authors of front novels deviated from this style. Like the subsequent war stories by Ernst Jünger and others, youth literature in 1914 and 1915 described a war of movement with little "judgment or expressed emotion" and with many "things" like boots, helmets, bodies, food, and artillery. When a fictional male youth arrived on the front, he became a monolithic, machine-like German soldier. He was loyal and fierce, and he lacked all personality.[16]

Authors for youth war literature almost always described a war of movement in the stories written after 1914, even though they contradicted the conditions of trench warfare and stalemate on the Western front. In the climax of most war novels, the protagonist or another character earned the Iron Cross. In the handful of stories in which soldiers did die, the deaths were always the hero's death, a glorious one for the Fatherland. Industrial killing in the First World War undermined the idea that war was noble and chivalrous, but in 1914 and 1915 the idea persisted. Airmen on the Western front respected their enemies by throwing wreaths on their victims. Foreign officers taken prisoner signed parole cards, left prisoner-of-war camps, and had a shave and a meal in town. Aristocrats and middle-class elites still ran the armies of Central and Eastern Europe, and for them war was like dueling, a way to win and maintain honor. Chivalry, a key concept in the "the myth of the war experience," led to the publication in youth literature of slogans like "many enemies—much honor." Georg Gellert, editor of the *Berliner General-Zeitung* and the most successful author of youth literature during the war, invoked such myths when he elevated a male youth's extreme perils into an enviable situation: "How happy he would have been to give his life to prove his service to the Fatherland." Far from a brutal dragging by Achilles, the hero's death palliated pain, and soldiers never died in anguish. There were no Hektors in the German youth literature of the First World War. Every soldier's death was peaceful or glorious.[17]

This war literature justified determination and fantastic courage to young readers. In the front novels and stories, the young protagonists almost always survived ferocious battles and showed extraordinary bravery. The male youth's military acumen and composure invariably brought about a dramatic victory, often single-handedly. In other words, the stories were gross exaggerations. "Hold out," a young soldier thought under heavy fire, with enemy bayonets flashing and all his comrades dead or wounded. "Just come through with honor." He fired his weapon and killed all the enemies. One boy protagonist captured a thousand prisoners. In another novel, five men alone killed eight hundred Russians. Danger only whetted soldiers' appetites for more war: "I would most like to be sent back into the battle—to victory!" a soldier thought after a fierce counterattack, relaxing with coffee and a cigar.[18]

Optimism about a German victory was often personified in representations of Hindenburg. Looming larger than life in a picture book, he was portrayed as a gigantic Zeus, with one foot in Germany and one in Russia, commanding

"In the Thick of the Fight." Cover of *Im Schlachtgetümmel des Weltkriegs: Der Kampf im Feindesland* (Berlin: Jugendhort, 1915) by Georg Gellert, the most popular war author for youths.

troops advancing on Petrograd. While poems extolled Hindenburg's military genius, fiction emphasized the general's personal magnanimity, and stories elevated him to nothing short of cult status.[19]

Although many characters had a manhood based on honor and chivalry, far more had strenuous masculinity, killing coldly for victory and seeking brutal revenge. German soldiers, without specific provocation, became ruthless and bloodthirsty. Crack units of shock troops fought ferociously; cavalry massacred and wrought havoc; schoolboys turned soldiers felt "holy fury" and "bitter hate" in the midst of battle; one soldier strangled a reprobate prisoner to death; another brutally beat a treasonous Frenchman and watched him gurgle his last words. The language was graphic and coarse, as in this description that accompanied a picture of a bayonet attack:

> Like wild devils our Styrians and Tyrolers cut and jabbed, a deafening cry filled the air, and we hit with rifle butts so madly that the Serbians' skulls shattered, and though some good comrades bit the dust, the enemy could not withstand the vehement attack.

The soldiers often took pleasure in the killing and the destruction:

> Oh, the joy to shoot the piece of junk into flames and to pepper it until disturbed ants overwhelmed their piles, a swarming mass of fleeing troops backwards over the fields into the village! And after them, on them, mercilessly! Spoil their return home! Hunt them to the interior of France, or nail them down so that they can't even bend a German hair.

Other times, the authors portrayed the killing of enemies as target practice:

> The first—jumps up!—shot in the head!—dead! The second—jumps up!— shot in the head!—dead! The third, fourth, fifth, sixth, seventh, eighth, ninth—the same!

Some of the literature anticipated the erotic overtones of soldiering later made popular by Ernst Jünger.[20]

The War Penny Dreadfuls

The discourses in youth war literature circumscribed the meanings of the war for young people, and the war compositions discussed in Chapter 3 show that the masculinity, nationalism, and militarism in war pedagogy and this youth war literature were not just presented to youths but reproduced by them as well. Another set of evidence of this internalization comes from journal and archival reports about the market for penny dreadfuls. This literature that glorified war and Germany had little appeal among youths before 1914 became immensely popular during the war.

Before 1914 the penny dreadfuls were short detective, love, adventure, and "Wild West" stories cast in coarse and exaggerated language. Among the first imports of Anglo-American mass culture into Europe, they were cheap mass-consumer pleasures that brought businesses big profits but pitted adults against youths. Between 1900 and 1920, together with the cinemas, automats, jazz clubs, sport associations, and dance halls, they contributed to a mass consumerism in which teenagers forged a modern youth culture that was international in scope and asserted independence and differences from adults. After German presses first began publishing penny dreadfuls in translation in the 1870s, they grew immensely popular among youths of all social classes. The Berlin publisher Kolportagehefte alone printed over 25 million per year; this was an enormous number in a country with 12 million youths ages 6 to 18. Their commercial success exasperated both middle-class and Socialist reformers, who worried that they tarnished youths' good character and campaigned to ban them under the 1900 youth clause of the *Lex Heinze,* the law regulating pornography. In 1910 they succeeded in creating a central register to blacklist them. In the years preceding the war, their campaign gained momentum; it was in fact one of the few reform movements in which the entire political spectrum—Conservatives, Liberals, Catholics, and Socialists—reached consensus. However, the liberal German press laws and the powerful publishing interests thwarted any outright bans.[21]

In August 1914, a dozen publishers dropped the detective, crime, love, and cowboy stories and, in a new development, offered graphic narratives of the war from the perspective of the German army. Although some penny dreadfuls had depicted military adventures before 1914, the stories had been largely imports from Great Britain and the United States and thus were not nationalist. However, the British blockaded cultural imports, and by April 1916 publishers had printed no fewer than eighteen series and seventy issues that celebrated the war and German patriotism. The penny dreadfuls followed the model of other war literature in developing a masculinity based on fierce nationalism and war enthusiasm.[22]

To fight the war, the military needed the myth that soldiering made boys men. But this myth came into conflict with reformers who believed that, in the absence of so many men, male youths were increasingly endangered and wayward *(verwahrlost)*. Like mainstream youth war literature—that is, hardcover books—the penny dreadfuls earned praise for instilling enthusiasm for the war, but reviewers censured them for their "inordinate exaggeration" and excessive "stimulation of fantasy." Critics were disturbed by characters who had the powers of demigods: "Usually a young hero appears, the more like a boy the better, who achieves the most astonishing heroic deeds, weathers the most unbelievable dangers, and is completely responsible that our army wins this or that battle or conquers this or that fortification." The critics were above all concerned that the penny dreadfuls stimulated boys' imagination, goading them to behave inappropriately for their age:

> The urge for adventure, which arises powerfully in all our young boys due to the events of the war, is skillfully exploited and kindled by glorifying hundreds and thousands of young volunteer soldiers. Most join the army against the will or without the knowledge of their parents or guardians; they wear civilian clothing or the uniform of their military youth company, hide themselves in artillery cannons, boxes of ammunition, or automobile seats; end up in the middle of the fiercest battle; show themselves to be infinitely superior not only to soldiers in bravery, prowess, and sharp shooting but also to military leaders in acuity, resourcefulness, and strategy; and against powers ten times greater, they turn a hopeless situation into success lightning fast and are presented before at least a General, but possibly Hindenburg or the Kaiser himself, with the Iron Cross, in a neat uniform, introduced as a model soldier.

After 1916, when criticism in the pedagogical press became more common, Heinrich Wolgast and others pointed out that this content and language in fact differed little from that of many hardcover books, such as those by Georg Gellert. But their points went unheeded because publishers of hardcover war literature had close ties to army censors and officials who felt the stories were too beneficial to the war effort to ban. By contrast, the small publishers of war penny dreadfuls lacked financial and political influence. Moreover, publishers of hardcover literature kept quiet about the bans; they stood to benefit financially by forcing youths to buy their more expensive books. Consequently, Social Democrats, Liberals, Catholics, Conservatives, and middle-class as well as working-class parents agreed that youths needed to be kept from the penny dreadfuls. Under the 1851 Prussian Law of Siege and its equivalents in the other states, deputy commanding generals, acting as agents of the monarchs, had the wartime authority to issue decrees on the home front, and a broad spectrum of adults asked them to censor the penny dreadfuls. In 1915 and 1916 generals in four districts complied.[23]

Male youths made great efforts to circumvent these bans, however. Because the penny dreadfuls remained immensely popular, a black market for them quickly emerged, and boys rummaged through recycling bins, picking them out for resale. When one teacher in a public elementary school in Magdeburg tried to stymie this black market by pressuring schoolboys to give up their penny dreadfuls, he quickly collected over a thousand. In Essen, schoolboys were less cooperative. In order to confiscate the stories, the school board had to offer a day off from school for every public elementary school class that turned in a hundred issues. They were surprised when, in a few weeks, boys turned in thousands. Facing food protests, labor strife, and stalemate on the fronts, deputy commanding generals in the other twenty districts were hesitant to use their limited resources to keep lurid paperbacks from kids. Because the deputy commanding generals acted independently without any coordinating policy, youths and adults had ample opportunities to smuggle issues from the twenty districts that had not banned them. Furthermore, with police overburdened and state censorship offices weakened by shortages of personnel, publishers eluded the censors by distributing new titles before they got on the blacklist.[24]

Youth war literature followed the same basic plotlines of heroic acts and battlefield exploits during the war that it had before 1914, but three things changed. First, its share of the book market swelled. Second, before 1914, the authors of youth war literature had focused on adventure and Germany's rising place in the world. During the war, the authors continued this focus but also emphasized that boys nearing the age of conscription had to prepare to die for Germany and that youths of all ages now had to accept hardship, hunger, emotional deprivation, and death of loved ones to achieve victory. Third, whereas before 1914 most teachers and purveyors of good books dismissed youth war literature as a frivolous genre, during the war they strongly encouraged boys and girls to read it. They accordingly condoned the violent, graphic descriptions of battles and superhuman sacrifices that were legion in the stories published after August 1914. Youth war literature also reinforced the myths that the war ended Germany's political conflicts, reconciled previously hostile social groups, made patriotism respectable for the working class, elevated the German nation, and turned boys into men and girls into women. The high demand for war penny dreadfuls, which projected these myths in the most sensationalist ways, shows that boys in particular wanted fantasies that celebrated both heroism and violence.

Early in the war, civilian and military authorities recognized that these myths were strategically instrumental to waging war. The government therefore did not bother producing propaganda until much later in the conflict. Instead it relied on support from a public who published and bought patriotic collections of war stories, war sermons, military histories, war poems, patriotic songs, and soldiers' letters. Although the German armies endorsed many of the war books for youths, they generally did not commission authors to write them. In this way, youth war literature was part of a popular, not state-led, mobilization for war.

Just as the war loosened the authoritarian relationship between teachers and pupils, youth war literature implied that the conflict brought young people independence and status. Although fictional stories glorified female domesticity and selflessness, reinforcing prewar gender norms, they also depicted female youths free from the constraints of marriage and patriarchal control and able to achieve equality with their male peers. Likewise for male youths, war was portrayed as promising manhood and release from paternal authority. Adults' disapproval of war penny dreadfuls was part of a nascent generational conflict over how civilians understood the war: the sensationalist nationalism and militarism in the stories were condemned by adults but devoured by youths.

All the belligerents had a war literature before 1914 that in turn expanded after the outbreak of the war. Youths in the German-speaking regions of Austria-Hungary could find the literature published in Germany in their local bookstores and libraries, and many of the tropes in German war literature, in particular the theme of sacrifice, were in books for youths published in France and Great Britain. Still, current research suggests some German-language particularities. British publishers were cautious about offering boys sensationalist war stories. War had only a limited place, for example, in England's most popular male youth weekly, *The Boy's Own Paper.* French authors portrayed the French soldiers as fighting to make peace, destroy German militarism, and establish human rights in Europe. By contrast, German authors portrayed soldiers fighting to secure German's "position as a world power." German publishers sold books with stories in which male youths made nationalist exclamations such as: "I see tomorrow a great future brought to Germany. I see my Fatherland at the height of its power as *the* Empire of Europe—a goal we can all be happy to die for." Such crude war aims were nowhere to be found in books for youths sold in France and Great Britain.[25]

5

Organized Leisure and Patriotic
Voluntary Labor

In August 1914 liberal and conservative newspapers applauded the mass volunteering for the war. Over one million men from all different social milieus enlisted in the army, according to their reports. In addition, hundreds of thousands of women joined the Red Cross, the newly founded National Women's Service *(Nationaler Frauendienst)*, and various state, municipal, and charity welfare organizations. This apparent rush by both men and women to the colors advertised patriotism and convinced many that Germans of all sorts had put aside their selfish interests and ended the decades of political and social conflict. But the true magnitude of the volunteering was less than the newspapers claimed. Reporters inflated the number of soldiers as much as fourfold because they did not account for men who tried to enlist at multiple barracks. They also grossly exaggerated the number of men who were working class. By the fall of 1914, the army relied primarily on conscripts; the volunteers were generally upper-middle-class secondary school boys or lower-middle-class male youths from Protestant villages and small cities. Adult female volunteers were also overwhelmingly upper-middle-class. By December many families' savings ran out, and soldiers' wives stopped volunteering because they needed to earn income previously provided by their husbands as their welfare benefits did not cover all household expenses. Like all urban women, they were also overwhelmed by the shortages of food and coal and the inordinate time it took to acquire them.[1]

By 1915, at most a few hundred thousand women worked for the war without pay, but a conservative estimate is that 6 to 7 *million* youths and schoolchildren were volunteering regularly. Schoolchildren had always had more free time than adults for such activity, and in 1914 and 1915 they had even more leisure because administrators canceled school for victory celebrations and shortened the school day by half or two-thirds. The shift from a peacetime to a war economy released hundreds of thousands of working teenagers, and until employment reached full levels in the summer of 1915, they too had more time to volunteer. Teachers, reformers, and administrators warmly praised the ad hoc programs that got schoolchildren and youths to train militarily, knit things for soldiers, sell war bonds, collect recyclables, and work on farms and in offices. Mobilizing their voluntary labor accorded with both the Prussian education minister's first decree of the war that "it is not in accordance with the times that youths be idle," and with the goal of war pedagogy of allowing youths to "experience the greatness of the times." The Prussian education minister proclaimed that the mobilization of youths' voluntary labor was a "glorious chapter in the history of the world war," an achievement he extolled even in his private communications.[2]

Teachers, leaders of youth associations, and the estimated fifty thousand district youth workers in Germany were the key agents mobilizing youths for patriotic voluntary labor. The youth workers were especially important: their coordination of the world's largest network of recreational associations ensured that youths could not only volunteer but also attend patriotic entertainment events geared toward the war. Their expertise and experience gave Germany more potential to succeed in the mobilization than the Allied nations, none of which had state officials responsible for organized leisure or so many youth associations.

The Patriotic Voluntary Labor of Schoolchildren

The voluntary work of schoolchildren involved millions of small labors not available elsewhere to recycle materials and reduce shortages. Training with wooden guns, knitting socks and mittens for soldiers, and going door-to-door, asking for money or material were also reminders to all, young and old, rich and poor, that Germany's smallest citizens were enthusiastically contributing to the war production. For the duration of the conflict, government officials, politicians, and the pedagogical, liberal, and conservative presses praised schoolchildren effusively, casting them as examples for why Germany was destined to be victorious. Photographs showed that teachers chalked up amounts collected on the blackboard for display, suggesting that the amount collected was proportional to the school class's commitment to the war (see illustrations on page 111).[3]

The most conspicuous form of voluntary patriotic labor was the recycling drives and trips to the countryside to collect berries, mushrooms, kindling, and other useful items. Participation in these after-school activities was remarkably high, even in cities dominated by the Social Democratic Party, such as urban Hanover, where half of the city's thirty-two thousand elementary school children were regularly collecting recyclables in 1914 and 1915. *Pädagogische Zeitung* praised the record-breaking highs of the collections of 1917, including the Mittenwald School in Brandenburg, which brought in four tons of animal bones. Other schools held records in collections of coffee grounds, pinecones, cartridge cases, gold, silver, tin, scrap iron, bottles, paper, books, hay, herbs, seeds, chestnuts, shrubs, leaves, tires, clothing, wool, and hair. Most schools also allowed their pupils to leave school for days at a time to volunteer their services in hospitals, banks, military bureaus, post offices, fire stations, freight yards, welfare organizations, snow removal brigades, government accounting bureaus, and food and ration card distribution centers. Rural areas had a long tradition of releasing children during harvests, but the war also led to mass releases of urban schoolchildren for agricultural work. In Erfurt in the spring of 1917, schoolchildren left for a week to destroy hamsters and mice in an attempt to improve crop yield. Hundreds of thousands helped with all the harvests of the war, even in 1917 and 1918, when a good many had no shoes.[4]

Despite the enormous number of schoolchildren who volunteered their labor, the operation was largely decentralized and relied on the initiative of teachers, youth workers, and leaders of youth associations. A few Prussian civil servants expressed some interest in creating a central office to coordinate the efforts, but the prevailing opinion was that such a bureaucracy was costly and undermined the grassroots excitement and the popular patriotism. Only in 1917 did bureaucrats create the Central Office for War Help in Schools, which surveyed the amounts collected nationally. Just a handful of schools ever filled out its questionnaires, and it accomplished no real organizational work.[5]

For elementary school teachers, mobilizing schoolchildren's voluntary labor on their own initiative, like war pedagogy, was a way to convince the public of their patriotism and worthiness. Their strategy worked: they regu-

"Whoever Buys War Bonds Shortens the War": schoolchildren advertising war bonds. *Source:* Franz Führen, *Lehrer im Krieg: Ein Ehrenbuch deutscher Volksschullehrer* (Leipzig: Georg Kummer, 1936), plate 13.

Schoolchildren displaying sale amount after the eighth war bond drive. *Source:* Franz Führen, *Lehrer im Krieg: Ein Ehrenbuch deutsher Volksschullehrer* (Leipzig: Georg Kummer, 1936), plate 13.

larly won praise in the press, bureaucracies, and legislatures for mustering the patriotic efforts of schoolchildren in the collection activities. Teachers and schoolchildren aiming to advertise their patriotism competed against other schools in the sale of war bonds, and the rivalry grew so fierce by the spring of 1915 that complaints poured into the bureaucracy and press. School officials and the public were concerned that the drives had devolved into frenetic contests to rack up high figures; this unfortunate development undermined the principles of unity and harmony in the *Burgfrieden*. The concern was that the war bond drives gave the wealthier pupils, who sold the bonds more easily, more recognition than the poorer pupils. After the third war bond drive in the fall of 1915, officials therefore made sure that teachers and school directors stopped bragging about amounts collected. But they still gave out medals, plaques, and other honors.[6]

Another reason for organizing the voluntary labor of schoolchildren was to mitigate the disruption the war inflicted on schooling. Collecting money and material for the war proved to be a good activity to occupy schoolchildren on the eighteen victory holidays in the first year of the war. It also kept the schoolchildren out of trouble after the school day was shortened. In the secondary schools, organizing the boys into voluntary projects was a useful antidote to the restlessness caused by the exodus of almost all the upper classmen who volunteered for the army in the first months of the war. The withdrawal from school by so many left the impression to the remaining pupils that voluntary service on the home front was the least they could do for Germany. Encouraging them were teachers who thought it was more valuable than homework and would prevent the bad behavior that idleness might provoke.[7]

Calling their labor *voluntary* and *patriotic* was in many cases a misnomer. Pupils who participated in these activities had a variety of motives that had little to do with supporting the war effort. Schoolchildren volunteered in the agricultural projects to get food clandestinely on the black market *(hamstern)*. Others saw the war bond drives as an opportunity to embezzle and the recycling drives as a way to keep some goods for their families. The decision to participate in these projects was a calculation of carrot and stick. The choice was to go out into the fresh air, be called a patriot, and gain some respite from homework and supervision by adults, or to stay in school and be labeled an apostate. Getting out of school was easy. In addition to the victory holidays, officials in the Prussian and Bavarian education ministries permitted school directors to dismiss pupils for patriotic voluntary labor as they wished. In a climate of good will and lax administration, teachers disregarded ordinances and released pupils on their own as well. Perhaps the biggest motivation, which some derided as "reward pedagogy," was the bestowing of holidays on the schoolchildren who surpassed goals in the war bond and recyclable drives. This usually happened on the local level, but it also happened by decree of the Kaiser after the success of the third war bond drive in September 1915. Because teachers felt this practice undermined true patriotism, many wanted to eliminate it, but it proved too useful a motivation to ban outright.[8]

School directors' annual reports, however, mentioned very few cases where the motives were selfish and suggested that the most persistent reward was admiration from the public and the press. According to the Free Conservative daily *Die Post*, the war bond drives in schools were laudable not for raising money but for being "an experience that would resonate and bring patriotic sensitivity into their hearts years later." For the duration of the war, the pedagogical, liberal, and conservative presses praised schoolchildren effusively. Despite its hesitations about the independence they granted to schoolchildren, even the left-wing Social Democratic daily newspaper *Vorwärts* reluctantly praised the war bond drives.[9]

Mobilizing Girls

Before the war, the resources that Prussia and other states allocated to the "youth-saving" campaigns targeted mostly boys. Officials reasoned that boys needed more attention because national security depended on having reliable soldiers who would defend Germany's world power and citizens who would vote against the Social Democratic Party (women did not have the right to vote until November 1918). Men were also more dangerous than women, committing crimes at four to ten times the rate depending on the category, and held the jobs that required more investment in education. The 1911 *Jugendpflege* Decree in Prussia accordingly made funds available for patriotic associations for boys only, and in most large cities, continuation schools were compulsory for boys but not girls.

The war ended this one-sided focus on male youths. Leaders in the women's movement convinced state and military officials that domestic labor such as mending clothes and cooking nutritious meals was an indirect but vital contribution to war production. Activists in the National Women's Service and the Red Cross inspired more women to found and lead youth associations and use the funds available under the 1913 revision of the *Jugendpflege* Decree. Women gained better representation in the committees that doled out the state recreation and welfare funds as they replaced conscripted district youth workers. Among the youth workers in Frankfurt a.M., for example, by May 1916 women outnumbered men nineteen to fourteen. Female associations also benefited from a larger pool of potential members. Because the service, textile, and luxury goods industries, the main economic sectors in which women worked, released hundreds of thousands of employees in the transition from a peacetime to wartime economy, there were more laid-off female than male youths with excess free time. With male leaders invariably conscripted, recreational associations for male youths declined steeply over the course of the war, but associations for females grew even through the years of deprivation. In addition to the voluntary activities, girls participated more than ever in crafts, singing, hiking, swimming, gymnastics, and competitions in running and field sports like the sling shot.[10]

Schoolgirls shoveling snow. *Source:* Franz Führen, *Lehrer im Krieg: Ein Ehrenbuch deutscher Volksschullehrer* (Leipzig: Georg Kummer, 1936), plate 22.

Knitting in patriotic circles, cooking in soup kitchens, and giving care in hospitals and day care centers conformed with women's traditional domestic roles. In solicitations for young female volunteers, like "be true to the German man during the war and at the same time gain skills for the German man after the war," association leaders reinforced a traditional belief that a female patriot's highest calling was to be a wife and a mother. But many activities, particularly the sports competitions, reflected an emergent belief that girls needed to maintain physical fitness and independence in the years before marriage. Gender played a less visible role when associations organized girls to work alongside boys in the harvests and in singing and bringing flowers and sweets to soldiers in hospitals. After the fall of 1916, even middle-class daughters volunteered for heavy labor like shoveling snow and hauling coal, jobs normally reserved for sons. Hence, while the expanded associational life often confirmed traditional beliefs about female domesticity, it could also cut the other way, particularly as conscription transformed the home front into an overwhelmingly female world where women now made the decisions and did men's work.[11]

The Youth Workers and the Military Training of Male Youth

Lacking coercive powers, the district youth workers had not been particularly successful before the war in carrying out the objective of the 1911 *Jugendpflege* Decree of turning youths into good nationalists. However, between 1914 and 1916 they came closer to realizing their mission by providing recreational associations with material about the war, staging so-called patriotic evenings, and, most importantly, organizing military youth companies.

The youth workers had an assembly of objects for recreational associations to make youths excited about the war. These included lyric books with patriotic songs; traveling libraries with books about the current war or past ones; and slide shows to lend with titles such as "Airships and Airplanes," "Krupp, the Workshop of the 42 cm [gun]," "The Mobilization of Our Infantry and Our Navy," "Pictures from the Belgian Front," and "Russian Days in East Prussia." They also helped associations offer lectures with titles like "What Wartime Demands of Our Women and Girls," "The Duties of Youths to the Fatherland," and "Trench Spirit in the Home Army." Filled with descriptions of battles, pictures of trenches, and biographies of military heroes, journals for youth workers like *Achtern Ploog!* helped them provide local associations with patriotic material for their events.[12]

When theaters and music hall venues ended their patriotic shows and returned to the prewar repertory of comedies, adventures, and love stories, youth workers stepped in and for the duration of the war helped recreational associations drum up enthusiasm by staging their own patriotic evenings. They organized their own dramas, concerts, slide shows, poetry readings, discussions, and lectures on topics such as German colonies, the economic mobilization for the war, and weapon technologies including the zeppelin, the 42-cm gun, the submarine, and the fabrication of explosives through the Haber process of nitrogen fixation. These activities aimed not only to discourage youths from the alleged dangers of commercial recreation but also to forge a sense of community and reinforce the necessary endurance to win the war. Even late in the war, some of these patriotic evenings had standing room only. Organizers of patriotic evenings aspired to create atmospheres where an ideal of social harmony prevailed. In confirmation of the *Burgfrieden*, a woman wrote that the elements of the evenings—flags, flowers, refreshments, tablecloths, communal songs, poetry, costumes, slides, films, gymnastics, and music—brought "all classes in the community" together.[13]

Most youth workers thought their primary task was to help recreational associations run and found voluntary military youth companies (*Jugend-wehren, vormilitärische Jugendbereitung,* etc.). The companies offered 16- to 18-year-old boys an opportunity to participate in marches, drills, and, later, games and sports competitions. The exercises were limited to four hours weekly and, because they taught none of the important skills soldiers needed to survive trench warfare, had little military value. But they played a key role in making male youths excited about becoming soldiers. Both the military and the public took a keen interest in the companies because Germany's war depended greatly on the reliability of these male youths as future soldiers. Like the war bond and collection drives of schoolchildren, the marches and drills of the companies placed the young male participants in conspicuous spectacles, earning them recognition in the press for their patriotism.

In the spirit of the *Burgfrieden,* in the fall of 1914 youth workers and retired military officers tried to make the companies socially diverse. They did not have trouble at first. While most members of the Socialist youth organizations outright rejected the companies in the fall of 1914, over two thousand working boys in Düsseldorf—roughly half of all 16-, 17-, and 18-year-olds in the continuation schools—marched in military youth companies in September 1914. They did so voluntarily, as the deputy commanding general in

Military youth training: firing line. *Source: Schule und Krieg: Sonderausstellung im Zentralinstitut für Erziehung und Unterricht, Berlin* (Berlin: Weidmann, 1915), plate 34.

Military youth training: bicycle patrols. *Source: Schule und Krieg: Sonderausstellung im Zentralinstitut für Erziehung und Unterricht, Berlin* (Berlin: Weidmann, 1915), plate 34.

Düsseldorf did not begin to consider compulsion until late 1915. In Hanover and Wilhemshaven, the majority of continuation schoolboys were also participating voluntarily in February 1915. In the summer of 1915 the Krupp factories in Essen still had many companies as well. As late as the fall of 1915, the district of Charlottenberg (Berlin) had eighteen companies of working youths. At least one factory in Berlin had a company. The youth workers and military officers were disappointed when in October and November 1914 the companies began splintering along confessional and class lines. After the spring of 1915, they were also upset that participation was declining. Working-class male youths left due to the plentiful jobs in the war industries and their growing disillusionment with the war. But a core of participants—as many as one-fifth of eligible male youths—was still participating now and then in the summer of 1918, particularly in middle-class neighborhoods in big cities, and Protestant small cities, towns, and villages (see Figure 5.1).[14]

Because of the military companies' early successes—in some regions, such as the Bavarian Palatinate, over 80 percent of eligible male youths were par-

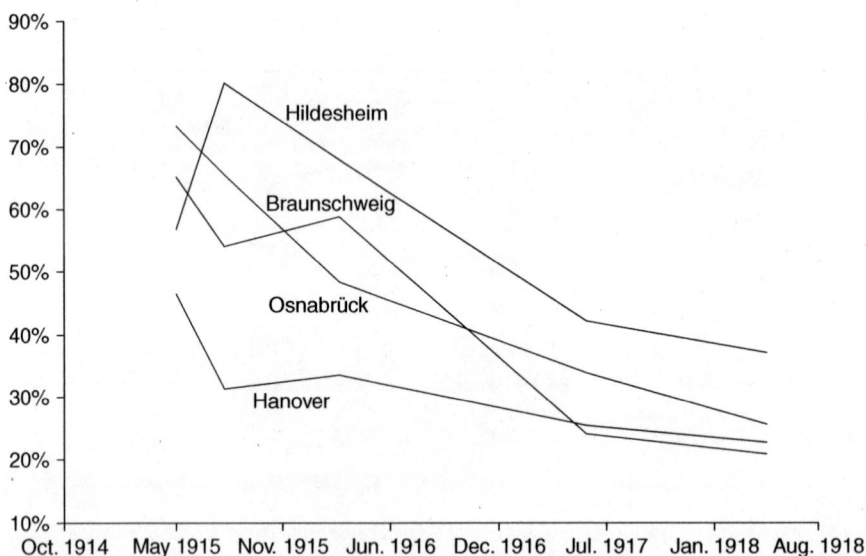

Figure 5.1. Male youths in military training as a percentage of all 16- and 17-year-olds, by county. *Source:* Reports, DCG, Hanover, 16 August 1915, 24 March 1916, 12 June 1917, and 10 May 1918, NHAH Hann. 122a Nr. 4490, Bl. 274, 299, 401, 445.

ticipating in the fall of 1914—they showed, according to one historian, that an authoritarian state now had an "almost total grasp" of youths and, according another, that officials believed "people now belonged entirely to the state." These characterizations are only partly true. In compulsory continuation schools, military training was sometimes part of the required physical education. In Prussia a decree in October 1914 by the trade and commerce minister, who oversaw the continuation schools, encouraged this policy. School boards and directors at continuation schools in Essen and much of Brandenburg and Schleswig required the schoolboys to participate, and their right to do so was upheld by the courts. The same legal prerogatives allowed directors of secondary schools to make participation compulsory as well. Further pressuring schools to put their pupils into military companies, the regional Prussian school authorities and the deputy commanding generals at times used stern language with directors whose secondary schools had lackluster records of military training.[15]

But schoolboys compelled to participate in military youth companies were the exception, and the evidence is marginal that the companies exacted "unconditional obedience" and constituted "totalitarian claims of the military." The prerogative to change the curriculum of continuation schools lay with individual municipal councils and school boards. These bodies were conservative before the war, but the *Burgfrieden* moved politicians in Prussia and Saxony to admit Social Democrats to school boards for the first time. In industrial cities like Höhscheid on the Rhine, the new Social Democrats on the board ensured that military youth companies for continuation school boys were strictly voluntary. Where the Social Democratic Party was politically weak, such as in small cities and the countryside, obligatory continuation schools were still uncommon. Most continuation schools did not institute compulsion, and most that did later rescinded it. In practice, directors of continuation schools lacked the teaching staff to lead military training and believed that the four hours of weekly drills took too much time away from the eight to twelve hours of vocational training they thought was critical for the war industries. In any case, fewer and fewer youths were in continuation schools after municipalities, the Reich War Office, and the state trade and commerce ministries released them to meet the surging demand for skilled labor in late 1915. The Prussian interior minister scuttled attempts by mayors and minor officials to make military training compulsory for working-class male youths who were not attending a continuation school. For secondary school boys, legal compulsion was negligible as well. In the first months of the war, the extent of the regulation was a decree from September 1914 that ordered teachers to be light on homework so that the schoolboys had time for military training. Although the War Ministry in May 1917 made military training a required course and created companies in every secondary school, this change was part of the Auxiliary Service Law, which conscripted the labor of all men age 17 to 60.[16]

Conservatives *proposed* making military training compulsory for all male youths. Reiterating an older argument from the debates preceding and following the 1911 *Jugendpflege* Decree, generals and state bureaucrats pointed out that those not participating in military training were precisely the ones least reliable and most in need of a patriotic education. When the enthusiasm for the military companies waned in late 1914, their cries grew louder to make the weekly exercises compulsory. But their bills never became law, in part because the reformers who originally founded recreational associations welcomed military training but categorically rejected compulsion. Prussian officials respected the consensus that teachers and youth workers achieved at a major conference led by Aloys Fischer in the fall 1916. All agreed that compulsion impeded patriotism and commitment to the war.[17]

In contrast to the induction into the army that broke down recruits, the military youth training empowered teenage boys, and by 1915 the boys themselves began to influence the content of the military training. In response to working youths' exodus from the companies, youth workers and army officers started a membership drive, attracting youths by substituting athletic activities for less popular drills and marches. The Prussian War Ministry provided funds for competitions in the triathlon, rounders, and soccer. In the duchy of Anhalt, medals were given out in these and other competitions. The companies, with the aid of the War Ministry, also sponsored free patriotic lectures, concerts, theater, films, and slide shows. They celebrated the Kaiser's birthday and distributed free patriotic magazines.[18]

Many boys were embarrassed that the guns used in the exercises of the military youth companies were toy wooden ones and pleaded to learn to shoot real arms, arguing it was a useful skill for a future soldier. An officer in Berlin reported: "Every new participant asks: 'When do I get a gun, when can I shoot?'" Making the participants imitate fire by clapping their hands had produced only "funny expressions." To the boys' disappointment, liberal and Social Democratic politicians rejected the use of real guns. In June 1915, the

War Ministry overruled this decision and allowed firearms in military youth training, provided the company was led by a registered shooting club. The stipulation limited the eligible companies to just a handful, a situation the public thought was fine. Wartime or not, parents did not like their boys playing with guns.[19]

Far from bringing new disciplinary controls over youths, the companies produced an unwanted brashness in some boys, according to state officials and conservative and liberal newspapers. While marching in their company, the pupils at one *Gymnasium* sang obscene songs. At least one youth company in Breslau developed into a social clique where members flaunted the armbands outside of practice, and their noise once transformed a local wine shop into a carnival. In military regalia, they sang, danced, ran up a bill of over 100 marks, and then split with their female dates without paying. In Munich in May 1915, a rumor circulated that a military youth company allegedly killed hundreds of people, "including a few mothers." Adults reacted to the smug young gendarmes:

> On Sundays these boys feel themselves called upon to be saviors of the Fatherland. I saw a little tot march in proudly with his gun and boast to his comrade: "We now have seized guns because we have to produce order again."

Parents and the public did not like boys acting like soldiers on the public streets.[20]

Youths had many motivations for joining military youth companies. Some went to get free meals. Others joined because some deputy commanding generals after August 1916 gave participants the privilege of choosing their garrison town upon conscription. Peer pressure was undoubtedly a factor. But in nationalist milieus the key reward was pleasing a public that hailed boys training for the army. For example, in Hanover in September 1915 thousands, including municipal and Prussian dignitaries, watched youths parade in about twenty companies and then attack each other, counterattack, fire wooden guns, and finally storm the trenches. The onlookers cheered. Mock battles became such spectacles that they attracted photographers and even film crews and moved the Social Democratic press to risk censorship and criticize the excessiveness. Typical was the reaction of the liberal *Vossische Zeitung*, which reported in January 1915 that the one thousand boy scouts who participated in military exercises had "jolly high spirits." The paper assured its readers that "as long as we have such boys, Germany can rest peacefully."[21]

The lyrics of songs for youth companies indulged in a masculine fantasy about power and militarism. A song, "German Army, You Fountain of Youth," invoked language of domination and superiority:

> ... The German army's powerful brawn,
> England's hoards of false mercenaries
> And all foreign people
> Have to bow to German strength and German courage.

Another song, "We Are the Youth Company," glorified the sacrifice of life for country:

> Yes, we are German
> Want to be German forever
> Always tried and true
> Fatherland, we are yours only;
> When we get the call, then we are there,
> Our life belongs to you.

Whatever their motivation, the male youths in the companies, like the schoolchildren in the voluntary projects, had to reconcile their opinion of the war with their choice to prepare to be soldiers and receive public recognition. Simulating a sanitized war of movement that contradicted combat in the trenches, the organizers of military youth training reinforced that war was exciting and that strenuous masculinity, aggression, and voluntary self-sacrifice were positive traits.[22]

Youths and schoolchildren in Germany volunteered their labor more expansively and consistently than those in the other belligerents. Pupils in France and Great Britain informally knit items for soldiers, worked the plantings and harvests, and collected money for soldiers' charities during class. But only in 1916, the year that the British war mobilization took a quantum leap nationally with the introduction of military conscription, did cities such as London undertake any major steps in marshaling the labor of schoolchildren. Current research suggests that the scale of the mobilization was accordingly smaller because the first mass organization of recycling and collection drives did not coincide, as it did in Germany, with the enthusiasm for voluntary activity accompanying the burst of patriotism in the first months of the war. Furthermore, the London Teachers' Association flat out rejected support for military youth training, and nationally in France and Great Britain there were few military youth companies outside elite secondary schools. Whereas over the course of the war Germany sent 1 million urban schoolchildren to work on farms, the French education bureaucracy was not able to carry out even relatively modest voluntary-labor programs, such as the one to cultivate 1,500 hectares nationwide. In France schools accordingly "failed with their mobilization of children," according to the leading expert. Austria-Hungary had more success in military training programs, particularly after the supranational state gave more resources to transnational companies in 1916 to contain Czech separatist ones, and rivalries among the empire's nationalities motivated teenage boys to get military training. The number of German youths who subsequently participated rose in regions such as Moravia where they were a minority. There an estimated half of all eligible male youths in 1916 and a third in 1917 were participating—more than in Germany. But the mobilization of schoolchildren's labor faltered after 1915 as the multinational empire fractured and ultimately collapsed.[23]

Germany was the most successful because it had the most developed network of youth associations in the world, and Prussia was the only major combatant state with official youth workers who coordinated resources and activities. The Prussian education minister was also singularly committed: the vast majority of his orders during the war had to do not with curriculum but with the productive use of schoolchildren's labor. A conservative estimate is that about half of the 13 million boys and girls age 6 to 18, approximately 25 percent of the total civilian population, did voluntary activity regularly. Their participation did not necessarily indicate enthusiasm for the war. Much evidence suggests, for example, that many girls who knit assiduously for soldiers harbored deep anxiety about the war. However, by mobilizing youths under the principle of voluntarism, state officials discovered a subtle but effective method to reinforce commitment to the war. Instead of force, crass indoctrination, or traditional disciplinary methods, they motivated the millions of schoolchildren and hundreds of thousands of youths by relying on peer pressure, esteem from the press and the public, and pupils' own joy in contributing. The activities, being voluntary, implied a conscious choice to help Germany and forced boys and girls to come to terms with the fact they were willingly working for the war.[24]

The voluntary activities also mitigated the authoritarian relationships between youths and adults while encouraging patriotic sacrifice and strenuous masculinity. The recycling and war bond drives were often unsupervised activities. Participants in the military youth companies gained recognition in the elaborate parades and war games that became public spectacles. The companies boosted the self-image of boys who would soon be men testing their bravery on the front. In their confidence, the male youths sometimes alarmed the public by asserting their superiority in aggressive masculine displays. Like war pedagogy and youth war literature, voluntary activity and premilitary training encouraged a commitment to the war, nationalism, and, for some boys, a fascination with proving manhood through military action.

6

Deprivation and the Collapse of Schooling

In the first year of the war, a sense of political unity moved teachers to soften the authoritarian relationship between them and their pupils. After 1915, the relationship relaxed further, only now the reason was not the social effect of the *Burgfrieden* and the Spirit of 1914 but the horrible deprivation affecting teachers and pupils alike. During the so-called Turnip Winter of 1916/17, when turnips were the only plentiful food, supplies of dairy, vegetable fats, meat, and wheat, the mainstay of the German diet, were almost nowhere to be found in major cities. Available coal was insufficient, and the temperature in Potsdam on one February day dropped to a bone-numbing –33° C. By 1918, the value of government rations was just 1,280 calories, half that of the prewar diet and well below the 1,600-calorie threshold that aid organizations today say is the bare minimum to avoid dying from starvation. Survival necessitated burning up extra calories while standing for long hours in line and roaming the countryside to find food from farmers on the black market. German families stopped maintaining and reproducing themselves in the most literal sense. Adolescents stopped growing, adults lost between twenty and fifty pounds, and, for the first time in Germany's modern history, deaths exceeded births. Even after the Turnip Winter, the shortages continued to create extreme hardship. The food shortage was not alleviated until the harvest in the fall of 1917 and then began again in December, though with less severity. Germans had not experienced mass starvation since 1848, but between 1915 and 1918 famine and cold killed an estimated seven hundred thousand German civilians, mostly because of susceptibility to disease. All the while, soldiers were dying by the hundreds of thousands and returning home wounded and traumatized by the millions.[1]

When coupled with personnel shortages, the effect of the deprivation proved disastrous to the school regime but beneficial to the softening relationships between teachers and pupils. As early as the spring of 1915, lack of teachers and buildings had forced consolidations of classes and the shortening of the school day by half or two-thirds. In the winters coal was often insufficient to heat classrooms, and schools had to close for weeks at a time. Teachers had to deal not only with the evisceration of personnel that diminished the quality of instruction but also pupils who arrived to class cold and hungry, fearing for loved ones on the front, traumatized by the millions of casualties, and exhausted from long waits and walks for food and coal. Teachers often did not see their pupils at all. Regular truancy to find food or to rest at home became a survival strategy. But because teachers were as overworked, hungry, cold, and distressed as their pupils, few had the will to be aggressive in punishing the truants. Suffering with the urban schoolchildren who showed signs of "nervousness, conditions of exhaustion, anemia, and other serious health disturbances," most could also no longer imagine comporting themselves like the haughty, imperious tyrants that so many were before 1914. They even went beyond their normal duties, as schools became the supreme welfare institution for schoolchildren, and many teachers became ersatz parents of sorts.[2]

While teachers put their energy into caretaking, state officials denied the unfolding catastrophe and bungled the distribution of food. Teachers increasingly sided with the starving urban masses who challenged the authority of the government for its incompetence, a development that contributed to the declining legitimacy of the state and spun Germany toward revolution.

Schoolchildren's Health and Administrative Incompetence

Germany depended on imports for half of its wheat and one-third of its fodder, but the military and municipal and state governments had not planned for the English food blockade and did not have a contingency food plan for a protracted war. In addition, Germany's federal system was poorly equipped to coordinate a national food policy; civilian administrations of the different states did not readily cooperate with each other. Under the Law of Siege, the deputy commanding generals, who could set domestic policy by decree, had plenipotentiary power only within their jurisdictions. They were answerable only to the Kaiser, and he was by most measures incompetent in matters of domestic administration during the war. Derided as a "sword without edges," the War Food Office, created first in 1916 to address this administrative weakness, issued numerous decrees but was never able to ameliorate the shortages and chaotic distribution.[3]

The war's assault on customary food habits began when supplies of wheat for bread ran low in December 1914—that is, before the shortages caused any real malnutrition. The absence of bread and the growing scarcity of meat, fats, and dairy led Germans to suspect that the health of schoolchildren was suffering. In response, various school districts and regional governments commissioned studies by doctors in the summer and fall of 1915. A circumspect physician for northern Charlottenberg-Berlin concluded in November that the health of children, including working-class ones, had not yet entered a level of immediate danger but "certainly could if the war continued." In 1916 the state school doctors were not as concerned. In Württemberg they concluded that the health of schoolchildren in both the city and countryside was "on average as good as or better than in peace time." In October 1916 state school doctors in Berlin reported that, based on a general study, "the overall level of health is extremely good." Bavarian state doctors reached the same conclusions.[4]

The credibility of these state school doctors plummeted during the Turnip Winter. The guidelines for establishing malnutrition were far from standardized, but denying that the health of schoolchildren had declined was laughable. When the state school doctors presented their health studies in the Prussian Diet in April 1917, elementary school teachers in attendance could only "shake their heads" in disbelief. Despite the prewar prohibitions on Socialism, during the debate teachers turned for support to the Social Democratic Party, whose organ *Vorwärts* had published studies that were at variance with the medical community's consensus. At the same time, Bavarian teachers scorned the state school authorities by publishing in their main professional journal a set of free compositions by schoolchildren depicting the hunger and the food riots. By the fall of 1917, the state authorities could no longer deny the alarming problem. A well-designed longitudinal study that measured eight hundred teenagers and schoolchildren in Munich in 1913, 1916, and 1917 concluded that they were now on average 2 to 3 centimeters shorter and 4 to 8 pounds lighter than before the war. Even those whose weights were normal had become more susceptible to disease.[5]

Further inciting teachers was Friedrich Schmidt-Ott, the Prussian education minister who replaced von Trott zu Solz in August 1917 and, in the first weeks of his tenure, mismanaged the coal shortage. Hoping to save fuel by not heating schoolrooms for a week in the middle of winter, he canceled the fall holiday and extended the Christmas holiday. The measure exasperated teachers who pointed out that the decree interrupted children's plans to work the harvest and forced children to do without heated classrooms during the coldest part of the winter. This was a problem because many families did not heat their apartments during the day and were relying on schools to provide warm spaces for their children in late December. One irritated teacher wrote that the authorities, "foolishly toppled by St. Bureaucracy, want to drive out our boys and girls into the Siberia threatening us in order to save heat and light." In Frankfurt, the measure unleashed panic among the local school authorities, who fired off a battery of desperate telegrams to Berlin and pleaded for an abrogation of the decree. Following orders from the War Ministry, the Prussian education minister did not budge. The teachers believed

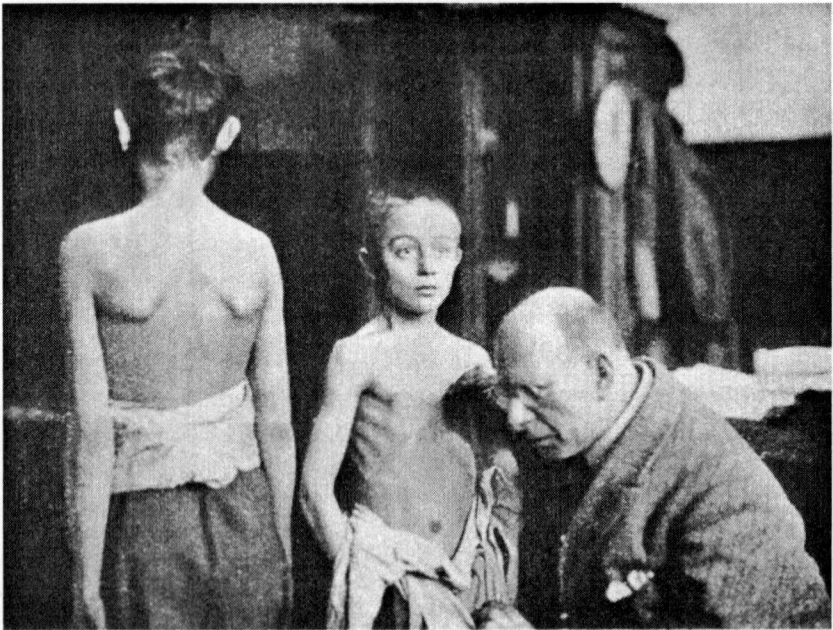

Doctor examining emaciated schoolchildren. *Source:* Walter Eschbach, *Kinderelend— Jugendnot, auch eine Bilanz des Krieges* (Berlin: E. Laub, 1925), 311.

the administration was incompetent because it had only shifted the burden of heating rooms from state schools onto families.[6]

The Dearth of Teachers

After 1915 the German school system functioned poorly at best and, in many cases, not at all. The primary cause of this disruption was the shortage of qualified teachers. At the end of the 1914/15 school year, one-third of Prussia's prewar 98,130 male elementary school teachers had volunteered or been conscripted; by January 1918 the portion had grown to two-thirds. The rate was similar for secondary school teachers and for teachers in the other German states. The constant scramble to find substitutes was Sisyphean. Whenever a new teacher was found, it seemed another was conscripted. It was common for one class to have four or five different teachers per year. Making matter worse, the substitutes were neophytes, retirees, or discharged soldiers physically or emotionally scarred from their war injuries. The reports of school administrators claimed that frequent changes of personnel lessened the teachers' control over their classroom. The emotional bonds may have been there, and in many cases increased, but according to one elementary school official, "the fabric that produces the intellectual bonds between pupil and teacher has been torn."[7]

Exacerbating the problem was the military's expropriation of schools in garrison and capital cities for use as hospitals, quarters, and offices. In Berlin, for example, more than 10 percent of all school buildings were occupied for the duration of the war. Administrators in some districts were able to improvise and hold classes in kitchens, dance halls, and attics, but in other areas they lacked resources, and school directors clashed over which schools should bear the burden. Shortages of coal forced the closing of classrooms for weeks and sometimes months during the war winters.[8]

The most common way to cope with the lack of resources was to shorten the school day. Early in the war, some schools amalgamated classes, but it became clear that bringing eighty to one hundred schoolchildren into a classroom with only fifty seats was impossible. "The children constantly touch each other," a teacher complained, "and the instruction flies over their heads." Most schools in Prussia shortened instruction to one-half day or a third of a day. In Munich in September 1915, just a handful of schools maintained full-time instruction (see Table 6.1). Half-time instruction did not necessarily

Table 6.1   School instruction in Munich elementary schools, September 1915

Extent of instruction	Number of schools
Full day	9
Half day	32
One-third day	10
None	4

Source: "Notbetrieb an den Volkshauptschulen während des Krieges 1914–1918," 22 September 1915, StdMünch Schulamt Nr. 911.

reduce class size in places like Mainz, where the average in elementary school increased from forty-seven pupils per class before the war to fifty-nine in the school year 1916/17. In the rural district of Mainz-Kotheim there were seventy-one pupils per class.[9]

The class consolidations increased teachers' work burdens tremendously. In financially strapped rural areas, it was common for teachers to work thirty to thirty-six hours in the classroom weekly, then grade the homework of over a hundred, even two hundred, schoolchildren, and finally plan lessons and fulfill administrative duties. All this was in addition to the sometimes tens of hours per week needed to find food and coal for their families. With the passing of the Auxiliary Service Law in December 1916, the military conscripted teachers' intellectual labor, such as preparing censuses of material goods and organizing collection drives. Since schoolteachers were on fixed salaries, their material conditions deteriorated in the inflation more rapidly than those of other groups. Overworked and undernourished, having lost weight and mental acuity, they quarreled with their equally exhausted administrators about the increased workload.[10]

Surging legitimate absences also hampered instruction, especially after the spring of 1916, when the Prussian education minister issued a series of decrees that permitted more extensive releases of schoolchildren for agricultural work. Individual teachers' lack of control over releases—school inspectors sometimes overrode teachers who wanted to keep the children in class—was frustrating and disruptive. Because of the evacuations to the countryside in 1917 and 1918, most children in Berlin were on farms weeks before the start of summer holiday. Consequently, on the last day of school in the summer of 1918, many elementary school classrooms were close to empty. Attendance in the secondary schools and the teacher-training colleges also faltered due to week-long collection drives and weeks and even months of voluntary work in agriculture, rail yards, and offices. The conscription of 17-year-olds into Auxiliary Service and their early volunteering for the army further cut into secondary school attendance.[11]

Rural schools, never well provisioned in peacetime, experienced particularly serious problems during the war. Instruction was regularly interrupted by releases for agricultural work, which was more common in the countryside than in the cities. In some villages, classes were held only twice weekly, and instruction was reduced from the prewar standard of twenty-five to thirty hours to just six per week in some schools. Consequently, many rural schools had to eliminate instruction in geography, natural science, poetry, drawing, singing, and gymnastics. Rural schools sometimes stayed closed for six months or longer because finding replacement teachers in the countryside was more difficult than in the cities. Reductions in rail transportation meant that some teachers were forced to travel extensively by foot, sometimes for three hours daily. In one extreme case, a rural school could only find a teacher four months out of his preparatory college, and he was responsible for three hundred pupils. The shortages of electricity and petroleum meant that rural teachers who taught all day, as most did, had no opportunity to correct papers at night in the winter. The lack of resources was even more stretched when one million urban schoolchildren were sent to farms from 1916 to 1918 for stays up to six months. Accommodating all the new guests was nearly impossible. "In school we didn't learn anything at all," wrote one pupil in her essay about her experience. "The children blabbed the whole time." Many pupils did not attend school at all because their hosts needed their labor on the farms, and truancy police were absent or inattentive. Many teachers and organizers proclaimed the stays in the countryside exacerbated the already loose discipline, both in school and at home.[12]

Officials alleviated some of this personnel shortage by hiring female substitutes, and almost all unemployed female teachers trained before 1914 found positions during the war. The portion of women teaching in urban schools rose from one-third in 1911 to over half in 1916. Furthermore, because the education ministries for the first time permitted women to teach coeducational classrooms, their proportion in rural schools increased from about an eighth to a quarter.[13]

However, the overwhelmingly male profession and state bureaucracy decried the alleged inability of female teachers to maintain classroom discipline. As one official put it, "they were no match for the boys." Some directors attributed the problem to the poor training of the substitutes—many were young women who had not yet passed their teaching exams. Male teachers also worried about the threat female teachers posed to their positions after the war. Consequently, officials in many regions made good on their promise that the training of new female teachers would be limited. Extreme need could not persuade state officials or even the Association of Prussian Female Elementary School Teachers, the main professional organization, to hire married female teachers. They believed motherhood took too much time to permit a woman to be a good teacher, and vice versa.[14]

A rural elementary school near Osnabrück offered a good example of these problems. Lacking a teacher for his school, the director reluctantly hired a female substitute. However, the schoolboys apparently held the same biases toward women as many male teachers. They gave her a hard time, and she quit. The class was forced to consolidate with a school one-hour walking distance away. The school administration continued to search for a new teacher but was offered only a wounded one from the front. The administration rejected him and insisted on having a healthy teacher to control the boys. After months, they were finally supposed to receive a male substitute, but in a bureaucratic blunder, they never managed to secure his release from the army. The school administration was exasperated when, in a letter from the front, the teacher requested his pay, though he had not taught a single day![15]

Truancy, Exhaustion, Plummeting Standards, and Sympathy

Almost all teachers and officials agreed that the disruptions and the deprivation substantially lowered academic achievement. When pupils participated in the collection drives after instruction, as was the case in most elementary schools, the activities diverted them from homework and drained their energy for the next school day. Enervated in addition by hunger, fear, traumatized family members, extra work burdens at home, and long searches for food, children were distracted, oversensitive, sluggish, and absent-minded. The thoughts of loved ones on the front made it difficult to concentrate and finish homework. Schoolchildren had even less incentive to get good grades after the Prussian education minister in 1915 and again in 1917 ordered teachers to be mild when promoting pupils to the next grade. For example, the fifty thousand schoolchildren in Berlin who went to the countryside in the spring and summer of 1917 were promoted to the next grade, even though they missed more than two months of instruction. In boys' secondary schools, an additional detriment to motivation was the prospect of imminent conscription at age 18 and an easy emergency final examination if the boy chose to volunteer at age 16 or 17. The easy advancements to the next grade "became almost a reward for laziness and ignorance." "The aftereffects," one official wrote, "will make themselves felt for a long time."[16]

Other factors further undermined basic instruction. Food riots forced teachers to release their pupils from instruction. Shortened train and tram schedules made punctual attendance by secondary school children difficult. During the Turnip Winter of 1916/17, the shortages of clothing produced acrimonious conflicts between parents who lacked the money for clothes, and directors of secondary schools who wanted to maintain their dress codes. Because of the acute lack of footwear, the Prussian governments in many provinces allowed pupils in all schools, including elite private ones, to attend instruction barefoot and encouraged all to wear wooden shoes.[17]

With the onset of the Turnip Winter, illegal truancy in elementary schools skyrocketed. Many female schoolchildren were forced to stay at home to cook, take care of siblings, and tend house while their mothers worked or searched for food. Boys and girls had to do the *polonaise*—the wry Berlin lingo for waiting in queues for food and coal that sometimes began in the dark of the early morning and lasted ten hours. In the winter months, the *polonaise* weakened the schoolchildren and impeded their completion of homework. In rural areas, the extreme shortage of labor also provided a constant incentive for truancy. "The smallest pretense," one official charged, served "many parents as an excuse to keep their children from school." Most police did not have the heart to discipline schoolchildren for arriving one or two hours late to school because of queuing for food. They were also dealing with problems more menacing to the social order, such as food riots and quadrupling crime rates, and conscription had depleted their ranks. Because teachers in Prussia did not have the prerogative to arrest and punish truants (only the police did), the jurisdiction limitations frustrated teachers who wanted to enforce attendance on their own. The "extremely limited authority" of the school police in Berlin charged 2,721 children with missing school in 1916/17. Although this figure was twice that of 1915/16, the rate was just twelve charges per thousand elementary school children per year. In reality, scores and sometimes hundreds per thousand were truant daily.[18]

Some teachers angrily dismissed accusations that these classroom conditions now posed a "national danger," but even those in the pedagogical press
who denied a general state of delinquency recognized that the shorter school
hours and overburdening of teachers hampered their pupils' good behavior.
As early as 1915, organizations such as the National Women's Service in Berlin were anxious that half-time instruction left millions of children without
adult supervision for much of the day. The anxiety intensified over the course
of the war, and many traced the origins of deviant street behavior and rising
property crime to truancy. In March 1916 Leopold Fischer, Berlin's school
superintendent, denied that Berlin's working-class pupils were in the throes
of a generalized juvenile delinquency. In February 1917, however, he organized a conference on delinquency and called for a more extended right to
corporal punishment for teachers of older pupils—a policy the editors of
Pädagogische Zeitung, who sympathized with the suffering of schoolchildren,
rejected. The breakdown of schooling hardened conservatives' demands for
severe disciplinary mechanisms, but they were impotent to stem the erosion
of state authority over schoolchildren. Teachers refused to be harsh with their
pupils. They could do little to reduce the truancy even if they so desired.[19]

While the state authorities bungled the labor, food, and coal shortages,
teachers and local administrations worked diligently to provide whatever welfare they could to schoolchildren. By 1917 enterprising municipalities were
serving schoolchildren ten times as many meals as in the year before the war
(see Table 6.2). The school meals placed hundreds of teachers and children
together for an activity that strengthened communal bonds. By 1916, teachers
were regularly supervising children whose fathers were in the army for two
hours after school. In Berlin they erected day care centers in at least one hundred elementary schools; they would have erected more, but many schools
had closed outright. Schools opened a few heated rooms for children after
regular school hours and during holidays and school cancellations. Teachers
consoled traumatized parents, especially mothers whose husbands were on
the front, and at the end of the war, *Pädagogische Zeitung* praised teachers for
not only having mobilized pupils patriotically but also serving as substitute
parents in times of need. According to the Prussian education minister, teachers were "in many communities the glue holding together the entire population." In his history of German education commissioned by the Carnegie
Foundation, the noted pedagogue Wilhelm Flitner claimed that in the years
of deprivation teachers' relationships to pupils, already softened in 1914 and

Table 6.2 Annual school lunches in Düsseldorf (in hundreds of thousands)

Year	Number of school meals
1914	179
1915	435
1916	2,331
1917	2,728
1918	2,147

Source: Verwaltungsbericht der Stadt Düsseldorf, für den Zeitraum vom 1. April 1914 bis 31. März 1918, 125.

1915 under war pedagogy, became closer: "Teachers and children came into a more confiding relationship than before. They no longer had an isolated lesson together, but rather a portion of life. After the war . . . teachers were no longer closed-off government educators."[20]

After 1915, schools became less about teaching than about helping schoolchildren endure the deprivation and muster the will for victory. Schools provided meals and warm heated spaces for pupils who had scarce food and coal at home. Teachers not only gave instruction on economic survival strategies but also offered a compassionate ear to schoolchildren grieving the loss of their brother or agonizing over their mothers' nervous condition. Despite the growing rates of absenteeism and widespread observations of indiscipline among young people, few had the heart to turn over their pupils to the school police or use the cane to bring them into line. In both elementary and secondary schools, teachers were suffering under the same miserable conditions as their pupils. In last years of the war, the priority was meeting the material needs and maintaining the human bonds that would allow Germans to hold out for a final victory. Many teachers remarked that this shared experience was incompatible with being cool and distant authoritarians and brought them closer to their pupils.

This deprivation and the collapse of schooling distinguished the Central European powers from the Western Allies. The conscription of men had far more serious consequences on schools in Germany because 80 percent of teachers there were male, compared to 40 percent in Great Britain and just 25 percent in France. Furthermore, in contrast to Germany and Austria-Hungary, France and Great Britain prevented severe shortages among their civilian populations and maintained or even improved nutrition. The British addressed public health issues, such as prenatal and infant care, so well that civilian mortality rates decreased significantly. As one scholar has argued, in England war was "good for babies." Having already suffered more on the home front than people in the Western Allied nations, the Germans were outraged at the armistice, which maintained the food blockade until July 1919, and the Versailles Treaty, which they believed punished them over and beyond their wartime suffering. Declining adult authority over youths likely led schoolchildren in France and Great Britain to skip school frequently, but absenteeism was greater in Germany because, in order to survive, pupils had to spend inordinate amounts of time searching for food. Because schooling was the most forceful instrument of state authority over children, social control in Central Europe disintegrated more extensively than in France or Great Britain.[21]

7

The Upheaval of Families

Conscription eviscerated schools of their personnel and severely eroded their social controls over children. Its effect on German families was no less merciless. Although soldiers returned on furloughs for convalescence, garrison duty, or work in factories, millions of fathers were absent entirely, and without their husbands' wages, mothers had to leave their children alone to make up lost income. At the same time, shortages forced mothers to spend inordinate amounts of time standing in queues and roaming through the countryside to get food on the black market. The bread shortages also made preparing meals time- and fuel-consuming. This family situation tended to accentuate prewar gender roles of siblings but upend relationships of authority between parents and children, particularly mothers and sons. Male teenagers who replaced conscripted men in enterprises and earned a man's wages gained status in their households by becoming the primary bread earners. Some girls earned more money as well during the war, but in general the lower average wages of female youths relative to their mothers' and brothers' forced more to stay at home. In this situation, many sisters lost status and independence, while their brothers gained them.

Absent Fathers

The military did not keep precise statistics on the number of children whose fathers were conscripted, but 4 million mothers of 7 million children under age 15—approximately one-third of all preschoolers and schoolchildren—received subsidies under the 1888 Reich law that compensated the families of soldiers in wartime. The actual number of children whose fathers were conscripted was higher, as many rural and middle-class families never received the aid. One social worker estimated in October 1915 that fathers were conscripted in 6, not 4, million families. Because men married on average at age 29 at the turn of the century, youths over 14 were less likely than preschoolers or schoolchildren to have fathers conscripted. The Berlin police nonetheless estimated in 1917 that one-third of working youths ages 14 to 18 had fathers in the army. Strained family budgets also forced civilian middle-class fathers to work in cities far from home.[1]

The separation of fathers from families on this unprecedented scale unleashed anxiety among state officials and welfare workers that families could not adequately support and supervise children. From an economic standpoint, their concerns were valid. The six marks weekly per child of state family aid, with additional supplements from local municipalities and charities, were sufficient only during the first months of the war. In 1914, the standard of living of many families on aid improved; some were even able to retrieve pawned goods and deposit money into savings accounts. But inflation quickly eroded the real value of their family aid, and it did not cover the costs of goods on the black market. Family aid did not even come close to indemnifying families for the lost wages of fathers, let alone their domestic labor.[2]

In addition to undermining the family economic unit, the absence of fathers removed the most potent authority over youths. During the war courts ruled that in the absence of fathers, mothers had full authority over children, including the right to punish, but customary discipline was patriarchal, and it was now absent in a third to half of all families. State officials and welfare workers panicked that unruly, fatherless youths threatened the social order. As evidence they pointed out that the fathers of almost all youths committed to state care for juvenile delinquency during the war were absent. Officials also believed that the fathers who remained on the home front were weak. As in German-speaking regions of Austria-Hungary, men on the home front were either older than 45 or considered unmanly for having failed their army medical inspection and thus incapable, in the minds of youth advocates, of restraining recalcitrant youngsters. When later remembering her life as a 16-year-old, Marlene Dietrich revealed this prejudice: "The few men we still saw were old or sick and were not real men."[3]

As debilitating as the economic and social deprivation associated with fathers' long absences was the emotional trauma. Children both pined and feared for their conscripted fathers. In a 1915 study of the "three dearest wishes" of 470 schoolchildren, for example, Munich researchers discovered that, after "victory," the most common responses were "the return of father and relatives," the "safe return of soldiers," and "no conscription of father or relatives." These wishes stood ahead of plentiful food, a longer life, a lasting peace, a healthy family, and success in learning. In their compositions, schoolchildren, particularly younger ones, regularly described their tears and worries about their fathers on the front. Even reuniting with a father returning on leave was an experience fraught with anxiety. A young elementary school girl wrote that when her father returned, "it had been so long and I was so happy [sic] that I hid myself behind the sofa, and then came the tears. We thought that this year would be better but it hasn't." Anecdotes from the pedagogical press show that teachers were overwhelmed in dealing with the grief and the conflicts it created. One teacher was despondent over an 8-year-old elementary school girl who cried regularly. She did not know how to console the girl when a schoolmate said: "Your father could be shot dead. I am happy that my father is at home." Another teacher agonized over a boy whose father was a prisoner of war and then died. The boy's mother mewled constantly about the misfortune, and the boy—normally attentive and diligent—went into shock. Every attempt to speak to him ended in tears.[4]

The reaction of individual youths to absent fathers varied greatly, however. When a girl imagined losing her father or, if he had already died and she described his death, the girl was expected to suppress her grief and show she could carry on stoically like a good patriot. Despondency over a conscripted father was common among younger schoolchildren, but male teenagers often took the absence in stride. In school compositions, impassivity over his absence implied their own early manhood. Like the adults who mentored them, middle-class male youths glorified their father-soldiers. Ernst Gläser, 12 years old at the outbreak of the war, wrote in his autobiographical novel: "And as in former days we had often given expression to our admiration for the heroes of Homer . . . so now we began, but with far more intensity, to transform ourselves symbolically into the ideal figures of our fathers." Once aloof disciplinarians, feared and scorned, fathers in absence became the imaginary idols of male teenagers. But police, teachers, parents, and youth workers also charged that in striving to be like their absent soldier-fathers, male teenagers became arrogant and undisciplined and took advantage of their allegedly weak mothers. By 1917, teachers, jurists, police, generals, youth workers, and newspaper reporters across the political spectrum agreed that the absence of fathers was the primary reason for the disturbing increase in mischief and crime.[5]

Overburdened Mothers

Exacerbating the problem of absent fathers was the enormous burden the war placed on mothers. When the consumer sectors of the German economy contracted in the fall of 1914 because of the mobilization for industrial war, tens of thousands of poor urban mothers no longer had income from so-called homework *(Heimarbeit)*—tailoring, cigar-rolling, luxury goods assembly, and other handwork done in their apartments. Homework had been critical to the survival of the poorest urban families, allowing mothers to earn while supervising preschoolers during the day and schoolchildren in the afternoon—the cost of day care made wage earning in factories unattractive or prohibitive. For mothers with conscripted husbands, family aid allowed them to hold out, if barely, for the first year of the war. But families in which the husband remained a civilian suffered even more if he lost his job in the recession that lasted through the spring of 1915. Thus, poor urban mothers with husbands at home were more likely to struggle economically in the first year of the war than were soldiers' wives. The former had few options because the textile and other factories that employed women laid off tens of thousands of workers and did not rehire many of them over the course of the war due to shortages of cotton. Accordingly, the better-off soldier's wife became an object of jealousy and derision in working-class neighborhoods, at least until 1916, when they began to suffer the same terrible hunger as other urban women.[6]

The war industries slowly outsourced homework production of gasmasks, uniforms, belts, baskets, and other military items, but despite regulations issued by the military, the compensation was meager, and most of the new jobs for women after the economic recovery in the spring of 1915 were in factories or mines. Hence, economic necessity drove hundreds of thousands of urban mothers to take wage jobs and abandon their children during the day. This development was disastrous for supervision because it coincided with personnel shortages that forced most elementary schools to institute half- or one-third-day instruction. At the end of the war a third of the women working in the Bavarian war industries were mothers. Half of them left their children with neighbors or relatives in informal day care, and 13 percent left their children unsupervised. Demand exceeded supply of slots for children in municipal day care programs, and the reliability of informal day care arrangements, for which most working mothers opted, was questionable during the food and coal crisis. It was not until late 1916 that the War Office recruited Marie-Elisabeth Lüders, the future Reichstag delegate of the German Democratic Party during the Weimar Republic, to study the problem of female labor. Through her reports the War Office became aware of the need for a labor policy that would successfully address the unrecognized work of mothering. By 1918, she was able to persuade the war industries to employ about 750 nurses to run day care centers so that mothers who manufactured armaments had supervision for their children. But the program was inadequate, providing only one nurse for every thousand female workers in the war industries.[7]

After 1915, working mothers from a broader range of social classes had burdens that forced them to leave their children unsupervised. The hardship derived in part from the pressure to earn money when families had spent their savings. Then in 1915 inflation began to reduce the real income of white-collar workers, lower civil servants such as elementary school teachers, and artisans and others in lower-middle-class trades. By the end of the war, their families were often worse off than the families of industrial workers, whose wages could keep better pace with inflation through collective bargaining. Without their husband's income and with family aid no longer sufficing, tens of thousands of middle-class mothers had to find work in their husbands' shops or in factories and smaller enterprises. Women of all social classes increasingly left their children at home while they stood in line, sometimes for ten hours a day, to buy scarce clothing, food, and coal for their families. Beginning in the Turnip Winter of 1916/17 and lasting until the fall harvest of 1917, urban mothers spent tens of hours monthly roaming the countryside looking for food. They returned home from these shopping and foraging trips exhausted but had to make do with foodstuffs like potatoes and turnips, which required more fuel and preparation time than the normal prewar diet of bread, sausage, and cheese. Cold, lonely, weakened by malnutrition, anxious that their husbands might die and that their families were starving, many no longer found it possible to be the model modern mothers—patient, nurturing, and attentive—that so many, particularly in the middle class, aspired to be. The deprivation incapacitated tens of thousands of mothers, such as

that of the 12-year-old diarist Ernst Buchner. Buchner's father, a patriotic
music teacher and an instrument seller, was impoverished by the war, and his
mother's malnutrition and hikes of tens of miles while ill to find food hastened her death in 1917. The devastated young Buchner then stopped writing
in his diary for several months.[8]

Fractured Households

Historians now doubt that German families were traditionally extended
and then became uniformly nuclear during industrialization. However, they
do not contest that fictive kinship grew to be less significant over the course
of the nineteenth century. Before industrialization, masters acting *in loco
parentis* had shared their urban households with apprentices and journeymen, but after industrialization the nuclear family was the norm in cities.
With a few exceptions, such as baker apprentices, the handful of pupils in
private boarding schools, and very poor families who took on lodgers, most
children of all social classes lived and ate exclusively with their mothers,
fathers, and siblings.[9]

The war tended to widen the household in a variety of ways. Extended
family filled in many gaps: uncles, father- and brother-in-laws, brothers, adult
sons, and other male kin visited more often and adopted paternal roles, like
disciplining children. Mothers also forged firmer kinship networks with
grandparents, aunts, sisters, cousins, sisters-in-law, and adult daughters.
Households expanded beyond the immediate nuclear family in garrison cities
and towns where the military quartered hundreds of thousands of soldiers in
private homes. Usually young men in their early twenties, they sometimes
encouraged the male adolescents in their host families to smoke cigarettes,
visit pubs, chase girls, steal property, and, in one obscene case, urinate in
school chalk boxes. They also conveyed the horrors of the front censored by
the press, and thereby spurred rising underground protest against the war.
Rotating strangers in and out of middle-class households undermined the
autonomy and privacy that families had taken for granted before 1914. Quartered soldiers, having access to food in the army, sometimes helped host families survive. The living situations reinforced the hosts' convictions that the
home front was united with the army. Hosts willingly sacrificed the autonomy and privacy of the nuclear family as a necessary step toward victory.
Those who did not were ostracized by their communities.[10]

Also fracturing families were the welfare agencies that provided day care, hostels, and school meals and took working-class children away from their parents. Working-class women were routinely questioned by boards of middle-class "ladies," who used their authority as the granters of welfare to impose their opinions about good behavior, proper hygiene, and child-raising. Family privacy was also violated by inspectors who entered homes to ensure proper potato storage and to prevent hoarding and consuming beyond rations. But the degree that this welfare constituted an intrusion of the state into private family life should not be exaggerated. Municipal day care services for schoolchildren with conscripted fathers and working mothers were uncommon and expensive. At the end of 1915, for example, Mainz had day care services for just six hundred schoolchildren, less than 3 percent of the children enrolled in the city's elementary schools. The services cost one mark per child per day—a price that was beyond the means of the neediest working-class mothers. By 1917, when personnel shortages worsened, the city had day care for just three hundred schoolchildren. Likewise, although the managers of the first hostel for working male teenagers in Frankfurt a.M. sought to instill "punctuality, orderliness, and cleanliness," they had only seventy beds by 1917. The only such hostel in Munich had just sixty.[11]

A far greater expropriation of family functions was the public kitchens that served millions of meals. Before 1914, the meal at home was held dear by all social classes because it reinforced family autonomy and belongingness. For the industrial working-class families it was also a cherished respite from harsh factory environs. Hence, after officials opened mass public kitchens in Berlin in July 1916 with capacity to serve 250,000 persons, it took weeks, despite good press, to convince Berliners to take advantage of the welfare. Germans were suspicious of public kitchens, but necessity forced millions to give up the meal at home. Diary entries indicate that the demise of the meal at home was regarded as an assault on family solidarity and identity. Furthermore, for middle-class Germans, dining en masse with workers of all classes was a humiliating reminder that the war had leveled them, ending their distinction from the less educated populace.[12]

New youth centers *(Jugendheime)* were yet another example of state institutions displacing family functions. On the one hand, these homes provided meeting spaces for slide shows, organizational discussions, choir practices, handiwork instruction, and knitting groups. The youth workers who oversaw them geared many of these activities to mobilize ideological support for the war. As the war fractured normal family life, these spaces became essential to maintain bonds and human contact, and they provided warmth during the frigid winters of 1916/17 and 1917/18. With fathers conscripted and mothers working or gathering food, the youth centers filled vacant familial roles. Reports claimed that youths visited them heavily. Citing their successes, the Prussian education minister decreed in May 1916 that the centers normally reserved for working youths in the evening should be open to elementary school children in the afternoons and that older schoolchildren were to supervise the younger ones. Many argued that Germany needed a law requiring youth centers in every city.[13]

The greatest disruption to the nuclear family was arguably the evacuation over the course of the war of one million urban elementary school children and their placement on strangers' farms for stays of one to six months, the so-called *Kinderlandverschickung*. The central organization that undertook this prodigious endeavor, *Landaufenthalt für Stadtkinder* (Respite in the Countryside for Urban Children), had state and military officials as members and sponsors, but it made policy decisions independently and even occasionally reprimanded government offices about delinquent dues. Operating on a shoestring budget that never exceeded 225,000 marks annually, it effectively organized schoolteachers to accompany the children on rail transports, rail authorities to make available special trains, municipalities and charities to provide the 50 pfennig per day compensation for the hosts, parish clergy and local aristocrats to greet the arriving children and locate suitable farmers, and, above all, schoolchildren willing to separate from their families and exchange their small labor to farmers in return for food. The program worked because of the remarkable degree of agreement it forged between city and countryside, despite some misguided claims otherwise. In 1917 alone, 575,000 children were sent to the countryside through *Landaufenthalt für Stadtkinder*, and an estimated additional 150,000 had extended stays on farms through private arrangements of their families. On the one hand, the *Landaufenthalt für Stadtkinder* can be considered the most successful child welfare program of the war and one of the very few food policies that did not provoke bitterness in cities or the countryside. On the other hand, it illustrated the absurdity and mismanagement of food policy. Germany was able to mobilize enormous resources to send over 1 million children to the countryside for long stays so they could eat, but it could not bring enough food to the less lucky ones in the cities.[14]

The success of the evacuation depended entirely on breaking up urban families. Pupils gathered in the schoolyard and marched to the station with their families, but the organizers kept parents off the train platform because they thought small dramas of goodbyes threatened smooth operation. The children did not learn of their destination until after the train departed, and the organizers refrained from telling parents afterward in order to prevent them from visiting their children and inveigling food on the black market from the farmer hosts. With boys and girls riding through the night in the same cars to unfamiliar destinations, the level of excitement on the rail transports was high, and there were reports that boys created disturbances like pinching the girls. When the trains arrived in the rural outposts, the villagers sometimes welcomed children with ceremonies of drums, trumpets, decorated wagons, and tables laden with eggs and cakes. Other times, the trains arrived with neither reception nor fanfare, and the chaperone had to march from village to village, looking for hosts for as many as ninety-five children. When the urban children finally settled in with their host families, most adapted well, according to the reports. They performed farm labor, sometimes went to school (though as often not), admired and played with farm animals, and, most of all, ate enough to gain weight. There were some complaints about boys who wanted to earn wages in the cities and about others who refused to work. But both letters home and school compositions demonstrated that the children were grateful to escape starvation in the cities. Unlike urban youths, who were regularly cited for misbehavior, the children in the countryside rarely raised an eyebrow. Surveys of children show that they were overwhelmingly impressed by the farmers' industriousness and religious faith. Children wrote poems thanking their hosts.[15]

Nevertheless, the program had the specific intention of severing poor children from their biological families. Its middle-class organizers wanted to provide, in the words of one organizer, an "orderly family life that so many [of the children] were missing." The Berlin Teachers' Association agreed that host parents accepted the urban children "as members of the family." In accordance with this principle, the children had to address their hosts as "father" and "mother" and use the familiar second-person pronoun, "du." Organizers reported that the rural hosts felt love toward the children, but there were numerous reports of homesickness. Even if "most children in the countryside felt as if they were at home," they also "acquired a great independence" in being far from their families. The experience for most children was sufficiently positive, however, that in 1918 many returned to their hosts from the previous year without registering and sometimes without even asking their hosts. The *Landaufenthalt für Stadtkinder* tried to prevent these "wild children" from returning to their hosts because of reservations about their "health and moral maturity."[16]

In the absence of fathers and mothers and with the fracturing of families, teachers, state bureaucrats, and youth workers were open to legislation to unify Germany's hodge-podge of youth and family welfare (both *Jugendfürsorge* and *Jugendpflege*). The bill took many shapes. A compromise with Protestant and Catholic associations, who feared it undermined their traditional authority, would have created independent youth agencies *(Jugendämter)* at the county and municipal level, with representation from schools, churches, and state medical boards. But the September 1918 conference convened to finalize the bill failed to introduce a single Reich law that organized the muddle of youth welfare and recreational organizations. The legislation was stymied by constitutional questions, and as the front collapsed in the fall of 1918, unifying fifteen German states and the representatives of hundreds of association behind Reich legislation was wishful thinking. The plans were ultimately dreams of a prosperous and efficient Germany that the more realistic Reich Finance Ministry never took seriously.[17]

The High Wages of Sons

Youth workers cited the positive socialization in the continuation schools for why working youths cooperated in the mobilization, despite the apprehensions in July 1914 and the disruptions in August. By the fall, offices and retail shops and nonessential industries like textiles, construction, and cigarette-rolling had laid off tens of thousands of teenagers, ending the full employment that working youths had enjoyed for two decades. Observers like Günther Dehn, a pastor in his early thirties who ran a youth association in a working-class neighborhood of Moabit (Berlin) and later wrote a celebrated ethnography of working youths, were delighted that these unemployed teenagers did not disturb the public or mill about aimlessly. They volunteered to load trains, bring in harvests, collect war materials, and, for male youths, march in military companies. Others who still held their jobs gave up cigarettes and candy and donated the money to patriotic causes. Some who were eligible even joined the army. Dehn claimed that before the war youths working in the metal factories had been good Socialists and staunch antimilitarists, but in August 1914 they either became reluctant supporters of the war or shed all inhibitions and joined the gay celebrators in patriotic song. Lower-middle-class male office and retail workers *(Kaufmänner)* were especially enthusiastic about the war.[18]

However, by the summer of 1915 social reformers had less confidence in working teenagers because tens of thousands were breaking their apprenticeships and shunning the continuation schools, Germany's world-respected institutions of social control (see Figure 7.1). Adults could do little to rectify the situation. Families impoverished by the war could no longer afford the opportunity costs of apprenticeships, particularly because their 18-year-old sons would be conscripted before beginning to earn a full wage. Apprenticeships also became less valuable as the war industries rationalized production and made work more automatic and easily learned. As the importance of skill declined, the value of youthful endurance grew, and factories zealously solicited hardy youths for unskilled and semiskilled work. The number of apprentices also decreased. In Berlin, for example, the number of artisanal apprentices fell from twenty-five thousand before the war to just seven thousand in 1917. The

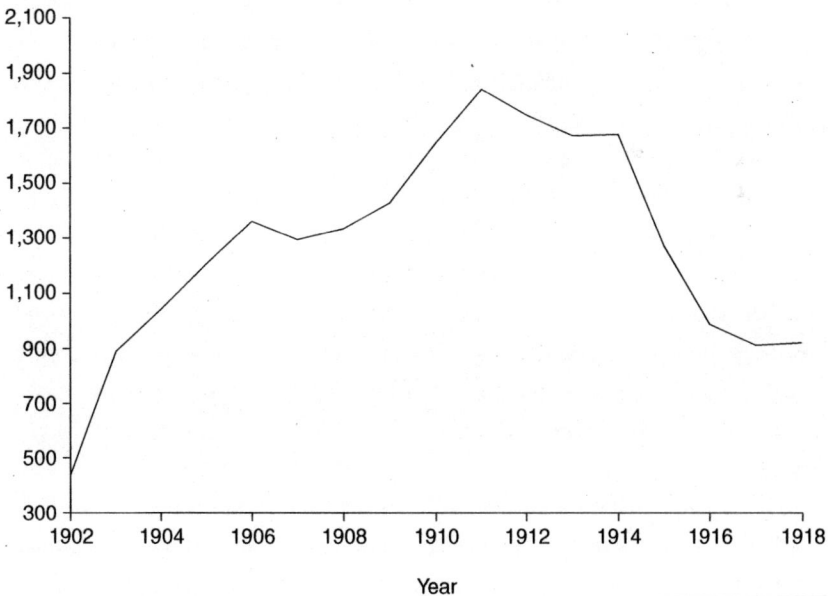

Figure 7.1. Apprentices in continuation schools in Düsseldorf, 1902–1918. *Source: Verwaltungsbericht der Stadt Düsseldorf, für den Zeitraum vom 1. April 1914 bis 31. März 1918,* 127.

situation was similar in other industrial cities. Continuation schools also became dysfunctional because the shortages of personnel and occupations of
buildings by the military reduced the customary eight to twelve hours of
weekly instruction to just four to six, often even less. Thousands of continuation schools closed outright. Continuation school teachers were exasperated
that, with compulsory military training for the pupils and the requirements of
the new Civic Education in Wartime curriculum, they had little time for the
technical and practical instruction that pupils arguably needed most for their
jobs. From 1914 to 1918, the number working youths attending continuation
schools declined in various cities by 50 to 95 percent.[19]

Making it easier to win releases from apprenticeships and obligatory instruction, the Reich War Office and the Prussian Trade and Commerce Ministry, which oversaw the continuation schools, favored loosening the labor
market over teaching skills and citizenship. Working youths could labor for a
few days in a munitions factory—enough, in most cases, to earn a permanent
release—and then take a less intense position elsewhere. Another strategy
was simply to flout apprenticeship obligations and stop attending continuation school. Many employers did not inform schools when their apprentices
earned a release. Some even illegally told the pupils simply not to attend
school. Further undermining attendance was the Auxiliary Service Law of
December 1916, which made releases for 17- and 18-year-olds automatic. In
any case, many school officials recognized that war production had to take
priority over vocational instruction.[20]

Social reformers were unnerved that the war had swept away two decades
of hard work in recasting apprenticeship and the paternalism it imposed on
working male teenagers. Some continuation school teachers claimed that the
boys who attended behaved well, but their observations were attributable
to the selection process—those who came were in practice doing so voluntarily. More complained that the releases stimulated a precocious arrogance
and egoism. At one continuation school in Munich, boys who had won releases loitered outside the school before instruction and inveigled their comrades to skip class. In one school in Baden, the released schoolboys "walk by
their comrades with proud contempt, barely give the teacher a dignified
look, smoke cigarettes, and pursue their nocturnal activities until the police
intervene."[21]

Records of work-exchange bureaus indicate that from the summer of 1915
through the end of 1918 male youths changed jobs on average three or four

times per year, finding higher paying positions in an extremely tight labor market. (By comparison, fewer than half of working youths changed jobs more than once in 1927, one of the more prosperous years of the Weimar Republic.) Because of their families' needs, increasing numbers found work in the metal industries. Machine factories alone employed fifty thousand more 14- and 15-year-olds in 1918 than they did in 1913, and youths' share of the industrial jobs rose from 16 percent in 1907 to over 25 percent in 1916. Countless coachmen were under 18 years old (their inexperience wrecked havoc on the streets of major cities). The high wages in skilled and semiskilled jobs in the war industries were particularly effective in enticing youths away from apprenticeships and the continuation schools. These high wages were the exception and not the rule: bakers, carpenters, cobblers, butchers, and waiters who quit their apprenticeships earned just 7 to 12 marks per week in unskilled work in the war industries, barely enough for food alone. However, even though the real wages of most Germans declined, nominal wages of skilled and semiskilled youths rose more quickly than those of female adults. Statistics from the munitions factories of Krupp in Essen and König and Bauer in Würzburg show that by the end of the war male youths' wages on average *exceeded* women's. An extensive police report confirmed these trends in other enterprises in Berlin too. As inflation eroded civil servants' salaries, continuation school teachers were exasperated that some of their pupils were earning twice as much as they were![22]

Extensive evidence from a variety of sources—complaints filed with the police, reports of school directors, articles in the pedagogical press, and observations by welfare workers—suggests that mothers found it difficult to discipline sons who were making more than they. Mothers also had difficulty preventing their sons from spending their leisure time in the commercial venues away from their families. Despite the sinking standard of living because of the inflation, thousands of mothers *supported* the compulsory savings plans imposed in April 1916 on working youths in Berlin. Civilian fathers, emasculated when their sons "assumed a patriarchal role [*den großen Herren spielen*]," also supported the ban. The editors of *Pädagogische Zeitung* claimed that the compulsory savings plans decreased parents' complaints that their sons were unruly.[23]

The extent that the discourses about male youths and their independence corresponded to reality is, of course, debatable. In their worry that male youths were indulging in the corrupting pleasures of pubs, cinema, tobacco, and other commercial leisure, reformers had also implicitly indicted working teenagers before 1914. Adjusted for inflation, the real wages of male youths declined from 1914 to 1918, and having less cash to spend on leisure in some cases, they were more subject to their parents' authority. But the preponderance of evidence throughout Germany suggests that in many families male youths' nominal and real wages rose relative to adult women's. Although Germans generally became more destitute, youths earning high wages in sectors like the metal industries gained status for stemming their families' descent into poverty. Furthermore, the context in wartime was wholly different than in peacetime: fathers were gone, and in a patriarchal society, their vacated authority was as often filled by mothers as by working sons.

The Household Labor of Daughters

Before 1914 reformers and state officials thought that mechanisms of discipline outside the family were not as pressing for female as for male youths because they believed that raising morally and politically reliable future soldiers and voting citizens was the most critical goal. Furthermore, fewer female than male teenagers had opportunities to earn high wages. Sisters also turned over a larger portion of their earnings to their parents than their brothers, took full control over their money three or four years after their brothers did, and, if unmarried, lived with their parents longer. Lacking the boys' pocket money, they had fewer opportunities to pursue the commercial leisure that was of such concern to reformers and officials. Young female office and retail workers had more independence in the 1920s because office and retail jobs were plentiful, and their increasing numbers provoked concerns that they were becoming libertine new women. But on the eve of the First World War, these young women made up just a fraction of the female labor force. The most common jobs were domestic service or aid to their biological mothers in household chores *(Hauswirtschaft)* and in homework, the assembly of goods at home *(Heimarbeit)*. In both of these occupations, female youths had less time and money for commercial leisure than male youths and were under closer supervision. In addition, as oral histories show, the presence of working-class girls on the street in Central Europe "stopped abruptly with puberty": domestic chores and fears that sexually mature female youths were vulnerable to predation led parents to keep them in the home. This supervision partly explains why five times as many male as female youths were prosecuted for crimes before the war.[24]

Reformers concerned about the morality of female youths before 1914 worried that they were abandoning traditional domestic service arrangements and subsequently becoming susceptible to prostitution and the Social Democratic Party, but hue and cry over female immorality was rare during the war. The Social Democratic Party was less threatening because of the *Burgfrieden*. Predatory young men were in the army, and the bordellos on the home front all but shut down. During the war, formal prostitution thrived only in the occupied territories in France, Belgium, and Poland. During the first year of the war, arrests of teenage girls for prostitution accordingly declined sharply. Some officials and women activists were concerned about the increasing numbers of female youths who migrated from the countryside to the city to work in the war industries, but no one to my knowledge ever recorded a case of a young female migrant who fell into prostitution. In any case, until 1916 the service, luxury goods, and textile industries, the economic sectors in which women worked, contracted. Although more female than male urban youths were unemployed and had free time, the energetic activism of middle-class women succeeded in getting them off the street. After 1916 almost all female youths who wanted jobs found them, but their earnings were on average much lower than those of male youths: censuses estimated that six to eight times as many male as female youths held the high-wage jobs in the war industries, and the boys earned on average earned twice as much. Mothers of families impoverished by the war reasoned that because they and their sons earned higher wages than their daughters, it made sense for them to take jobs in factories and leave their daughters at home to care for younger siblings, do homework for extra family income, and take care of household chores. City magistrates, state officials, and even Social Democrats encouraged this trend by offering girls more instruction in laundry, hygiene, infant care, and cooking in times of shortages. According to one estimate, the total number of female youths working in Germany *declined* by six thousand over the course of the war. Even if household labor required them to wait in the long food lines, adult women oversaw their behavior. The ratio of male to female youth prosecutions increased from 5.64 in 1913 to 6.2 in 1916, a trend suggesting (though far from proving, given the unreliability of statistics from the time) that crime rates were increasing faster for boys than for girls. As in Vienna during the war, the vast majority of youths who stole coal and food in gangs in German cities were boys. Standing in line or stuck at home, girls were not getting in trouble as much as boys.[25]

The experience of female youths varied greatly, of course. Although the total number of working female youths declined, the number in high-wage jobs in the metal and machine industries rose during the war from approximately 17,000 to 50,000, according to one estimate. These girls had more money to spend on commercial leisure. Many of them were domestic servants released by impoverished middle-class families. Exhausted from the heavy labor but flush with pocket money, these girls generally shunned voluntary and recreation activities in formal associations and forged an independent social life around the cinema, café, pub, and music hall. Free from the stern eye of their mistress, some became politicized after being exposed to the Socialist peace movement. Still, fewer female than male youths won independence during the war. Fewer had high-wage jobs—the machine and metal industries employed approximately four hundred thousand more male than female youths 17 years old and under. Most female youths had extensive obligations supervising younger siblings and keeping house.[26]

By 1915 hunger, exhaustion, cold, inflation, mass conscription, and emotional trauma had uprooted the traditional relationships of authority in nuclear families. Fathers, the main disciplinarians and wage earners, were to a large extent gone, and hundreds of thousands of mothers had to take on factory work and give up their jobs in homework that had allowed them to earn money while supervising children. Mothers of all social classes spent enormous amounts of time looking for food, and impaired supervision coincided with a shortened school day, giving boys and girls more free time. Even if they had the time to oversee their children, the burdens imposed by the war taxed their patience and diminished their attentiveness.

Because of mass conscription, factories and other enterprises offered male teenagers a man's wage, money that sinking families desperately needed. Hundreds of thousands of male youths broke their apprenticeship contracts and took the high-paying jobs in the war industries. Others ran small enterprises on their own, and many earned more than their mothers. By becoming the main breadwinners in their families while escaping the stern eye of their fathers, these male youths gained status and independence. Working female youths also had new opportunities to earn high wages and thereby gain independence, but generally they earned only half the wages of male youths. It was thus a rational survival strategy to encourage female youths to stay home to care for siblings and the household. This tended to lower the status of girls within families.

Other assaults on the nuclear family—the end of the family meal, the garrisoning of strange soldiers within private homes, and the mass sending of urban children to the countryside—further subverted traditional relationships of authority within families. When the men finally returned, families faced the enormous challenge of restoring the old relationships of authority. Exacerbating the problem was the demobilization decree that required male youths give up their jobs for the returning soldiers. Male youths then faced high systematic unemployment for the duration of the Weimar Republic.

The absence of men due to mass conscription in Germany, the uprooting of families, and the rising status of male youths was a phenomenon in all the belligerents, but only in Central and Eastern Europe did men's absence coincide with widespread hunger and severe shortages of necessary items such as coal and shoes. In Germany, as well as in Russia and Austria-Hungary, this deprivation exacerbated the upheaval by forcing urban family members to spend hours and hours weekly looking for food and making do with foodstuffs that took more fuel and effort to prepare. Youths in all the belligerents feared the death of their brothers, fathers, and uncles, but in Central and Eastern Europe they also feared for the survival of their families at home.

8

The Dwindling Controls over Sex, Crime, and Play

Teachers, clergy, state officials, and youth workers panicked after 1915 that more and more youths were becoming "delinquent" *(verwahrlost, verwildert)*. Assessing the meaning and truth of this charge presents somewhat of a conundrum. Such a fear was prevalent in the peaceful and prosperous decades before the war, when reformers and officials worrying about the dangers of urbanization and youth wage labor founded new institutions of social control such as continuation schools. Before 1914 the belief that delinquency was rising had less to do with any reality of increasing bad behavior (per capita crimes in some categories were in fact declining) than with the turn-of-the-century progressive urge to make society more orderly. The category of delinquency was malleable enough to change perceptions of it over time. Delinquent youths were those who committed crimes or had psychiatric disorders but, depending on the person, time, and place, also included those who loitered, smoked cigarettes, used vulgarities, played too loud, or did anything else that annoyed a grownup. Before 1914 adults sometimes cited increasing crime as hard evidence of escalating delinquency. Many did not understand how per capita rates are a more meaningful statistic than aggregate incidents or how rising nominal rates involved the introduction of new categories of crimes, more vigorous surveillance, and notoriously inaccurate records.[1]

There is good reason to doubt, however, that the charges of rising delinquency after 1915 were a result of changing social perceptions. Charges of delinquency would be expected to multiply during wartime, but the fact is they did not rise at first. With hundreds of thousands of casualties, and the nation deeply at risk, Germans wanted civility at the outbreak of the war. Patience for frivolity and tolerance for social transgressions were especially low in August and September 1914, when the casualty rate was the highest of the entire war and, until the First Battle of the Masurian Lakes, the risk of occupation by Russia was the most threatening. Nevertheless, officials, clergy, teachers, and youth workers marveled at how *well-behaved* young people were during this time. The charge of delinquency reappeared after 1915, not because of changing perceptions but because the hardship of the war increased, participation in patriotic activities waned, theft of food and coal became a way to survive the deprivation, and, above all, the capacity of adults to shape and control youths diminished.[2]

The decline in adult authority over youths was partly due to mass conscription of the police, which limited the state's power of surveillance, and to administrative incompetence, which after 1915 increasingly turned Germans of all ages against the regime and its ruling elites. The decline in authority was also due to the breakdown of schooling, the fracturing of families, the decreasing supervision at work, and the increase in real and nominal wages of male and some female youths relative to their parents, which earned them status within their families and opened the world of commercial leisure to them. Social controls over female youths were somewhat maintained by the growth of their recreational associations. In addition, the new onus on girls to maintain households in the absence of their mothers kept many off the street. But youths of all social classes had more opportunities than before the war to socialize without adult supervision. When their behavior violated standards of civility set at the outbreak of the war, middle-class officials, clergy, teachers, and youth workers naturally charged that delinquency was rising.[3]

The context of this new autonomy—inflation, hunger, cold, grief for the millions of dead and wounded, anger about a war that increasingly seemed senseless, and a deluge of violent representation of combat—was nothing to cheer. In order to have adequate nutrition and warmth after the fall of 1916, youths, like older Germans, stole and violated food regulations. Working male youths turned to coarse language and physical brutality to express their displeasure over the disruptions in their lives. At the same time, male youths who had been inundated with positive images about the war incorporated the war's violence into their games. Toys revolved around arms and battles; war games on the street grew increasingly violent as boys acquired guns and makeshift hand grenades; and criminal acts by secondary school boys often involved fantasies about combat. According to shocked teachers, parents, clergy, youth workers, and state officials, the participants asserted a premature, aggressive manhood. Boys expressed more bravado and strenuous masculinity in part because families, employers, and the state had less authority over them than before. If they supported the war, boys were also empowered by a public who exalted them as future soldiers; if they opposed it, they were backed by an antiwar movement that demanded mass strikes for revolution.

The Decline of Male Youth Associations

In their delirium in August 1914, many teachers and youth workers thought that youths had overcome any prewar delinquency and were showing themselves to be almost unconditionally devoted to victory. According to youth workers, the patriotism and good behavior in many cases continued into 1916. During the calendar year of 1915, for example, patriotic youth associations in the affluent neighborhoods of Charlottenburg and Spandau (Berlin) suffered from personnel shortages, but in the second half of 1916 they enjoyed an Indian summer of sorts and boasted their highest rates of participation ever. In working-class Neukölln (Berlin) in 1915 and 1916, associational life flourished as it had before the war. The youth worker there led two thousand children in star gazing, brought six hundred to the Urania theater for a patriotic film, and organized activities related to maintaining order, such as lecture evenings, bond drives, courses in handiwork and cooking, visits to museums, communal hikes, and athletic competitions.[4]

Nevertheless, membership in male youth associations on the whole dwindled. Conscription ravaged the leadership, and the army appropriated youth centers for hospitals, food distribution offices, and housing for prisoners of war. As early as January 1915, budget shortfalls forced communities to cancel plans for new courses, playgrounds, sport leagues, athletic fields, and youth centers. In Nassau-Hessen youth workers reported that after 1916 youth associational life for boys in many places came to a complete standstill. A year after complaining that forty-four of his colleagues were conscripted, the youth worker in Neukölln was himself conscripted and served for a period of three months. No one replaced him during his tour of duty. The strenuous work schedules of male working youths sapped their energy and militated against participating in recreation or patriotic labor. Working male youths' relatively high wages also gave them pocket money to forgo the associations for commercial pleasures, such as the cinema, theater, pubs, and penny dreadfuls. Fatigue and hunger dampened younger boys' desire to participate in associational life. Above all, the military training of male youths took priority over all other activities. A decree in 1916 by the Prussian education minister, who oversaw the disbursement of state funds for youth recreation, demanded that other recreational activities "fall into the background." The breakdown of male youth associations began in certain regions in early 1915 and became almost universal during the Turnip Winter of 1916/17.[5]

The once effusively patriotic spirit in recreational activities now steadily waned. Instead of kindling youths' excitement for the war, youth workers resigned themselves to foster "the resolve to carry on [*durchhalten*]." As one claimed, the "favorable moment of August 1914" had disappeared. Now the goal was to "endure," in both emotional and economic senses. Courses for leaders of youth associations outlined procedures for how to dispel rumors, discuss the military deadlock, cope with food and coal shortages, and prevent exaggerated complaints from reaching soldiers on the front. Youth associations became organs for informing 14- to 18-year-olds about emergency decrees.[6]

A good example of the decline of male youth associations was the fate of the Young Germany League, the nationalist and militarist umbrella organization founded in 1911. Most of its leaders had volunteered for the army in 1914. Many members also volunteered if they were 18 years old, or were 16 or 17 years old and had their parents' permission. By the summer of 1917, the few remaining leaders decried the appearance of so-called wild youth associations—informal groups unregistered with the police and likely without grownup mentors—that "shot up like mushrooms out of the earth and competed with one another fiercely." In 1918 the Young Germany League fell apart. A leader of one local chapter wrote to the interior minister in May 1918: "Because of the long war, it is not known here who the leadership of the League can turn to speak about a revitalization of our Young Germany business."[7]

The Decrees Curbing Commercial Leisure

The euphoria of youth workers and teachers in August 1914 stemmed partly from their initial belief that the war purged Germany of drinking, smoking, and other allegedly sordid pleasures. During the mobilization, youths turned to what they believed were healthier forms of recreation—for girls, knitting items for soldiers, and for boys, marching in military companies. With youth unemployment high in the fall of 1914, few teenagers had pocket money to buy alcohol and tobacco. Most who did refrained from conspicuous consumption because it seemed impertinent to smoke or get drunk while fathers, brothers, and uncles were marching off to war. Limiting access to commercial leisure, municipalities banned public dancing and shut down lurid variety shows *(Tingel-Tangel)*.[8]

Replacing prewar commercial leisure were highly praised patriotic evenings of slides, songs, lectures, and, especially popular, films about the war. For the first time, the films shown in the cinemas were almost all German. Before 1914, German film companies controlled only 15 percent of the domestic market; most films were imported from France, Great Britain, and the United States. But the blockade and a ban on imports invigorated the German film industry. In 1914 and 1915, "soldier kitsch" films about the war dominated the showings with titles like *War Marriage (Kriegsgetraut)*, *The Watch on the Rhine (Die Wacht am Rhein)*, *The Call of the Fatherland (Das Vaterland ruft)*, *On the Field of Honor (Auf dem Felde der Ehre)*, and *German Women, German Loyalty (Deutsche Frauen, Deutsche Treue)*. These films reproduced the ideals of the *Burgfrieden* and the Spirit of 1914, depicting reconciliation and celebrating the patriotism and sacrifice of individuals across social classes. The cinemas also showed newsreels of the film companies Eiko-Woche and Messter-Woche that cheered German victories and displayed soldiers' bravery in sanitized images from the front. Reformers expressed elation about how these new patriotic films offered an opportunity for youths to experience the "great times" and encouraged their good behavior.[9]

The sanguine outlook on youths deteriorated in late 1915 and early 1916. Personnel shortages forced male recreational associations to trim their offerings, while working male youths, growing bored with the drills and perhaps disillusioned with the war, abandoned the military companies. Between the spring and fall of 1915, working-class youths like grownups stopped patronizing the cinemas that showed the "soldier kitsch" patriotic films. German cinemas returned to the tried-and-true formulas of comedies and sensationalist dramas that social critics claimed endangered young people. Although the real income of most youths had declined, and families needed it to survive, by the end of 1915 the increase in real wages relative to women gave youths an upper hand in demanding that their families permit them to go to the cinema and buy alcohol, tobacco, and penny dreadfuls. For their part teachers and youth workers were upset that parents could not restrain their children from consuming nonpatriotic commercial leisure.[10]

Youths clearly needed an escape from the particularly intense labor in the war industries. Operating a lathe to make shells, for example, required exhausting, repetitive motions for twelve hours a day or longer under loud, hot, and dangerous conditions. But teachers, policemen, military officers, and youth workers fretted that instead of sacrificing for the war effort and showing respect for their elders, working youths sought pleasure as a way to assert adult status prematurely. When the number of youths seeing "trash films" *(Schundfilme)* surpassed prewar levels by the end of 1915, adults across the political spectrum railed that the younger generation was becoming, in the words of a rural Bavarian, "cheekier and more immoral." Most alarming to adults were youths who flaunted their high wages in displays of conspicuous consumption like smoking tobacco:

> A young man in workers' clothes entered the store, a boy between sixteen and seventeen years old. He requested cigars and picked out one for 40 pfennig a piece; he took ten of these and paid with a five-mark note. He got a one-mark note in return, which he rolled with tobacco and lit up. . . . A sign of the times!

Apocryphal or not, countless stories such as these played into middle-class fears that the war was, in their words, encouraging working youths' "false self-confidence," "hedonism," "frivolity with money," "defiance and ostentatiousness," "swagger," "craving for status," and "craving to be a big man" *(Großmannssucht)*. The image of the cocky, precocious, insouciant male working youth was parodied in a lyric published by Karl Ettinger, the Jewish patriot who wrote for the arts weekly *Jugend,* in 1918:

> My old people are in the war—hurrah!
> I'm free of supervision
> And my mama
> Doesn't bug me much!
> Nothing stops me from gabbing,
> I don't care about God and the world—
> I am seventeen years old
> And earning a mound of money!

> A cigarette jaunty in the mouth,
> So I set off,
> Taking wide steps like a draft horse,
> Like the master of show-off.
> What the adults say leaves me cold,
> Because I have a good job:
> I am seventeen years old
> And earning a mound of money!

Many pointed out that this behavior was also common in peacetime, but Germans across the political spectrum claimed that such conspicuous consumption was increasing. In any case, it was not commensurate with "the seriousness of the times."[11]

To the delight of reformers, the deputy commanding general in the army district of Cassel took action in October 1915. Using his powers under the Prussian Law of Siege, he banned youths from visiting pubs and attending the cinemas. His decree then became a model for deputy commanding generals in Hessen, Westphalia, Hanover, East Prussia, West Prussia, Bavaria, and Hamburg, some of whom in addition prohibited loitering, smoking, or penny dreadfuls. These bans had broad support from most welfare groups and all political parties, including the Social Democrats. The deputy command generals canvassed opinions before issuing their decrees, and the only adults to oppose them were those with financial interests—cigarette companies, cinema owners, and publishers of penny dreadfuls.[12]

The effectiveness of the bans was doubtful. Conscription gutted police forces of personnel, and after 1915 they were devoting their limited resources to enforcing food regulations and containing bread riots. The deputy commanding generals had little executive power to enforce the regulations. They had authority over garrisoned troops, not the local police, and rightly feared public wrath if they took the draconian step of calling in the army to stop youths from smoking, loitering, drinking, and attending the cinema. The bans were initially a deterrent, but young people quickly realized they could get around them. In Munich and Hamburg, tobacconists claimed they had difficulties determining the age of youths—most did not have identification papers. Tobacco companies strongly resisted shutting down the vending machines that made cigarettes available to Germans of all ages. After two months of flagrant violations, the deputy commanding general in Hamburg abrogated his ban on youth smoking. Youths quickly learned that they could ignore the ban on smoking in Hanover, Munich, and the other cities as well. Friedrich Wilhelm von Loebell, the Prussian interior minister, warned that the bans were for these reasons not feasible.[13]

More successful than the bans in stemming consumption was the introduction of compulsory savings plans *(Sparzwänge)* for young workers. First decreed in March 1916 by the deputy commanding generals in the army districts in Berlin and Cassel, the plans required that wages over 24 marks per week earned by youths under 18 years of age be deposited into savings accounts for the duration of the war. The generals acted after the public urged them in citizen letters of complaint to stop youths from squandering their earnings on commercial pleasures. The public also wanted to halt "the increasing insubordination toward those persons whose authority they would otherwise have respected," such as clergy, teachers, employers, youth workers and, in particular, mothers whose husbands were in the army. Most of the Socialist and Christian unions in regions outside Berlin opposed the bans, claiming that they usurped parental authority. But their opposition was timid. Furthermore, breaking the party line, some union officials publicly supported the plans as well, agreeing that mothers were incapable of getting their sons to save, fathers were no longer masters, and male youths were spending their high wages frivolously. The compulsory savings plans were instituted in Berlin without major conflict in part because a provision allowed for youths to apply for exemptions if they showed family need. The plans in Berlin and Cassel established over ninety thousand savings accounts for young workers. Many felt that they stanched the consumer spending of working youths, contained inflation, and reasserted adult authority.[14]

By contrast, the compulsory savings plan issued in Hanover failed because the deputy commanding general planned to introduce it in 1916 on May Day, the traditional Socialist holiday. Three young workers from a machine factory in Linden (Hanover) planned a strike in the previous week, possibly at the instigation of delegates to the Jena conference of oppositional Socialist youths one week earlier. They rallied another thousand comrades who had gathered publicly for the holiday festivities. The protest then spread to nearby Braunschweig, where 500 youths gathered to announce their decision to strike until the decree was repealed. The next day, eight hundred youths joined, including three hundred young female workers. The deputy commanding general raised the exemption to twenty-four marks, from sixteen. But on 3 May, eight hundred youths in Braunschweig continued to protest. When a delegation of youths went to Hanover to ask the union to arbitrate their position with the deputy commanding general, a Social Democratic official barked, "What do you Braunschweig hotheads [*Großschnauzen*] want here?" The adult leadership unanimously rejected the strike actions. But then bread riots broke out at the potato market in the center of Braunschweig. Protest over food now coincided with a political strike, and the deputy commanding general perceived the threat to the social order to be real and dangerous. He pleaded with the union and the Social Democratic Party in Braunschweig to contain the strike while still refusing to abrogate the measure. But the next day an additional 120 female youths at the A.E.G. plant joined the strikers, and young people gathered in the city and skirmished with the police. Such a fracas ensued that the deputy commanding general called in the military, which countered the crowds with cavalry and rubber bullets. Under intense pressure from the rank and file, union officials that night agreed to a sympathy strike. Faced with a breakdown of the social and political order, the deputy commanding general abrogated the decree completely on 5 May, to the jubilation of the young organizers.[15]

The strike was singular in many respects: it was successful, limited to Braunschweig (and a smaller one in Hanover), and the only one of such magnitude organized anywhere by youths alone during the war. Nevertheless, the strike figured prominently in discussions of state policy toward youths. Because it stimulated more strikes against the war, industrialists and deputy commanding generals in other areas were leery of instituting compulsory savings plans. Some doubted whether the plans achieved their goals, pointing out that the very youths whose profligate spending was to be curtailed found ways for evasion. For example, many youths in Berlin sought work in Brandenburg just outside the city boundaries, where the compulsory savings plan was not in force. Outside Berlin and Cassel, social policy did little to contain young male wage workers' access to commercial leisure. Other cities and deputy commanding generals rejected the plans because they were an administrative burden. Furthermore, the success of the strike emboldened oppositional Socialist youths to take more aggressive action.[16]

The Rise in Youth Crime

Anxiety about an alleged increase in youth crime led reformers in the 1890s and 1900s to found recreational associations, continuation schools, and censorship boards to supervise adolescents. Fear of crime also moved reformers and Prussian officials to set up juvenile courts that forsook traditional fines and jail sentences for therapeutic measures such as foster care *(Fürsorgeerziehung)*, which addressed the roots of crime in poverty, negligence, and abuse. The reformers were optimistic about their work when youth crime rates began to fall in the years before the war. Whether their optimism was justified is difficult to determine. Even with access to more accurate data like victim reports rather than prosecution records (the only statistics available from the era of the First World War), criminologists today rarely reach consensus on the causes for the rise or fall in crime. Lagging prosecution or shrinking categories of deviance may have been as important a cause for the drop in youth crime as the reforms that prevented malfeasance. But on the eve of the war, few grasped the theoretical conundrums of crime rates. Reformers like the eminent jurist and criminologist Franz von Liszt declared that lower crime rates were the result of better policing and care of youths. Liberal Germans believed they could make more progress on youth crime in the future.[17]

To gleeful teachers and youth workers, the war at first seemed to be exactly that kind of progress. Aggregate indictments and convictions of youths fell unexpectedly in the fall of 1914 to the lowest level in over two decades. Directors of reformatories applauded the hundreds of delinquent youths who volunteered for the army, and youths released from prison during the mobilization confessed they felt a new sense of modesty and responsibility. According to youth association leaders, the tough, recalcitrant hooligans *(Halbstarke)*, who had shunned regular work and preyed on vulnerable passersby, quit their mischief overnight and became good German patriots. The fall in youth crime reinforced convictions that the Spirit of 1914 was real.[18]

The jubilation ended in 1915, when youth crime inched up, raising public alarm (see Figure 8.1). It is impossible to determine the cause of the increase with any certainty, but the Munich police was likely correct when they argued that the uptick was not an effect of broadening categories of crime or shortages of food. The arrests of youths for violating wartime emergency acts were negligible, the deputy commanding general had not yet issued the bans on youth leisure, and the food shortages were not yet serious. According to the police, youth crime rose because fathers, masters, and teachers were absent; young people were more easily excitable; and unsupervised play, such as boys' war games on the street, incited transgressions. According to their analysis, apprentices whose masters were conscripted committed the majority of embezzlement cases. In a reverse of prewar trends, 13-, 14-, and 15-year-old boys committed more crimes than 16- and 17-year-olds. These younger youths did not steal necessary items like food or coal but rather cartridges, flashlights, and other props for their war games. Some also stole to buy train tickets to the front and satisfy their curiosity about combat. In their desire to imitate soldiers, younger boys broke the law by carrying rifles and other weapons. The police in Munich as well as Berlin and Stuttgart were especially alarmed by the increase in the number of 12- to 15-year-olds who committed crimes in gangs.[19]

In the first half of 1916, police and youth workers suggested that economic necessity was now increasingly motivating youths to commit crimes. But crime was also incited by jealousy of peers who smoked, attended the cinema,

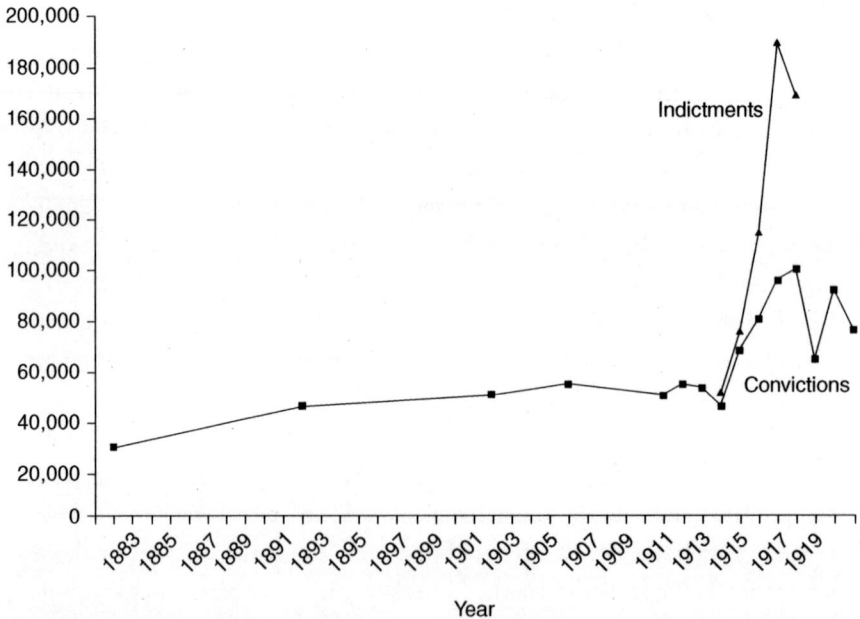

Figure 8.1. Youth crime in Germany, 1882–1921. *Note:* Data on indictments is available only for the period 1914–1917. The 1918 data is based on an extrapolation from the first six months of the year. *Sources:* "Die Vergehen Jugendlicher im Jahre 1918," *Haus und Schule* 40 (November 1918): 48; Moritz Liepmann, *Krieg und Kriminalität in Deutschland* (Stuttgart: Deutsche, 1930), 98; and *Statistik des Deutschen Reichs*, vols. 257, 272, 297, 301, 302, 304, 342, 346 (Berlin, 1913–1928).

wore nice clothes, displayed other signs of gentlemanliness, and in general flaunted the fruits of their high wages. Much theft was caused by "a craving to be a big man." In addition, the shortened school day left 12- to 14-year-olds without adequate supervision. Few parents provided day care for this age group, and with many mothers working and male youth associations in steep decline, the boys played in the streets for a good deal of the day. With the peer group's influence growing and parents' discipline declining, thefts by bands of elementary school boys continued to rise. Another impetus to crime was the policy of commuting sentences upon conscription, which eliminated punishment as a deterrent for boys nearing 18 years of age. Von Liszt agreed that these were the main causes for the rise in youth crime, though he added that an increase in fantasy incited by the cinema and the war penny dreadfuls played a role as well. Others pointed out that convictions for crimes against the state and public order from 1913 to 1917 fell by 56 percent for adult women but rose by 32 percent for youths. Overall, prosecutions of youths quadrupled and convictions doubled from 1914 to 1918; to officials and newspapers reporters, this was a vexing indicator that state authority over youths was lapsing.[20]

By the summer of 1916, hunger rather than fantasy, excitability, inadequate supervision, or craving for status became the overwhelming cause of youth crime, as it was for Germans of all ages. Because government rations were at the starvation level, buying food on the black market or stealing it became a necessary strategy to survive. Rising crime was now less linked to age than to access to food. In fact, in certain categories, adult crime rose faster than youth crime. Convictions for property crimes, for example, rose by 82 percent from 1913 to 1917 for adult women but by only 57 percent for youths.[21]

Nevertheless, more youths than ever were violating the laws of the state. The statistics on crime likely underestimated the lawlessness. Because conscription depleted the ranks of policemen, and experiments in deputizing civilians failed, more youths got away with crimes than in peacetime. The burdens of the police in Hamburg were so great that they stopped processing denunciations of youth misbehavior and demanded that residents send their complaints to schools or welfare associations, who had little personnel to discipline, let alone the will. Because of the food crisis, the Berlin police also allocated few resources to combat juvenile delinquency. According to a school director in Munich, the police cared "little or not at all about the excesses of youth; city and state grounds are insufficiently patrolled." The amount of crime overwhelmed the German justice system. After the Turnip Winter, the courts processed only serious infractions against youths, such as theft or embezzlement. Convictions of male youths for crimes against the public order under the war regulations in fact *fell* from 1,172 in 1915 to 320 in 1917, and the rise in youth crime was therefore not likely to be a consequence of prosecutorial zeal. Judges and prosecutors lacked the heart or means to sentence large numbers of youths, as the growing gap between the number of indictments and convictions suggests (see Figure 8.1).[22]

Deprivation, declining family support, and insufficient police surveillance were the reasons why increasing numbers of male youths turned to criminal gangs like the "wild cliques" that called themselves "the Apaches" and "the Black Hand." Youths had organized themselves informally in groups on the street before the war, but the wild cliques had a self-consciousness lacking in earlier groups. They also did not shy from organized theft as a way to survive. In Hamburg in March 1917, for example, gangs of thirty to fifty boys, some as young as 12 years old, regularly coordinated assaults on freight yards and coal wagons to get supplies for their families.[23]

Courtship and Sexuality

Before the war boys and girls met and courted on the street, at family social events, in street cars, on group hikes, or within recreational associations. Middle-class youths also courted in the salons of their parents, who, in the so-called calling system, kept watch over their children and enforced scruples against premarital sex. The boys and girls often sealed their romantic relationships at dances. Working youths sealed them at dances as well but also treated girls in cafes, shops, racetracks, pubs, and the cinema. Prohibitions on premarital sex were less strict in working-class than in middle-class families, and sexual contact before marriage among working youths was common. Because the apartments of working-class families were small, and the so-called moral police *(Sittenpolizei)* kept watch over sex and courtship in public areas, young couples sought abandoned rooms, often with great difficulty, for their love-making.[24]

The war uprooted much of the rules and controls that shaped courtship, and it gave youths more independence in the ritual. Because of the absence of fathers, the overburdening of mothers, the decline in policing, and the availability of rooms of associations that had closed during the war, unsupervised courtship thrived in Germany's large cities. In practices such as courtship parades, middle-class youths released from their parents' watchful eyes began to imitate the wooing rituals of the working class. In these acts, working youths also donned markers of middle-class youths, such as the colored caps that secondary school boys were required to wear. Courtship accordingly became a ritual in which the participants could use public space and consumer items to circumvent the restrictions imposed by their parents and social class.[25]

New courtship practices evolved among the youths who loitered near automats and market fairs in Berlin. According to a secondary school director, those who frequented these areas had been exclusively apprentices and working youths before 1914, but by October 1917, boys from secondary schools were also loitering there. Male and female youths exchanged the coveted colored secondary school caps and wooed in a way that the director found immoral. Many working boys hopped around ostentatiously, a jaunty cap on the head, a cane in one hand, and a cigarette in the other, imitating the dress and style of the affluent dandy. The Prussian school authority in Berlin ordered all teachers to use the strictest discipline against these youths. But while teachers could punish secondary school boys, they had no authority over the working youths, and the police were impaired. The courtship parades continued. In February 1918 a director of another secondary school got fed up and intervened by taking down names, but was exasperated when the youths gave aliases. The gatherings continued to grow in size. According to the director's candid report, truckloads of boys and girls arrived on Sundays, and sometimes over five hundred male and female youths loitered from 4:30 in the afternoon until 9:00 at night. In a classic execution of the monkey parade, the boys "made chains and bumped into girls and passersby." The consequence of the director's "interventions" was that the youths fled, "howling loudly," to other public spaces in the city. He discovered that many of the youths were former secondary school boys who had discontinued study or young workers who had acquired the colorful caps illegally. The mixing of social classes in courtship rituals made middle-class parents anxious that their children were consorting with the riffraff. The director had the same opinion, calling the working female youths in the parades "bad elements."[26]

Similar types of courtship patterns emerged in Munich. In February 1918, the police reported that every afternoon since September 1917 continuation school girls were strolling in groups of two or three while holding arms in a monkey parade. They made "jaunty and conspicuous glances" at apprentices, young soldiers, and continuation school boys and then engaged them in lengthy conversations. One resident denounced two girls who sat in the middle of a bench with five boys on each side. Although the police admitted that this behavior was "harmless," they nevertheless believed it "harbored moral dangers," piquing the fantasies of on-looking "male lechers" who strolled the neighborhood. The gathering spot was in a heavily trafficked square and disturbed the more modest public by displaying "love scenes and comedies of jealousy."[27]

More widespread than these courtship parades were the challenges to adult authority by teenage soldiers and their sweethearts who publicly displayed affection. Teenage soldiers were a new phenomenon—the army lowered conscription from age 20 to 18 during the war and allowed 16- and 17-year-olds to volunteer. Boys now wore uniforms that had previously marked a rite of passage into male adulthood and in wartime conferred particular status and prestige. The male youths themselves often still had love interests who were their age or younger, however, and the public did not know how to react to a garrisoned or furloughed soldier kissing a teenage girl. Some onlookers complained to the police when they guessed the age of the couple, but denunciations were rare. Apparently, most people turned the other way because they understood that, whatever his age, a soldier had a claim on some affection by virtue of his war service. Germany did not face an outbreak of "khaki fever" (the mass fawning of soldiers by female youths that in Great Britain set off a moral panic), but uniformed male teenagers and their sweethearts nonetheless gained independence in their love relations because the boys enjoyed the status previously accorded only to men 20 years old or older.[28]

Less public but equally unsupervised socializing among boys and girls flourished in the "wild" recreational associations not registered with the police. Pastors and the police discovered in Berlin that wild associations of the Wandervogel—boys and girls who took the Wandervogel name but had no links to the national umbrella association—rented cheap small rooms on less populated streets. They used the rooms to sing, sometimes past midnight, and to dance, though forbidden. Because these groups did not register through a mentor, they violated the Reich Association Law, and the police consequently intervened. They discovered that the youths respected decency and morality— during communal overnights in tents or hay-barns, girls and boys slept in separate quarters. The same was true of communal bathing, though two members admitted that the youths transgressed this ban now and then. The participants never consumed alcohol, but many smoked, despite the bans. Although the boys wore the caps of secondary school boys, they were overwhelmingly young salesmen, handworkers, and technicians. Concerned with more pressing matters such as strikes and food riots, the police requested that the behavior stop but did not charge them.[29]

The war offered new opportunities for boys and girls to mingle in other ways. Schoolboys told their parents they were skipping school to help in harvests but then strolled unsupervised with sweethearts. They also found empty rooms in which to entertain girls. The Wandervogel had for years sponsored coed nest "evenings," but during the war, informal groups of boys and girls took outings together as well. In general, authorities were upset by the increase in unsupervised socializing between the sexes.[30]

Our knowledge of sexual contact between boys and girls is limited to the few arrests and expulsions from school for statutory rape. In consensual cases, the youths had occasion to engage in hetero- and homosexual sex because parents were absent and no one could stop it. Middle-class secondary school children generally did not have extensive sexual contact during their teenage years, but middle-class teenage boys looked for it in younger female working-class youths. With fathers in the army and mothers searching for food, they found opportunities for sex parties. In Berlin the police discovered that on one street with many bars, teenage girls, some still in elementary school, let boys "embrace and kiss them and also touch them on their breasts and under their skirts." Warnings to stop this behavior had little effect. In one of their few mass interventions, the Berlin police organized an investigation and made sixty-six arrests in August and September 1917. It turned out that eleven of these youths were middle-class pupils in secondary schools; the rest were working youths or elementary school children. This mixing of social classes in commercial leisure later flourished during the Weimar Republic.[31]

Male youths sometimes explicitly linked militarism and sexuality. For example, teachers confiscated this broadside machine-typed by two secondary school boys in 1915:

War Clauses for a Newly Installed Women's Free Corps

- Each woman must be provided with a *Büchse* [rifle, womb, tin can], not too big and not too small, to satisfy all claims. Front-loaders are preferred. Rear-loaders are satisfactory only in absence of the first.

- Each woman who holds a round of munitions longer than five weeks in the *Büchse* has to walk for nine months with a pack fit for a field marshal.
- With advent of any special circumstances that would make a truce desirable, a red flag is to be waved, which the enemy will respect.
- During an invasion, the woman must stand ground until the enemy completely retreats. . . .
- With the retreat of the enemy, the enemy must be taken with all possible force, in order to bring upon him all possible losses. . . .
- The women must provide for a good and dry storage place in order to make the enemy aware of their standpoint.
- The goal is to make the enemy as weak as possible.
- Because the enemy likes fishy places, his advanced guard is to be lured into the closest thicket in order to bring him toward easy expression of his full power and encircle him.
- Circumspect women can also capture the enemy while practicing drawing a sword or cartridge from its case, so that it is unable to fight.
- "The Destruction of All Standing Armies" remains the battle cry even after the peace treaty.

On the one hand, this treatise was a set of puerile double-entendres linking weapons to penises, vaginas, wombs, and pubic hairs and military tactics to coitus, ejaculation, menstruation, pregnancy, and heavy petting. On the other hand, it endorsed male domination and, in the last precept, revealed the protofascist idea that the war should continue until the German army defeated its enemies militarily—that is, that there should be no negotiated peace, just the annihilation of the Allies' military force, and if there was a peace, Germans should fight on anyway.[32]

War Play on the Street

The maligning of children's street play momentarily ceased after August 1914, when, in an unexpected metamorphosis, most children played war instead of cops and robbers or cowboys and Indians. Playing soldier, conservatives argued, was good. It transmitted "militarism . . . unnoticed to youths" and aided the mobilization by teaching boys to follow orders. Most teachers agreed and encouraged their pupils. In school compositions from 1915, elementary school children in Breslau took joy in describing their elaborate props and regalia: massive graves for the dead, paper helmets with feathers, uniforms, cavalry with lances, tents, epaulets, swords, iron crosses, pails for cannons, barbed wire, battery walls, trenches, sketches of battlefields, toy machine guns, and paper arrows emblazoned with black crosses for German airplanes. They wrote how they sometimes joined 150 boys in epic battles. Girls playing Red Cross nurses bandaged wounds and administered cherry juice for medicine. According to the pastor Günther Dehn, children zealously played soldier in working-class Moabit (Berlin), whose population had previously repudiated such war games. As in German-speaking Austria-Hungary, the incorporation of the war into street play was yet another reason for teachers and youth workers to cheer the war.[33]

Within months, however, civilians began denouncing the street war play. The grievances stemmed partly from hypersensitivity induced by war traumas and fears for loved ones on the front. They also resulted from the perception that the levity and chaos of war games mocked "the seriousness of the times." The reality was that half-time instruction in school and the numerous victory holidays gave schoolchildren more free time for unstructured play. Furthermore, absent fathers, overburdened mothers, and understaffed police forces impaired supervision of street activity. Teachers under war pedagogy had encouraged their pupils' fascination with military weapons, and the urge to imitate soldiers made guns common objects of theft. Schoolboys fired real ones while playing soldier, and the number of injuries to children caused by firearms increased. Aware of the market for military playthings, an enterprising dealer in Leipzig manufactured toy hand grenades, composed of two screws fastened to a long threaded nut. The devices were filled with explosives that detonated upon impact. Enterprising salesmen also found a ready market for stink bombs. By the spring of 1916, these accoutrements were available in the same shops that sold schoolbooks.[34]

The war games grew louder, rougher, more persistent, violent, extravagant, and, above all, disturbing to the public. As early as December 1914, a woman praised teachers for "awakening in our youths a proclivity for military activity" but condemned schoolboys' war play, which had "nothing at all of military discipline," simply a brutal recasting of the cops and robbers and cowboy and Indian games. She was shocked to see legions of boys with guns marching down the street. Others in Munich confirmed that throngs of boys, lacking guns and hand grenades, hurdled bolts and scrap metal. In January 1916, even the Bavarian war minister felt the situation had gotten out of hand. In a memo to the interior minister, he condemned the "excrescence in the playing of soldier, such as the carrying of guns, swords with company insignias, ribbons and trimmings of enlisted officers, and edelweiss." Wearing such paraphernalia was already banned, however. In June 1916 the *Berliner Volkszeitung* claimed the same was happening in the capital city. The street harbored "fierce battles," and boys cavorted with air pistols, makeshift hand grenades, and stink bombs. Their targets were the public—"the neutrals," in the boys' words. Many of these informal boy battalions gave themselves names, such as the "Cossackean Little Fathers" (the Cossacks were particularly feared Russian soldiers). In big cities and rural areas alike, war games escalated into large battles among gangs of boys vying for neighborhood turf and resulted in serious bodily injury. In the first months of the war, middle-class adults who had previously frowned on playing on the street did not object to the war games because they believed the play was patriotic, but after 1915 they retracted their position. "All the horrible depictions of the war," one conservative youth association leader wrote, "awakened a desire for adventure, led to a reckless use of weapons in soldier play, and fostered a tendency toward cruelty."[35]

War Mischief of Middle-Class Boys

Before 1914, playing with toy soldiers was fabulously popular among middle-class male youths in Germany. Like youth war literature, this war play elevated soldiering to the supreme masculine ideal. It also stimulated fantasies that prompted tens of thousands to volunteer in August 1914. But before the war most of the toys sold in Germany were nonmilitary items like dolls, trains, and chemistry sets. Toy manufacturers refrained from placing nationalist markers on their goods because they feared crass German militarism would offend the foreign customers who bought 80 percent of their wares. The British blockade and loss of foreign customers forced toy manufacturers to cater primarily to the market in Central Europe after August 1914, however. The manufacturers sensed that their middle-class German customers wanted military toys above all other playthings. In the months leading up to Christmas 1914, they set up toy displays in department stores with almost exclusively miniature infantry, submarines, zeppelins, planes, 42-cm guns, and other military items. They advertised their wares as good gifts for getting sons excited about the war, and in contrast to the convention before the war, put clear nationalist markers on their items. Demand for military toys waned considerably over the course of 1915, but the slackening demand likely had

more to do with the impoverishment of families than with declining fascination with the war. Middle-class families continued to buy new toys that celebrated the war, such as the board games "Hunt for the Emden" and the
submarine adventure "U-1000." Air-powered toy rifles and machine guns
sold well throughout the war. Memoirs of middle-class children who grew up
in the war invariably recalled that play with military toys was one of their
main amusements.[36]

Uniforms and medals were as popular as military toys, but trade in real
military items disturbed parents, teachers, and officials. Some secondary
school boys placed the colored insignias of their class caps on the buttonholes
of their collars, imitating the symbolic ranks of soldiers. Others wore real
medals and epaulettes of officers that they bought on the black market, even
though the police banned the practice and teachers who had served in the war
thought it was "obnoxious."[37]

Sometimes boys' war fantasies led them to break more serious laws. The
"bright and talented" secondary school boy Klaus (alias), for example, was a
proud member of the School Navy League and tried to enlist when the war
broke out. He was rejected because he was only 15 but told his friends at
school that he had been accepted as a telegraphist in the navy and was undertaking training. Later, he told his friends he was wounded at the battle at
Helgoland and received the Iron Cross (he had purchased one on the black
market). He also claimed that his heroics won him a promotion to noncommissioned officer, which he documented with a telegram falsified on his own
toy machine. Most days he wore a uniform with a black-white-red cord and
the epaulettes and insignias of his rank of noncommissioned officer, but because many other boys wore uniforms, his teachers noticed nothing amiss.
Only later did they discover his forged service book in which he listed his
casualties, battles, promotions, and permission to remain on the home front
for twenty-five weeks, during which he continued to go to school. After his
14-year-old friend pleaded to let him become a naval telegraphist too, Klaus
forged a service book for him and produced two falsified transportation
cards on his typewriter, and the two of them set off. In Wittenberg, Klaus
told his friend he had received new orders and had to return to Berlin alone.
An investigation began after a postal employee notified the police about a
postage stamp Klaus had falsified.[38]

Similar fantasies about war emboldened five secondary school boys in
Danzig to buy laboratory equipment, rent a room to install it, and manufacture

mines and explosives. As prices for materials increased, they began to steal their supplies from their schools. What began as petty theft "developed eventually into a youthful atmosphere of robbing romantics." They carried away carpets, furniture, cakes and wine, even a state-coffer. At the trial, the prosecutor agreed to have the sentences against the boys' parents commuted because of the "present war psychoses." He also cited the lack of paternal authority: three of the five boys had lost their fathers, and their school was suffering from a shortage of teachers. The defense made the case that, because of the war, the mothers had little time for their children, and the youths lacked supervision: "in such abnormal times of war the offenses of the youths could not be recognized as normal crimes." Only one participant, who was tried as an adult, received a sentence.[39]

Other play inspired by war fantasies was less innocent. Middle-class secondary school boys acquired guns for their soldier games and fired them, breaking windows and wreaking other havoc. Secondary schools reported that one negative effect of the war was the tendency for younger pupils to engage in "violence against fellow pupils," particularly if their fathers were conscripted. One of the most sensational cases of gang activity dates from the spring of 1915 in the resort gambling town of Zoppot, West Prussia. According to reports, fifty to sixty boys, from both elementary and secondary schools, broke into restaurants, hotels, and summer homes that had been boarded up for winter. The boys allegedly shattered 150 glass windows, destroyed thermometers and dishes, and cut up sofas. Part of this band of youths then made numerous break-ins into other hotels, shops, and businesses, where they stole delicacies and flashlights, among other things. The magistrate of Zoppot alone suffered 10,000 marks worth of damages. Tellingly, the boys confessed that their excesses had been incited by refugees who had told them stories about the invasion of East Prussia. The boys called their game "Russian."[40]

The press, teachers, the police, and youth workers were all hesitant to assert that juvenile delinquency had gripped all or even most youths. Typically, a report bemoaned the ignominious state of youth but then claimed that the problem did not affect youths of all classes and regions and was by no means general. Even as late as 1918, police and secondary school directors wrote that the war was "a more severe discipliner of youths than parents or schools." Nevertheless, the practical ability to exercise authority over youths diminished. Even if the coercive power of the German military in theory expanded under the Law of Siege, none of the deputy commanding generals had the stomach to call out the garrisoned troops to fight youths who smoked tobacco, loitered, or kissed in public. They did not have much help from the exhausted, overstretched local police who faced starving, angry crowds.[41]

On the one hand, male youths increasingly reproduced in their play the violence that authors of youth war literature and teachers under war pedagogy had celebrated, and secondary school boys in particular had burning fantasies to become soldiers. On the other hand, hunger and cold motivated theft by gangs of preteens and so-called wild cliques, which became a permanent feature on the street after 1918 and reminded Germans of the weakness of the Weimar Republic in the realm of law and order. A key legacy of the war was that hundreds of thousands of particularly male youths grew up inured to lawlessness and violence. Mass conscription gave youths more autonomy in the other belligerents too and played a role in creating the modern youth culture that flourished in the 1920s. This culture was international in scope, and its sin qua non was independence from adults. But unlike the situation in the Western Allied nations, youths' rising autonomy in Central Europe coincided with starvation, cold, crime, and, after 1918, violent dreams of revenge.[42]

9

Propaganda and the Limits on Dissent

Because of the stalemates on the Eastern as well as Western fronts, teachers after 1915 no longer benefited from the cadence of military victories and their opportunities to celebrate the present. By April 1917 one out of ten prewar male teachers in Prussia was dead, and the remaining were cold, hungry, and overworked. The excitement about war pedagogy—its new subjects, methods, activities, and media—wore off, as articles endorsing it declined steadily in the most influential journals for elementary school teachers such as *Pädagogische Zeitung* and *Leipziger Lehrerzeitung*. In January 1916, a handful of pedagogues broke the long silence and openly criticized the war curriculum. Over the course of 1916 until the summer of 1917, a few more spoke out as well, risking disciplinary actions by administrators and accusations of betrayal by others. Most teachers either supported war pedagogy or were too fainthearted to criticize it.[1]

Sensing that teachers might not universally support a peace through military victory *(Siegfriede)*—that is, the total destruction of the Allies' military force, in accordance with Carl von Clausewitz's precept that had become dogma in the Prussian Army—the education and war ministries took a more active role in school curricula after 1915. Abandoning their earlier reliance on teachers' spontaneity and innovation, officials distributed and demanded that teachers use propaganda calling for a peace with territorial acquisitions that would allow Germany to dominate world trade and secure its status as a world power. Aiding the ministries in the goal of drumming up support for annexations and military victory was the radical nationalist German Fatherland

Party. Although it had little success with big-city elementary school teachers, it won the support of teachers and administrators in Catholic and Protestant secondary schools and Protestant elementary schools in the countryside and small- and medium-sized cities.[2]

Teachers at all levels continued with the patriotic mobilization, in the sense that they summoned pupils to "hold out" for victory. While they devoted fewer lessons to the war, many retained to varying degrees a curriculum that presented the war as necessary and honorable. In contrast to the heyday of war pedagogy, war was rarely a central theme of instruction after 1915. Personally, many, perhaps even most, teachers sympathized with the July 1917 Reichstag Peace Resolution of the Progressive, Center, and Majority Social Democratic Parties, which called for an immediate end to the war without annexations or reparations. But professionally they adhered to official policy and obeyed the regional governors and school inspectors who enforced it. Poems, dictations, free compositions, Bible stories, and mathematical exercises about war continued to have a place in their repertoire, and most teachers still found stories of heroism from the corpus of youth war literature written in 1914 and 1915 useful for instilling the courage to endure. Even teachers skeptical about the war could reluctantly support a curriculum designed to sway opinion in favor of military victory during and immediately after the negotiations of the Treaty of Brest-Litovsk in January 1918 and during the military offensive in the spring of 1918, when it seemed for one last time that Germany might win the war and gain something for its sacrifices. School directors observed a growing "indifference" about the war among schoolchildren. They also claimed, however, that most pupils, even in working-class neighborhoods, still believed that Germany's army was superior and therefore would win the war. The shock that Germany had lost led many schoolchildren to search for internal enemies who had allegedly foiled the country's military victory.

The Paucity of Protest

Until the summer of 1917, only a small minority of teachers were politically to the left of the mainstream Social Democratic Party, which accepted the idea that a peace with "real guarantees," in Chancellor Bethmann-Hollweg's purposely vague formulation, was necessary to secure Germany's borders from future attack. Teachers at all levels generally refrained from public criticism of the war for many reasons: they feared foiling a possible victory, letting down colleagues and family on the front, and impairing their case for school reform after the war. They also knew that the military and the government ruthlessly smothered the peace movements led by the radical Socialists Karl Liebknecht and Rosa Luxemburg, on the one hand, and the middle-class publicist Ludwig Quidde, winner of the 1927 Noble Peace Prize, on the other. Almost all teachers rejected the pacifism of iconoclasts like the pedagogues Friedrich Wilhelm Foerster, Gustav Wyneken, and Heinrich Wolgast. In any case, the opposition expressed by these three men was at best tepid. Wyneken even expressed hopes in August 1914 that the war was infusing Germany with the community spirit he had long aimed to create through youth culture. In my research, I found no teacher or pedagogue, not even one, who unambiguously dissented against war pedagogy until early 1916. Even until the summer of 1918 there were just a handful of dissenters, and over the course of the war no pedagogical journal ever indicated that officials had censored it (newspapers and other journals usually printed notices of their violations). Until the front collapsed, the vast majority of teachers who voiced their views remained squarely in the middle-class mainstream. They wanted a peace that brought gains, even if that required holding out and suffering for a military victory.[3]

The little public criticism of war pedagogy that there was began when Liebknecht denounced the "hate sermons" in religious instruction just after he and Otto Rühle became the first to violate the *Burgfrieden* by voting against the second Reichstag war credits bill in March 1915. Joining him in the criticism was Anna Blos, the pioneering historian of women and future Reichstag delegate, who condemned teachers for encouraging their pupils "to delight in gruesome battle reports." These criticisms from Social Democrats had little influence on either elementary school teachers, who supported the moderate Progressive Party, or secondary school teachers, who supported the right-wing National Liberal and Conservative Parties. In any case, Liebknecht and Blos were far from the mainstream in the Social Democratic Party; most functionaries at this time supported the *Burgfrieden* to maintain their new rights, such as to serve on school boards.[4]

In 1915 several non-Socialist authors, taking a cue from a talk given by Foerster, faulted teachers for encouraging their pupils to hate Germany's enemies. Their censure was not an attack on war pedagogy as a whole but

a reproach of teachers who condoned practices like pupils singing Ernst
Lissauer's popular ditty, "Hate Song against England":

> We hate you with enduring hate,
> We won't let you from our hate
> Hate on water and hate on land
> Hate of the head and hate of the hand
> Hate of the hammer and hate of the court . . .
> We have only one enemy: England.

Some countered that expressing hate was to be expected of children in war,
but the consensus among teachers and clergy was that crude expressions were
insipid and un-German. Teachers would do better instilling courage, selflessness, and endurance, and the Bavarian and Prussian education ministers
agreed. This condemnation of teachers who encouraged hate was the only
sustained criticism of war pedagogy in the liberal and pedagogical press in
1915. Notably, even the teachers who had qualms about inculcating enmity
invariably praised the use of the war in instruction.[5]

Overt dissent against war pedagogy began in January 1916. In the previous fall the middle-class peace movement had found more sympathizers after Ludwig Quidde, Albert Einstein, Max Weber, and others signed a petition against annexations, and Quidde published his incendiary pamphlet,
Shall We Annex? At the peace conference that Quidde organized in November 1915, the participants created a committee "to work against the militarization of youth and support education in pacifism." With collections of
schoolchildren's war compositions available in the bookstores since the summer, the peace activists had ample documentation about the effects of war
pedagogy. Apparently shocked by what they read, Foerster, Wolgast,
Wyneken, and other luminaries signed a petition published widely in the
pedagogical press in January and February 1916. In the petition, the authors
dared:

> It is time to break the silence and for everyone to consider the great
> responsibility that education has had for the alarming spread of scorn,
> hate, national arrogance, thirst for revenge, and joy in the pain of other
> nations.

The petition was arguably the first direct, publicized attack on war pedagogy.[6]

The pacifists' charge introduced a degree of polarization among teachers and
school officials. The Prussian governor in Frankfurt an der Oder immediately

denounced the signers of the petition and urged teachers to continue to draw upon the experience of war to instill patriotism and respect for the monarchy. "The general feeling of international brotherhood and mania for international peace has no place" in schools, he claimed in a directive to his school inspectors. "Germany's peace and security are guaranteed only by its army and navy." The editors of *Hamburgische Schulezeitung* hailed the Prussian governor for assailing the "killjoys and dishonorable pacifists *(Völkerversöhner),*" and the editors of *Der Volksschullehrer,* one of the few pedagogical journals to endorse the peace movement before 1914, also denounced the signers, claiming their views were "far more suspect" than those who discussed the hate expressions of schoolchildren in 1915. Although in March 1916 the provincial school authorities in Berlin reiterated the ban on instilling hate of the enemy, they, like the governor in Frankfurt an der Oder, directed their school inspectors to inform teachers of the need to support a military victory unconditionally. With the military clamping down hard on the peace movement, editors of education journals skeptical of aggressive war aims did not respond to the Prussian governor's directive. The exception was *Pädagogische Zeitung* in Berlin, which declared in early March that the Frankfurt governor's directive was excessive. Together with the pacifists' letter, this reaction by a central organ of German elementary school teachers sounded the alarms in the offices of the deputy commanding generals, who suddenly wondered whether the commitment of teachers to the war was precarious in their regions as well.[7]

For a year and a half following the pacifists' condemnation, a small but growing group of teachers and professional pedagogues publicly criticized a curriculum centered on the war. They also endorsed a negotiated peace and denounced those who exhorted their pupils to hold out for military victory. Max Romanowski, a private tutor and a frequent contributor to the pedagogical press, rebuked teachers for silencing discussions of peace in the classroom. He attacked the central principle of war pedagogy, charging, "The solution of the day is nothing more than: War! War! Every other interest is suffocated." A Latin teacher denigrated schools for "celebrating a nationalism that grew into an orgy of chauvinism." In a controversial book for German youths published in 1916 and banned by deputy commanding generals, Foerster ridiculed the war literature used by teachers, claiming it created false illusions and incited misguided enthusiasm for war. In October 1916 a group of teachers in Baden held a peace demonstration. During the discussions that led to the July 1917 Reichstag Peace Resolution, *Schulblatt der Provinz Sach-sen,* an erstwhile proponent of war pedagogy, published an article that be-moaned teachers' exhaustion from shortages and overburdening. As a remedy, it suggested the elimination of all lessons devoted to the war. Such proposi-tions, unthinkable in the heyday of war pedagogy in 1914 and 1915, demon-strated the degree to which a curriculum centered on the war was falling out of favor.[8]

After the fall of Chancellor Bethmann-Hollweg in July 1917 and the more severe censorship under the so-called military dictatorship of Generals Hin-denburg and Ludendorff, the pedagogical and liberal press refrained from actively publishing dissent against war pedagogy. Nevertheless, passive dis-sent was expressed through publishing fewer articles on war lessons. For ex-ample, whereas *Leipziger Lehrerzeitung* published close to two hundred arti-cles on war pedagogy in 1914 and 1915, it published just four in 1917. Not surprisingly, in the last years of the war there was no equivalent to Jannel's *Kriegspädagogik,* the massive 1916 survey of war-pedagogy literature pub-lished in 1914 and 1915. The priority after 1916 was to maintain instruction and fortify endurance, not to have theoretical or practical discussions on im-plementing the highest-minded goals of a war curriculum. The absence of both nationalist discourses and criticisms of war pedagogy suggested that teachers thought the war was terrible but nevertheless did their duty and helped pupils "hold out" for a victorious peace. For the small but growing numbers of dissenters from this view, fear of censorship or retaliation from the conservative school inspectors kept them quiet.

Propaganda in Schools

In 1914 and 1915 the education ministers did not issue major directives on war pedagogy except to endorse retroactively the changes in lesson plans that teachers had already undertaken. When the enthusiasm for war pedagogy diminished in 1916, however, state and military officials took a more active role. They also began to use schoolchildren as nodes for disseminating pro-annexationist propaganda and other material to encourage older Germans to endure the hardship necessary for a victorious peace. The education min-isters recognized that schoolchildren were good targets for propaganda be-cause they were from all social milieus and came into daily contact with a government official. The war ministries saw war pedagogy and its ideological mobilization as part of a strategy to convince Germans that they could win the war.

The feature-length films of the War Press Office, first available in 1917, were arguably the most influential propaganda because showing films was cheaper and more impressionable than handing out pamphlets to eight million pupils. The War Press Office met obstacles from some directors and officials in the education ministries who distrusted celluloid and claimed it aroused dangerous fantasies and abetted deviant behavior. Many of them persisted in their bias against film throughout the war, supporting the bans on the cinema and systematically turning down offers of war films from enterprising companies. But Germans of all ages adored films. Despite the inflation and growing poverty, cinema attendance grew by 50 percent over the course of the war, and by 1918, film rivaled reading as the most important entertainment medium, particularly for schoolchildren and working youths. Cinemas, which had discretion in the films they screened, continued to gear some of their content toward the war because though war as a subject declined in popularity, it remained in demand, and in German cities, as in Vienna, films about the war were deemed to be patriotic, in contrast to the staples of comedies, romances, and detective stories. With the rubberstamp of the War Ministry, most school directors yielded previous opposition to films. In Hamburg, for example, the municipal school authorities regularly ordered that teachers recommend war films to their pupils. Schools in districts without cinemas were able to get funds from the War Ministry to erect theaters to show films on the war.[9]

The War Ministry wanted to excite schoolchildren through films like *Die Möwe*, a feature-length documentary about the German cruiser. The effect of such films, however, was not exactly what they intended. The films impressed upon the schoolchildren the heroism of soldiers, the cunning of generals, and the wonders of warplanes, submarines, and ships. But the showings of the films—usually in rented private cinemas that required a field trip—broke the rhythms of the school regime and further loosened the already slackening authority over the schoolchildren. Screenings of the War Press Office's *East Prussia and Its Hindenburg* in the spring of 1917 to eight hundred to one thousand pupils at a time provoked considerable indiscipline in Düsseldorf, for example. Because the theater had only 750 seats, hundreds of pupils had to stand during some showings. Filled to capacity with the schoolchildren, the theater was mayhem. According to the cinema manager, the teachers had "absolutely no authority over the children." They entered "the theater noisily and full of bluster and make deafening sounds, clapping together the chairs, reading out loud, and whistling." These antics sometimes resulted in property damage. Like the collection drives, the showing of films gave schoolchildren opportunities to meet and socialize with their peers for a patriotic purpose with minimal adult supervision. Like war pedagogy more generally, they loosened adult authority and impressed schoolchildren with Germany's military technology and power.[10]

The War Press Office's less subtle way to firm up resolve for the war was to distribute pro-annexationist propaganda. The materials were part of the agency's 1917 program in "patriotic instruction" *(vaterländischer Unterricht)*, which it directed primarily at soldiers. The caption of one such material, a poster of an armored knight, read: "Hell-burning indignation and holy rage will double the strength of every German man and woman, whether they are devoted to battle, work, or patient sacrifice." Believing that the duration of the war undermined the resolve for victory, the municipal school authorities in Hamburg strongly recommended this material to teachers. They also suggested using it at parent-teacher evenings. The shortages of paper and minimal resources of the War Press Office limited the distribution of this propaganda, with most of it going to secondary schools, where the teachers were more receptive than in elementary schools.[11]

In contrast to earlier war bond drives, which teachers and pupils had undertaken without prodding, the fourth drive in 1916 involved the War Press Office. Officials had grown concerned about the fitness of teachers and the public to raise money when they were hungry, cold, overworked, and perhaps fed up with the war. They accordingly began coordinating an advertising blitz for war bonds with haunting posters like Fritz Erler's 1917 image of the assault soldier with a gas mask, two grenades, and the tough, intense stare that became the icon of German wartime masculinity. At this point policies became more coordinated. The Prussian education minister von Trott zu Solz no longer assumed teachers and school inspectors would universally participate in war bond drives. Ordering them to help, he began centralizing the drives of pupils in the teacher-training colleges.[12]

After the summer of 1916, the education ministries, goaded by the War Ministry, issued their own prowar curricular directives. Von Trott zu Solz requested, for example, that all elementary and middle schools distribute and discuss the chancellor's Reichstag speech from 9 November 1916, which emphasized the guilt of France, England, and Russia in fomenting the war. Furthermore, in a decree issued in May 1917 he demanded that teachers act to prevent the growing mistrust of the Kaiser. In cooperation with the Central Institute for Education and Instruction, he sponsored fifty elementary school teachers from each province to attend a course on delivering patriotic lectures. The aim of the course was to instruct teachers in how to disseminate prowar ideas in schools, and its curriculum covered material about battleships and submarines. In April 1917 von Trott zu Solz worked with the Central Institute, which had organized the 1915 "School and War" exhibition, to distribute slide shows about the war and to offer teachers courses in how to use them. In urgent and desperate language, state bureaucrats pressed teachers to cultivate in class and at parent evenings the necessary endurance to win the war—that is, to dispel rumors and reiterate General Ludendorff's insistence to "hold out for victory."[13]

The number of teachers and pupils indifferent to war pedagogy increased after 1915, but so did the number who attacked the pacifists. Secondary school teachers and members of the Conservative and National Liberal Parties in particular denounced the few teachers who opposed holding out for a military victory. Their views gained credibility from the growing prestige of the Fatherland Party. Founded in July 1917 by Generals Erich von Ludendorff and Wolfgang Kapp, the leader of the notorious 1920 putsch, the party began a massive campaign to sway popular opinion in favor of a victorious peace, substantial reparations, and territorial gains. The Fatherland Party was particularly successful in mobilizing administrators, school inspectors, secondary school teachers, and Protestant elementary school teachers in small cities and the countryside, as well as numerous left-liberal pedagogues, including Theobald Ziegler. Its propaganda penetrated not only the education bureaucracies but also the independent professional groups of teachers; the Saxon Teachers' Association in early 1918 hosted a Pan-Germanist who called on all to join the party. Even though school had been canceled on dozens of days because of the shortages, the school inspector in the district of Culm in West Prussia gave teachers a day off in January 1918 to attend a meeting of the party. Supporters of the Fatherland Party published textbooks for teachers that outlined lessons on the necessity of annexations in Poland and Belgium. In response to teachers becoming outlets for the distribution of its propaganda, the editor of *Welt am Montag* quipped, "Wouldn't it be simpler to make the program of the Fatherland Party a new subject in the curriculum?"[14]

Like secondary school teachers throughout Germany and elementary school teachers in the Protestant small cities and countryside, elementary school teachers in big cities supported nationalist war aims in principle, but after the disastrous winter of 1916/17, material circumstances compelled many of them to want an immediate peace. They had less access to food than rural and small-city teachers and suffered more than secondary school teachers, who were better paid, and even many factories workers, who weren't on fixed salaries and could renegotiate wages in the inflation. Furthermore, although the Fatherland Party held a position of neutrality on domestic issues and had prominent left-liberal pedagogical reformers like Ziegler as members, urban elementary school teachers knew that its top leaders came from political circles that supported the authority of clerical school inspectors, whom they detested. The party's leaders had also previously opposed school reform on the model of the *Einheitsschule*.

Yet until the summer of 1918, urban elementary school teachers were hesitant to criticize the Fatherland Party. This was partly because censorship of anti-annexationists escalated after the July 1917 Peace Resolution, and teachers faced disciplinary action from the school inspectors for involvement in the pacifist movement. It was also because schoolteachers wanted to protect their image as good patriots to improve public support among elites for national school reform. Furthermore, though hungry and exhausted, many still hoped, like other moderate Germans, for victory as compensation for all their sacrifices. On the one hand, few urban elementary school teachers ever criticized the war. On the other hand, their journals never endorsed the Fatherland Party's platform. I did not evidence that urban elementary school teachers passed out literature for the party. From July 1917 until the summer of 1918, elementary school teachers opposed to the war were quietist.

However, when the front collapsed in the summer of 1918, urban elementary school teachers sided with the Social Democratic parties and denounced the Fatherland Party in the left-liberal press (the pedagogical press still remained silent). In August 1918, for example, the *Berliner Morgenpost* charged that teachers who distributed prowar pamphlets knew it was illegal because it brought the war aims debates and therefore politics into the classroom, but they protected themselves in this "unconscionable poisoning of youth" by acting *en masse*. The Independent Social Democratic Party called for public protest after it discovered in August 1918 that teachers in secondary schools were distributing a leaflet that called the Peace Resolution of July 1917 "treason to the Fatherland." Propaganda from Fatherland Party material was also distributed in girls' secondary schools, the teacher-training colleges, and elementary schools in Prussia's eastern provinces and Berlin's suburbs, where party officials hoped to mobilize parents by way of their schoolchildren. Only in September 1918 did the education minister warn the provincial school authorities and the Supreme Command, which underwrote the Fatherland Party, that distributing political content to pupils was prohibited. His directive was too little too late, however, to protect a generation of secondary school boys from all over Germany and elementary school boys in Protestant small towns and the countryside from propaganda claiming that Germany's aggressive war aims were legitimate.[15]

The Persistence of War Pedagogy

The growing silence on the war curriculum that reigned after 1915 did not necessarily indicate opposition to it. For example, the *Leipziger Lehrerzeitung* had few articles on curricular issues in the last years of the war. Nevertheless, in the face of imminent defeat, it published one in November 1918 that praised teachers for placing the war at the center of school life. In the summer of 1916, the Leipzig Teachers' Association denounced the municipal school board because the board, hoping to counter pupils' plummeting academic performance, ordered the teachers to return to the prewar lesson plans. Such a return involved forsaking the newfound liberty to innovate, and Leipzig's teachers were among the leaders in the German pedagogical reform movement. They hence faulted the board for denying them the pedagogical freedom to discuss the "great events of the time for the heart and soul" of youth. In October 1916 the teachers pursued the same strategy as in the first year of the war. They argued that having pedagogical freedom was necessary to mobilize schoolchildren for the war. Their strategy worked: the Saxon education minister decided in their favor.[16]

In general, teachers cut the crudest jingoism from war pedagogy, but after 1915 they persisted in using much of the content and methods from the first years of the war. Many even followed the exhortations of school inspectors and state governors, who in 1916 and 1917 urged teachers to make war lessons "the foundation of instruction" and all other subjects "supplementary." Elementary school teachers led excursions to war exhibitions and hung and discussed war maps. For a donation to a war welfare fund, they let their pupils drive nails into doors as a mark of their patriotism. Teachers had their pupils write letters to soldiers and published ones the pupils had received in memorial war books. In 1917 and 1918, they strove to eliminate foreign words from instruction, collecting fines for uttering Latin cognates and cutting instruction in the French and English languages whenever convenient. They had their pupils collect newspaper and magazine articles about the war. Despite the severe interruptions to schooling, school directors reserved time for ritualized, patriotic war ceremonies. Before a so-called war consecration hour in August 1916, one director made the elementary school boys wait outside the hall in anticipation. He then sprung the doors open. A lieutenant, a former teacher who had earned the Iron Cross, gave a lecture about the war, and the director observed what he believed was the Spirit of 1914:

> [The pupils'] souls were opened great and wide, and capable, with the help of their divine friend, Fantasy, to grasp greatness, holiness, *heroism!* . . . How many boys wanted to jump up and shake the hand of the honored teacher out of joy and pride!

In general, acclaim for the positive effect of the war on education was less common after 1915 than before, but the pedagogical, liberal, and conservative press continued to praise the war for giving more freedom to teachers and making it possible to introduce reform teaching methods and more nationalist curricula.[17]

Protestant as well as Catholic female elementary school teachers also stayed the course on war pedagogy after 1915. At the time of the July 1917 Reichstag Peace Resolution, the editor of *Die Lehrerin,* the leading weekly for female schoolteachers, recommended war books with political speeches and battle stories from the first year of the war. In 1917 and 1918, the *Monatsschrift für die katholischen Lehrerinnen* was singularly committed to war pedagogy. Although its nationalism was far less effusive than in 1914 and 1915, its war dictations in 1918 instilled pupils with the idea that victory was necessary at all costs. Authors in the journal discussed using class time for war prayers and patriotic war work and suggested lessons for teaching war poems and war plays. The slogans were the same as in 1914: Allow "the children to experience the great times" and "devote service to the Fatherland." "The war is a great pedagogical God," one teacher claimed. "It helps us to ennoble the will of the child, to educate her in selflessness and joy in sacrifice." She believed it was easy to place the war in the middle of instruction in geography, history, singing, dictations, reading, writing, and religion. She assigned a poem entitled, "Loyal until Death."[18]

War pedagogy changed after 1915, becoming less reliant on the creativity and initiative of teachers themselves. The war curriculum became more standardized and accordingly lost some of its home-grown populism. The change was partly due to the availability after 1915 of the first textbooks and readers about the war that school directors and inspectors urged teachers to use. In part because exhausted teachers did not want to gather material on their own, they accepted using the textbooks. Most widely recommended by administrators was Hans Korsch's *War Lessons,* a four-volume set. The textbook, intended for teachers (pupils were not expected to buy it), was sober by the standards of youth war literature. It had photographs of generals and royal families, maps of all the main battles, and information on civic education and social spending in Germany, England, and France. It also had sections on the army and various types of weapons. It claimed the causes of the war were Serbia's and France's desires for power, Germany's economic competition with England, and Russia's Pan-Slavism and need for a warm-water port. It offered a twenty-page chronology of the war.[19]

More lurid than Korsch's textbook were the plentiful school readers of soldiers' letters, war lyrics, patriotic speeches, and battle descriptions after 1915. The literature perpetuated the myths of the *Burgfrieden* and the Spirit of 1914, reproduced the Kaiser's "I know no parties, I now know only Germans" speech, and contradicted the stalemate by depicting current combat as a war of movement. In these battles soldiers detonated railway bridges and smashed the enemies with zeppelins, cavalry, submarines, torpedo boats, and bayonet-wielding infantry. Officers commanded battleships, 42-cm centimeter guns, and infantry attacks with hand grenades. The Germans were invariably victorious, and the soldiers earned the Iron Cross. The stories recognized the hardships of the war—deaths of soldiers and shortages of food and coal in fact figured prominently. One poem captured the silent pain of a mother burying her son, for example. In a section on "humanity in war," one reader depicted a German soldier who saved a wounded Frenchman and wept at the pictures of his family. But like war pedagogy in 1914 and 1915, the readings always cast the hardship in patriotic terms; they glorified the tribulations as exemplary of the German people's "joy in sacrificing."[20]

Youth War Literature after 1915

The school readers mirrored how authors of youth literature wrote about the war after 1915. Some of these authors did not invoke themes of jubilation or renewal, and the language became dry and technical, the soldiers portrayed as automatons doing their duty. The authors occasionally described it as "terrible" or in cynical, dark, and ominous language. But they continued to invoke themes of heroism and adventure. Without bloodshed, soldiers saved comrades on sinking ships, extinguished fires in munitions depots while under attack, and ventured out of bunkers for missions during artillery barrages. Numerous stories focused on Hindenburg. The single most popular figure in biographical and anecdotal articles, he was hailed as one of Germany's all-time greatest leaders. These biographies disseminated his optimism about German nationalism and military superiority. They quoted the general: "When with God's help the entire German people remains unified in its will to victory, a world full of enemies can no longer get us." The predominant war stories after 1915 were about zeppelins, warplanes, torpedo boats, submarines, cruisers, and mine layers. One of the most popular was the chronicles of the *Emden*, the German cruiser torpedoed in the Indian Ocean in 1914 after it had sunk sixteen British ships and forced seven others to surrender cargo. (While the *Emden* sank, its landing crew was destroying British Cable and Wireless installations on Direction Island; captured by the British, the landing crew broke out, hijacked a fishing boat, and hightailed to the safety of Germany via Turkey.) In addition to the *Emden*, the authors celebrated the exploits of a handful of warships: the torpedo boat *S 90*, the submarine *U 9* piloted by the legendary Captain Otto Weddigen, and the cruisers *Möwe* and SMS *Wolf*. In these depictions, the superiority of German technology made victory swift. The stories portrayed the war not as a horrifying war of attrition but as an exciting adventure with the big toys of the generals.[21]

Religious ideas that justified submission to the policy of war became increasingly common after 1915. Poetry, fiction, and nonfiction asserted that neither politicians nor citizens but rather God alone determined destiny in the war, implying that a youth could thus end the war only through faith, patriotism, and self-sacrifice. For characters in a host of articles, novels, poems, and short stories, a spirited toleration of war misery built character, ensured victory, and preserved national unity and greatness. Wounded soldiers refrained from telling their loved ones about their injuries, and children who endured the absence of their fathers were called heroes. This willingness to submit matched the strident language of the High Command's request after 1915 for Germans to hold out for victory until Germany's enemies were annihilated.[22]

Because the paper and labor shortages after 1915 made publishing books and long magazines expensive, this more dispassionate youth war literature was not produced in the same quantities as the earlier Spirit-of-1914 books and articles. The extreme shortage of paper after 1917 also made new publications prohibitively costly and in some places illegal. Lending libraries remained full of the earlier war books but had trouble making new purchases after 1915. Thus, for purely material reasons, the ideas of war in 1914 and 1915 dominated over the later, less positive ones.[23]

Schoolchildren and the Post-1915 Curriculum

Officials and school directors often bemoaned the "indifference" and "depressed mood" among schoolchildren after 1915. The directors of secondary wrote that responses to victories were sometimes now just queries about whether they would get the day off from school. Although the Prussian education minister denied the existence of this apathy, he stretched to find evidence for a counterview. In October 1917 he speciously reasoned that the compositions from the "School and War" exhibition, erected in the spring of 1915, showed that pupils were enthusiastic. At the start of the war, teachers marveled at the excitement schoolchildren showed for the new technologies of war, but some now reported that children were indifferent to visual stimuli of submarines, airplanes, zeppelins, and cruisers. In follow-up questions to the slide show "The Air War and Its Heroes" shown in Frankfurt in the fall of 1917, the images evoked little patriotism from the pupils.[24]

After 1916 the mobilization of children for the war was more successful in secondary than elementary schools. The new war readers generally targeted the wealthier children in the secondary schools and the private elementary ones *(Vorschulen)*. Because of the inflation and shortages, poorer children could not afford the war readers and textbooks, and subsidies were uncommon. Elementary schools depended on financing from municipalities, and even early in the war, strained budgets compelled school districts such as Düsseldorf's to refrain from purchasing new teaching materials. Continuing financial problems forced more and more school districts to do the same—

insolvency threatened communities due to the inflation and the prodigious expense of providing welfare to the hungry. Recognizing that working- and lower-middle-class families could not afford books, the Prussian education minister forbade elementary schools in January 1916 to require their pupils to purchase new readers.[25]

More secondary than elementary school teachers were committed to holding out for a military victory. Secondary school children were also more likely to come from middle-class families who supported aggressive war aims and encouraged reading war literature and volunteering for patriotic work and pre-military training. Because secondary school teachers distributed the propaganda of the Fatherland Party, they arguably made these middle-class teenagers more susceptible to the idea that Germans should reject a negotiated peace and fight to the last man. In 1917 and 1918 secondary school teachers regularly had pupils reproduce the annexationist position in their cumulative final exams. After 1915 until the end of the war, officials agreed that secondary school children had, with some notable exceptions, shown considerable seriousness, patriotic enthusiasm, willingness to sacrifice, and consciousness of duty. The war experience had "deepened youths' love of the German soil," and it had evoked "much latent youthful heroism." According to the Prussian school authorities in Magdeburg, "a certain craving" set in when secondary school children were kept away from patriotic voluntary activity.[26]

Elementary school children in big cities were more inclined to accept a negotiated peace after 1915, but a good proportion of them never gave up working for the war effort. They participated in the collection drives and voluntary labor in the summer and even the fall of 1918, after the front collapsed. They were willing to hold out for a military victory particularly at auspicious times. For example, after 1915 teachers noticed that in the "community meeting" in the progressive Berthold-Otto elementary school, during which the pupils chose the themes for the following week's instruction, pupils were increasingly less enthusiastic about the war, and they returned to the prewar curriculum. After the Eastern offensive in Russia in 1917, however, the pupils began to take an interest again. The atmosphere was now less celebratory and more serious, but according to one of the teachers:

> Most [of the pupils] had a resolute commitment to victory; they are aware of our power. If anyone dares to show doubt, the others grow indignant. We must be victorious. Therefore, we will be victorious. And every one of these children is prepared to do everything he can within his powers. . . .

[In January 1918] the pupils were indignant about the strikes, which they felt to be a betrayal of the soldiers in the trenches. . . . They are proud and happy to be able to experience these times.

In the fall of 1917, teachers gave pupils good reasons to hold out for victory: the war was still off German soil, and Russia was soon likely to surrender. In 1918 Germany then defeated Russia, occupied huge swaths of Poland and the Ukraine, the bread basket of Europe, and made an advance on Paris, breaking the stalemate on the Western Front. Having built a more trusting relationship with their pupils over the course of the war, the teachers needed just the real possibility of victory to redress the disillusionment and prod their pupils to hold out for a favorable end and be rewarded for their years of suffering.[27]

War pedagogy in the fall of 1914 had been largely a spontaneous reaction of teachers and administrators, with little or no centralized coordination. This populism ebbed after 1915. In the first year of the war, many teachers had their pupils cull war poems and soldiers' letters, a practice that reinforced the idea that patriotism originated in the people. But in 1916 and 1917 officials in the Prussian Education Ministry sensed that grief and deprivation had sapped many teachers of their will to carry out war pedagogy and began to pressure teachers directly to mobilize schoolchildren, particularly in summoning their voluntary labor. They asked to get schoolchildren to hold out for a military victory. Teachers now relied more on propaganda like films, textbooks, and slide shows on the war sponsored by the education ministries or the newly created War Press Office and the Fatherland Party. Whereas teachers in 1914 and 1915 portrayed the war as thrilling and purifying, most portrayed it from 1916 to 1918 as a solemn rite of sacrifice and duty.

But even without the ministers' encouragement, elementary school teachers in Protestant villages, towns, and small cities, as well as many in Catholic and Protestant large cities, were committed after 1915 to muster schoolchildren's economic and ideological support for victory. For the course of the war, most progressive educational reformers either openly supported the war or kept quiet. Like many others in the middle class, a good number abandoned the Progressive Party for its pacifism in the fall of 1917 and placed their hope in the Fatherland Party with its platform of a victorious peace with territorial gains. Elementary school teachers could be more nationalist than state officials. When moderate education officials, hoping to halt declining academic achievement, urged elementary school teachers to stop frequent discussions of the war and return to the pre-1914 curriculum, many of them lashed out, indignant that the government was undervaluing their patriotic efforts. Like youth workers and authors of youth literature, elementary school teachers of all sorts accepted that suffering was a necessary condition for victory. After 1915 they thought that the war was positive in at least one sense: it encouraged schoolchildren's devotion to Germany.

Although secondary school teachers were hesitant to replace their humanities or science curricula with patriotic war content, the majority were resolved to make the necessary sacrifice for the decisive German victory that would bring annexations and reparations. After the July 1917 Peace Resolution, most secondary school teachers turned to the Fatherland Party and its rabidly nationalist propaganda. Secondary school boys, who were primarily middle class, were accordingly the social group among youths most committed to continuing the war until Germany achieved a military victory. They became more politically radicalized than most other social groups.

10

Politicization and Repression

The July 1917 Reichstag Peace Resolution and the subsequent founding of the Fatherland Party accelerated political polarization in Germany. On the right, the fall of Chancellor Bethmann-Hollweg initiated the authoritarian rule by Generals Hindenburg and Ludendorff. The generals instituted a more severe regime of censorship and tried to silence the growing criticism of aggressive war aims, but they could not prevent increasing numbers of working-class Germans from wanting an immediate negotiated peace. In April 1917 and then again in January 1918, industrial workers in Berlin and other cities organized the war's largest strikes, demanding democratic reforms such as universal manhood suffrage and peace without annexations. Although Hindenburg brutally repressed the strikes and was able to contain overt antiwar protest until October 1918, he could not end the tacit opposition of millions against the government and the war.[1]

This political polarization infused youth associations as well. Exhaustion, material deprivation, and a growing disillusionment with the war led working youths as early as 1915 to quit the voluntary patriotic organizations. Times of scarcity and rising domestic burdens made production for the family, not the war, the priority. Although exact estimates are difficult to determine, working-class youths and women made up half of the participants in the great antiwar strikes of April 1917 and January 1918. Ideologically opposed to them were middle-class youths, particularly secondary school boys, who trained in the military companies and volunteered for patriotic projects until the end of the war. These circumstances—working youths rejecting their alleged patriotic duty, on the one hand, and middle-class boys and girls gladly supporting and sacrificing for the war, on the other—fed anger on both sides. The most outstanding example of this political polarization was in the youth movements.

Voluntary Labor, Military Youth Training, and Social Class

After 1915 the 14- to 18-year-olds who volunteered for patriotic projects were primarily from either middle-class families throughout Germany or lower-middle-class ones in the Protestant small and medium-sized cities not devastated by the food crisis. Because schoolchildren age 6 to 14 were not working, and the school day shortened considerably, they volunteered at higher rates than those a few years older. Elementary school children whose parents did not need their labor to get food continued to collect recyclables and work in agriculture until the end of the war, but children in less fortunate families, including previously lower-middle-class ones who had since fallen into poverty, were forced to quit the voluntary projects. Perversely, the press and state bureaucracies praised the volunteers but not the suffering ones, and they thereby linked patriotism to being middle- and lower-middle-class.[2]

Early in the war the organizers of military youth training had hoped that social class would not play a role like this. But creating classless, pluralist patriotic organizations, a goal grounded in the ideals of unity under the *Burgfrieden* and the Spirit of 1914, was utopian. As early as October 1914, numerous secondary school boys had formed companies separate from those of working youths. By the spring of 1915, military youth training was segregated by social class and confession; municipalities, secondary and continuation schools, and religious and patriotic youth groups all had exclusive companies. This situation was criticized for reproducing the "splintering" of youth associations that frustrated so many before the war. Disappointed, the deputy commanding generals abandoned their ideals.[3]

Membership rates for the first year of the war indicate that voluntary military youth training was most popular in areas without organized Socialist youth associations and outside the rural Catholic milieu. After the winter of 1914/15, support for military training from urban working youths further eroded because of the return to full employment, longer hours of factories, growing disillusionment with the war, lack of charismatic leader, and exhaustion from the deprivation. In March 1915 the municipal continuation schools in Berlin had only seventeen military companies and a total of 1,930 members—a figure that represented just 7 percent of the eligible male youths. Detailed evidence on membership rates from the army district of Hanover, where the deputy commanding general asked leaders to keep careful records, shows that most working youths in Braunschweig and Hanover—cities that had especially active Socialist youth organizations—shunned military companies after December 1914. In nonindustrial Protestant regions, the participation rates were by contrast high: 50 percent as late as the summer of 1915 and just below that through the summer of 1916. While participation declined steeply thereafter, particularly during the Turnip Winter, a core of youths continued to support the companies in the last two years of the war (see Figure 5.1). In December 1916, the beginning of the Turnip Winter, over 84 percent of secondary school boys in the province of Hanover and the duchies of Oldenburg and Braunschweig were practicing regularly. One newspaper report estimated in February 1917 that the district of the 9th Army Corps (Hamburg and its rural environs) had twenty thousand members in youth companies. Although the figure was surely an exaggeration—extrapolated for Protestant Germany as a whole, it was about a third of those eligible—the report nevertheless attested to the perception of enthusiasm for the companies among a core of male youths.[4]

Social class also determined who participated in the large agricultural projects that the press and state bureaucracy praised as examples of steadfast patriotic sacrifice. These programs began in 1915 out of the military youth companies in Düsseldorf, where officers organized two thousand teenage boys to bring in harvest. With the passing of the Auxiliary Service Law in December 1916, which required that civilian males age 17 and older provide their labor to the War Office, the various education ministries began to organize agricultural and industrial brigades *(Jungmannen)* along this model. Schoolteachers, the press, and the bureaucracy saw these brigades as patriotic voluntary activity because the boys also had the option of getting paid, practical experience working in offices instead. The War Office distributed uniforms to boost the pride of the seventy-five thousand mobilized boys and instituted elaborate courses in leadership of the brigades. In most cases, these brigades broke into small platoons and worked on farms, unsupervised by any teacher or youth worker.[5]

Instead of being hailed as heroes solving the food crisis, they were derided by the farmers for whom they worked. Prejudiced against the leisured urban middle class and angry at state and military officials for requisitioning their livestock and crops, the farmers—particularly Catholic ones who had turned against the war but many Protestant ones as well—thought the boys were arrogant and physically weak. They turned many away, despite the severe shortage of labor in agriculture. Problems of provisioning plagued the brigades. Many boys went without adequate food and slept on straw in cramped, makeshift barracks. Because of conscription, most young men were absent on the farms; sometimes the only adult male was a prisoner of war. Without guidance, a few boys shirked work and spent their days smoking cigarettes and pursuing love relationships. In the summer of 1917, low morale and poor leadership had led some individuals and even entire commandos to defect. The entire program was in grave doubt.[6]

These problems did not undermine the participants' conviction that they were sacrificing for the war. The boys had given up their schooling, and most for the first time in their lives did heavy manual labor. They also apparently worked hard despite the mismanagement, and schoolteachers and the press consistently praised them for their patriotism. The experience then contributed to the political polarization: the boys observed how one group that had turned against the war, the rural population, snubbed them despite their sacrifice. They also saw how another group, their peers who worked in factories, earned lucrative wages for the same heavy labor that they did voluntarily. In addition, they read or heard from their teachers that these working youths had spent their money on alleged frivolous commercial pleasures like the cinema and, worst of all, had turned against the war.

The male youths in military training and agricultural projects had various motivations, and some doubtlessly participated because of pressure from teachers, family, and peers. But whatever their reason, these middle-class male teenagers isolated themselves from working youths while developing a fascination with soldiering, comradeship, and sacrifice for Germany. Almost all in the cohort born from 1896 to 1904 who after 1918 joined anticommunist paramilitary groups and radical-right organizations had been participants in a military company. One youth recalled in his 1932 memoir, for example, how as a 17-year-old he was proud to march in his military youth company and to volunteer for the agricultural projects. He returned from voluntary work in the summer of 1918 disgusted with the "war weariness" of much of the population. As the front collapsed, he realized it was too late for him to join the army, and in January 1919 he joined a *Freikorps* regiment to fight against "Bolshevism" and "the seeds of pacifism and internationalism."[7]

Military youth training was a development largely confined to Central Europe during the war, and only in Germany did it isolate a minority of enthusiasts who tended to be middle and lower middle class. In France and England, the number of youths participating was negligible; hence, the Western Allies never gave a cohort of youths who did not serve in the army a chance to practice being a soldier and earn public admiration for it. In the German-speaking areas of Austria-Hungary, nationality was a more salient factor than social class. At first, the lack of youth workers made it more difficult to organize companies, but whereas the German states devoted less and less resources to the military youth companies, the Austro-Hungarian state gave more. In contrast to Germany, participation in the Austro-Hungarian companies in 1916 increased to an estimated half of eligible youths. The companies soon after declined as cold, hunger, exhaustion, and parents' concern militated against participation. Yet they maintained moderately high levels of participation in regions like Moravia and Bohemia, where Germans were a minority and felt threatened by nationalist eruptions within the crumbling supranational state.[8]

The Socialist Youth Movement under National Integration

An exception to the general decline of state and paternal authority was the vigorous surveillance, arrest, and punishment of Socialist youths who publicly protested the war. The number of these dissenters—an estimated ten thousand—was small. With the exception of them and a few hundred in the middle-class youth movement, almost all of Germany's 10 million teenagers either supported the war or were ambivalent or fearful enough to shun antiwar activism. The unpopularity of protest suggests that teachers, youth workers, and authors of youth literature succeeded in mobilizing youths to hold out for victory and keeping them away from the peace movement. It also shows that despite personnel shortages and declining legitimacy, state and military authorities still had the will and might to quash opposition.

Almost all historians agree that oppositional Socialist adolescents ceded from the Central Office that oversaw the mainstream youth organizations of the Social Democratic Party in part because the youths wanted peace, and the party supported war. East German historians and memoirists argued that these oppositional youths ceded because they supported peace *and* an immediate Socialist revolution and found inspiration in Karl Liebknecht and Rosa Luxemburg, the most outspoken critics of the war and among the first to break the party line on the *Burgfrieden*. Overlooked is that many sided with Liebknecht and Luxemburg not because they embraced immediate revolution but because they hated the paternalism of Friedrich Ebert, the chairman of the party. After the Social Democratic Party depoliticized the Socialist youth organizations in 1908, Liebknecht and Luxemburg became steadfast advocates of giving youths their autonomy back. Teenagers looking for mentors to oppose Ebert's paternalism and to support antiwar activism turned to Liebknecht and Luxemburg, among the only Germans who championed youths' engagement with politics during the war. Ludwig Quidde and his small group of middle-class pacifists did not involve youths to any significant extent. The only other youth organization working for peace, the middle-class Central Working Group for the Youth Movement *(Centralarbeitsstätte für die Jugendbewegung)* led by the 23-year-old future sexologist Max Hodann, was small and distributed almost no propaganda. For those who wanted peace, oppositional Socialist youths aligned with the radicals Liebknecht and Luxemburg had the only game in town: from 1914 to 1916 they organized arguably the largest and most sophisticated antiwar movement in Germany, and the only significant one open to young people. So whether or not they were committed revolutionaries, Socialist youths who wanted to work for peace had little choice but to join an organization undertaking conspiratorial agitation and calling for the overthrow of the state in a worldwide proletarian revolution.

In demanding independence from the Social Democratic Party while brazenly distributing illegal propaganda, these teenagers forged a rebellious and politically charged Socialist youth subculture. After 1918 the cohort's youthful radicalism in turn shaped the rough style and tactics of the German Communist Party. Heroes to the far left but traitors to liberals, conservatives, and Majority Social Democrats alike, these rebels called for mass strikes to end the war. Their actions helped justify the legend of "the stab in the back," the narrative later popularized by Hindenburg that the German army would have won the war if the home front had remained steadfast. The activities of oppositional Socialist youths also polarized the workers' movement and destabilized the political system after 1918.[9]

The opposition of Socialist youths to the war began in reaction to the Social Democratic Party's vote for the war credits in August 1914. The vote, which sealed the *Burgfrieden,* was ostensibly an agreement to cooperate in the defense of Germany, but many functionaries also saw it as an opportunity to end the party's isolation caused by so-called negative integration. Under this policy, the Social Democratic Party accepted the Prussian-German constitution and renounced an immediate revolution but, hoping to maintain its base of support, also founded working-class cultural associations strictly separate from the middle class and accordingly "negatively" integrated its constituents into Germany. Many working-class Socialists had entrenched traditions of antimilitarism, disdain for bourgeois culture, and rough cultures of drinking and brawling. The Social Democratic Party pursued negative integration while also trying to win votes from the middle classes. Thus, to rectify its members' bad reputations, it subdued crass antimilitarism in its youth and other organizations and promoted "respectable" behaviors like moderation with alcohol. The party nonetheless remained firmly opposed to imperialism and discouraged its constituents from adopting middle-class nationalism. By agreeing to the *Burgfrieden,* however, the Social Democratic Party adopted a new policy, so-called *national* integration, under which the party put Germany ahead of its own immediate, particular interests and agreed to get the working class to support the war. The Social Democratic Party hoped that national integration would convince the ruling parties that workers were good Germans and deserved full political rights. Right-wing Social Democrats who supported this strategy were in particular elated when, two weeks after the historic vote for the war credits, Chancellor Bethmann-Hollweg announced a "new orientation," which gave official recognition to the Social Democratic Party and the Socialist labor unions, and promised that political reform would follow the war, provided that the party maintained the *Burgfrieden.*[10]

The degree to which the Social Democratic Party implemented national integration is a matter of debate, but in few places was the attempt more brazen than in the youth movement. *Arbeiter-Jugend,* the Socialist youth weekly edited by Karl Korn and Heinrich Schulz in the Central Office, followed the lead of middle-class recreational associations and tried to mobilize youths for the war. Korn and Schulz also wanted to contain radicalism and augment the respectability of Socialist youth organizations by vehemently opposing their autonomy. Above all, they urged their young readers to be patriotic, make sacrifices, and disengage from class struggle. On 14 August 1914 *Arbeiter-Jugend* admonished the youths who said the *Burgfrieden* was a betrayal of Socialist principles. Three weeks later, in an article entitled "To the Front, Comrades!" the editors made an official call upon youths to help bring in the harvest (thousands of middle-class schoolchildren were already volunteering). Their plea for national integration was plain: they urged "proletarians to rush to the border" and claimed that in this war "the prince like the pauper offers his last drop of blood." In an article that infuriated tens of thousands of Socialist youths, *Arbeiter-Jugend* cast dead soldiers as heroes in a homage in mid-September to Ludwig Frank, the founder of the Association for Young Workers who, against all expectation, volunteered for the army in August 1914 and died in the Battle of the Marne. In the subsequent months, *Arbeiter-Jugend* published articles with titles like "The Will to Bravery" and "War as Experience." It compared the adventures of the German cruiser *Die Emden* to Odysseus' adventures in *The Odyssey*. Such patriotic language, encomiums for dead soldiers, enthusiasm for military enterprise, and cozying up to middle-class nationalists had few precedents in Socialist youth culture. Before the war, centrist and right-wing Social Democratic functionaries sought to contain youths' autonomy and suppress their radical antimilitarism, but few ever encouraged youths to imitate bourgeois nationalists or make heroes of the soldiers who died for Germany.[11]

Another attempt to integrate working-class youths into the nation early in the war was the support that right-wing Social Democrats gave to premilitary training. Their endorsement had precedents. In 1912 the chairman of the Social Democratic Party August Bebel suggested that military training of youths would prepare the working class for service in a future citizen's militia, fulfilling the nebulous commitment in the Erfurt Program (the Social Democratic Party's party line after 1891) to give youths an "education in defense" *(Erziehung zur allgemeinen Wehrhaftigkeit)*. Likewise, the leaders of the Worker Gymnastics League entertained the introduction of military training into their programs to achieve parity with the middle-class groups and gain access to state funds and municipal spaces and equipment under the 1911 *Jugendpflege* Decree. But fearing they would send the wrong message and contradict key Socialist tenets, both the Social Democratic Party and the Worker Gymnastics League ultimately rejected such a policy in the years before the war.[12]

In August 1914, however, a handful of Social Democratic newspapers tacitly endorsed the education minister's guidelines on the military training of male youth by printing them without comment. In addition, newspapers in Kiel, Magdeburg, and other cities actively urged male teenagers to partici- pate. Most scandalously, leaders of several regional gymnastics organizations and district youth committees, including Eduard Adler, the chair in Schleswig-Holstein, offered to help deputy commanding generals found mil- itary companies. In Hamburg, Karl Hense, a leading trade union official, and Emil Krause, editor of the feuilleton in the Social Democratic *Hamburger Echo*, agreed at a meeting with middle-class youth workers to form one as well. Facing an exodus of working-class youths who thought the Social Democratic organizations were now militarist, Ebert issued a circular on 5 September asking the district youth committees to advise their young members not to join military companies. But because the censor frowned on its publication, some branches did not know that the party was opposed to premilitary training. In Hamburg, young Socialists composed a wry ditty, "The Death Song of Youths," that attacked the apparent support for military companies and the policy of national integration in the Hamburg Socialist Youth League:

> Youth League and military youth company,
> There is only similarity.
> All of them are alike,
> The poor, the rich, the old, the tykes.

The situation seemed so bad that representatives from thirty-five district youth committees met in Berlin on 29 October, and all but three resolved to censure Social Democratic participation in military youth companies. But again, the censor forbade publication of the resolution. Making matters worse, Schulz towed the party line on military training only half-heartedly, issuing a circular from the Central Office in May 1915 that gave it tacit support. Similarly, Korn scorned opponents of military training, claiming that the nationalist language in the education minister's guidelines for the programs was "harmless" and that the lack of working-class participation was problematic because it irked middle-class political parties and newspa- pers and endangered the *Burgfrieden*. Even in 1918, long after the Majority Social Democratic Party had signed the Peace Resolution and close to two million Germans were dead, Schulz insisted that the working class had "love of the Fatherland" and denied that the state was a "solicitor of the ruling classes."[13]

National integration of working-class youths rightly seemed feasible to Social Democratic leaders in August and early September 1914. Memoirs of German workers corroborate police reports that on Sedan Day (2 September) 1914, thousands of working-class male youths in Berlin celebrated the military victories of August by waving the German flag. Anecdotal evidence suggests that thousands were still participating in military youth companies at this time as well. But as demands by prominent industrialists and the middle-class political parties for territorial annexations grew louder in the fall of 1914, tens of thousands were alienated by Korn and Schulz, who in their patriotic slogans seemed to condone military training. Most irritating to these youths was that the *Burgfrieden* hardened the gag rule—they could not even debate in their organizations whether the war was justified. Youths in cities like Berlin, Hamburg, and Stuttgart who had fought with the Social Democratic Party leadership before 1914 over independence and the right to vocalize antimilitarism turned to Liebknecht and Luxemburg, whose antiwar agitation legitimated their contempt for the party leadership and the war. In June 1915 these youths also gained confidence in their cause (though not in their methods) when Hugo Haase, Karl Kautsky, and Eduard Bernstein—three Reichstag delegates representing the left, center, and right, respectively, in the Social Democratic Party—condemned the war in their impassioned plea, "The Commandment of the Hour." Soon afterward national integration of youths backfired. Over the course of 1915 and 1916, dozens of district youth organizations ceded from the Central Office and aligned themselves with the internationalist, oppositional Socialist youths calling for mass strikes to end the war. Even though working male youths were earning higher nominal wages after 1915, subscriptions to *Arbeiter-Jugend,* the best indicator of participation in the Social Democratic Party youth organizations, dropped from 108,000 before the war to 53,000 in April 1916 and just 31,000 in April 1918.[14]

Despite the defections, the Central Office remained stubbornly committed to the *Burgfrieden*. Korn rightly pointed out that condoning the protests by teenagers would have invited police repression and probably outright closing of the Social Democratic youth organizations. He also doubted that teenagers passing out antiwar broadsides and newspapers could win a struggle against formidable foes like the Prussian police and the army. His diagnosis of youth radicalism was that hotheads over 18 years old were corrupting younger innocents and seducing them to espouse a self-defeating stance. At a conference in the summer of 1917, he persuaded the representatives of the district organizations still loyal to the Majority Social Democratic Party that the common practice of having youths lead youths, the sine qua non of the youth movement, needed to end. Germans over 18 years old were thereafter banned from the youth organizations and asked to join the Social Democratic Party instead. The representatives also affirmed that the Social Democratic youth organization was "not a fighting organization with party-political goals." Thereafter, Social Democrats in cities like Magdeburg and Hanover tried to found new organizations to replace the defected groups.[15]

With thirty-one thousand members at the end of the war, organizations loyal to the Central Office had support from working-class teenagers who either thought the war was justified or ignored politics and simply enjoyed the hikes, lectures, and other sponsored events. Such was the attitude of the teenager at the Social Democratic youth center in Bremen who argued in January 1916 with the 18-year-old journalist and left radical Wilhelm Eildermann. Eildermann wrote in his diary that the disputant insisted that no one could stop the war and feared that England would annex Germany and force everyone to speak English. Eildermann was outraged by the teenager's abandonment of antimilitarism. He also noted that the entertainment that evening was "dilettante theater on a level under a night-club act," far from the political discussion and action that he wanted youths to engage in. This apoliticism of the Social Democratic youth organization in Bremen was similar to Magdeburg, where the district youth organization fiercely resisted opponents of the *Burgfrieden* and, in one of the few cases during the war, managed in May 1917 to increase membership over prewar levels.[16]

Despite the wholesale defections by youths who resented the paternalism of the Central Office, the Majority Social Democratic youth leaders in many places tightened censorship and hardened discipline. For example, in Frankfurt, adult leaders scolded youths for "loud talking and laughing" and expelled a female member for riding a man's bicycle and a male member for saying "shut up." According to the protocol book, youths were also expelled for smoking and making disturbances. In Magdeburg, leaders regularly scolded youths in their local journal for "taking on the tasks of men and women" and participating in the "wild nonsense"—code for protest against the war. Their tone was shrill and condescending when they upbraided youths in bold type for violating the gag rule and urging members to quit the mainstream Social Democratic organizations for the opposition: "Whoever distributes propaganda for the separation of working youth places himself outside the working youth."[17]

The Social Democratic Party's Central Office for Working Youths risked implementing national integration in part because it hoped that appeasing the state and the nationalist middle classes would serve its youth organizations. The benefits came, but they were too little too late to pacify the membership exasperated with the paternalism and the support for the war. The Central Office's new access to the interior and war ministers was useful only a few times. When in 1915 police in several cities coerced working male youths to join military companies, and a deputy commanding general threatened to conscript males in the birth cohorts 1896 and 1897 promptly at age 18 if they did not participate in premilitary training, the Central Office appealed to the ministers, who found the objections warranted and intervened on the Party's behalf. But the German chancellor's office's first gesture toward Social Democratic youths in 1914—an edict giving the Socialist youths permission to serve as volunteers in military hospitals—was unexceptional. It was not until September 1916 that Ebert got Prussian authorities to extend price discounts on rail travel to youths in the Social Democratic organizations (youths in the middle-class organizations had enjoyed these breaks since 1911). It also took two and a half years of war for Ebert to get the Prussian House to approve money to help build Social Democratic youth centers. In Württemburg, where Socialist youths almost universally opposed the *Burgfrieden*, and in Bavaria, where few youths were in opposition at all, he had no such success.[18]

On balance, support of Germany's entry into the war, the *Burgfrieden*, and national integration disrupted the Social Democratic youth organizations to the point of dysfunction. Gutting the administration, 1,995 leaders were by March 1915 conscripted, and another 783 had volunteered for the flag. Although many joined because their conscription was imminent and volunteering gave them a choice of regiments, hundreds were following Ludwig Frank in support of Germany and the new Social Democratic policy of national integration. Exacerbating managerial constraints caused by these personnel shortages, Friedrich Ebert and other salaried functionaries were themselves overburdened with war duties and did not attend to the youth organizations diligently. Although Ebert nominally remained the youth organization's chairman, in practice he delegated most administration to his deputies Korn and Schulz, whose paternalism and strident patriotism repelled tens of thousands of members. In addition, personnel shortages prevented the organizations from offering retraining courses to the teenagers who lost their jobs in the consumer industries in August and September 1914. In March 1915, only 229 of the 740 district youth committees responded to the survey sent out by the Central Office; of these, just 35 were offering courses and lectures. By contrast, 128 had had such programs in the previous year. Whereas in 1910 the Social Democratic Party's Central Office distributed 1.2 million leaflets, brochures, and pamphlets, between August 1914 and March 1915 it distributed just eighty-four thousand. Because the military expropriated buildings, and funds were increasingly short, 70 percent of the 391 youth centers *(Jugendheime)* operating before 1914 closed outright by the end of the war. Furthermore, the Social Democratic Party had to accept the Reichstag's abrogation of workplace protections for youths that the party had diligently won and maintained in the previous decades. Even if the resources were available, the youths themselves were not. The new twelve-, fourteen- and in some cases seventeen-hour days of working teenagers after the summer of 1915 left time for smoking and drinking but not for organized recreation.[19]

The only positive development in the Social Democratic youth organizations during the war was the rise in the number of female participants. Before the war they composed just one-fifth of the membership and even less of the leadership; by 1918, half of the members and two-fifths of the leaders were female. The change ushered in more so-called girl evenings and courses for female youths seeking to become Social Democratic Party officials. Unlike the middle-class associations for female youths, which emphasized preparation for marriage and motherhood, the Socialist associations introduced more gender equity during the war. Male and female youths went hiking and socialized together, and the experiences of female youths in the war convinced them that women needed full political and legal equality.[20]

The Protest of Oppositional Socialist Youths

Except for disputes over premilitary training, protest against the war by Social Democratic youths was remarkably muted in the first months of the war. Most followed their leaders in respecting the *Burgfrieden*. They feared arrest for doing otherwise, and like Europeans everywhere, they hoped that the war would be short. A teenager needed immense courage to raise a voice against a war that millions seemed to celebrate and almost no one condemned publicly. Although the German working class on the whole was privately skeptical about the war, the excitement of the mobilization swept up tens of thousands of working-class youths who, like their middle-class counterparts, yearned for adventure and hoped to demonstrate their patriotism and manhood on the front. In Leipzig in August and September 1914, Social Democratic youths heard few protest speeches but witnessed dozens of comrades in their cohort who, against all expectations, volunteered for the colors. The parents of Karl Ottinger, who begged his father for permission to join the nationalist Boy Scouts in August 1914, were among the many members of the Social Democratic Party who had trouble keeping their children away from patriotic middle-class organizations.[21]

After 1914, however, Willi Münzenberg, the 26-year-old budding propagandist and future Communist publishing magnate safe in exile in neutral Switzerland, mobilized opposition to the *Burgfrieden* widely and effectively. The bastard son of an abusive Junker, Münzenberg had honed his resourcefulness after 1905 as a 15-year-old orphan working a dead-end job sorting scrap leather in a shoe factory in Erfurt. As one of the first members of the local Socialist youth group, he developed a talent for recruiting and organizing. In 1908, the 18-year-old grew frustrated with the depoliticization of the youth organizations—in a letter Ebert personally rebuffed his pleas for autonomy. After his boss fired him for protesting Prussia's inequitable three-class voting system, Münzenberg fled to Switzerland and joined a radical Socialist youth organization. At age 22, he was appointed editor of *Freie Jugend,* the Swiss Socialist youth newspaper, and two years later he made the paper financially independent. With signature bombast, he also proclaimed himself in 1914 "National Secretary of the Autonomous Youth Socialist Movement of Switzerland."[22]

From Switzerland, Münzenberg used his organizational skills to foment protest against the war by youths in Germany. After his rallies in Zurich against the Socialist betrayal of antimilitarism and internationalism failed to have any tangible effects, he sent out invitations in December 1914 for a youth conference to be held in Zurich the following Easter. Attended by sixteen delegates from ten countries, including three from Germany, the conference preceded by six months the Zimmerwald Conference that historians often mark as the beginning of the organized international Socialist antiwar movement. (International Socialist women held a secret meeting three weeks prior to the youth conference, but they were acting autonomously without support from their home institutions.) The delegates at the

youth conference represented over thirty thousand dues-paying members
and were able to set up an effective mechanism for distributing antiwar propaganda. The delegates broke with the previous International Socialist Youth
Secretary, Robert Dannenberg, who had hung the sign, "Closed indefinitely
because of the war," on the door to his office in Vienna. In his place they
elected Münzenberg, who bragged that the international Socialist youth
movement, previously "a poorly functioning exchange of letters," had become a real political bureaucracy. His most important activities, which the
conference helped organize, were publishing the oppositional newspaper,
Jugend-Internationale, and overseeing the complex and dangerous operation
of smuggling it into Germany. In September 1915, when the antiwar confer-
ees first met at Zimmerwald, the first issue of *Jugend-Internationale* was already in the hands of German Socialist youths. Young sympathizers in
Germany sent Münzenberg the addresses of recipients in code on postcards
with patriotic raptures on the cards to evade the censors. They also slipped
messages into jars of marmalade and under cigar cases with false bottoms.
Undercover agents hoodwinked Münzenberg by posing as representatives of
German Socialist youth associations and obtaining distribution lists. In this
way German counterintelligence succeeded in identifying hundreds of oppositional Socialist youths, many of whom were arrested or, if they were
male and older than 17, sent to the front. Münzenberg nevertheless managed
to regroup and maintain the integrity of his smuggling operation. *Jugend-
Internationale* lasted longer than any other illegal antiwar newspaper distributed in Germany during the war. Münzenberg's courier services were also
essential to exiles like Lenin for maintaining contact with revolutionary Socialists in Germany, like the Sparticists.[23]

Under Münzenberg's direction, *Jugend-Internationale* aroused interest
among Socialist youths because it was singular in its condemnation of the war
and the *Burgfrieden,* and it urged reviving the autonomy and antimilitarist
activism that the creation of the Central Office had smothered in 1908. With
a brashness unlike anything else available in Germany, the newspaper trashed
military youth companies and mocked the timidity and cowardice of Ebert,
Schulz, and Korn. The new Youth International, the organization run by
Münzenberg in Switzerland, resolved at the April 1915 conference that "war
was the result of the ruling class' imperialist policy in all capitalist countries."
Jugend-Internationale took the position of Lenin, in whose inner circle Münzenberg intimately traveled from February 1916 to April 1917, that youths

should engage in class struggle to foment a proletarian revolution to end the war. *Jugend-Internationale* solicited articles from the most radical antiwar Socialists, including the Germans Liebknecht and Karl Radek, the Ukrainian-born radical expelled from the Social Democratic Party, and the exiled Russians Lenin, Trotsky, and Zinoviev. Münzenberg acknowledged that *Jugend-Internationale* was crass and lacked theoretical sophistication, but the budding propagandist recognized that defaming established authorities and calling for mass action rallied youths bitter about the Social Democratic Party's opposition to antimilitarism and autonomy.[24]

The publishing of *Jugend-Internationale* inspired autochthonous protests. Eyewitnesses reported that in 1915 several hundred working-class youths protested in front of the Reichstag on 28 May and 1 August, and over one thousand youths in Berlin and hundreds in other cities condemned the war publicly on May Day. Rank-and-file Socialists of all ages in Stuttgart were among the earliest vocal opponents of the *Burgfrieden*. In the summer of 1915 their youth organizations declared independence from the Central Office, boycotted *Arbeiter-Jugend*, and publicly demanded an immediate peace. The leadership still committed to the *Burgfrieden* apparently denounced the youths to the police, who made twenty arrests. Nevertheless, in February 1916 the youths published the first issue of their oppositional newspaper, *Morgenrot,* in which they mocked and attacked the Central Office. Socialist youths in Hamburg had traditions of opposing adult authority before 1914 and were among the few Germans anywhere who protested the war on the day the *Burgfrieden* was announced. In 1915 hundreds attended secret open-air meetings disguised as star-gazing events, where they sang the old fight songs and made speeches against the war. In March 1916, they expressed outrage that the adult leadership brooked the military's ban on Münzenberg's "dirty newspaper," *Jugend-Internationale.* Party leaders, disgusted with youths' hostility toward the *Burgfrieden* and concerned that funds could be better spent elsewhere, closed the Socialist youth organization. In the next few weeks more than half of the Socialist youths joined their own autonomous Free Youth Organization of Hamburg and began publishing an oppositional newspaper, *Proletarier-Jugend,* with support from the left radical Ernst Thälmann, the future chairman of the German Communist Party.[25]

By the end of 1915, Socialist youths in German industrial cities were founding networks in opposition to the leadership of the Social Democratic Party. A pamphlet written in Berlin in December 1915, for example, was circulated among Socialist youths in Düsseldorf until the police seized it. It asserted the need for "youth independence from adults" and charged that, because of the demand for passivity, sixty-four district Socialist youth organizations had already seceded from the Central Office. It also criticized the middle-class youth movement for encouraging enthusiasm for premilitary training and the war. This propaganda was having its desired effects. Four months later, the Düsseldorf police seized the transcript of an inflammatory speech addressed to a gathering of left-wing working-class youths angry that the Social Democratic Party had cut off their funding. According to an undercover agent, the youths condemned the Social Democratic Party's calls to hold out for victory. The youths left the hall after the speech singing, "Toward the Red Rising Sun, Comrades in the Fight!" During the meeting they formally seceded from the Central Office, founded the "New Free Youth Movement," raised almost 300 marks, and vilified the *Burgfrieden*.[26]

This agitation culminated in a conference of close to sixty Socialist youths from all over Germany at a vegetarian restaurant in Jena on Easter weekend (21–22 April) 1916. The participants set a conspiratorial tone to the meeting by taking extensive precautions to prevent police surveillance and by sponsoring a keynote address by Karl Liebknecht, now a fugitive. After two days of discussion, the delegates signed a declaration endorsing the program of the Sparticists, who during their first meetings in early 1916 had called upon youths to lead protests and offered financial support. The youths demanded an end to what they felt were a host of repressive state practices: the militarization of factories, the compulsory savings plans, and the ban on youth participation in political organizations under the 1908 Reich Association Law. Drawing on the language of the 1912 Meissner Oath of the middle-class Free German Youth, they proclaimed that youths had to follow "the urge for independence. . . . [and] to find themselves in independent organizations, in order to make their own independent decisions and pursue new goals," such as "fighting for peace." Above all, they resolved to secede formally from the Social Democratic Party's Central Office and to join with Münzenberg's Internationalists to muster antiwar protest. Karl Korn called the Jena conference "grotesquely romantic," but the participants in fact set up an effective practical apparatus to publish and distribute antiwar broadsides and newspapers. They also organized protests for both May Day and International Youth Day in early September. Above all, the solidarity gave the participants the self-confidence to take more radical action.[27]

During the first few days of May 1916, just one week after the Jena conference, oppositional Socialist youths in Hanover and Braunschweig helped defeat the compulsory savings plans in what became the largest wartime strike by youths in Germany, the third largest of any age group in Lower Saxony, and one of the few successful ones in the province. In the memory of the participants, it was the single most important event of the war and the revolution—more important than the 1917 February or October Revolutions in Russia, the general strikes for peace in April 1917 and January 1918, or even the armistice and outbreak of the revolution in November 1918. For adults as well youths in Lower Saxony, it constituted a turning point in the transformation of spontaneous riots over shortages of food and coal into protests with conscious political aims. In subsequent strikes during the war, youths began playing an active organizing role. In the weeks that followed the strike, youths organized a conference in the Lower Rhine district, where they resolved to engage in a broader political movement for their rights. They rejected, for example, the proposed bill to ease restrictions on youth membership in unions because it did not rescind the clauses in the 1908 Reich Association Law that prohibited youths from participating in political meetings.[28]

In Berlin immediately after the strike, oppositional Socialist youths distributed a flurry of incendiary literature that demanded greater independence for youths because the aging Social Democratic Party had sold out the working class to the war and the ruling elites. These youths helped organize sixty thousand Berliners to demonstrate in sympathy for their incarcerated hero Liebknecht on 27 and 28 June 1916 at Potsdamer Platz. In a report they wrote on their actions, they used the old fight language banned for youths by the party since 1908: "We will also show that youth is a factor in the class struggle, one that the general proletarian movement cannot do without." Youths in Berlin also began printing broadsides exhorting soldiers to desert and organizing, albeit with limited financial resources, underground railroads to convey them into Denmark. Despite the police intervention, they staged the first International Youth Day on 2 September 1916, with demonstrations announcing a peace platform.[29]

In 1916 oppositional Socialist youths in Hamburg and Bremen were particularly assertive of their independence. While they supported the peace resolutions of the Jena conference, they refused to ally with any political group, not even the Socialist Youth International. In addition, the events in

Braunschweig were an explicit inspiration to radical leaders like Paul Fröhlich, who organized thousands of youths to protest in marches in May, June, and August, including one during which two thousand participants shouted, "Down with the War!" This action drove the deputy commanding general to dissolve their organization and threaten the members with prison and stiff fines. The Social Democratic Party and unions in Hamburg strongly encouraged parents to keep their children away from these radicals. Nevertheless, in December 1916, four to five hundred youths gathered for a secret protest organized by word of mouth.[30]

In November and December 1916 in Essen, where the Socialist youth movement had been quiet since the outbreak of the war, the police observed that "radical elements" had become active and aimed to attract three-fourths of all local Socialist youth groups into their camp. One 16-year-old was caught in January 1917 distributing twenty-five copies of *Freie Jugend*, the voice of the antiwar Free Youth Movement in the province of Hanover. This issue, produced on a typewriter, included Liebknecht's "treasonous" slogan, "Down with the War, Down with the Government." One section of the paper was devoted to describing gatherings of youths for hikes in the countryside near Remschied. On their return on the railroads, the young workers sang Socialist songs and hailed Liebknecht to the disturbance of the other passengers.[31]

The extreme deprivation during the Turnip Winter of 1916–1917 hampered antiwar agitation, but conferences in Hanover and Stuttgart during Easter weekend 1917 allowed oppositional youths to regroup. In Halle on May Day 1917, the "Free Socialist Youth" organized an illegal demonstration, with seven hundred youths waving red flags, carrying torches, and singing the *Internationale*. In the memory of one participant, it was "our proudest day during the war." In Dresden on May Day, five to six hundred youths marched through the street and sang the *Internationale*. According to *Jugend-Internationale*, "hired henchmen" shouted at them to stop and disperse, and the police made twenty arrests. The other youths came to the rescue, storming the police building, climbing through the windows, and screaming, "Out with our brothers and sisters!" The police apparently gave in, and the previously arrested youths marched away singing the *Internationale*, saluting Liebknecht, and chanting "Down with Militarism!" Another conference held in Halle in early July 1917 founded an organization code-named the "Cobbler Center" *(Schusterzentrale)* to prepare Germans for mass strikes to end the war. In Hamburg in August 1917 youths announced a mass protest on broadsides posted in almost every city district; the young organizers succeeded in attracting several thousand protesters, whom they led in a parade to a pavilion on the Alster frequented by "war profiteers," pelted it with rocks, and chanted "Against war! For Freedom!" The protest was one of the largest antiwar demonstrations to that time in Hamburg among Germans of any age. Police in Leipzig and Dresden reported that youths were *the* vanguard of the antiwar movement during the mass political strikes of April 1917.[32]

The obstacles to maintaining this kind of protest were enormous. On the one hand, the ten to twelve hours daily of factory work limited time and energy for activism. On the other hand, the police and the army increasingly sabotaged the underground organizations. Except for *Jugend-Internationale,* none of the half-dozen oppositional newspapers founded in 1916 managed to publish more than a few issues before police shut down their operations, arrested the editors, and meted out prison sentences. Furthermore, the army promptly conscripted the most spirited antiwar male youth leaders when they turned 18. Police in all the German states stepped up their surveillance of oppositional Socialist youths following the Jena conference. Arrests and prison sentences were relatively easy to undertake. Just owning copies of *Jugend-Internationale* was deemed a crime. Aiding the police were bitter Majority Social Democratic Party leaders who denounced oppositional youths to the authorities. By the summer of 1917, the military and the police gained the upper hand. A police report in Hamburg in January 1918 claimed that "one can no longer talk of a self-contained radical youth opposition."[33]

In the last eighteen months of the war, however, working Germans of all ages joined in protest actions. In April 1917 they staged the war's first mass political strikes, demanding an immediate peace without annexations, an end to marshal law and forced labor, reinstatement of the right of association, release of political prisoners, and election reform, including eliminating the three-class voting system. The military took over the factories and incarcerated the strike leaders. The unions and both the Majority and Independent Social Democratic Parties were reluctant to support the strikers in subsequent actions, but shopfloor stewards in Berlin and grassroots labor leaders in other cities organized the great 1918 January strike for the same political demands. Newspaper and police reports estimated that close to half of the seven hundred thousand participants in Berlin were women or youths. Furthermore, of the hundred and fifty strikers arrested by the Berlin police, twenty-eight were youths under 18 years old. A consequence of the much larger protest movement was that Socialist youths no longer needed their own separate organizations to express dissent. Nevertheless, thousands of oppositional Socialist youths in Hamburg, Berlin, and Stuttgart continued to meet illicitly on hikes over the course of 1918. In May 1918, for example, over two thousand gathered in the woods outside Berlin to celebrate Karl Marx's 100th birthday and chant "Let's do it like Russians! Down with the war! Long live the revolution!"[34]

As many as one-half of Socialist youths never joined this opposition. In Frankfurt a.M., for example, only a minority of Socialist youth organizations ever allied with the Internationalists. In Bavaria, radical Socialists were not active at all among working-class teenagers. Tens of thousands of working and nonworking youths participated in informal modes of resistance to the war. Some boys of conscriptable age obtained and spread knowledge about how doctors could declare them unfit for military service. The quadrupling of crimes by youths against the state and the public order also suggests an implicit protest against the war. But it remains sadly true that the vast majority of German teenagers either shunned politics or participated in the nationalist popular mobilization.[35]

Still, Münzenberg and other left Socialists radicalized a core of German youths by transforming opposition to the war and long-term yearnings for independence into support for class struggle and illicit action. Such actions included harboring fugitives like Liebknecht, aiding military deserters, holding secret meetings, singing banned fight songs, making inflammatory speeches, evading police surveillance, and distributing antiwar propaganda. They established that youths would not only have a central role in future radical-left politics but would also use conspiratorial means to achieve their goals, if necessary. The vigor with which these youths embraced radical left politics after 1918 stemmed in part from their claim to moral authority in having righteously opposed the war. They condemned those who had condoned the disaster that resulted in the deaths and impoverishment of millions. Because they felt the leaders of the Weimar Republic had been complicit in the *Burgfrieden,* they could categorically reject the new political order. Although their numbers were small, they constituted an ardent core of the left wing that polarized German politics after 1918.

Demonstrationsstreik

Um des schnöden Geldsacksmillen ist die Welt in ein schauriges Blutbad verwandelt worden. Unter dem trügerischen Schein der Vaterlandsverteidigung werden seit drei Jahren Väter und Brüder zur Schlachtbank geschleppt. Unter Entbehrungen, Not und Leid müssen sie für ein mörderisches Pharisäertum gegen ihre eigenen Interessen Blut vergießen. Während das arbeitende Volk dem Hungertode nahe, feiern die herrschenden hinter den Kulissen bei festlichem Gelage den profitbringenden Massenmord. Der Drang nach Frieden, die Empörung, der Schrei nach Freiheit und Brot wird von den Regierenden nur mit einem heuchlerischen Wortschwall erwidert. Aber, das nicht um endlich einmal dem Wahnsinn ein Ende zu bereiten, sondern nur um das Volk zu beruhigen, es für das im kapitalistischen Interesse liegende Durchhalten gefügig zu machen

——— in ganz Deutschland ———

Aber nicht von den Besitzenden, sondern von dem Willen des Volkes hängt es ab, die schreckliche Kriegsfurie zu ersticken. Der Zorn über die Millionen bereits Gefallener und verkrüppelter Mitmenschen, muß den Krieg gegen unsere eigenen Volksmörder und Verräter entfachen und die Brandfackel in das tyrannische Gebäude brutaler Willkür und Unterjochung zündend werfen. Zu lange schon, Arbeitsschwestern und -brüder, haben wir unter Murren und Jammern die blutigen Fesseln getragen. Drei Jahre hindurch hat man mit kostbarem Menschengut gespielt, in der unverantwortlichsten Weise Frauen und Kinder zu Witwen und Waisen gemacht. Wo ist dann die deutsche Freiheit, für die sorgenvolle Mütter ihre Söhne opfern müssen? Zeigt sie sich darin, daß jede freie Meinung unterdrückt, daß Volksvertreter, wie Liebknecht, und andere für viele Jahre ins Zuchthaus wandern müssen, daß selbst Frauen, wie es in Düsseldorf geschah, bis zu sechs Jahren Zuchthaus verurteilt, oder auch daß willensfeste jugendliche Arbeiter, wegen sozialistischer Gesinnung und Betätigung in Fürsorgeanstalten gesteckt werden? Der Belagerungszustand ist eine Galgenstätte deutscher Freiheit!

Am 2. und 3. September ruft die sozialistische Jugend aller Länder ihre Klassengenossen zu gewaltsamen Kundgebungen gegen das herrschende System infamer Entrechtung und schmachvoller Unterdrückung auf.

Ob alt, ob jung! Männer, Frauen und Mädchen! Es gilt die Tat!

Der internationale Jugendtag muß ein gewaltiger Ansturm des revolutionären Arbeiterheeres, des jungen Proletariats, gegen die bestehende kapitalistische Gesellschaft, die einzig und allein die Millionen grausam Gemordeten zu verantworten hat, sein! Erst der Massenkampf des internationalen Proletariats wird Freiheit und dauernden Frieden bringen!

Jeder agitiere dafür, daß am 2. und 3. September alle Betriebe ruhen und die streikende Arbeiterschaft sich zu Demonstrationsveranstaltungen versammelt!

gegen den Krieg, am 2. und 3. September 1917

An euch Arbeitsbrüder im bunten Rock! ergeht der Mahnruf:

„Wenn sich das bis zur Verzweiflung getriebene Volk nun endlich einmal zur revolutionären Tat aufrafft, den Vernichtungskampf wagt, unerschüttert das Banner der Revolution entfacht, dann kämpft mit uns! Widerhandelt den Befehlen! Schießt nicht auf Vater und Mutter! auf mutige Kämpfer für die Sache des internationalen Proletariats, die auch die eure ist! Werdet selbst Soldaten der Revolution!

Druck und Verlag Union-Druckerei, Zürich.   Die sozialistische Jugendbewegung Deutschlands.

Faksimile 25.

Broadside announcing illegal antiwar strike organized by oppositional Socialist youth. *Source:* Wolfgang Breithaupt, *Volksvergiftung 1914–1918* (Leipzig: K. F. Koehler, 1925), plate 25.

The Polarization of the Middle-Class Youth Movement

The middle-class youth movement offers an especially vivid narrative of conflict and political polarization because the members published their views copiously in their journals. The youth authors became embroiled over control of the leadership. Female youths took over most of the positions, and defending their new status robustly, they irritated conscripted former Wandervögel. These young soldiers were also infuriated by those under 18 years old who rejected their leadership, and the youth movement revisited its old conflict over the age of members. The authors lastly fought over war aims, which polarized the movement between a racist, radical nationalist camp of young soldiers who wanted annexations through a military victory, and a small group of youths on the home front who condemned the war.

The war at first halted most normal activity in the Wandervogel because it seemed inappropriate to hike aimlessly through the countryside while older members risked their lives on the front. Taking a cue from their mentors Wyneken and Foerster, who despite their pacifism at first greeted the war positively for its possibilities for social reform, the youths embraced the idea that war purified the mind, rejuvenated the soul, cultivated noble idealism, and destroyed crass materialism. This support for the war contrasted to their position before 1914, when they were hesitant to declare their love for Germany because such expressions flirted with the political concerns of adults. Patriotism had been dormant, however, in their visits to historical battlefields, predilection for German folk culture, unreflective acceptance of the monarchy in rituals like the celebration of the Kaiser's birthday, participation in the war games sponsored by the Young Germany League, and love for national songs from the Thirty Years War and the wars of liberation. Imbued with heroic war literature and the myth of the war experience in the secondary schools, most male Wandervögel saw the war as a great adventure and spectacular exploration of their ethos. They were among the most spirited participants in the victory celebrations of August 1914. Almost every eligible male in the Wandervogel and a good number in the Free German Youth volunteered for the army in the fall of 1914. Those female and younger male youths who remained on the home front enthusiastically did voluntary patriotic service like working in hospitals, bringing in harvests, knitting items for soldiers, caring for small children, helping in collection drives, tending victory gardens, and preparing packages to send to soldier. The first war issue of

Wandervogel, in October 1914, declared that "for us Wandervögel, there is only one single thought: in magnificence and fortune, in death and distress, only you, Fatherland." It also published letters affirming the patriotism of the members. The introduction to the 1915 edition of the Wandervogel song book declared: "The Wandervögel have embraced war, which has freed the profound national idea from everything else and made it central for us. We have to become more German than ever." Editors of their journals *Wandervogel, Führerzeitung,* and *Freideutsche Jugend* excised foreign words.[36]

The rush to join the army by male Wandervögel meant that activity resumed at the end of 1914 only because female members stepped in and ran the organizations. Although most Wandervogel branches accepted girls before the war, the male leadership had generally given them little voice. During the war, however, female Wandervögel boldly asserted their right and need to participate in youth-led hikes, campfires, and "nest" evenings. The new female leaders also proved adept at reviving dormant groups and even increasing membership in 1916 in some regions over prewar levels. Girls took over the editorships of *Wandervogel* and published an issue every month after January 1915 until the end of the war. They argued that they needed to hike to develop their bodies and purify their souls in order to be future companions of Wandervogel men (they never went so far as to reject their future roles as mothers and wives). By 1916, older girls were leading hiking groups of mixed sexes. Such commingling had been uncommon before the war, and the new practice alarmed the Bavarian education minister, who banned it. The new power of female youths also provoked soldiers and male members on the home front. Some angrily demanded that the girls step down from the leadership and threatened, "if this doesn't happen peacefully, then bring on the weapons!" But no matter how much the boys complained, one female author maintained, the girls were going to run the Wandervogel during the war if it was to survive.[37]

The war also empowered male youths too young to be conscripted and ignited generational conflict. In some groups, 15- and 16-year-olds replaced the older secondary school boys and university students who had been the leaders but were now in the army. Groups began to admit 12- and 13-year-old elementary school boys to fill their depleted ranks. This new youthfulness changed the dynamics within the organizations. Memoirs attested that the youngest members felt more independence and were more loyal to the younger leaders. In contrast to the prewar period, "no mentor, like an older university student or teacher, dampened the joy of coming together." In leaflets, articles, and letters to the editors, younger Wandervögel attacked the influence of older members who, according to one author, had introduced the "un-German materialism and shallowness of the last decades." Most of these older members—"old" here meant over 18, or over 20, depending on the author—were front soldiers, who fulminated against an ungrateful home front for driving them out of their beloved organization. The younger members' stance against them was far from universal; many Wandervogel groups welcomed soldiers on leave to their "nest" evenings. Furthermore, the basic shape of this conflict—between the older generation who wanted to maintain membership in the Wandervogel into their 20s and the younger generation who wanted to take control—preceded the war. But the war exacerbated it, charged it emotionally, and linked it to national defense. The petty turf battles of the teenagers at home outraged the soldier Wandervögel, but from the front they were powerless to stop the younger generation.[38]

The problems posed by military training especially aggravated the conflict between members serving or wanting to serve in the army and the rest who remained loyal to the principle of independence and "self-education." Before the war both the Wandervogel and the Free German Youth were leery of state influence on their associations. This position contrasted with that of groups like the German Boy Scouts, which organized their activities around military hierarchy and discipline. Wandervogel groups did join the Young Germany League, but the League in practice merely doled out funds and organized large athletic competitions. It exerted no sway over the internal activities or organizational structure of Wandervogel groups. The military youth companies were, by contrast, believed to be far more of an intrusion by the state. Led mostly by retired officers for four hours weekly, the companies placed the participants under military discipline and hierarchy in drills and marches. This practice challenged the principle of self-determination so central to the youth movement. As patriotic secondary school boys, most male Wandervögel recognized their duty to defend Germany and participated enthusiastically in public military youth companies, many until the end of the war. Others rejected the public companies and, in order to have some degree of self-determination, formed their own, exclusive ones. Pointing out that Wandervogel boys usually won athletic competitions, still others claimed that hiking was a form of premilitary training. As a matter of principle, the Free German Youth lobbied vehemently against the War Ministry's 1916 plans to make participation in military youth companies compulsory (the plans were never carried out). By 1917, most members of the Free German Youth began to inveigh against military training of youth. Their argument, printed in *Freideutsche Jugend*, was that it treated youths "like a blind mass." This mobilization against the bill, which also ensued in the pages of the journal *Wandervogel*, baptized the members of the youth movement in national politics. It also hardened differences between the members on the home front who were forming a nascent antiwar movement and those members, particularly those serving on the front, who believed male youths had a duty to risk their lives for Germany.[39]

These developments—girls taking over leadership positions, younger members excluding older soldiers, and Free German Youth opposing military training—incited a group of more nationalist members to break further with the tradition of apoliticism. These youths, soldier Wandervögel and their sympathizers, made public demands for a military policy of annexations and a domestic policy of racial purity. Before the war, only a handful in the youth movement had advocated anti-Semitism and territorial expansion, as most believed that such national and international politics were the vile affairs of adults. By 1916, however, approximately a third took the extreme nationalist political position in favor of annexations, according to one historian's estimate. Furthermore, a set of more vocal proponents, including Otger Gräff and Dankwart Gerlach, broke with the tradition of political quietism. Through their organizations, the Greifenbund and the Young German League (*Jungdeutscher Bund*, not to be confused with the *Jungdeutschlandbund*, the Young Germany League), they popularized racist emblems like the swastika and terms like *Aryan* and *Volksgemeinschaft* (racial community). Anticapitalist and anti-Christian, they called for financial and agricultural reform. They imagined creating "settlements," rural communities of youth movement members. At first, these nationalist youths in the Greifenbund and the Young German League professed they were apolitical, but by July 1918 they shed all veils in a broadside that endorsed the creation of a *Volksgemeinschaft* through colonies in the Eastern occupied areas, an expansion of the German Empire, conscription of all men into the army, and a Socialist economic system that maintained private property. They claimed that their views were similar to those of the Social Democratic Party except that they supported an aggressive foreign policy and rejected Marxist historical materialism. The parties closest to their views, they asserted, were the Fatherland Party and a (not-yet-founded)

"German National People's Party." Few of these so-called *völkisch* (racial and nationalist) youths joined the Nazi Party until much later during the Weimar Republic, but their platforms had an uncanny similarity to its creeds.[40]

Opposing this large *völkisch* wing were Hodann and his Central Working Group for the Youth Movement, the smaller rival to the oppositional Socialist youths undertaking peace activism. The Central Working Group had support from middle-class pacifists like Ludwig Quidde, the right-wing Social Democrat Eduard Bernstein, the publicist and former Progressive *(Nationalsozialer Verein)* Reichstag delegate Helmuth von Gerlach, and the long-time peace activist and editor Minna Cauer. It aimed to bring the working-class and the middle-class youth movements together. In the fall of 1914, it opened a center in Berlin and published critiques of the proposals to make military training of male youth compulsory. But unwilling to risk imprisonment for violating the *Burgfrieden,* its members did not distribute antiwar propaganda like the oppositional Socialist youths.[41]

Although its left wing was not especially radical during the war, the middle-class youth movement became politicized as a whole. As one author argued, in 1913 it had transformed as a result of the Meißner Oath from hiking groups into a movement with a cultural mission; during the war, it entered a third stage, ending its insularity and taking on political goals. Bearing out this observation, approximately two-thirds of the articles in *Freideutsche Jugend* during the war were political, according to one member's judgment. Furthermore, at the Easter 1918 meeting, representatives of the umbrella organization Wandervogel agreed with the Free German Youth that they needed to emerge from their isolated communities and engage in public life. Numerous authors in *Freideutsche Jugend*, like those on the right, argued that for a rebirth of Germany, youths needed to energize politics. Their suggestions for accomplishing this rejuvenation were vague and utopian. Most wanted a *Volksgemeinschaft,* though without the racist and nationalist elements of those in the Greifenbund and Young German League. Some proposed making the youth movement a substitute for parliament and political parties. Others advocated creating settlement or education communities composed of youths who would sponsor political lectures, magazine articles, discussion evenings, and letter exchanges. Still others wanted to found youth consumer cooperatives to solve the problems of capitalism. Those following Hodann even argued for making contact with the Social Democratic Party and ending aristocratic privilege and the three-class voting system. The Free German Youth shared this nebulous utopian socialism with the *völkisch* nationalists, but they clashed over their position on the war. As early as 1915, the Free German Youth issued implicit condemnations of the war in its journals, but the censor prevented them from publishing articles in outright opposition.[42]

The growing polarization alarmed Knud Ahlborn, the editor of *Freideutsche Jugend*. He tried to maintain the prewar apoliticism of the Free German Youth, and until November 1918 he followed "a program of not having a program" and a policy "of not having goals," but the authors in his and other journals became politically assertive nonetheless. In the summer of 1915, the future belletrist Walter Benjamin and others founded a new journal, *Aufbruch*, that reached out to oppositional Socialist youths and made veiled criticisms of the war. In 1916, they reproduced the slogan, "Let the ruling classes tremble before the youth revolution. . . . Youths of all classes, unite!" By the fourth issue, the censors shut down *Aufbruch*. Against Ahlborn's advice, the Free German Youth delegates at the Göttingen meeting in 1916 agreed to support Friedrich Wilhelm Foerster, whose faculty in Munich censored him for signing the letter condemning war pedagogy and speaking out openly against the war. At another meeting in the fall of 1917, almost all the delegates were infuriated by a nationalist lecture on the "soul of the German people." They subsequently endorsed the Reichstag Peace Resolution of July 1917, announced their sympathy with the February Revolution in Russia, welcomed the pacifist Gustav Wyneken back into the organization, and agreed to combat chauvinism and "such catastrophes as we are today experiencing." Although Ahlborn realized that the Free German Youth held "a passionate creed against the war as mass murder," he feared the censor and insisted that they express their views only orally. In the summer of 1918, Alfred Kurella, the leader of the so-called Berlin Circle and future founding director of the Communist Youth International, nonetheless attacked the *völkisch* nationalists in the youth movement for their "groundless war enthusiasm" and their valuing of war in itself. All this inflammatory content provoked counterattacks from the right wing in the Wandervogel and the Greifenbund.[43]

After 1915 the longing for a peace that was immediate *and* gave Germans something for their sacrifice posed a dilemma that made Germans of all ages ambivalent about continuing the war. Most people accordingly fell somewhere in the middle of the spectrum between prowar and antiwar positions. However, significant numbers increasingly took harder lines, and by the summer of 1917 Germany became polarized politically, dividing between those who wanted a negotiated, immediate peace and those who wanted to continue the war until a final military victory.

This polarization characterized much of German youth culture as well. It manifested itself within the context of the deteriorating patriotic mobilization, on the one hand, and the decline of adult authority, on the other. Middle-class youths, especially males in secondary schools, hoped for the military victory that their teachers told them was the only possible kind of peace, and they tended to devote themselves assiduously to the war effort until the end of the war. By contrast, working youths increasingly turned against the war and, in a behavior that suggested disdain for patriotic sacrifice, spent their adult wages on consumer pleasures like tobacco, alcohol, and the cinema. At the same time, oppositional Socialist youths revived the tradition of rebuffing adult authority and engaged in vibrant, illegal political protest against the war. Their activities in 1915 and 1916 contributed to the split of the Social Democratic Party in 1917 and helped inspire the mass strikes for peace in April 1917 and January 1918. In quarrels over policy, the middle-class Wandervogel and the Free German Youth also became polarized. The disputes were on the one hand an intensification of issues that predated the war, such as whether girls could lead and whether the younger youths should exclude the older youths. On the other hand, members broke with prewar traditions of shunning high politics, and the movement divided between those who supported peace and later became Communists and those who supported war and later joined fascist paramilitary groups.

Conclusion

The First World War was a catalyst of jingoism, progressive reform, and conspiratorial agitation, an upheaval that not only mobilized millions of young people to more zealous devotion to Germany but also undermined old authoritarian relationships and spurred thousands to foment proletarian revolution. Before 1914 moderate nationalism and militarism had penetrated some schools, youth literature, and recreational organizations, but after the outbreak of the war chauvinist discourses became more brash and pervasive. In the prewar period, reformers and state officials assiduously built institutions such as the postelementary continuation schools and the offices of the district youth worker to exert more control over youths. In 1914 and 1915 the military youth companies, war bond drives, recycling brigades, and knitting hours in some ways expanded this apparatus. But in other ways these institutions gave youths more independence. War pedagogy early in the war substantially loosened authoritarian relationships in schools. Then, after 1915, both schooling and other youth institutions broke down as a result of mass conscription, the British blockade, and the resulting starvation and personnel shortages. Despite the militarization of society, paternal authority over youths declined. In a climate now more conducive to challenging adult authority, thousands of left-wing youths angry about the abandonment of antimilitarism organized spirited opposition to the war, the government, and the Majority Social Democratic Party. Many more youths, particularly those from middle-class families, remained fiercely committed to the war and internalized the violence and nationalism prominent in school and popular literature.

All the belligerents introduced new curricula based on the war to various extents, but Germany stood out for having pupils read that a nation's right to be a world power justified making war and for implementing methods that softened a previously authoritarian teacher-pupil relationship. Because it had by far the largest network of youth associations, and its fifty thousand state-paid youth workers had no equivalent, Germany was also able to mobilize young persons' voluntary labor more widely than the other belligerents. Even though the military training of male youth faltered after 1915, none of the Allies came close to mustering the resources for it that Germany did. Mass conscription undermined adult authority everywhere, but it caused particular problems in Germany because three times as many of its teachers were male. Above all, only in Central and Eastern Europe did the absence of police, teachers, judges, and fathers coincide with terrible deprivation that forced young people to steal in order to survive.

This history of youth in the First World War challenges interpretations that emphasize continuity in early twentieth-century Germany. The cohort born from 1900 to 1908 indisputably had a youth and childhood fundamentally different than those just a few years older. The rapid pace of change and the consequent sharp differentiation of experience by age led many to become conscious of belonging to a war youth generation, distinct from the better known and more visible front generation of war veterans. Of course, real conditions after 1918, notably the high unemployment suffered by young men and women, also roused this consciousness. Identity with a unified national war youth generation was ultimately an imagination and a social construct. The war experience of boys and girls born from 1900 to 1908 varied too much according to geography, religion, age, gender, social class, political persuasion, and particular family situation to create memories that could make a single generational consciousness possible. Nevertheless, as the sociologist Karl Mannheim argued in his seminal 1928 essay on generational formation, the breakdown of the old social order during the First World War and the differing experiences in this process according to age was a precondition for the generational consciousnesses within specific milieus. For example, before and during the war, novels and plays by young German-speaking authors highlighted the conflict between fathers and sons. After 1918, this literary theme grew more pronounced in a narrative of how the fathers lost the war and left their sons a sick nation, despite the sons' best efforts on the home front. Within the middle-class women's movement, those born after 1900 doubted the benefits of political emancipation and united in opposition to older women who had claimed that equality justified women's newly won political rights. Above all, both the Nazi and Communist parties endorsed generational revolt as a tactic to mobilize those born after 1900.[1]

The Erosion of Adult Authority

My analysis of German education from 1900 to 1918 suggests that the German Empire had more potential to break the severity of schooling than most historians have assumed. Before the war teachers and pedagogical theorists presented numerous proposals for school reform, but they had little success introducing softer teaching methods and eliminating the inequality in the education system. The outbreak of the war then ushered in a new era of putting reform teaching methods into practice more widely and vigorously. Scholars have generally claimed that these reforms were a result of the 1918/19 Revolution, but an equally important stimulus was the perceived spirit of unity at the outbreak of the war. From August to November 1914, officials in Germany's school administrations relaxed their demands for adherence to strict methods and prescribed lesson plans and allowed teachers to experiment with creative practices such as having pupils write free compositions about the war and select articles and poems from newspapers about combat for their reading assignments. The officials agreed with teachers that these practices, which the press called war pedagogy, would effectively mobilize pupils for the war by making the battlefront and the perceived national unity more immediate and exciting. Contrary to historians' claims that educators were mere tools of the authoritarian state, teachers generally undertook war pedagogy willingly, with minimal goading from administrators. The militarism and nationalism of German school curricula became more strident and pervasive precisely because schoolteachers themselves took advantage of the opportunities opened by their patriotism to dismantle the old authoritarian approaches to education.

War pedagogy also empowered elementary school teachers in their attack on the inequity in their profession. They now demanded with ever greater conviction that the government allow them to attend university, eliminate the elitist clerical school inspectors, and advance pupils into secondary schools on merit, not ability to pay. Because they felt indebted to the working classes for their support of the war and recognized that the war had revealed a dearth of talent among government officials, even some conservative-minded teachers in Germany's exclusive secondary schools were hard pressed to find counter-arguments that such reforms were fair and necessary. Discussion of reform did not wane after 1916, despite the hunger, overburdening, and millions of casualties. Both the personnel to run schools and the coal to heat them dwindled, making it impossible to maintain regular instruction, let alone carry out further progressive change. But the liberal and conservative press recognized the work that teachers did to persuade their pupils to hold out for victory. Few teachers liked the war after 1915, but most hoped desperately for a victory. Just a handful ever publicly opposed it in part because they assumed that their commitment and sacrifice for Germany would justify reforms during peacetime. This was especially true after the chancellor in 1917 called a government conference, which convened in 1920, on how to reform the education system after the war.

The immediate legacy of the war for German elementary school education was to make it less controversial to experiment with child-centered methods that respected the pupil's individuality and mitigated the teacher's authority. After the unexpected and disastrous defeat, elementary school teachers seemed to forget their experiments with nationalist mobilization under war pedagogy, but they did adapt the reform spirit of August 1914 to an era of relative peace under the liberal laws of the Weimar Republic. Thousands were able to open new schools that eschewed the strict drill method, forbade insulting and beating pupils, fostered candid dialogue in the classroom, worked closely with parents and communities, and reduced the distance between teachers and pupils through field trips and festivities. In the 1919 elections, Protestant elementary school teachers voted overwhelmingly for the German Democratic Party, led by former members of the Progressive Party who signed the July 1917 Reichstag Peace Resolution and had long supported educational reform. Their representatives in the Weimar Assembly succeeded in inserting many favorable articles into the constitution, including making teaching a subject at the universities, requiring school inspectors to be teachers themselves, and guaranteeing that admission to secondary school be based on talent and motivation. In early 1920, many believed that, despite the lost war, the *Burgfrieden* had paid social and political dividends.[2]

At the 1920 conference, however, secondary school teachers ridiculed the elementary school teachers' call to reform the *Gymnasien* and *Oberrealschulen*. The delegates quarreled about religious instruction, and their disagreements

ultimately thwarted any broad consensus. Almost everyone declared the conference a failure. In the subsequent years, few secondary schools altered their
staid curriculum and methods, and in small towns and rural areas of Prussia,
many elementary school teachers remained unreceptive to the new pedagogy.
In practice, the Weimar Republic lacked the money to finance advancement
into secondary schools based on merit. The lack of progress beyond the initial
year of the Republic coincided with a surplus of teachers who could not find
employment in the mid-1920s, further discrediting the new political system.
The 1929 Wall Street crash exacerbated these problems and moved tens of
thousands of teachers to join the Nazi Party. Unlike many progressive schoolteachers, the Nazis did not forget the Spirit of 1914 and paid homage to the
work of teachers who had mobilized pupils for the war. War pedagogy was
their model when they introduced a far more nationalist curriculum and loosened authoritarian pedagogical practices by empowering pupils to challenge
their teachers through the Hitler Youth and the threat of denunciation.[3]

The war undermined adult authority over youths in areas beyond education, too. Of course, the surge of patriotism in August 1914 seemed to actual-
ize the goals of the 1911 Prussian *Jugendpflege* Edict, which financed patriotic, sport, and confessional associations and tried to lure working youths
away from the Social Democratic organizations. Hundreds of thousands of
working youths previously susceptible to Socialism joined the military youth
companies and volunteered in the harvest brigades. But authority over youths
eroded as the army conscripted 13 million men. Four to six million fathers
were gone, and the continuation schools founded before 1914 to control
working youths crumbled. Male youths earning high wages indulged in commercial pleasures like tobacco, cinemas, and penny dreadfuls, which continuation schools and recreational associations had aimed to contain. With police
understaffed and courts overburdened, boys and girls—like the urban populations more generally—easily refused to obey regulations like food rationing
that would have starved them. Teachers, police, reformers, and youth workers
all complained that, even though most youths remained patriotic and well-
behaved, growing ranks of them rejected the laws of the state and, according
to social workers, had become juvenile delinquents *(Verwahrloste)*. In order to
survive the awful deprivation after 1916, teenagers and even 11- and
12-year-olds formed criminal gangs to steal food and coal—most German
cities had had little youth gang activity of this kind before 1914. Criminal
convictions of youths skyrocketed. Even the behavior of those youths still

committed to the war became rougher, particularly in war games that disregarded middle-class decorum.

Many in this cohort carried over this disrespect for authority into the postwar period. For example, during the revolution, 16-year-old boys in a Munich
Gymnasium formed their own "pupil's council," which declared among other
things that schoolboys no longer had to salute their teachers. A coterie of
working male youths maintained their antiauthoritarian gangs—so-called
wild cliques—to survive the economic problems that were particularly harsh
for young people after the war. During the British blockade that lasted until
the summer of 1919, millions of working youths had to give up their jobs for
the demobilized soldiers. Exacerbating their unemployment was their numbers. Youths born from 1900 to 1914 made up the largest birth cohort in
Germany, and they competed viciously for jobs in an economy that never fully
recovered. From 1890 to 1914, teenagers enjoyed full employment in a buoy-
ant job market, and after Germany recovered in 1915 from the short economic contraction following the declaration of war, their labor became so
valuable that their wages rose relative to those of adults. Compulsory savings
plans in cities like Berlin restrained their spending power, but in other places
they displayed their new economic status through conspicuous consumption
on the street and in the pubs, cinemas, and tobacco shops. But after the war,
the cohort born after 1900 did not enjoy full employment for almost two decades, let alone maintain the high status they achieved in the war as primary
bread earners in their families. Compounding their frustration, the moderate
political parties ignored their plight, and members of the wild cliques frequently crossed over into Communist fighting organizations. Tens of thousands of youths continued their disrespect for adult and government authority
into the postwar period, and their presence on the street highlighted the
Republic's failure in the realm of law and order.[4]

The disrespect for authority was no less prominent among middle-class
male youths. Feeling disenfranchised and alienated by the lost war, tens of
thousands joined autonomous organizations, so-called *Bünde*, that admitted
no adults, rejected the democratic politics of the new Republic, and required
members to respect the group's discipline and hierarchy. Most of the *Bünde*
also demanded that their members place loyalty to the group above family,
professional, and civic obligations, challenging the traditional basic sources of
authority in parents, employers, and the state. In addition, tens of thousands
of patriotic youths joined counterrevolutionary paramilitaries that challenged

the new Republic with guns. Politics in Germany was volatile before 1914, but even the radical right had then accepted constitutional procedure, the rule of law, and the necessity of adjudicating conflict through debate, persuasion, and negotiation. Many middle-class male youths now rejected the authority of the state, followed only their charismatic *Freikorps* commanders under the *Führerprinzip* (leadership principle), and carried out politics through assassinations and aggressive displays of military power.[5]

Strenuous Masculinity and the Contradictions in Femininity

Strenuous masculinity—the ideal of toughness, risk-taking, soldiering, action, and youthful vigor—was a limited model of manhood before 1914, when the prevailing view was that manliness involved emotional self-control, years of wisdom, and the calming demeanor necessary to support a family. In prewar Germany, service in the military commanded immense prestige in both professional life and the marriage market. However, women liked military men not so much for their bravado than for their cleanliness, handiness, thriftiness, respectfulness and cheerfulness—all the virtues that made for a good husband. Even the duel, often seen as the supreme expression of strenuous masculinity, was—with the exception of competitions among university students—almost always fought to preserve the dignity of a woman. William Gurlitt, author of the influential 1907 prescriptive tract, *Erziehung zur Mannhaftigkeit (Education in Manliness)*, argued that boys became men by striving for "truthfulness, courage, endurance, fidelity, and nobility." Writers in the pedagogical press generally agreed that masculinity required firmness, not brutality or toughness. Furthermore, even if working-class men had a penchant for bravado, brawling, and heavy drinking, a genteel masculine respectability tied to moderation and support of the family was preached by the Social Democratic Party and gained favor in the decade before 1914. Men in the labor movement rejected the association of masculinity with imperialism, and the antimilitarism of the Social Democrats meant that soldiering for the nation was for them insipidly bourgeois. Those members of the Social Democratic Party like Karl Liebknecht who called for more radical action, such as a general strike to bring about a revolution, even if it resulted in violence, were a minority.[6]

For hundreds of thousands of male youths across the political spectrum, however, the war encouraged and legitimated strenuous masculinity. Under the *Burgfrieden,* the government censored the most trenchant criticisms of German militarism, and even certain Socialist circles supported military youth training. The glorification in youth literature and educational curricula of fantastically brave soldiers in a frenetic war of movement undermined any expectations that manhood required reason, self-restraint, and support of family. In addition, the loosening restrictions on belligerent expressions in school and the nationalist imperative of war pedagogy and military youth companies encouraged boys to embrace militarist violence and extreme na-tionalism. The future role that young men were expected to play as soldiers defending the nation, and their consequent rising status on the home front, further reinforced the ideal of strenuous masculinity. The highest masculine ideal was to not be afraid of "dying on the altar of the Fatherland." Some of the evidence demonstrating the hegemony of strenuous masculinity in war was the increasingly brash, complex, and violent war games on the streets and the graphic descriptions of war and the claims to German superiority in pop-ular youth literature and schoolboys' original compositions. The most con-spicuous evidence that strenuous masculinity had replaced Victorian concep-tions of manhood was that after 1918 the curled mustaches and prominent beards of dignified male statesmen like Otto von Bismarck and Paul von Hindenburg had gone out of style, replaced by the beardless athletic face of the modern man. On the far right, the model was the clean-shaven, fierce young storm trooper depicted in Fritz Erler's widely distributed 1917 war bond poster, an icon for German fascists after the war.[7]

Wartime discourses on female youths paradoxically idealized the domes-ticity of girls while recognizing their new independence. On the one hand, teachers, reformers, and administrators emphasized that schoolgirls should prepare to make extraordinary sacrifices to care for their families; a domestic self-abnegation commensurate with the sacrifice of soldiers on the front was for girls the highest expression of patriotism. The most persistent discourses in the daily and pedagogical press about female youths were pleas that they save their spending money, buy yarn, knit socks and sweaters, and donate them anonymously as gifts to soldiers. This practice was supposed to be the supreme expression of young women's special capacity for love. The domestic ideal also moved administrators of continuation schools to expand curricula on cooking, knitting, mending, child-raising, and infant hygiene. The Ger-man Female Teachers' Association called upon the state to require all girls to participate in a mandatory year of domestic service without compensation to develop these skills. Although this comprehensive plan never came to fruition, it indicated the general view (even among leaders in the women's movement) that the war had proven how the state needed female youths to attend more assiduously to their families and their domestic role. In practice, if a female youth's or schoolgirl's mother had to find work outside the home because her father's conscription impoverished her family, she likely spent more time than before 1914 cleaning, cooking, mending, and supervising younger siblings. Because the wages of female teenagers were far below those of males, a mother's rational strategy was to keep her daughter at home and send her son to work in the armaments industries. For these reasons, the war generally tied schoolgirls and female youths more closely to the home. Not surprisingly, given the changes that coterminously fostered independence, some girls recalled how they hated this imposition of domesticity, but there was little opposition in general to this gender ideal in the middle classes.[8]

On the other hand, mass conscription liberated millions of female youths from male authority, and young women welcomed this new autonomy. Marlene Dietrich, 15 years old at the outbreak of the war, recalled: "Our life with women became so comfortable that we often thought about whether it was desirable to have men in our midst, men who would again take over the leadership and be the rulers at home." Such spaces and activities that excluded boys and men proliferated not just in families but in the rising numbers of female recreational and knitting groups. Female teenagers took over the leadership of the Wandervogel and asserted their right, against highly critical male youths, to develop their bodies (albeit for the purpose of preparing for motherhood). Novels and magazines stressed young women's natural gifts for domestic tasks but also celebrated their new responsibilities as nurses in military hospitals. The frequent portrayal in fiction of girls as auxiliaries who bound the wounds of soldiers under heavy fire suggested that they could contribute to the war and achieve equality with boys while keeping true to their special gift for nurturing.[9]

The war especially empowered female youths in both wings of the Socialist movement. Among all the youth organizations in Germany, the Social Democratic ones stood out for their defense of radical equality between the sexes, but rank-and-file male members before 1914 usually had less progressive views on gender than the leaders, and working-class parents generally frowned on their daughters participating in party politics. Just 20 percent of the membership in the Social Democratic youth organizations was female in 1914, a smaller portion than in the middle-class youth movement, despite the latter's more conservative views on gender. During the war the number of female youths in the mainstream Social Democratic organizations more than doubled, however. The increase was in part due to a larger pool for new members, particularly the tens of thousands of working girls who left their positions as domestic servants for jobs in the war industries and no longer faced prohibitions by their mistresses on attending Social Democratic functions. Female membership also increased because the leaders insisted more vocally than before that boys and girls should socialize together and that the "bourgeois" and Catholic organizations prepared girls to be only housewives and mothers. By the end of the war, more than half of the regular participants and 40 percent of the leadership in the mainstream Social Democratic organizations was female. In addition, thousands more female youths became radicals in oppositional Socialist politics. In 1916 and 1917 police arrested girls as frequently as boys for distributing illegal leaflets against the war, and dozens of female teenagers delivered fiery oratory. Radical male teenagers invited girls to informal political clubs where they discussed the ideas of Rosa Luxemburg that the mainstream organizations had banned. Hundreds of working girls staged sympathy strikes during the uprisings in Lower Saxony.[10]

These experiences help explain the contradictions in this cohort's conceptions of femininity after the war. On the one hand, the war ended with female youths asserting independence. Flouting prewar prohibitions on erotic public expressions, some greeted returning soldiers with kisses and schnapps and, according to one eyewitness, allowed themselves to be taken to bed to satisfy the young men who had endured years of sexual deprivation. Almost immediately after the armistice, male and female youths began doing the new dances imported from the United States like the foxtrot and one-step, despite the continued bans on public dancing. Hundreds of thousands subsequently took on the qualities of the new woman. Bobbed hair, loose clothing, and the penchant for cigarettes projected independence, nonconformity, and social and political equality with men—an implicit rejection of gender ideals stressing motherhood. Replacing the calling system in which a mother oversaw her daughters' prospective boyfriends were self-regulated courtship rituals that flourished particularly in urban dance halls and became the sine qua non of modern youth culture. In forging intimate relationships on their own, female and male youths wrested control over a key rite of passage from adults and wrote the rules of courtship themselves. On the other hand, the new woman was as much legend as reality. In contrast to the women a few years older who won suffrage rights in 1919, the war youth generation was less interested in the feminist movement. Younger members of the League of German Women spurned the "egalitarian feminist concept of citizenship" and instead emphasized that only their motherly qualities could nurse a sick nation. Millions of women in this cohort voted for the Nazi Party in the early 1930s, even though the party made no secret that it wished to take away women's political rights. The attraction of the Nazis was their valuing of motherhood, a vocation glorified during the war but, they believed, denigrated by the Republic.[11]

The Radicalization of the Left

Most of those who were youths or schoolchildren during the First World War led uneventful lives after 1918, but a significant number became radicalized by the war. On the left, these were the oppositional Socialist youths who were in disbelief not only that the Social Democratic Party endorsed the *Burgfrieden* but also that a third of its youth leaders renounced their antimilitarism and volunteered for the army. They were further incensed by the support of many Socialist groups for military youth companies and the publication in *Arbeiter-Jugend* of homages to fallen soldiers. Knowing that youths would have a hard time swallowing all this, Friedrich Ebert, the chairman of the Social Democratic Party who directly oversaw the Socialist youth organizations, hoped to educate the young members about the *Burgfrieden*. But like recreational associations for male youths more generally, formal Socialist youth organizations disintegrated due to conscription and lack of funding. Paternal authority within the Social Democratic Party in turn diminished, and the teenagers opposed to the adult leadership revived the practice, which had been smothered after the enactment of the Reich Law of Association in 1908, of organizing politically. Aided by the 26-year-old Willi Münzenberg, the future Communist media mogul who from Switzerland oversaw a complex smuggling operation of agitation pamphlets and broadsides, these oppositional Socialist youths organized in 1915 arguably the most vigorous antiwar and pro-revolution movement of any age group. In Berlin, Hamburg, Düsseldorf, Braunschweig, Hanover, Leipzig, Dresden, and Stuttgart, as well as many smaller cities, hundreds and in some cases thousands met on hikes under the cover of darkness and sang the old antimilitarist and political fight songs. In part because the government conscripted, exiled, or jailed the most vigorous adult male opponents, other formal antiwar protest movements in Germany did not reach this magnitude before 1917. Through infiltration and arrests, the political police gained the upper hand in crippling this movement in the spring of 1917. By that time, however, the youths had managed to galvanize workers of all ages, including women exasperated by the disastrous food shortages in the winter of 1916/17 and emboldened by the February Revolution in Russia. Although we know few details, police reports attested that youths played a major role in the mass strikes for peace and revolution in April 1917 and January 1918.

After 1918 youths active in this antiwar movement rejected the Majority Social Democratic Party outright. In their minds it had sold the workers out to the war, and thus only the internationalists in the Communist Party, founded in January 1919, represented the interests of working youths. Whereas the Social Democratic Party vigorously opposed any youth involvement in politics during the war, radicals like Karl Liebknecht and Rosa Luxemburg happily turned to them to mobilize antiwar protest and prepare the working class for revolution. Youths angry about the war hence developed loyalties to radical Communists. Regardless of their previous positions on Marxism, they came of age in a milieu that rejected the Weimar Republic for failing to overthrow private property and purge middle-class elites from the army, the judiciary, and the bureaucracy.

Biographical evidence suggests that the absence of paternal authority and the increased autonomy of working youths hastened their radicalization. For example, Willi Bohn, 14 years old when the war broke out, was an apprentice in a Berlin law firm specializing in criminal defense. After most of the firm associates and staff were conscripted in the summer of 1915, the partners gave him new responsibilities, including filing briefs daily in court. This experience awakened his political consciousness. He began meeting regularly with five other working-class teenage boys to formulate theory against the war. Notably, all of these boys' fathers were conscripted. The group also began to engage other teenagers in political discussions about the war. After 1918 Bohn became a committed member of the Communist Party. Oskar Hippe, also 14 years old at the outbreak of the war, was the son of a poor but staunch monarchist. As an apprentice at a coffin manufacturer during the first year of the war, he was beaten regularly and forced to sleep in an attic. When his master was conscripted, the 16-year-old Hippe broke his apprenticeship contract and found high-wage work in the Berlin metal industry, far from his stern father in Gotha. There he became an active member of the oppositional Socialist youth movement. He discussed the war and politics in the bathrooms during his break and began distributing smuggled leaflets printed by Münzenberg in Switzerland. He joined the Spartacists when he was just 16 years old. He was likely one of the thousands of 13- to 17-year-olds who gathered for a rally in Berlin in mid-December 1918 that demanded an end to conscription, a six-hour day for workers under 16 years of age, voting rights for 18- and 19-year olds, and a law repealing the right of teachers to mete out corporal punishment.[12]

Working-class newspapers during the Weimar Republic regularly pointed out that the participation of male youths in communist violence was disproportionately high. More recently, a random sample of men prosecuted following the armed "March Campaign," the violent action organized by the Communist Party in Saxony in 1921, revealed that approximately half of the several hundred sentenced were in the war youth generation. The newspapers asked readers to be lenient on these "juvenile delinquents" because they had suffered greatly from deprivation during the war. After the Wall Street crash in 1929, the majority of violent Communist street fighters, who physically fought the Social Democrats and the Nazis, were men born from 1900 to 1910.[13]

The middle-class youth movement also became politicized as a result of the war, spinning off a left wing that wanted an immediate, negotiated peace and an anti-Semitic and racist right wing that wanted to continue the war until a final military victory. Then, after the abrogation of censorship in October 1918 and Germany's descent into revolution in November, the members flocked to the political extremes. Flaunting the ban on politics in youth associations, in October Karl Bittel, a leader in the Free German Youth, mimeographed editions of "Political Memos," which addressed the explosive issues of peace and domestic political reform. In December, he joined the Independent Social Democratic Party because it refused to join the Weimar coalition of the Center, Democratic, and Majority Social Democratic parties. Knud Ahlborn, the editor of *Freideutsche Jugend* who had insisted that the Free German Youth refrain from endorsing political parties, also joined the Independent Social Democratic Party that month. In the Berlin Circle, Alfred Kurella, Max Hodann, and others joined the Communist Party. Still others like Hans Koch put the utopian socialist visions into practice. With twenty male and female youths, he founded a commune in Blankenburg near

Donauwörth. The moral impropriety of its members led to their arrest in the summer of 1919.[14]

The Radicalization of the Right

The shock of defeat and anger against those on the home front who called for an immediate peace moved many in the middle-class youth movement toward radical nationalism and militarism and polarized the war youth generation politically. Furthermore, the German right awakened during the wartime campaign for annexations to the possibility of mobilizing youths for their cause. Before the war, Pan-Germanists and other radical nationalists had endorsed state-sponsored youth organizations such as the Young Germany League, but they ignored the youth movement until the war illuminated its members' nationalist convictions and willingness to challenge the moderate establishment. Radical right politicians were impressed by the legend that at the battle at the Belgian village of Langemarck in November 1914, volunteers from the youth movement sang *Deutschland, Deutschand über alles*, while marching into French machine guns to their deaths. Radical right politicians also recognized that Walter Flex's 1916 novel *The Wanderer between Two Worlds*, which became a cult classic among right-wing youths, disseminated the myth that the war elevated the ideal of "unselfish charismatic leadership with loyal followers." Although the right wing of the middle-class youth movement supported annexations, it was fiercely independent and rejected affiliation with the Fatherland Party. But hundreds of former Wandervögel entered the various *Freikorps* to fight revolutionaries and maintain order during the revolution. The Wandervogel Squadron, which in early 1919 fought against insurgents in Poland, had equal numbers of seasoned soldiers, young men who spent a brief time on the front, and teenagers who had never seen combat. Spin-offs of the Wandervogel—so-called *Bünde* like the Artamans and the Eagles and Hawks—later provided key leaders to Hitler's SS. Wandervögel on both the right and the left stated in oral interviews that the war was the turning point in their lives, the time when they became political aware and active.[15]

This polarization within the youth movements suggests that a key legacy of the war was that male youths became susceptible to violent right-wing movements. Fascists in Italy and Germany came to power after 1918 by relying heavily on males who did not serve in the First World War or served only a limited and usually bloodless tour of a few months. Their movements were led by disaffected front soldiers angry about defeat or, as it was construed in Italy, "mutilated victory," but youths without combat experience eagerly filled the ranks. In Italy in late 1922 the average age of a fascist squadrist was just over 23 years old, and the cohort born 1901 to 1905, which was never conscripted, was the most disproportionately overrepresented, making up 40 percent of the squadrists in Bologna, for example. Similarly, about half of the members of the Nazi Party and the SA who joined before 1933 were too young to be conscripted during the war. Germans of all ages cast their ballots for the Nazis in elections, but males born from 1900 (the last birth year conscripted in the summer of 1918) to 1908 (the birth year of the youngest German schoolboys in 1914) galvanized the right and carried out its violence. As teenagers or men in their early 20s, they also overwhelmed the *Freikorps* and other fascist paramilitary organizations before the rise of the Nazis. Boys as young as 14 practiced with groups like the Jungwolf. According to some estimates, by the mid-1920s more than half the members in the Stahlhelm were too young to have served in the war. Officers considered these youths among the most reliable and radical militia troops.[16]

The previous chapters suggest that defeat and revolution radicalized these most spirited agitators of fascism because their experiences in the war raised unrealistic expectations about military superiority and the prospect for victory. By immersing pupils in war stories and glorifying destruction and killing, teachers under war pedagogy transmitted the German military's particularly violent tactics and dogmas, including the stubborn belief in the necessity of a *Siegfriede*, Clausewitz's dictum, which teachers and the High Command alike crudely interpreted as meaning that ending the war required complete annihilation of enemy military forces. By contrast, before 1914 conservative curricula and prohibitions on exposing youths to politics shielded most German schoolchildren from the violence of the colonial wars. Furthermore, even though the middle classes venerated military service before 1914, the vast majority of army recruits had little or no experience in killing and using violence. After 1914, however, the details of making war became central in the lives of hundreds of thousands of middle-class youths in particular. Encouraged by war pedagogy, heroic war literature, and military youth companies, these youths eagerly studied the string of victories on the Eastern front that resulted in the favorable treaty at Brest-Litovsk in January 1918. The radical nationalist Fatherland Party also entered the fray, intensifying propaganda targeted at teachers and pupils and winning over thousands of secondary school boys to extreme positions on annexations and the necessity of a total military victory. In the spring of 1918, the army broke the stalemate and advanced on Paris, as these youths had assumed it would. The collapse of the Western front in the summer of 1918 was therefore unreal to these male youths. The events of November 1918 stoked their hatred of the workers and Socialists, who they believed had robbed Germany of victory by seeking the cowardly negotiated peace. To them, the workers and the Socialists were the same internationalists who before 1914 had never recognized or supported the Fatherland. In the last year and a half of the war, right-wing middle-class boys in the youth movement developed intense hatred of internationalists and pacifists. It is doubtful that these youths would have maintained their anger if German had won the war. But defeat and then a revolution led by internationalist and pacifist Socialists crystallized hatred in nationalist youths, turning an even broader cohort of victory watchers into right-wing radicals.[17]

After 1918, these male youths reasoned that traitors at home foiled military victory. During the war, they saw that the youths who volunteered for patriotic projects and premilitary training came primarily from their own milieu—middle-class families in big cities or families of a variety of classes in Protestant villages, towns, and small cities. There were numerous exceptions to this generalization, but in general rural Catholic and urban working boys fled the patriotic labor projects and military youth companies after the first six to twelve months of the war. Furthermore, after 1915 the liberal and conservative press vilified urban working youths for seeking high wages, splurging on the cinema, demanding a negotiated peace, and organizing strikes to end the war. As teenagers, those who became Nazis in this cohort dreaded that the war would end before they could volunteer. Stunned by defeat and denied the opportunity to prove their manhood, they, more than ordinary soldiers, began to believe the legend that the army was not conquered on the battlefield but stabbed in the back by the working class and the Republican government. Even secondary school boys who later had pacifist leanings invariably recalled their burning desire to get to the front before the war ended.[18]

For middle-class secondary school boys, October and November 1918 marked their political awakening. For example, with the front collapsing, five boys in the Helmholtz *Realgymnasium* in Berlin-Schöneberg approached their school director with a leaflet they had written by hand and asked for permission to publish and distribute it in school. Ashamed of the impending defeat and threatening chaos, they called for all Germans born in 1901 and 1902 to heed the Spirit of 1914 and volunteer to bleed and die for the Fatherland: "We want to remain free like our fathers; better death than to live in slavery." A similar desperation overcame 15-year-old Werner Best, later the chief legal adviser to the Gestapo. In his memoirs he claimed he was politicized by diligently following the events of the war, practicing regularly in a military youth company, and preparing and giving a speech in school on war guilt. When the front collapsed, he felt responsible for the moral and political rebirth of Germany. Though engagement with politicians was illegal for minors, he acquired brochures of the Pan-Germanists and met their chief propagandist, Heinrich Claß. His memoirs claimed that his friends and classmates shared his views. In his diary the 16-year-old Heinrich Himmler denounced rural southern Bavarians for wanting peace and expressed a burning desire to join the war. At age 18 he was mortified at the unexpected defeat. Martin Matthiessen, born in 1901 and later an SS general, recalled the joy he took in patriotic voluntary labor and his military youth company during the war. He remembered his teacher who followed the principles of war pedagogy and discarded "the usual distance between teacher and pupils." Ernst von Salomon's autobiographically inspired account of a youth born in 1901 who joined the *Freikorps* after 1918 resonated with the same themes:

> Every appeal to patriotism found an echo in him. Naturally he regretted he was too young to take part in the events which were described to him as the "Great Experience." The sight of wounded soldiers, of black-veiled widows, the casualty lists in the newspapers, the reports from the front, the accounts of gains and losses—all these things exercised a stronger influence on him than the watery soup dished up each day, and even made him wish that the war would last long enough for him to take part in it himself. . . . [He] had a rabidly patriotic teacher and immediately on being appealed to by him reported for duty [to the *Freikorps*].

Von Salomon himself "had only one wish: that the war would last long enough for us to take part in it." Because it did not, he joined the paramilitary *Freikorps* to fight against the revolutionaries who, he believed, had lost the war for Germany.[19]

My survey of the autobiographies of early Nazis born from 1900 to 1908 collected in 1934 by the Columbia sociologist Theodore Abel suggests that for almost all of these male youths, defeat and revolution in November 1918 thwarted their nationalist and militarist dreams and inflamed their hatred of the alleged Socialist traitors. Even the 40 percent of the autobiographers who had themselves been working youths upheld this belief in betrayal. Although they mostly accepted progressive social policy, they fulminated against the pacifism among their Socialist-influenced working-class peers who had scorned them during the war for training in military youth companies. A key cause of their anger was their dashed hopes to volunteer in the army, as most of those born after 1899 saw limited combat, if any. Denied this opportunity to demonstrate their manhood on the front, they sought a continuation of the war at home in paramilitary organizations. For example, a Berliner born in 1900 who pursued an apprenticeship in sales remembered being enthusiastic about the war and entering a military youth company in 1915. In September 1918 he arrived in Serreville, France, and before he saw any real action was shocked by the revolution in November. Returning to Berlin, he joined a paramilitary group and fought the Spartacists. Another early Nazi remembered playing war games before 1918 that resulted in bloody heads and police intervention; a civilian for the entire war, he volunteered during the revolution at age 18 in a militia and fought the Communists. A 17-year-old wrote about "victories" and saw "how our honest soldiers held out with valor against despair and an entire world of enemies." He then cursed the "Marxists" who "exploited the deprivation at home for criminal goals" and ended the war before the *Siegfriede,* the decisive military victory. Bucking working-class politics, a male 16-year-old factory worker suggested to the chair of the local patriotic society that citizens be armed to suppress the Socialist revolt. When he and the chair held a meeting and no one showed up, he claimed, he "first learned to hate the spirit of the November betrayal."[20]

The experience of male youths during the First World War can by no means alone explain the rise of German fascism. Men born from 1900 to 1908 often became fascists for the same reasons as those born earlier or later. Anger at the Republic for neglecting their economic woes, signing the Versailles Treaty, and failing to maintain law and order were some of many possible reasons. Furthermore, many early Nazis born in this cohort blamed Jews as well as Socialists for the lost war, but there is little evidence that these men had age-specific war experiences that turned them into anti-Semites. War pedagogy in fact emphasized the heroism of ancient Jewish war heroes like Joshua, Samson, David, and the Maccabees. The anti-Semitism of these Nazis originated elsewhere in frustrations they shared with German fascists of all ages. But there was a set of age-specific explanations for why so many youths were attracted to nationalist and militarist groups and had political awakenings in October and November 1918: during the war they experienced war pedagogy, fantasized about soldiers described in war literature, made sacrifices in patriotic voluntary labor and military youth companies, believed that the working class shirked patriotic duties, and then were denied their great wish to fight for Germany's glory on the front. Fervid nationalists during the war, they saw their unwavering belief in the German army's superiority quashed by defeat and revolution. Their reaction was to cry, rage, and seek blame. Their entry into nationalist paramilitary groups and the Nazi Party after 1918 developed out of frustration with having sacrificed and trained to defend Germany but never having a chance to demonstrate their patriotism and manhood on the front.[21]

The Ten Commandments of a
War Pedagogy

Theobald Ziegler's "Ten Commandments of a War Pedagogy" was first published in the *Schwäbische Merkur*, 10 September 1914, and was reprinted in almost every pedagogical journal.

1. Thou shalt attend to discipline and order among the schoolchildren and continue to fulfill your duty now as before because you are responsible to your people more than ever for the next generation. But don't be a school-tyrant, today less so than ever, and also understand the art of looking the other way. And don't give them too much homework: They have to read the newspaper daily.

2. Thou shalt not let the war become an amusement for the schoolchildren because it is indeed a serious matter. Therefore don't celebrate every victory with a day off from school, and don't think that you have to make a festival out of every collection drive or other contribution to the war by your pupils.

3. Thou shalt raise your schoolchildren to be citizens. You now have the best opportunity to do that because the war is a teacher of first rank.

4. Thou shalt teach more interestingly than it has since been your duty because the thoughts of schoolchildren now easily wander. Therefore relate all instruction to the daily and hourly events. Don't let the easy opportunity slip by. When it is difficult, go ahead and do it anyway *(da ziehe sie getrost an den Haaren herbei).*

5. Thou shalt more than before make every lesson a German lesson and teach your schoolchildren the style of General-Quartermaster von Stein. You can do this in Latin and mathematics too.

6. Thou shalt read Schiller in German lessons, as much as you can and want because he is the manliest of our poets. For the moment, raising aesthetes no longer has any value.

7. Thou shalt speak of battles in history class and be happy—knock on wood—that you're allowed to do that again. Your boys are interested in them and can put them to good use right away during the breaks between classes. And you should gently point out the march of God in history being revealed to us today so amazingly and wonderfully.

8. Thou shalt not fret nervously about the prescribed lesson plans. If it is prescribed to discuss rural India, then make a war lesson out of it and lead your fifth graders on the path from Metz to Paris or the Masurien Lakes. Not barbarians but reasonable and patriotic men run the school administrations.

9. Thou shalt think about whether there is not truly a difference between man and woman and between the heroism of a man and the heroism of a woman. Therefore, even if you are already the state education counselor, you may ask yourself whether co-education is again a problem because we need masculine men and feminine women. Every group has its particular gift and task in the war.

10. Thou shalt be happy that the "Century of the Child" is out because that was a totally foolish slogan. The leaders of our army are men between the ages of fifty and seventy, and the touching boys who marched to war as the youngest will from their tough manly work return home as serious men and place their stamp on the time afterwards.

Notes

Abbreviations

Bl.	*Blatt* (two sides of a page)
DBA	*Deutsches Biographisches Archiv*
DCG	Deputy commanding general
Gym.	*Gymnasium*
Kjp.	District youth worker *(Kreisjugendpfleger)*
KPSK	Provincial school administration in Prussia (*Königliches Provinzialschulkollegium,* or *Provinzialschulkollegium* in November 1918)
KPSK-Berichte	Annual reports of above in GStA I. HA Rep. 76. VI Sec. I. Gen. z: 243
KSinsp.	Prussian or Bavarian District School Inspection
Min. Ed.	Education Ministry (*Kultusministerium, Ministerium der geistlichen und Unterrichts-Angelegenheiten, Ministerium für Kirchen und Schulangelegenheiten,* or *Ministerium für Wissenschaft, Kunst und Volksbildung*)
Min. Int.	Interior Ministry
Oberreal.	*Oberrealschule*
Pol.	Police *(Polizeipräsident, Präsidium der Polizei, Polizei-Verwaltung, Polizeidirektion, Polizeiinspektion, Polizeiamt)*
Reg. Präs.	Prussian provincial governor *(Regierungspräsident, Königliche Regierung zu—)*
Sch. Dep.	Municipal school board *(Schuldeputation, städtische Schulverwaltung, Schulkomission, Schulleitung)*

Introduction

Epigraph: Alfred Mann, "Aufsätze von Kindern und Jugendlichen über Kriegsthe-mata," in *Jugendliches Seelenleben und Krieg,* ed. William Stern (Leipzig: J. A. Barth, 1915), 88. [Unless otherwise noted, all translations in this book are my own.]

1. Hagen Schulze, *Freikorps und Republik, 1918–1920* (Boppard am Rhein: Harald Boldt, 1969), 51; Hans Gerth, "The Nazi Party: Its Leadership and Composition," *American Journal of Sociology* 45 (1940): 517–541; Hermann Weber, *Die Wandlung des deutschen Kommunismus: Die Stalinisierung der KPD in der Weimarer Republik* (Frankfurt a.M.: Europäische, 1969), 26–27; and Dirk Schumann, *Politische Gewalt in der Weimarer Republik, 1918–1933: Kampf um die Straße und Furcht vor dem Bürgerkrieg* (Essen: Klartext, 2001), 139–142.

2. On creating reliable citizens, see Friedrich Paulsen, *German Education: Past and Present* (London: T. Fisher Unwin, 1908), 136–150; Mary Jo Maynes, *Schooling in Western Europe: A Social History* (Albany: State University of New York Press, 1985), 33–85; John Gillis, *Youth and History: Tradition and Change in European Age Relations, 1770 to the Present* (New York: Academic, 1974), 95–183; Detlev Peukert, *Grenzen der Sozialdisziplinierung: Aufstieg und Krise der deutschen Jugendfürsorge von 1878 bis 1932* (Köln: Bund, 1986), 37–162; Michael Childs, *Labour's Apprentices: Working-Class Lads in Late Victorian and Edwardian England* (Montreal: McGill-Queen's University Press, 1992), 28–50, 140–156; Joseph Kett, *Rites of Passage: Adolescence in America 1790 to the Present* (New York: Basic Books, 1977), 189–224; Maurice Crubellier, *L'Enfance et la jeunesse dans la société française, 1800–1950* (Paris: Armand Colin, 1979), 77–98, 143–334; John Springhall, *Coming of Age: Adolescence in Britain, 1860–1960* (Dublin: Gill and Macmillan, 1986), 38–64, 109–189; and Edward Ross Dickinson, *The Politics of German Child Welfare from the Empire to the Federal Republic* (Cambridge, MA: Harvard University Press, 1996), 11–112. On radical political movements and youth, see Michael Kater, *Hitler Youth* (Cambridge, MA: Harvard University Press, 2004), 36–45; Sean McMeekin, *The Red Millionaire: A Political Biography of Willi Münzenberg, Moscow's Secret Propaganda Tsar in the West* (New Haven, CT: Yale University Press, 2003), 3, 32–38; Isabel Tirado, *Young Guard! The Communist Youth League, Petrograd, 1917–1920* (Westport, CT: Greenwood, 1988), 204–206; and Hilary Pilkington, *Russia's Youth and Its Culture* (New York: Routledge, 1994), 48–64.

3. Abigail Green, *Fatherlands: State-Building and Nationalism in Nineteenth-Century Germany* (New York: Cambridge University Press, 2001), 189–222; Paulsen, *German Education,* 236–261; Maynes, *Schooling,* 134; Derek Linton, *"Who Has the Youth Has the Future:" The Campaign to Save Young Workers in Imperial Germany* (New York: Cambridge University Press, 1991), 48–97; Peter

Dudek, *Jugend als Objekt der Wissenschaft: Geschichte der Jugendforschung in Deutschland und Österreich, 1890–1933* (Opladen: Westdeutscher, 1990), 92; and P. W. Musgrave, *Society and Education in England since 1800* (London: Methuen, 1968), 81.

4. Walter Laqueur, *Young Germany: A History of the German Youth Movement* (London: Routledge & Kegan Paul, 1962), 3–83; Klaus Saul, "Der Kampf um die Jugend zwischen Volksschule und Kaserne: Ein Beitrag zur 'Jugendpflege' im Wilhelminischen Reich, 1890–1914," *Militärgeschichtliche Mitteilung* 9 (1971): 115, 142–143; Jürgen Reulecke, "Bürgerliche Sozialreformer und Arbeiterjugend im Kaiserreich," *Archiv für Sozialgeschichte* 22 (1982): 320; Linton, *Young Workers,* 98–164; Edward Ross Dickinson, "Citizenship, Vocational Training, and Recreation: Continuation Schooling and the Prussian 'Youth Cultivation' Decree of 1911," *European History Quarterly* 29 (1999): 112–113; Laurence Munoz, "Le sport catholique en France au début du vingtième siècle," *Stadion* 27 (2001): 59; Childs, *Labour's Apprentices,* 152; and Kett, *Adolescence in America,* 190–192, 194.

5. Susanne Miller, *Burgfrieden und Klassenkampf: Die deutsche Sozialdemokratie im Ersten Weltkrieg* (Düsseldorf: Droste, 1974), 31–74; Wolfgang Kruse, *Krieg und nationale Integration: Eine Neuinterpretation des sozialdemokratischen Burgfrie-densschlusses, 1914/15* (Essen: Klartext, 1994), 30–51, 90–115; Jeffrey Verhey, *The Spirit of 1914: Militarism, Myth and Mobilization in Germany* (New York: Cambridge University Press, 2000), 52–57; Friedhelm Boll, "Die deutsche Sozialdemokratie zwischen Resignation und Revolution: Zur Friedensstrategie 1890–1919," in *Frieden, Gewalt, Sozialismus: Studien zur Geschichte der sozialistischen Arbeiterbewegung,* ed. Wolfgang Huber and Johannes Schwerdtfeger (Stuttgart: Ernst Klett, 1976), 182–216; and William English Walling, *The Socialists and the War* (New York: Henry Holt, 1915), 131 (quotation).

6. Miller, *Burgfrieden,* 54–55 (quotations), 244–245; Reinhard Rürup, "Der 'Geist von 1914' in Deutschland: Kriegsbegeisterung und Ideologisierung des Kriegs im Ersten Weltkrieg," in *Ansichten vom Krieg,* ed. Bernd Hüppauf (Königstein /Ts.: Forum Academicum, 1984); Verhey, *Spirit of 1914,* 110–111; and David Welch, *Germany, Propaganda and Total War, 1914–1918* (London: Athlone, 2000), 12–19.

7. On the variable moods of August 1914, see Verhey, *Spirit of 1914,* 89–96; Thomas Raithel, *Das "Wunder" der inneren Einheit: Studien zur deutschen und französischen Öffentlichkeit bei Beginn des Ersten Weltkrieges* (Bonn: Bouvier, 1996), 499; Christian Geinitz, *Kriegsfurcht und Kampfbereitschaft: Das Augusterlebenis in Freiburg* (Essen: Klartext, 1998), 175–182; and Michael Stöcker, *Augusterlebnis 1914 in Darmstadt* (Darmstadt: Eduard Rother, 1994). On working-class and rural opposition, see Kruse, *Krieg und nationale Integration,* 54–61, 90–98, 84–94, 223; Benjamin Ziemann, *War Experiences*

in Rural Germany, 1914–1923 (New York: Berg, 2007), 15–28; Klaus Dieter Schwarz, *Weltkrieg und Revolution in Nürnberg* (Stuttgart: Klett, 1971), 106–130; Volker Ullrich, *Die Hamburger Arbeiterbewegung am Vorabend des Ersten Weltkrieges bis zur Revolution, 1918/19* (Hamburg: Ludke, 1976), 140–220; Erhard Lucas-Busemann, *Zwei Formen von Radikalismus in der deutschen Arbeiterbewegung* (Frankfurt: Roter Stern, 1976), 145–152; and Friedhelm Boll, *Massenbewegungen in Niedersachsen, 1906–1920* (Bonn: Neue Gesellschaft, 1981).

8. For figures on conscription, see Ziemann, *War Experiences*, 31. Approximately 10.5 million men were on regular duty at any given point after 1915.

9. Peter Merkl, *Political Violence under the Swastika: 581 Early Nazis* (Princeton, NJ: Princeton University Press, 1975), 28, 149–153, 238–239, 270–282, 302–304; John Tosh, *A Man's Place: Masculinity and the Middle-Class Home in Victorian England* (New Haven, CT: Yale University Press, 1999), 5–6, 170–194; George Mosse, *Fallen Soldiers: Reshaping the Memory of the World Wars* (New York: Oxford University Press, 1990), 132–134, 166, 186; and the autobiographies of early Nazis born 1900 to 1908 in boxes 1–8, HIA-TAC.

10. Ute Daniel, *The War from Within: German Working-Class Women in the First World War* (New York: Berg, 1997), 139–140, 160; Reichsjustizministerium und Statistisches Reichsamt, *Kriminalstatistik für das Jahr 1917*, vol. 304, *Statistik des deutschen Reichs* (Berlin: Putkammer & Mühlbrecht, 1923), 22–31; and Waldemar Zimmermann, *Die Einwirkung des Krieges auf Bevölkerungsbewegung, Einkommen und Lebenshaltung in Deutschland* (New Haven, CT: Yale University Press, 1932), 350–351.

11. Karen Hagemann, "Military, War, and the Mainstreams: Gendering Modern German Military History," *Gendering Modern German History: Rewriting Historiography*, ed. Karen Hagemann and Jean Quartet (New York: Berghahn, 2007), 69; and Ute Frevert, *Women in German History: From Bourgeois Emancipation to Sexual Liberation* (New York: Berg, 1989), 151–167.

12. Demographic data are based on the 1919 census: Reichsjustizministerium und statistisches Reichsamt, *Bewegung der Bevölkerung in den Jahren 1914 bis 1919*, vol. 276, *Statistik des deutschen Reichs* (Berlin: Puttkammer & Mühlbrecht, 1922), iv. See also Klaus Tenfelde, "Großstadtjugend in Deutschland vor 1914: Eine historisch-demographische Annäherung," *Vierteljahrschrift für Sozial- und Wirtschaftsgeschichte* 69 (1982): 182–218.

13. Ernst Buchner [Eduard Mayer], *1914–1918: Wie es damals daheim war: Das Kriegstagebuch eines Knaben* (Leipzig: Die neue Zeit, 1930), 34; and Jo Mihaly [Piete Kuhr], *Da gibt's ein Wiedersehen! Kriegstagebuch eines Mädchens, 1914–1918* (Freiburg: Kerle, 1982), translated as *There We'll Meet Again: A Young German Girl's Diary of the First World War* (Gloucester: Walter Wright, 1998), 101, 141. On the expected content of war diaries, see "Das Kriegstage-

buch," *Freie Bayerische Schulzeitung* 15 (27 August 1914): 232; and Anny
Schulze, "Kriegstagebücher," *Die Lehrerin* 32 (1 May 1915): 34–36. The Nazi
memoirs are in HIA-TAC.

14. Wilhelm Deist, *Militär und Innenpolitik im Weltkrieg, 1914–1918* (Düsseldorf:
    Droste, 1970), 85–86, 98–99; Kurt Koszyk, *Deutsche Pressepolitik im Ersten
    Weltkrieg* (Düsseldorf: Droste, 1968), 69–70; and Verhey, *Spirit of 1914*, 15,
    142–146.

15. For an overview of these types, especially lower-middle-class working youths,
    see Günther Dehn, *Großstadtjugend: Beobachtungen und Erfahrungen aus der
    Welt der großstädtischen Arbeiterjugend* (Berlin: Carl Heymann, 1922), 66–72.
    On unifying a "discursive" and "realist" approach to class, see Geoff Eley
    and Keith Nield, *The Future of Class in History: What's Left of the Social?*
    (Ann Arbor: University of Michigan Press, 2007), 166. The term *war youth
    generation* was popularized by Günther Gründel, *Die Sendung der jungen
    Generation* (Munich: Beck, 1932), 31–42.

16. Maureen Healy, *Vienna and the Fall of the Habsburg Empire: Total War and
    Everyday Life in World War I* (New York: Cambridge University Press,
    2004), 211–257; Stephen Harp, *Learning to Be Loyal: Primary Schooling as
    Nation Building in Alsace and Lorraine, 1850–1940* (Dekalb: Northern
    Illinois University Press, 1998), 159; and Tara Zahra, *Kidnapped Souls:
    National Indifference and the Battle for Children in the Bohemian Lands,
    1900–1948* (Ithaca, NY: Cornell University Press, 2008), 79–105.

1. The Pedagogy of Obedience and Its Critics

1. The classic account of this view is Hans Ulrich Wehler, *The German Empire*
   (Berg: Lemington Spa, 1985), 118–124. See also Jürgen Kocka, "Asymmetri-
   cal Historical Comparison: The Case of the German Sonderweg," *History
   and Theory* 38 (1999): 46; and Heinrich August Winkler, "A Pioneer in the
   Historical Sciences," *Central European History* 24 (1991): 13.

2. On fathers see William Hubbard, *Familiengeschichte: Materialien zur
   deutschen Familie seit dem Ende des 18. Jahrhunderts* (Munich: C. H. Beck,
   1983), 58; Heidi Rosenbaum, *Formen der Familie: Untersuchungen zum
   Zusammenhang von Familienverhältnissen, Sozialstruktur und sozialem
   Wandel in der deutschen Gesellschaft des 19. Jahrhunderts* (Frankfurt a.M.:
   Suhrkamp, 1982), 356–359, 457–459; Heidi Rosenbaum, *Proletarische
   Familien: Arbeiterfamilien und Arbeiterväter im frühen 20. Jahrhundert
   zwischen traditioneller, sozialdemokratischer und kleinbürgerlicher Orientier-
   ung* (Frankfurt a.M.: Suhrkamp, 1992), 231–293; Gunilla-Friederike
   Budde, *Auf dem Weg ins Bürgerleben: Kindheit und Erziehung in deutschen
   und englischen Bürgerfamilien, 1840–1914* (Göttingen: Vandenhoeck &

Ruprecht, 1994), 153–156, 413; Robert Wegs, *Growing Up Working Class: Continuity and Change among Viennese Youth, 1890–1938* (University Park: Pennsylvania State University Press, 1989), 61–62; and
the testimony of a secondary school boy's father in Realschule Marktbreit, Munich, 29 July 1918, BHStA Mk, Nr. 20893. See also Robert Griswold, *Fatherhood in America: A History* (New York: Basic Books, 1993), 13–15, 19.

3. The best overviews of the educational system under Wilhelm II are *Das Unterrichtswesen im Deutschen Reich*, vols. 1–4, ed. W[ilhelm] Lexis (Berlin: A. Asher, 1904); and Paulsen, *German Education*, xi–xx, 197–299. On the exclusionary structures of the educational system, see Detlef Müller, *Sozialstruktur und Schulsystem: Aspekte zum Strukturwandel des Schulwesens im 19. Jahrhundert* (Göttingen: Vandenhoeck & Ruprecht, 1977), 253, 287–297; Fritz Ringer, *Education and Society in Modern Europe* (Bloomington: Indiana University Press, 1979), 54–55, 70–81; William Learned, *An American Teacher's Year in a Prussian Gymnasium* (New York: Carnegie Foundation, 1911), 357; Marjorie Lamberti, *The Politics of Education: Teachers and School Reform in Weimar Germany* (New York: Berghahn, 2002), 18–20; and I. L. Kandel, "Germany," in *Comparative Education: Studies of the Educational Systems of Six Modern Nations*, ed. Peter Sandiford (London: J. M. Dent & Sons, 1918). For the statistics on secondary school opportunities, see Peter Lundgreen, "Die Bildungschancen beim Übergang von der 'Gesamtschule' zum Schulsystem der Klassengesellschaft im 19. Jahrhundert," *Zeitschrift für Pädagogik* 24 (1978): 109.

4. Lothar Mertens, "Das Privileg des Einjährig-Freiwilligen Militärdienstes im Kaiserreich und seine gesellschaftliche Bedeutung," *Militärgeschichtliche Mitteilungen* 39 (1986): 59–66.

5. James Albisetti, *Schooling German Girls and Women: Secondary and Higher Education in the Nineteenth Century* (Princeton, NJ: Princeton University Press, 1988), 41, 45 (quotation), 46–48, 51; James Albisetti, "The Feminization of Teaching in the Nineteenth Century: A Comparative Perspective," *History of Education* 22 (1993): 253–263; and Harald Reissig, "Die Lehrerseminare in Preußen im Ersten Weltkrieg" (Ph.D. diss., Freie Universität, Berlin, 1987), 54–55. See also Anne Digby and Peter Searby, *Children, School and Society in Nineteenth-Century England* (New York: Macmillan, 1981), 43; and Wegs, *Viennese Youth*, 87–88, 95.

6. Theobald Ziegler, *Allgemeine Pädagogik* (Leipzig: B. G. Teubner, 1906), 84 (quotation); S. J. Curtis, *Education in Britain since 1900* (Westport, CT: Greenwood Press, 1970), 174; and Budde, *Bürgerleben*, 206–207, 365–368.

7. Andrew Lees, *Cities, Sin, and Social Reform in Imperial Germany* (Ann Arbor: University of Michigan Press, 2002), 226–227; John Tilden Prince, *Methods of Instruction and Organization of the Schools of Germany* (Boston: Lee & Shepard, 1897), 32–33, 64, 101; Thomas Alexander, *The Prussian*

Elementary Schools (New York: Macmillan, 1918), 333–344; C. H. Lepping-
ton, "Some Characteristic Differences between English and German
Education," *Charity Organization Review* 13 (1903): 189; I. L. Kandel,
"Germany," 129, 124–130; Reissig, "Lehrerseminare," 29–73; and Learned,
American Teacher's Year, 354–356. Schools in Great Britain could be as strict
and abusive as those in Germany, but British schoolboys were far more
likely to resist through acts like school strikes. Stephen Humphries,
*Hooligans or Rebels? An Oral History of Working-Class Childhood and Youth
1889–1939* (Oxford: Basil Blackwell, 1981), 54–120.

8. Albisetti, *Schooling German Girls*, 56; and Reissig, "Lehrerseminare,"
290–292.

9. On female teachers, see *Statistisches Jahrbuch für den preußischen Staat*, ed.
Köngliches statistisches Landesamt 14 (Berlin, 1917), 222–223, and 15
(Berlin, 1918), 229; Rainer Bölling, "Elementarschullehrer zwischen Diszipli-
nierung und Emanzipation: Aspekte eines internationalen Vergleichs (1870–
1940)," in *Staat, Gesellschaft im 19. Jahrhundert: Mobilisierung und Disziplinier-
ung Bildung*, ed. Karl-Ernst Jeismann (Stuttgart: F. Steiner, 1989), 331, 334;
Albisetti, "Feminization of Teaching," 255. The evidence for the authoritarianism in schools is overwhelming. See Folkert Meyer, *Schule der Untertanen:
Lehrer und Politik in Preussen, 1848–1900* (Hamburg: Hoffmann und Campe,
1976), 200 (quotation); Hans Jürgen Apel, "Gymnasiallehrer mit 'Verständnis
und Taktgefuhl für die heranwachsende Jugend,'" in *Bildung*, ed. Jeismann,
320–21; Wolfgang Scheibe, *Die reformpädagogische Bewegung (1900–1932)*
(Weinheim: Beltz, 1974), 67–73; Mary Jo Maynes, *Taking the Hard Road: Life
Course in the French and German Worker' Autobiographies in the Era of Industrialization* (Chapel Hill: University of North Carolina Press, 1995), 86–99; Jürgen
Reulecke, "Von der Dorfschule zum Schulsystem," in *Fabrik—Familie—Fei-
erabend*, ed. Jürgen Reulecke and Wolfhard Weber (Wuppertal: Peter Hammer, 1978), 247–248; Franz Wenzel, "Sicherung von Massenloyalität und
Qualifikation der Arbeitskraft als Aufgabe der Volksschule," in *Schule und
Staat im 18. und 19. Jahrhundert*, ed. Ursula Aumüller-Roske et al. (Frankfurt
a.M.: Suhrkamp, 1974), 379–382; *Kindheit im Kaiserreich: Errinerungen an
vergangene Zeiten*, ed. Rudolf Pörtner (Düsseldorf: Deutscher Taschenbuch
Verlag, 1987), 105, 115; *Schule und Leben: Die Schulzeit in der Erinnerung
grosser Persönlichkeiten*, ed. Walter Klatt (Darmstadt: Winklers, 1961), 71, 95,
97, 120, 141, 189; Rosenbaum, *Formen der Familie*, 168–173; and Rosenbaum,
Proletarische Familien, 93. Teachers in German-speaking Austria-Hungary
treated pupils as they did in Germany. See the colorful descriptions in Stefan
Zweig, *The World of Yesterday* (Lincoln: University of Nebraska Press, 1964),
28–36. A lone dissenter from the dominant view is Dorle Klika, *Erziehung und
Sozialisation im Bürgertum des wilhelminischen Kaiserreichs* (Frankfurt a.M.:
Peter Lang, 1990), 390–391.

10. Helmut Sienknecht, *Der Einheitsschulegedanke* (Berlin: Beltz, 1968), 148–157; Rainer Bölling, *Volksschullehrer und Politik: Der Deutsche Lehrerverein 1918–1933* (Göttingen: Vandenhoeck & Ruprecht, 1978), 78–79; Rainer Bölling, *Sozialgeschichte der deutschen Lehrer* (Göttingen: Vandenhoeck & Ruprecht, 1983), 88–90; Marjorie Lamberti, "Radical Schoolteachers and the Origins of the Progressive Education Movement in Germany, 1900–1914," *History of Education Quarterly* 40 (2000): 25–32; Dudek, *Geschichte der Jugendforschung*, 98; and "Ist die Auswahl der Kreisschulinspektoren in Preußen eine Rechte?" *Pädagogische Zeitung* 42 (15 May 1913): 386–387.

11. Derek Linton, "Reforming the Urban Primary School in Imperial Germany," *History of Education* 13 (1984): 207–219; Wilhelm Flitner, *Der Krieg und die Jugend* (New Haven, CT: Deutsche Verlags-Anstalt, 1927), 243–244; and Lamberti, "Radical Schoolteachers," 27.

12. Emil Saupe, *Deutsche Pädagogen der Neuzeit* (Osterwieck am Harz: Zickfeldt, 1927), and Wilhelm Zils, *Geistiges und künstlerisches München in Selbstbiographien* (Munich: Kellerer, 1913), reprinted in DBA NF II 697, 421–424; Ulrich Hermann, "Pädagogisches Denken und Anfänge der Reformpädagogik," in *Handbuch der deutschen Bildungsgeschichte*, vol. 4, ed. Christa Berg (Munich: C. H. Beck, 1991), 155, 166; Georg Kerschensteiner, *Education for Citzenship* (New York: Rand McNally, 1911), 15–34, 97–110; and Scheibe, *Reformpädagogische Bewegung*, 171–210.

13. Scheibe, *Reformpädagogische Bewegung*, 81–109.

14. Hartwig Fiege, *Geschichte der hamburgischen Volksschule* (Hamburg: Erziehung und Wissenschaft, 1970), 80–82, 107–108; Gunther Böhme, *Das Zentralinstitut für Erziehung und Unterricht und seine Leiter* (Neuburgweier: Schindele, 1971), 31; Scheibe, *Die reformpädagogische Bewegung*, 67–75, 83; and Heinz Lemmermann, *Kriegserziehung im Kaiserreich: Studien zur politischen Funktion von Schule und Schulmusik, 1890–1918* (Lilienthal: Eres Edition, 1984), 255 (quotation).

15. Thomas Alexander and Beryl Parker, *The New Education in the German Republic* (New York: John Day, 1929), 121; James Albisetti and Peter Lundgreen, "Höhere Knabenschule," in *Bildungsgeschichte*, ed. Berg, 238; James Olson, "The Prussian Volksschule: A Study of the Social Implications of the Extension of Elementary Education" (Ph.D. diss., New York University, 1971), 102–103; and Lamberti, "Radical Schoolteachers," 45–46.

16. On working-class drinking culture, see Robert Goodrich, "Confessional Drinking: Catholic Workingmen's Clubs and Alcohol Consumption in Wilhelmine Germany," in *Histories of Leisure*, ed. Rudy Koshar (New York: Berg, 2002), 237; James Roberts, "Drink and the Labour Movement: The Schnapps Boycott of 1909" in *The German Working Class*, ed. Richard Evans (London: Croom Helm, 1982); and Ulrich Linse "'Animierkneipen' um 1900: Arbeitersexualität und bürgerliche Sittenreform," in *Kirmes-Kneipe-*

Kino: Arbeiterkultur im Ruhrgebiet zwischen Kommerz und Kontrolle (1850–1914), ed. Dagmar Kift (Paderborn: Ferdinand Schönigh, 1992), 237–238. On tobacco, see Richard Klein, *Cigarettes Are Sublime* (Durham, NC: Duke University Press, 1993); Matthew Hilton, "Leisure, Politics, and the Consumption of Tobacco in Britain since the Nineteenth Century," in *Leisure*, ed. Koshar, 321, 324–326; and Humphries, *Hooligans or Rebels*, 121–140, 149.

17. Scott Curtis, "The Taste of a Nation: Training the Senses and Sensibility of Cinema Audiences in Imperial Germany," *Film History* 6 (1994): 445, 449 (quotations); Lynn Abrams, *Workers' Culture in Imperial Germany: Leisure and Recreation in the Rhineland and Westphalia* (London: Routledge, 1992), 172–177; and Jürgen Kinter, "'Durch Nacht zum Licht': Vom Guckkasten zum Film Palast: Die Anfänge des Kinos und das Verhältnis der Arbeiterbewegung," in *Kirmes*, ed. Kift, 138.

18. Dehn, *Großstadtjugend*, 70; and Mack Walker, *German Home Towns: Community, State, and General State, 1648–1871* (Ithaca, NY: Cornell University Press, 1971), 73–75. See also Beth Bailey, *From Front Porch to Back Seat: Courtship in Twentieth-Century America* (Baltimore, MD: Johns Hopkins University Press, 1988), 13–22; and David Fowler, *The First Teenagers: The Lifestyle of Young Wage-Earners in Interwar Britain* (Portland, OR: Woburn, 1995), 110–132.

19. Thomas Lindenberger, *Straßenpolitik: Zur Sozialgeschichte der öffentlichen Ordnung in Berlin, 1900 bis 1914* (Bonn: Dietz, 1995), 124–127, 131; Linton, *Young Workers*, 44; Dickinson, *Politics of German Child Welfare*, 38; and Wegs, *Viennese Youth*, 68–72. On leisure and the street, see also see also Kathy Peiss, *Cheap Amusements: Working Women and Leisure in Turn-of-the-Century New York* (Philadelphia: Temple University Press, 1986), 56–114, 139–184; Scott W. Haine, "The Development of Leisure and the Transformation of Working Class Adolescence, Paris 1830–1940," *Journal of Family History* 17 (1992): 451–476; Kathleen Alaimo, "Shaping Adolescence in the Popular Milieu: Social Policy, Reformers, and French Youth, 1870–1920," *Journal of Family History* 17 (1992): 419–438; Childs, *Labour's Apprentices*, 95–109, 115–135, 159–160; and Gillis, *Youth and History*, 62–64.

20. Waldemar Zimmermann, "Die Erwerbsarbeit der Kinder und Jugendlichen," in *Handbuch für Jugendpflege*, ed. Frieda Duensing (Langensalza: Hermann Beyer & Söhne, 1913), 204; Christina Benninghaus, *Die anderen Jugendlichen: Arbeitermädchen in der Weimarer Republik* (Frankfurt a.M.: Campus, 1999), 79; Dehn, *Großstadtjugend*, 72–78; and Linton, *Young Workers*, 19–47, 52. See also Harry Hendrick, *Images of Youth, Age and Class and the Male Youth Problem* (New York: Oxford University Press, 1990), 15–47, 58–65; Springhall, *Adolescence in Britain*, 145–147; Childs, *Labour's Apprentices*, 20–21, 89–92; and Humphries, *Hooligans or Rebels?* 59–62.

21. Dickinson, "Citizenship, Vocational Training, and Recreation," 114–116, 128; Derek Linton, "Between School and Marriage, Workshop and Household: Young Working Women as a Social problem in Late Imperial Germany," *European History Quarterly* 18 (1988): 387–408; Nancy Reagin, *A German Women's Movement: Class and Gender in Hanover, 1880–1933* (Chapel Hill: University of North Carolina Press, 1995), 77–81; and Linton, *Young Workers,* 14, 73–97

22. Manfred Zwerschke, *Jugendverbände und Sozialpolitik: Zur Geschichte der deutschen Jugendverbände* (Munich: Juventa, 1973), 14; Saul, "Der Kampf um die Jugend," 115, 142–143; Reulecke, "Arbeiterjugend im Kaiserreich," 320; Dickinson, "Citizenship, Vocational Training, and Recreation," 112–113; Linton, *Young Workers*, 172; and the contributions to *Jugendpflegeverbände,* ed. Hertha Siemering (Berlin: Carl Heymanns, 1918), 6, 97–98, 133–134. See also David Macleod, *Building Character in the American Boy: The Boy Scouts, YMCA, and Their Forerunners, 1870–1920* (Madison: University of Wisconsin Press, 1983), 15–20, 37; Kett, *Adolescence in America,* 190–194; Crubellier, *L'enfance et la jeunesse,* 309–334; Springhall, *Adolescence in Britain,* 147–156; Munoz, "Sport catholique," 59; and Childs, *Labour's Apprentices,* 152.

23. Ulrich Aufmuth, *Die deutsche Wandervogelbewegung unter soziologischem Aspekt* (Göttingen: Vandenhoeck & Ruprecht, 1979), 38–42, 49; Fritz Borinski and Werner Milch, *Jugendbewegung: The Story of German Youth 1896–1933* (London: German Educational Reconstruction, 1945), 7–11; Harry Pross, *Jugend, Eros, Politik: Die Geschichte der deutschen Jugendverbände* (Bern: Scherz, 1964), 75–86; and Laqueur, *German Youth Movement,* 3–31.

24. Dietmar Schenk, *Die Freideutsche Jugend 1913–1919/20: Eine Jugendbewegung in Krieg, Revolution und Krise* (Münster: Lit, 1991), 53–54; Jürgen Reulecke, "Männerbund versus the Family: Middle-Class Youth Movements and the Family in Germany in the Period of the First World War," in *Upheaval of War: Family, Work and Welfare in Europe 1914–1918,* ed. Richard Wall and Jay Winter (New York: Cambridge University Press, 1988), 442; Laqueur, *German Youth Movement,* 30; Aufmuth, *Wandervogelbewegung,* 47; John Springhall, *Youth, Empire and Society: British Youth Movements, 1883–1940* (London: Croom Helm, 1977), 61; and Macleod, *Boy Scouts,* 271–272.

25. Borinski and Werner, *Jugendbewegung,* 12–13; Aufmuth, *Wandervogelbewegung,* 43 (quotation); Schenk, *Freideutsche Jugend,* 45–47, 57–63, 69; and Laqueur, *German Youth Movement,* 31–37

26. Gerhard Ille, "Jugendbewegung und Erster Weltkrieg," in *Der Wandervogel,* ed. *idem* and Günter Köhler (Berlin: Stapp, 1987), 189 (first quotation); Laqueur, *German Youth Movement,* 53–54, 57–64, 75–82, 100; Pross, *Jugend, Eros, Politik,* 133–134, 165 (second quotation), 171–173; Schenk, *Freideutsche Jugend,* 70–83, 81 (fourth quotation), 83 (third quotation); and Karl Wil-

libald, *Jugend, Gesellschaft und Politik im Zeitraum des Ersten Weltkrieges* (Munich: Neue Schriftsreihe, 1973), 127–129.

27. On girls in the Wandervogel, see Marion E. P. de Ras, *Body, Femininity and Nationalism: Girls in the German Youth Movement 1900–1934* (New York: Routledge, 2008), 89–90, 97, 189–190.

28. Richard Evans, "'Red Wednesday' in Hamburg: Social Democrats, Police and Lumpenproletariat in the Suffrage Disturbances of 17 January 1906," in *Rethinking German History: Nineteenth-Century Germany and the Origins of the Third Reich,* ed. Richard Evans (Boston: Allen & Unwin, 1987); and Roberts, "Drink and the Labour Movement."

29. Carl Schorske, *German Social Democracy, 1905–1917: The Development of the Great Schism* (New York: Russel & Russel, 1955), 98; Heinrich Schulz, "Die proletarische Jugendbewegung," in *Jugendpflegeverbände,* ed. Siemering, 422–423; Alex Hall, "Youth in Rebellion: The Beginnings of the Socialist Youth Movement, 1904–1914," in *Wilhelmine Germany,* ed. Evans, 248–253; Reinhard Höhn, *Sozialismus und Heer: Der Kampf des Heeres gegen die Sozialdemokratie,* vol. 3 (Bad Harzburg: M. Gehlen, 1969), 480; Erich Eberts, *Arbeiterjugend 1904–1945: Sozialistische Erziehungsgemeinschaft— Politische Organisation* (Frankfurt a.M.: dipa, 1979), 25–26; and Linton, *Young Workers,* 122.

30. Walter Sieger, *Junge Front: Die revolutionäre Arbeiterjugend im Kampf gegen den Ersten Weltkrieg* ([East] Berlin: Neues Leben, 1958), 34–38; Schorske, *German Social Democracy,* 98–100; Linton, *Young Workers,* 124; Hall, "Youth," 250; and Eberts, *Arbeiterjugend,* 27.

31. William Walling, *The Socialists and the War* (New York: Henry Holt, 1915), 10, 15, 22, 65–79; Roland Stromberg, "La patrie en danger: Socialism and War in 1914," *The Midwest Quarterly* 18 (1977): 268–286; Horst Klein, "Zur Kriegsfrage in der Geschichte der deutschen Sozialdemokratie: Mit der Erblast der Kriegskredite von 1914 in den NATO-Krieg 1999," *Beiträge zur Geschichte der Arbeiterbewegung* 42 (2000): 7; Boll, "Die deutsche Sozialdemokratie," 210–211; and Schorske, *German Social Democracy,* 66–86, 100 (quotation), 101;

32. Eberts, *Arbeiterjugend,* 29–32; Schorske, *German Social Democracy,* 103–108; Sieger, *Junge Front,* 40–43; and Saul, "Der Kampf um die Jugend," 103–105, 109–110.

33. Wilhelm Eildermann, *Jugend im ersten Weltkrieg: Tagebücher, Briefe, Erinnerungen* ([East] Berlin: Dietz, 1972), 311; Schulz, "Die proletarische Jugendbewegung," 424–430, 425 (quotation); Sieger, *Junge Front,* 45–47; Höhn, *Sozialismus,* 484–485, 491; Hall, "Youth," 256–59; Linton, *Young Workers,* 129, 134; and Ebert, *Arbeiterjugend,* 35–38, 42–44.

34. Karl Heinz Jahnke, Rudolf Falkenberg, Bernd Ferchland, Werner Lamprecht, Horst Pietschmann, and Siegfried Scholze, *Geschichte der deutschen*

Arbeiterjugendbewegung, 1904–1945 ([East] Berlin: Neues Leben, 1973), 133; McMeekin, *Willi Münzenberg*, 24; and Linton, *Young Workers*, 127–129.

35. Linton, *Young Workers*, 130, 135–136; and Sieger, *Arbeiterjugend*, 49–58.

36. Humphries, *Hooligans or Rebels?* 211–214, 238 (quotation); and Peukert, *Grenzen der Sozialdisziplinierung, 128–139.*

2. The Constraints on Chauvinism

1. The best synthesis of this interpretation is again Wehler, *German Empire*, 51–191.

2. Verein für Christliche Erziehungswissenschaft, "Ideale von Knaben und Mädchen unter dem Einfluß des Krieges: Aus der Arbeitsgemeinschaft für experimentell-pädagogische Forschung der katholisch-pädagogischen Vereine Münchens," *Völkerkrieg und Jugendführung* (Donauwörth: n.p., 1916), 13.

3. Horst Joachim Frank, *Geschichte des Deutschunterrichts: Von den Anfängen bis 1945* (Munich: C. Hanser, 1973), 511–518, 512 (first quotation), 528–531, 544–557; Joachim Hohmann and Hermann Langer, *"Stolz, ein Deutscher zu Sein . . .": Nationales Selbstverständnis in Schulaufsätzen, 1914–1945* (Frankfurt a.M.: Peter Lang, 1995), 12–13; *Kindheit*, ed. Pörtner, 188–198; Margret Kraul, *Gymnasium und Gesellschaft im Vormärz* (Göttingen: Vandenhoeck & Ruprecht, 1980), 101–111, 120–122; Jakob Vogel, *Nationen im Gleichschritt: Der Kult der "Nation in Waffen" in Deutschland und Frankreich, 1871–1914* (Göttingen: Vandenhoeck & Ruprecht, 1997), 75–77, 89, 144–162; Reiner Bessling, *Schule der Nationalen Ethik: Johann Georg Sprengel: Die Deutschkundebewegung und der deutsche Germanistenverband* (New York: Peter Lang, 1997), 38, 45, 95–116; Gerhardt Petrat, *Schulerziehung: Ihre Sozialgeschichte in Deutschland bis 1945* (München: Ehrenwirth, 1987), 225–236; Hermann Hesse, "Weltgeschichte," in *Krieg und Frieden* (Zurich: Fretz & Wasmuth, 1946), 101–102; Marieluise Christadler, *Kriegserziehung im Jugendbuch: Literarische Mobilmachung in Deutschland und Frankreich vor 1914* (Frankfurt a.M.: Haag-Herchen, 1979), 8–20; Lemmermann, *Kriegserziehung*, 146–171, 155 (second and third quotations); and Synes Ernst, *Deutschunterricht und Ideologie* (Frankfurt a.M.: Peter Lang, 1977), 211–213.

4. Douglas Skopp, "Auf der untersten Sprosse: Der Volkschullehrer als Semi-Professional im Deutschland des 19. Jahrhunderts," *Geschichte und Gesellschaft* 6 (1979): 383–402; Eugene Anderson, "The Prussian Volksschule in the 19th Century," in *Entstehung und Wandel der modernen Gesellschaft: Festschrift für Hans Rosenberg*, ed. Gerhard Ritter (Berlin: De Gruyter, 1970), 266, 276–277; Hildegard Milberg, *Schulpolitik in der pluralistischen Gesellschaft: Die politischen und sozialen Aspekte der Schulreform in Hamburg, 1890–1935* (Hamburg: Leibniz-Verlag, 1970), 89–91; Bölling, *Sozialgeschichte*

der deutschen Lehrer, 51–52; Bölling, *Volksschullehrer,* 9–10, 19, 24–25, 74–75; Hartmut Titze, "Lehrerbildung und Professionalisierung," in *Bildungsgeschichte,* ed. Berg, 356; Bernd Weber, *Pädagogik und Politik vom Kaiserreich zum Faschismus: Zur Analyse politischer Optionen von Pädagogikhochschullehrern von 1914–1933* (Königstein/Ts.: Scriptor, 1979), 84; Apel, "Gymnasiallehrer," 315; Meyer, *Schule der Untertanen,* 200–203; and Höhn, *Sozialismus,* 319.

5. On German instruction, see Marjorie Lamberti, "Elementary School Teachers and the Struggle against Social Democracy in Wilhelmine Germany," *History of Education Quarterly* 32 (1992): 93; Kraul, *Gymnasium,* 105; and the tables on the weekly *Lehrpläne* in *Bildungsgeschichte,* vol. 4, ed. Berg, 220–221, 276–278. On history, see James Albisetti, *Secondary School Reform in Imperial Germany* (Princeton, NJ: Princeton University Press, 1983), 254 (quotation), 254–256, 282; James Olson,"Nationalistic Values in Prussian Schoolbooks prior to World War 1," *Canadian Review of Studies in Nationalism* 1 (1973): 51; Hilke Günther-Arndt, "Monarchische Präventivbelehrung oder Curriculare Reform? Zur Wirkung des Kaiser-Erlasses vom 1. Mai 1889 auf den Geschichtsunterricht," in *Bildung,* ed. Jeismann, 271–272; Karl Dietrich Erdmann, "Geschichte, Politik und Pädagogik—aus den Akten des Deutschen Historikerverbandes," *Geschichte in Wissenschaft und Unterricht* 19 (1968): 10–11, 13; Lamberti, "Elementary School Teachers," 84–85; Alfred Kelly, "The Franco-German War and Unification in German Schoolbooks," *1870/71–1989/90: German Unifications and the Change in Literary Discourse,* ed. Walter Pape (New York: Walter de Gruyter, 1993); and Walter Langsam, "Nationalism and History in the Prussian Elementary Schools under William II," in *Nationalism and Internationalism,* ed. Edward Earle (New York: Columbia University Press, 1950), 248.

6. On antimilitarism, see Höhn, *Sozialismus,* 332–334; and Lemmermann, *Kriegserziehung,* 48 (quotation), 76–77. Lemmermann's strongest evidence for the militarism in schools comes, not surprisingly, from the First World War. On politics, see Helmut Becker and Gerhard Kluchert, *Die Bildung der Nation: Schule, Gesellschaft und Politik vom Kaiserreich zur Weimarer Republik* (Stuttgart: Klett-Cotta, 1993), 370; and Albisetti, *Secondary School Reform,* 256, 306. The Reich Law of Association of 1908 codified the custom in families on refraining from discussing politics with youths. Budde, *Bürgerleben,* 371–375; and Saul, "Der Kampf um die Jugend," 105. On the military, pacifism, and international history, see Manfred Messerschmidt, "Militär und Schule in der wilhemischen Zeit," *Militärgeschichtliche Mitteilung* 23 (1978): 51–76; Roger Chickering, *Imperial Germany and a World without War: The Peace Movement and German Society, 1892–1914* (Princeton, NJ: Princeton University Press, 1975), 170–175; Katharine Kennedy, "Regionalism and Nationalism in South German History Lessons, 1871–1914," *German Studies Review* 12 (1989): 11–33; and Olson, "Prussian Volksschule," 159.

7. Julianne Eckhardt, "Imperialismus und Kaiserreich," in *Geschichte der deutschen Kinder- und Jugendliteratur,* ed. Reiner Wild (Stuttgart: J. B. Metzler, 2002), 179.

8. Christadler, *Kriegserziehung,* 21–40, 68–85, 106–177; Irene Dyhrenfurth, *Geschichte des deutschen Jugendbuches* (1942; reprint, Zürich: Atlantis, 1967), 144–173; and Eckhardt, "Imperialismus und Kaiserreich," 182–202.

9. Joe Dubbert, *A Man's Place: Masculinity in Transition* (Englewood Cliffs, NJ: Prentice Hall, 1979), 122–131; James Steakley, "Iconography of a Scandal: Political Cartoons and the Eulenberg Affair in Wilhelmine Germany," in *Hidden from History: Reclaiming the Gay and Lesbian Past,* ed. Martin Duberman, Martha Vicinus, and George Chauncey (New York: New American Library, 1989), 248–249; Ute Frevert, "Soldaten, Staatsbürger: Überlegungen zur historischen Konstruktion von Männlichkeit," in *Männergeschichte—Geschlechtergeschichte,* ed. Thomas Kühne (New York: Campus, 1996), 82–85; Klaus Vondung, "Apokalyptische Erwartung: Zur Jugendrevolte in der deutschen Literatur zwischen 1910 und 1930," in *"Mit uns zieht die neue Zeit": Der Mythos Jugend,* ed. Thomas Koebner, Rolf-Peter Janz, and Frank Trommler (Frankfurt a.M.: Suhrkamp, 1985), 526; and Mosse, *Fallen Soldiers,* 54–68.

10. Giesela Wilkending, "Mädchenliteratur von der Mitte des 19. Jahrhunderts bis zum Ersten Weltkrieg," in *Jugendliteratur,* ed. Wild, 220–246; Ronald Fullerton, "Towards a Commercial Popular Culture in Germany: The Development of Pamphlet Fiction, 1871–1914," *Journal of Social History* 12 (1979): 489–511; and Rudolf Schenda, *Die Lesestoffe der kleinen Leute: Studien zur populären Literatur* (Munich: C. H. Beck, 1976), 80–94; and Dyhrenfurth, *Jugendbuch,* 168–175.

11. John Fout, "Sexual Politics in Wilhelmine Germany: The Male Gender Crisis, Moral Purity, and Homophobia," in *Forbidden History: The State, Society and the Regulation of Sexuality in Modern Europe,* ed. John Fout (Chicago: University of Chicago Press, 1992); and Zweig, *World of Yesterday,* 25–26 (first and second quotations); Heinrich Wolgast, *Das Elend unserer Jugendliteratur* (Hamburg: Selbstverlag, 1899), 23–24, 120–146; Christa Kamenetsky, *Children's Literature in Hitler's Germany: The Cultural Policy of National Socialism* (Athens: Ohio University Press, 1984), 11–15; Christadler, *Kriegserziehung,* 21–40, 24 (third quotation); Gerhard Holtz-Baumert, *Überhaupt brauchen wir eine sozialistische Literatur: Skizzen vom Kampf um eine sozialistische, deutsche Kinderliteratur mit einem Dokumenten-Anhang* ([East] Berlin: Kinderbuch, 1972), 12, 23, 31–37, 108–110; and Lamberti, "Elementary School Teachers," 95–99.

12. On muscular Christianity and masculinity, see John Springhall, "Building Character in the British Boy: The Attempt to Extend Manliness to Working-Class Adolescents, 1880–1914," in *Manliness and Morality:*

Middle-Class Masculinity in Britain and America, ed. A. Mangan and James Walvin (Manchester: Manchester University Press, 1987), 54; George Mosse, *The Image of Man: The Creation of Modern Masculinity* (New York: Oxford University Press, 1996), 49–50; Dubbert, *A Man's Place*, 122–140; *Muscular Christianity: Embodying the Victorian Age*, ed. Donald Hall (Cambridge: Cambridge University Press, 1994); John Higham, "The Reorientation of American Culture in the 1890s," in *Writing American History* (Bloomington: Indiana University Press, 1970), 78–80; Springhall, *Youth, Empire*, 24; and Kett, *Adolescence in America*, 221–224. On the Boy Scouts, see Michael Rosenthal, *The Character Factory: Baden-Powell and the Origins of the Boy Scout Movement* (New York: Pantheon, 1986), 160, 175; Henri van Effenterre, *Histoire du scoutisme* (Paris: Université de France, 1947), 42; Karl Seidelmann, *Die Pfadfinder in der deutschen Jugendgeschichte* (Hanover: Hermann Schroedel, 1977), 27–41; Christoph Schubert-Weller, *"Kein schönerer Tod . . .": Die Militarisierung der männlichen Jugend und ihr Einsatz im Ersten Weltkrieg, 1890–1918* (Munich: Juventa, 1998), 127–157; Robert MacDonald, *Sons of the Empire: The Frontier and the Boy Scout Movement* (Toronto: University of Toronto Press, 1993), 16–18; *Jugendpflegeverbände*, ed. Siemering, 51–53; Hendrick, *Male Youth Problem*, 221–223; and Macleod, *Boy Scouts*, 77–78, 190–194.

13. Heinrich Muth, "Jugendpflege und Politik: Zur Jugend- und Innenpolitik des Kaiserreichs," *Geschichte in Wissenschaft und Unterricht* 12 (1961): 600, 604–605; Brigette Naudascher, *Freizeit in öffentlicher Hand: Behördliche Jugend Deutschland von 1900–1980* (Düsseldorf: Bröschler, 1990), 45–48, 171; Christa Hasenclever, *Jugendhilfe und Jugendgesetzgebung seit 1900* (Göttingen: Vandenhoeck und Ruprecht, 1978), 36–41; Hildegard Böhme, "Zentral-Organisationen und Organe," in *Handbuch für Jugendpflege*, ed. Duensing, 524–525; Kohlrausch, "Der Zentralausschuß für Volks- und Jugendspiele in Deutschland" in *Jugendpflegeverbände*, ed. Siemering, 18–22; Saul, "Der Kampf um die Jugend," 99–107, 104 (quotation); and Schubert-Weller, *Die Militarisierung der männlichen Jugend*, 56–69. Many officials were cognizant of the semantic distinction between *Jugendfürsorge* and *Jugendpflege*, but in practice the public still conflated the terms.

14. Muth, "Jugendpflege," 607; Saul, "Der Kampf um die Jugend," 113–115; Dickinson, "Citizenship, Vocational Training, and Recreation," 133–136; and Linton, *Young Workers*, 141 (quotation).

15. Dickinson, "Citizenship, Vocational Training, and Recreation," 120; and "Bericht über die Sitzung der Kreisjugendpfleger," Ortsausschuss für Jugendpflege, Frankfurt a.M., 27 April 1916, HessHA 405 Nr. 3838, Bl. 289–290. An account of the most popular *Jugendpflege* journals among district youth workers in Nassau-Hessen appears in "Bericht über die Tätigkeit des Kreisjugendpflegers des Untertaunuskreises im Jahre 1918," 1 February 1919, HessHA 405 Nr. 3839, Bl. 256–267.

16. Linton, "Young Working Women"; Linton, *Young Workers,* 165–185; Reagin, *German Women's Movement,* 43–70; and Michael Teitelbaum and Jay Winter, *Fear of Population Decline* (New York: Academic, 1985), 18–36.

17. See reports by youth workers Steitz, Biedenkopf, 10 January 1917, HessHA 405 Nr. 3838, Bl. 364; Abicht, Hauptausschuss für Jugendpflege in Charlottenburg, 12 January 1916, LABr Pr. Br. Rep. 2a Reg. Potsdam II Gen. Nr. 1577; and Bertsche, Unterweserwaldkreis near Monatabaur, 31 December 1916, HessHA 405 Nr. 3838, Bl. 416ff, and 29 January 1918 and 9 January 1919, HessHA 405 Nr. 3839, Bl. 103ff, 291–293.

18. Kjp., Frankfurt a.M., 9 February 1915, HessHA 405 Nr. 3838, Bl. 48ff; Linton, *Young Workers,* 140 (quotation); Muth, "Jugendpflege," 611–617; and Saul, "Der Kampf um die Jugend," 113.

19. Major General von Bailer, "Der Jungdeutschlandbund," in *Jugendpflegeverbände,* ed. Siemering, 43–49; Schubert-Weller, *Die Militarisierung der männlichen Jugend,* 172–193; Muth, "Jugendpflege," 610–611; and Saul, "Der Kampf um die Jugend," 118–123.

20. Linton, *Young Workers,* 159–160 (quotations).

21. Hans Jürgen Ostler, "'Soldatenspielerei?' Vormilitärische Ausbildung bei Jugendlichen in der österreichischen Reichshälfte der Donaumonarchie, 1914–1918" (M. A. thesis, Hamburg University, 1990), 42; Dickinson, "Citizenship, Vocational Training, and Recreation," 137–138; Linton, *Young Workers,* 13 (quotation); and Saul, "Der Kampf um die Jugend," 123.

3. War Pedagogy in the Era of the *Burgfrieden*

1. On university professors and the war, see *Aufrufe und Reden deutscher Professoren im 1. Weltkrieg,* ed. Klaus Böhme (Stuttgart: Reclam, 1975), 24–26, 30–31; Klaus Schwabe, *Wissenschaft und Kriegsmoral: Die deutschen Hochschullehrer und die politischen Grundlagen des ersten Weltkrieges* (Göttingen: Musterschmidt, 1969), 21–45; Weber, *Pädagogik und Politik,* 43–203; and Verhey, *Spirit of 1914,* 161–173.

2. On Theobald Ziegler, see DBA NF (II) 1446, 273–290. The only scholarship to date that recognizes the degree to which war pedagogy used reform teaching methods is by a lay historian. Bernd Moiske, "Formeln, Schüler, Krieg: Mathematisch-naturwissenschaftliche Fachpädagogik um die Zeit des ersten Weltkrieges," in *Lehrer helfen siegen: Kriegspädagogik im Kaiserreich,* ed. Arbeitsgruppe "Lehrer und Krieg" (Berlin: Diesterweg, 1987). Overviews of education during the war are not comprehensive in periodization, content, or types of schools. See Walther Jannel, *Kriegspädagogik: Berichte und Vorschläge* (Leipzig: Akademische Verlagsgesellschaft, 1916); Ulrich Bendele, *Krieg, Kopf und Körper: Lernen für das Leben—Erziehung zum Tod* (Frankfurt a.M.: Ullstein, 1984); Rainer Bendick, *Kriegserwartung und Kriegserfahrung: Der*

Erste Weltkrieg in deutschen und französischen Schulgeschichtsbüchern (1900–1939/45) (Paffenweiler: Centaurus, 1999), 93–245; Eberhard Demm, "Deutschlands Kinder im Ersten Weltkrieg: Zwischen Propaganda und Sozialfürsorge," *Militärgeschichtliche Zeitschrift* 60 (2001): 51–98; Stefan Goebel, "Schools," in *Capital Cities at War: Paris, London, Berlin, 1914–1919*, vol. 2 (New York: Cambridge University Press, 2007); Eckhard Emminger, "'Und der ganze Unterricht muss auf die große Uhr des Weltkrieges eingestellt werden!' Die Auswirkungen des Ersten Weltkrieges auf die Volksschule im Königreich Bayern, 1914 bis 1918" (Ph.D. diss., Augsburg University, 1988); Flitner, *Krieg und die Jugend;* Lemmermann, *Kriegserziehung,* 254–379; and Reissig, "Lehrerseminare."

3. War pedagogy, an educational movement in the first years of the war, should not be confused with "patriotic instruction" *(vaterländischer Unterricht),* whose materials the War Press Office published in 1917 and 1918 for officers, enlisted soldiers, and a general reading public. Wilhelm Ziegler, *Grundlagen für den vaterländischen Unterricht: Unter besonderer Berücksichtigung des bisher vom Kriegspresseamt verbreiteten Unterrichtsmaterials* (Berlin: Kriegspresseamt, 1918). Even otherwise excellent overviews on the transition of schooling from the German Empire to the Weimar Republic have left out the wartime reform methods entirely. See, for example, Becker and Kluchert, *Die Bildung der Nation,* 246.

4. *Kriegserlasse für die preußische Volksschule,* ed. Julius Schapler and Friedrich Groeteken (Arnsberg: Stahl, 1918), 44 (quotation); and Min. Ed., Munich, 19 October 1914, StaaMünch RA Nr. 53885.

5. Peters, "Kriegspädagogik in der ländlichen Fortbildungsschule," *Hannoversche Schulzeitung* 50 (27 October 1914): 690 (quotation); Schepp, "Unsre Schulen in der Kriegszeit," *Lehrer-Zeitung für Ost- und Westpreußen* 45 (3 October 1914): 812; and "Krieg und Volksschule," *Katholische Schulzeitung für Norddeutschland* 31 (17 September 1914): 614–615.

6. "Die Sedanfeier verboten?" *Vossische Zeitung* (first quotation) and "Die Schule während des Krieges," *Deutsche Tageszeitung,* both 31 August 1914, and "Schulausfall am Sedantag," *Berliner Lokalanzeiger,* 1 September 1914, all in BA-Li 8034 II 6938, Bl. 129, 130; "Krieg und Schule," *Katholische Schulzeitung für Norddeutschland* 31 (25 September 1914): 627; "Keine Siegesfeiern in den Volksschulen" and "Zwei Verfügungen," *Der Volksschullehrer* 8 (26 November 1914): 712 (second quotation); and "Soll zur Feier großer Siege der Unterricht ausfallen oder nicht?" *Der Volksschullehrer* 8 (10 December 1914): 734–736.

7. "Krieg und Unterricht," *Pädagogische Zeitung* 43 (19 November 1914): 808–809; and Schapler and Groeteken, *Kriegserlasse,* 45 (quotation).

8. As reprinted in "Der Krieg und der Lehrplan der Volksschulen," *Pädagogische Zeitung* 44 (11 November 1915): 555 (quotation). See also "Die diesjährigen

Kultusdebatten im preußischen Abgeordnetenhaus," *Der Volksschullehrer* 10 (13 April 1916): 117.

9. "Volksschulsorgen der 'Kreuzzeitung'," *Pädagogische Zeitung* 41 (29 August 1912), 685; and Bölling, *Volksschullehrer*, 24–25.

10. L. Viereck, "Schulverfassung," *Jahresberichte über das höhere Schulwesen* 30 (1915): ii.35 (quotation); and "Aus dem preußischen Abgeordnetenhause," *Deutsches Philologen Blatt* 23 (1915): 507.

11. W. Knebel, "Unterricht in Kriegszeit," *Deutsches Philologen Blatt* 22 (1914): 639 (quotation); Josef Häußner, *Der Weltkrieg und die höheren Schulen Badens im Schuljahr, 1914–1915* (Karlruhe: Gutsch, 1915), 23; and L. Eicke, "Latein," *Jahresberichte über das höhere Schulwesen* 30 (1915): vi.6. See also the following in *Das humanistische Gymnasium* 26 (1915): E. Gründwald, "Burgfrieden!" 1–8; R. Lück, "Vaterländischer Kriegsabend," 16–18; and "Unsere jungen Griechen und Römer," 146.

12. "Zentralinstitut für Erziehung und Unterricht," *Hannoversche Schulzeitung* 51 (20 April 1915): 193 (quotation); V. H. Friedel, *The German School as a War Nursery*, trans. from the French (New York: MacMillan, 1918), 31–32; and Böhme, *Zentralinstitut*, 31.

13. "Die Kriegsführung der Kinder: Zur Ausstellung 'Schule und Krieg'," *Berliner Tageblatt*, 14 August 1915, LABe STA Rep. 20–01 Nr. 402, Bl. 93; "Vorträge während der Ausstellung 'Schule und Krieg,'" GStA I. HA Rep. 77 Tit. 924 Nr. 8 Bd. II, Bl. 89–90; L. Pallat, "Das Zentralinstitut für Erziehung und Unterricht in den zwei ersten Jahren seines Bestehens," *Monatsschrift für höhere Schulen* 16 (February–March 1917): 65–79; and Zentralinstitut für Erziehung und Unterricht, *Schule und Krieg: Sonderausstellung* (Berlin: Weidmann, 1915).

14. "Schule und Kriege," *Vorwärts*, 29 April 1915; "Schule und Krieg," *Jugendführung* 2 (1915): 25–26; and Min. Ed., Berlin, 13 October 1917, KPSK-Berichte, Bd. II, Bl. 8.

15. Woldemar Goerlitz, "Der Krieg und der gymnasiale Geschichtsunterricht," *Monatsschrift für höhere Schule* 14 (1915): 233; A. Hedler, "Vom Krieg in der Schule," *Deutsches Philologen Blatt* 23 (1915): 492; "Worte an die deutsche Jugend und ihre Führer," *Frankfurter Schulzeitung* 32 (15 January 1915): 14 (first quotation); Max Engel, *Leipzigs Volksschulen im Zeichen des Welkrieges: Auf Grund von Einzelberichten und unter Mitarbeit von Lehrern und Direktoren* (Leipzig: Dürr, 1915), 7 (second quotation); Schwabe, *Hochschullehrer*, 24; "Volkskrieg," *Schulblatt der Provinz Sachsen* 53 (14 October 1914): 541; and "Wie das neue Deutsche Reich entstand," in *Der Weltkrieg im persönlichen Ausdruck der Kinder: 150 Schülerkriegsaufsätze* ed. Max Reiniger (Langensalza: Beltz, 1915), 31–32.

16. "Laßt die Jugend die große Zeit erleben!" *Lehrer-Zeitung für Ost- und Westpreußen* 45 (19 September 1914): 784; Georg Kerschensteiner, "Der Krieg

als Erzieher," *Der Volksschullehrer* 8 (10 December 1914): 729–730; Graf, "Wie ich in diesen schweren Tagen meine Kinder unterrichte," *Badische Schulzeitung* 53 (3 April 1915), 105 (third and fourth quotatios); M. Hartmann, "Kriegspädagogische Betrachtungen," *Deutsches Philologen Blatt* 23 (20 January 1915): 43; K. Weise, "Mathematik," *Jahresberichte über das höhere Schulwesen* 30 (1915), xii.1–4; K. A. George, "Eine Kriegsausstellung in der Schule," *Deutsches Philologen Blatt* 23 (16 June 1915): 354 (last quotation). For a bibliography with close to two thousand citations of articles and books written in 1914 and 1915 on war pedagogy, see Jannel, *Kriegspädagogik*. On the denouncements of hate in schools in 1915, see Chapter 9 in this volume.

17. Paul Samuleit, *Wie unsere Jugend den Krieg erlebt* (Berlin: Sigismund, 1917), 35 (first quotation); and W. Schütz-Westerfeld, "Zeitkunde," *Frankfurter Schulzeitung* 33 (1 November 1916): 196 (second quotation). The first textbook with a war pedagogy curriculum was arguably H. Korsch, *Kriegsstunden: Stoffe und Darbietung für die Schule* (Leipzig: List & von Bressendorf, 1915–1916). On the new war media, see Wolfgang Natter, *Literature at War, 1914–1940: Representing the Time of Greatness in Germany* (New Haven, CT: Yale University Press, 1999), 174–186; Verhey, *Spirit of 1914*, 115–185; Klaus Vondung, "Deutsche Apokalypse 1914," in *Das wilhelmische Bildungsbürger-tum* (Göttingen: Vandenhoeck & Ruprecht, 1980); Wilhelm Pressel, *Die Kriegspredigt 1914–1918 in der evangelischen Kirche Deutschlands* (Göttingen: Vandenhoeck & Ruprecht, 1967); Karl Hammer, *Deutsche Kriegstheologie 1870–1918* (Munich: Kösel, 1974), 54–59; Heinrich Missalla, *"Gott mit uns": Die deutsche katholische Kriegspredigt 1914–1918* (Munich: Kösel, 1968); Bernd Ulrich, *Die Augenzeugen: Deutsche Feldpostbriefe in Kriegs- und Nachkriegszeit, 1914–1933* (Essen: Klartext, 1997); and Manfred Hettling and Michael Jeismann, "Der Weltkrieg als Epos: Philipp Witkops 'Kriegs-briefe gefallener Studenten,'" in *Keiner fühlt sich hier mehr als Mensch . . . : Erlebnis und Wirkung des Ersten Weltkriegs*, ed. Gerhard Hirschfeld (Essen: Klartext, 1993). An estimated 1.5 million patriotic war poems were sent to newspapers in August 1914 alone. Julius Bab, *Die deutsche Kriegslyrik, 1914–1918: Eine kritische Bibliographie* (Stettin: Norddeutscher Verlag für Literatur und Kunst, 1920), 25.

18. H. Kölling, "Die Aktualität des Unterrichts," *Pädagogische Zeitung* 43 (10 September 1914): 690–691; Blanckenhorn, "Lehrplan und Krieg," *Der Volksschullehrer* 9 (26 August 1915): 405; Göhrs, "Kriegsrechnen und Kriegszeichnen," *Hannoversche Schulzeitung* 51 (18 May 1915): 236; Eduard Stemplinger, "Kriegsjahresberichte 1914/15 der bayerischen gymnasialen Anstalten," *Deutsches Philologen-Blatt* (1914): 747–749; "Krieg und Zeichenunterricht," *Der Volksschullehrer* 9 (9 December 1915): 576; Paul Hildebrandt, "Wie unsere höheren Schüler den Krieg erleben," in *Wie Deutschlands Jugend den Weltkrieg erlebt*, ed. Wilhelm Müller (Dresden:

Mitteldeutsche Verlagsanstalt, 1918), 65; "Das Kriegsgedicht in der Schule,"
Preußische Volksschullehrerinnen-Zeitung 10 (15 May 1916), 38 (last quotation); and
"Jahresberichte der höheren Schulen," *Deutsches Philologen Blatt* 23 (6 January
1915): 16. On the change in history curricula, see "Stoffverschiebungen im
Geschichtslehrplan zugunsten der neuesten Geschichte," *Zentralblatt für die
gesamte Unterrichtsverwaltung in Preußen* (2 September 1915): 693–700. Most
elementary and secondary school teachers were already doing this, however.
See, for example, "Der Weltkrieg im Geschichtsunterricht," *Schulblatt der
Provinz Sachsen* 54 (13 January 1915): 21. On the celebrations, see "Helden
und Kinder," *Vossische Zeitung,* 9 September 1915 (long quotation); Reform-
realgymnasium und Oberrealschule Berlin-Weissensee, *Bericht über das
Schuljahr, 1914–1915,* 22–24; "Jahresbericht der höheren Mädchenschule F.
Sicknberger," 16 November 1915, Staatsarchiv Munich RA Nr. 56447; "Die
Siegesfeier in den Schulen," *Hamburger Nachrichten,* 4 December 1916,
StHam 361–2 I Oberschulbehörde I B 26 Nr. 1; "Siegesfeiern und Schulfrei!"
Die Wahrheit, 1 July 1916, GStA I. HA Rep. 76 VI Sec. I. Gen. z: 3 Bd. XIII,
Bl. 96; and "Vom eisernen Hindenburg," *Pädagogische Zeitung* 45 (20 January
1916): 40.

19. Emminger, "Volksschule," 105–119, 109 (second quotation), 117 (first
    quotation); Bendick, *Kriegserwartung,* 132 (third and fourth quotations); and
    Reissig, "Lehrerseminar," 194.

20. "Der Krieg und die Schule," *Deutsche Tageszeitung,* 16 February 1915, BA-Li
    8034 II 6938, Bl. 144.

21. "Aus der Schule—für die Schule," *Tägliche Rundschau,* 8 December 1914,
    BA-Li 8034 II 6938, Bl. 138–39 (first quotation); K. Foltz, "Niederschriften
    und Aufsätze," *Pädagogische Zeitung* 43 (15 January 1914), 646; and Eduard
    Spranger, "Schule und Krieg," *Schulblatt der Provinz Sachsen* 54 (19 May
    1915), 231–232 (last quotations).

22. [Max] Brahn, "Krieg und Schule," *Leipziger Tageblatt,* reprinted in *Han-
    noversche Schulzeitung* 50 (13 October 1914), 667 (first quotation); T. F.
    Schmidt, "Die Einheitsschule," *Vossische Zeitung,* 26 February 1916 (second
    quotation); and W[ilhelm] Rein, "Die Einheitsschule," *Vossische Zeitung,* 4
    March 1916; and Dudek, *Geschichte der Jugendforschung,* 142 (third quotation).

23. Eugen Wolbe, "Schulbetrieb in Kriegszeiten," *Der Tag,* 22 September 1914,
    BA-Li 8034 II 6938, Bl. 132–133; Verhey, *Spirit of 1914,* 40–42, 65; W.
    Woclick, "Zeitgemäßes aus der Schule," *Hamburger Nachrichten,* 25 April
    1915, StHam 361–2 I B 26 Nr. 1, Bl. 63; and Bartscht, "Auch ein Kriegs-
    echo!" *Katholische Schulzeitung für Norddeutschland* 31 (17 September 1914),
    613 (quotation).

24. H. Tussing, "Der Krieg im Rechenunterricht," *Katholische Zeitschrift für
    Erziehung und Unterricht* 64 (March 1915), 122 (quotations); and "Lehrplan
    und Krieg," *Erziehung und Unterricht* 22 (26 June 1915), 101–102. On the

lesson plans before the war, see Paul von Glizycki, "Das Volksschulwesen," in *Unterrichtswesen,* ed. Lexis, 125–128; Scheibe, *Reformpädagogische Bewegung,* 72; and Albisetti and Lundgreen, "Höhere Knabenschulen," 253.

25. "Zeitung und Schule," *Der Tag,* reprinted in *Der Volksschullehrer* 9 (9 December 1915), 576; Lorenz Treutler, *Krieg und Schule: Anregungen und Vorschläge für Erziehung und Unterricht in der Volks- und Fortbildungsschule* (Stuttgart: Muth, 1915), 28 (last quotation); H. Dittmar, "Kind, Krieg, Zeitung," *Die Praxis der Landschule* 25 (August 1916), 241–243; Robert Hänsel, "Die Kriegszeitungssammlung in der Gewerbe-Klasse," *Die ostdeutsche Fortbildungsschule* 10 (June 1917): 73–78; Rudolf Czasche, "Schul-Kriegsschriften," *Deutsches Philologen-Blatt* (25 April 1917): 285–286; and *Kriegsnachrichten der Oberrealschule in Eppendorf* 29/30 (April–May 1917), in StHam 361-2 I B 29 Nr. 3.

26. On the physical school environment before the war, see Alexander and Parker, *New Education,* 3 (quotation); Learned, *American Teacher's Year,* 351; Leppington, "German Education," 189; Scheibe, *Die reformpädagogische Bewegung,* 70, 91–92, 140–142; and Saupe, *Deutsche Pädagogen,* 424. On the environment during the war, see "Das Kriegsbild in der Schule," *Der Volksschullehrer* 9 (8 July 1915): 319; *1914–1918: Kriegs-Gedenkschrift des Andreas-Realgymnasiums* (Berlin: Nauck, 1919), 6–8; and Paul Matzdorf, "Wie wir den Krieg miterleben," in *Deutschlands Jugend,* ed. Müller, 48–49.

27. Engel, *Leipzigs Volkschulen,* 81 (first quotation); Hildebrandt, "Höhere Schulen," 65, 67–68 (second quotation); and Alexander and Parker, *New Education,* 329 (last quotations).

28. Alexander, *Prussian Elementary Schools,* 334 (quotation); H. Stern, "Noch einmal Aufsatz und Niederschrift," *Pädagogische Zeitung* 42 (27 November 1913): 882–885; and Otto Ludwig, *Der Schulaufsatz: Seine Geschichte in Deutschland* (Berlin: Walter de Gruyter, 1988), 275–276, 288–291.

29. Adolf Jensen and Wilhelm Lamszus, *Unser Schulaufsatz ein verkappter Schundliterat* (Hamburg: Janssen, 1910), 10 (quotation); Karolina Fahn, *Der Wandel des Aufsatzbegriffes in der deutschen Volksschule von 1900 bis zur Gegenwart* (Munich: Oldenbourg, 1971), 75–78; Ludwig, *Schulaufsatz,* 306–307, 314; Christadler, *Kriegserziehung,* 306–316; Scheibe, *Die reformpädagogische Bewegung,* 150–154; Frank, *Deutschunterricht,* 361–371; and Wilhelm Lamszus, *Das Menschenschlachthaus: Bilder vom kommenden Krieg* (1912), ed. Johannes Merkel and Dieter Richter (Munich: Weissmann, 1980).

30. "Weisung betreffend die Schulrevision," *Zentralblatt für die gesamte Unterrichts-verwaltung in Preußen* (1908), 379–384, 382; K. Foltz, "Niederschriften und Aufsätze," *Pädagogische Zeitung* 43 (1 August 1914), 646; Willy Müller, "Zur Einführung in den neuen Grundlehrplan für die Volkschulen Groß-Berlins," *Pädagogische Zeitung* 43 (30 April 1914), 349; and Fahn, *Aufsatzbegriff,* 54–59. For examples of free compositions written in 1913 and 1914, see Karl Linke,

Der freie Aufsatz auf der Unterstufe, Mittelstufe, und Oberstufe (Braunschweig:
Westermann, 1916), 5–9, 168–210.

31. *Kinderaug' und Kinderaufsatz im Weltkriege,* ed. O[tto] Karstädt (Osterwieck:
Zickfeldt, 1916), 1 (quotation); Engel, *Leipzigs Volksschulen,* 27–28; "Laßt die
Jugend;" "Aus dem Kriegsschuljahre 1914/1915 der Volksschule Lörrach,"
Badische Schulzeitung 53 (5 June 1915): 179; and Werner Dackweilr, "Der
große Weltkrieg im Dienst unseres Aufsatzes," *Naussische Schulzeitung* 13 (15
April 1915): 58–59. On exhibitions, see "Schule und Krieg," *Der Volksschul-
lehrer* 9 (13 April 1915): 177; Arndt-Gymnasium, *Jahresbericht* (Berlin, 1915),
17; "Kriegs-Schulmuseum," *Schulblatt der Provinz Sachsen* 54 (2 June 1915):
261; and the following correspondences: LABe STA Rep. 20–01 Nr. 402, Bl.
134, 138, 183, 189; StDüss III 1702, Bl. 281; and StKöln Best. 561 Nr. 277,
Bl. 7. On decrees of administrators, see Blanckenhorn, "Lehrplan"; Peters,
"Kriegspädagogik;" and "Verfügung der Schulabteilung der Regierung
Stettin," *Amtliches Schul-Blatt für den Regierungs-Bezirk Stettin* 28 (1915), as
reprinted in Klaus Saul, "Jugend im Schatten des Krieges: Dokumentation,"
Militärgeschichtliche Mitteilung 34 (1983): 128.

32. The collections are *Kinderaufsatz,* ed. Karstädt; *Schülerkriegsaufsätze,* ed.
Reiniger; *Aus eiserner Zeit: Freie Kriegsaufsätze von Meeraner Kindern,* ed.
Arthur Fröhlich (Leipzig: Wunderlich, 1915); *Die Kinder und der Krieg:
Aussprüche, Taten, Opfer und Bilder,* ed. Hans Floerke (Munich: G. Müller,
1915); *Das Kind und der Krieg: Kinderaussprüche, Aufsätze und Zeichnungen,*
ed. Max Schach (Berlin: G. Müller, 1916); *Das Buch Michael: Mit Kriegsaufsätzen, Tagebuchblättern, Gedichten, Zeichnungen aus Deutschlands Schulen,* ed.
Hermann Reich, 2nd ed. (Berlin: Weidmann, 1918); and *Jugendliches Seelenleben und Krieg,* ed. William Stern (Leipzig: Barth, 1915). I included in the
analysis only the seventy-six compositions that had personal or unique content
in this archival collection: Stadtknabenschule III Stadtarchiv Darmstadt, St
63 18/1, 1915–1916. Schoolchildren's compositions were also published in
Hp., "Schuldiplomatie im Schüleraufsatz," *Pädagogische Zeitung* 44 (30
September 1915): 277; "Unsere Schule im Dienste des Vaterlandes," *Monatsschrift für katholische Lehrerinnen* 28 (February 1915): 91–92; "Kriegstagebücher," *Monatsschrift für katholische Lehrerinnen* 28 (October 1915): 545–546;
"Ein Tag aus der Kriegszeit, den ich nie vergessen werde," *Monatsschrift für
katholische Lehrerinnen* 28 (June 1915): 343; "Zwei Kinderaufsätze," *Frankfurter Schulzeitung* 32 (1 April 1915): 55; Wilhelm Zeuch, "Der große Krieg
im Spiegel des freien Aufsatzes," *Pädagogische Zeitung* 44 (20 May 1915):
249–253; "Volksschülerpoesien zum Krieg," *Badische Schulzeitung* 54 (13 May
1916): 160–161; "Schulaufsätze im Kriege," *Freie Bayerische Schulzeitung* 18
(12 April 1917): 35–36; Wintermantel, "Über Aufsatzunterricht und
Kriegsaufsätze," *Badische Schulzeitung* 55 (20 May 1917, 1 June 1917, and 10
June 1917): 123–124, 130–131, 138–140; and "Ein Schüleraufsatz aus einer

Landschule 1915" and "Aus Schüleraufsätzen in einer Mittelschule," *Freie Bayerische Schulzeitung* 19 (24 January 1918): 12.

33. Gustav Spiegelberg, *Über 800 Aufgaben über den Weltkrieg, 1914/15, zu freien Aufsätzen und Niederschriften in Schulen* (Halle: Gesenius, 1915), 33; "Freie Aufsätze für die Kriegszeit," *Monatsschrift für katholische Lehrerinnen* 28 (June 1915): 343–344; Friedrich Brücker, "Die Konzentration des Unterrichts im Weltkriege," *Katholische Zeitschrift für Erziehung und Unterricht* 65 (1916): 39; Fritz Elsner, "Die Schule und der Krieg," *Für unsere Mütter und Hausfrauen* 26 (17 September 1915): 101, reprinted in Saul, "Jugend im Schatten des Krieges," 132–134; E. Leupolt, "Der Krieg und der Schulaufsatz", *Hannoversche Schulzeitung* 51 (28 September 1915): 467–468; and Hildebrandt, "Kriegs-Themata im Schulaufsatz," *Vossische Zeitung*, 2 April 1915.

34. "Wenn ich König von Italien wäre," in Hp., "Schüleraufsatz," 277; and "Wenn meine Mütter hexen könnt'," in *Kriegsaufsätze*, ed. Fröhlich, 21.

35. Quotations in order: "Steh' ich in finst'rer Mitternacht," in *150 Schülerkriegsaufsätze*, ed. Reiniger, 50; "In Gedanken," in *Kriegsaufsätze*, ed. Fröhlich, 48–49; "Ein Tag aus der Kriegszeit, den ich nie vergessen werde," *Monatsschrift für katholische Lehrerinnen* 28 (June 1915): 343; and Erich J., "Ein Gang über das Schlachtfeld von Dieuze-Vergaville 24. August 1914," in *Das Buch Michael*, ed. Reich, 179.

36. Quotations in order: Untitled, in *Jugendliches Seelenleben*, ed. Stern, 109; Distel, "Ein Soldatenbegräbnis auf dem Nordhäuser Friedhof," in *Kinderaufsatz*, ed. Karstädt, 134; "Abschied," in *Kriegsaufsätze*, ed. Fröhlich, 3; Martha Krone, untitled, *Kinderaufsatz*, ed. Karstädt, 34; and Blanckenhorn, "Lehrplan und Krieg," 405.

37. Quotations in order: "Vor dem Sturm auf einen feindlichen Schützengraben," in *Schülerkriegsaufsätze*, ed. Reiniger, 45; Fr. Kaestner, "Was ein Krieger erzählt," in "Der Krieg: Aus den Aufsatzheften der Stadtknabenschule III Kl. I Schulj. 15/16," H. 6, Stadtarchiv Darmstadt St 63 18/1 1915–1916, Bl. 1; and "Bald wird die Trompete blasen," in *Kriegsaufsätze*, ed. Fröhlich, 72.

38. Quotations in order: Müller, "Ich stieße alles nieder!" in *Kinderaufsatz*, ed. Karstädt, 53; untitled, in *Jugendliches Seelenleben*, ed. Stern, 91; and "Ein Feldbrief aus dem Jahre 1813," in *Kriegsaufsätze*, ed. Fröhlich, 116–119. See also Untitled, in *Kinderaussprüche*, ed. Schach, 35; K. Bernhardt, "Wo hast du den Weihnachtsbaum herbekommen?" in *Kinderaufsatz*, ed. Karstädt, 95–96; Schorschel, untitled, in *Die Kinder und der Krieg*, ed. Floerke, 144–145; and the two untitled compositions in *Jugendliches Seelenleben*, ed. Stern, 88, 107.

39. Alfred Mann, "Die Aufsätze von Kindern," *Jugendliches Seelenleben*, ed. Stern, 91; and E. Hylla, "Krieg und jugendliches Seelenleben," *Pädagogische Zeitung* 44 (26 August 1915), 407.

40. Anny Schulze, "Unterrichtliches aus der Kriegszeit (Kriegslyrik)," *Die Lehrerin* 32 (22 May 1915): 60 (last quotation); Elisabeth Seifarth, "Der

Unterrichtserfolg in der Kriegszeit," *Die Lehrerin* 32 (18 December 1915):
297–298; "Auch für den Krieg," *Monatsschrift für katholische Lehrerinnen* 28
(May 1915): 296–297; "Unsere Schulen und der Krieg," *Die höhere Mädchenschule* 27 (26 October 1914): 412–418; Olbrich,"Kriegsaufsätze der
Oberprima einer Studienanstalt," *Frauenbildung* 14 (1915): 62; Mihaly, *Girl's
Diary,* 54, 96; "Freie Aufsätze für die Kriegszeit;" Schulze, "Kriegstagebücher;" and "Verfügung der Schulabteilung der Regierung Stettin." For
statistics on coeducation, see *Statistisches Jahrbuch für den preußischen Staat*
14 (Berlin, 1917), 222–223, and 15 (Berlin, 1918), 229.

41. "Eine Schlacht an einem heißen Sommertage 1870" and Windolf, "Der
Überfall eines französischen Bagagetransportes," both in *Kinderaufsatz,* ed.
Karstädt, 249–250, 121–122 (quotations); Elfriede Paul, *Ein Sprechzimmer
der Roten Kapelle* (East Berlin: Militärverlag der DDR, 1981), 12; Mihaly,
Girl's Diary, 18, 54; Verein für Christliche Erziehungswissenschaft, "Ideale
von Knaben und Mädchen;" and *Kindheit,* ed. Pörtner, 99–102, 138, 143,
177–197.

42. Helma Riefenstahl, "Die allgemeine vaterländische Erziehungsaufgabe der
Lehrerin in großer Zeit," *Monatsschrift für katholische Lehrerinnen* 28 (March
1915): 124 (quotation); "Kriegslehren für die Frauenbildung," *Frauenbildung*
15 (1916): 120; and Alfred Kühne, "Krieg und Fortbildungsschule," *Die
deutsche Fortbildungsschule* 24 (1 December 1915): 721–732.

43. "Unsere Schulen und der Krieg," *Die höhere Mädchenschule* 27 (26 October
1914): 413 (quotation); Min. Int., Munich, 1 October 1914, StdMünch
Schulamt Nr. 911; "In den Berliner Gemeindeschulen," *Vossische Zeitung,*
22 August 1914; Buchner, *Kriegstagebuch,* 26; "Schulen sollen den Arbeitern
keine Konkurrenz machen," *Vorwärts,* 28 August 1914, BA-Li 8034 II 6938,
Bl. 129; Sophie Rehm, "Von der Arbeit der Mädchen," *Wandervogel* (Febru-
ary 1915): 27; Marlene Dietrich, *Marlene* (New York: Grove Press, 1989), 7;
Henny Koch, "Wodurch es Ursel vergönnt war, etwas 'ganz Großes' zu tun,"
Der Jugendgarten 41 (1916): 258; and "Krieg und Schule," *Die deutsche
Fortbildungsschule* 23 (1 November 1914): 894. See also Elke Koch, "'Jeder
tut, was er kann fürs Vaterland': Frauen und Männer an der Heilbronner
'Heimatfront,'" in *Kriegserfahrungen,* ed. Hirschfeld et al.; *Kindheit im Ersten
Weltkrieg,* ed. Christa Hämmerle (Wien: Böhlau, 1993), 265–335; and
Christa Hämmerle, "'Wir strickten und nähten Wäsche für Soldaten . . . :'
Von der Militarisierung des Handarbeits im Ersten Weltkrieg," *Homme* 3
(1992): 104–118.

44. "Kriegsernährung" and "Rechenaufgaben zur Brotfragen," both in *Preußische
Volksschullehrerinnen-Zeitung* 8 (15 March 1915): 180–181; Luise Hesse, "Aus
der Zeit für Schule und Leben," *Monatsschrift für katholische Lehrerinnen* 28
(February 1915): 87 (first quotation); A[nny] Schulze, "Zehn Kriegszeitge-
bote," *Frauenbildung* 14 (1915): 100 (second quotation); and "Wie erzieht die

Schule die Jugend zum sparsamen Brotverbrauch?" *Monatsschrift für katholische Lehrerinnen* 28 (February 1915): 89–90.

45. "Kriegszeichnungen von Schülern," *Der Volksschullehrer* 9 (12 August 1915): 379–380; and "Kriegszeichnungen unserer Schüler," *Vossische Zeitung,* 16 June 1915 (first quotation).

46. Fr. Blencke, "Über den Eintritt unserer Schüler in das Heer: Brief an eine Mutter," *Deutsches Philologen Blatt* 23 (21 July 1915): 431–432; Bernhard Rensch, *Lebensweg eines Biologen in einem turbulenten Jahrhundert* (Stuttgart: Fischer, 1979), 29; Willy Sägebrecht, *Nicht Amboß, sondern Hammer sein: Erinnerungen* ([East] Berlin: Dietz, 1968), 33; Häußner, *Schulen Badens,* 57; "Die höheren Lehranstalten in den preußischen Landtagsverhandlungen," *Das humanistische Gymnasium* 26 (1915): 78; Reissig, "Lehrerseminare," 115; and KPSK-Berichte.

47. Verein für Christliche Erziehungswissenschaft, "Ideale von Knaben und Mädchen," 10, 13; Irmgard Meyer-Otto, "Wie die Schüler der Berthold Otto-Schule den Weltkrieg erleben," in *Deutschlands Jugend,* ed. Müller, 77 (quotation); Walter Brecht, *Unser Leben in Augsburg, damals: Erinnerungen* (Frankfurt a.M.: Insel, 1984), 217–221, 243, 280; Uwe Schütz, *Gustav Heinemann und das Problem des Friedens im Nachkriegsdeutschland* (Münster: Agenda, 1993), 25–29; Bettina Goldberg, *Schulgeschichte als Gesellschaftsgeschichte: Die höheren Schulen im Berliner Vorort Hermsdorf (1893–1945)* (Berlin: Edition Hentrich, 1994), 62; Buchner, *Kriegstagebuch,* 35, 80; and Theodor Eschenburg, *Also hören Sie mal zu* (Berlin: Siedler, 1995), 77–79, 93, 98–99.

48. On Austria-Hungary, see Eduard Golias, *Die Kinder und der Krieg: Ernstes und Heiteres aus der Welt der Kleinen* (Vienna: F. Tempsky, 1915), 12, 16 (first and second quotations); Richard Rothe, *Die Kinder und der Krieg: Beitrag zur grundlegenden Gestaltung der Ausdruckskultur* (Vienna: A. Haase, 1915), 136–137; Zahra, *Kidnapped Souls,* 83; and Healy, *Vienna,* 245. On Italy, see Andrea Fava, "War, 'National Education' and the Italian Primary School," in *State, Society and Mobilization in Europe during the First World War,* ed. John Horne (New York: Cambridge University Press, 1997). On France, see Stephen Harp, "War's Eclipse of Primary Education in Alsace-Lorraine, 1914–1918," *The Historian* 57 (1995): 496; Stéphane Audoin-Rouzeau, *La guerre des enfants, 1914–1918* (Paris: Armand, 1993), 24–37, 25 (last quotation); Mona Siegel, *The Moral Disarmament of France: Education, Pacifism, and Patriotism, 1914–1940* (New York: Cambridge University Press, 2004), 20; and Jean-Jacques Becker, *The Great War and the French People* (New York: St. Martin's, 1986), 155–160.

49. Goebel, "Schools," 202 (quotation, emphasis mine); Curtis, *Education in Britain,* 178–179; and David Parker, "'Talent at Its Command': The First World War and the Vocational Aspect of Education, 1914–1939," *History of Education Quarterly* 35 (1995): 237–259.

50. Ostler, "Vormilitärische Ausbildung," 104, 176 (quotations); Zahra, *Kid-napped Souls,* 86–87; Healy, *Vienna,* 215–241; and Oskar Jászi, *Dissolution of the Habsburg Monarchy* (Chicago: University of Chicago Press, 1971), 436–447.

51. Audoin-Rouzeau, *Guerre des enfants,* 28; Jacques Ozouf and Mona Ozouf, "Le thème due patriotisme dans les manuels primaires," *Le mouvement social* 49 (October–December 1964): 15 (first quotation); Siegel, *Education,* 18–50; and Bendick, *Kriegserwartung,* 200–205, 210 (last quotation).

4. The Content and Popularity of War Literature

1. Mosse, *Fallen Soldiers,* 7–8.

2. Natter, *Literature at War,* 127–142, 174–186; Max Lobsien, *Unsre Zwölfjähri-gen und der Krieg* (Leipzig: Säemann-Schriften, 1916), 7–8; Robert Dinse, *Das Freizeitleben der Großstadtjugend* (Berlin: Archiv für Jugendwohlfahrt, 1932), 47; and the catalog of the Staatsbibliobiothek Berlin, Abteilung Jugendschriften.

3. See Chapter 10.

4. J[ohannes] Tews, "Der Volksunterricht im Kriegsjahr," *Berliner Tageblatt,* 26 February 1915, in Bundesarchiv R 8034 II 6938, 149; Schenda, *Lesestoffe der kleinen Leute,* 98; "Kleinliches," *Das Kränzchen* 29 (1916–17): 330 (quotation); Tony Schumacher, *Wenn Vater im Krieg ist* (Stuttgart: Levy & Müller, 1915), 210; "Der Krieg und unsre Kinder," *Gesundbrunnen* (1916): 98–99; "Eine pädagogische Tat," *Jugendschriften-Warte* 23 (January–March 1916): 1–2; and Taiji Azegami, *Die Jugendschriften-Warte: Von ihrer Gründung bis zu den Anfängen des "Dritten Reiches"* (Frankfurt a.M.: Peter Lang, 1996), 131–141.

5. "Wer hat angefangen," *Der gute Kamerad* 29 (1914/15): 54 (quotation); *Kindheit,* ed. Pörtner, 155; and Gerhard Füllkrug on "Der Krieg" in *Deutsche Mädchen-Zeitung* 48 (1916): 2–4; 49 (1917): 34–36; and 50 (1918): 9–10.

6. "Kasperle und der Krieg: Eine Szene für das Kasperletheater," *Meidinger's Kinder-Kalender* 21 (1918): 125–128.

7. Agnes Sapper, *Kriegsbüchlein* (Stuttgart: Gundert, 1915), 28 (first quotation); Alfred Sternbeck, *Der Weltkrieg in Frankreich* (Berlin: Meidinger, 1915), 30 (second quotation); Kurt Küchler, "Von der Schulbank in den Krieg," *Scherls Jungdeutschlandbuch* 2 (1915): 349 (third quotation); Paul Baumann, *Unser Kriegsbuch* (Berlin: Montanus, 1915), 160; Thea Harbou, "Ein altes Fräulein," *Du junge Wacht am Rhein!* (Stuttgart: Levy & Müller, 1915); E. Herbold, "Was deutsch sein heißt," *Mädchenpost* 3 (19 March 1916): 396–397; Maria Mancke, *Marie von Felseneck: Landwehrmanns Einzige* (Berlin: Weichert, 1917), 14; and Fr. Hörnig, "Der Kriegsfreiwillige," *Neuer deutscher Jugend-freund* 70 (1915): 17–41.

8. Maximilian Kern, "Ich hatt' einen Kameraden," *Der gute Kamerad* 29 (1914/15), serialized; Wilhelm Momma, *Wir halten aus!* (Reutlingen: Enßlin & Laiblin, 1914), 33; Fr. Hörnig, "Einig und stark!" *Neuer deutscher Jugendfreund* 69 (1914): 419–432; A. Oskar Klaußmann, "Hans Däumling in Uniform: Eine Feldzugsgeschichte," *Für die Kinderwelt* 10 and 11 (1915/16): 78–80, 85–87; "Der Feigling," *Neuer deutscher Jugendfreund* 71 (1916): 310–327; and Max Karl Böttcher, "Die jungen Feinde," *Meidinger's Kinder-Kalender* 20 (1917): 61–72

9. Wilhelm Momma, *Der jüngste Rekrut: Eine Erzählung für der Jugend aus den Kämpfen in Flandern* (Stuttgart: Levy & Müller, 1916), 18–19; Else Ury, "Eva, das Kriegskind," *Der Jugendgarten* 41 (1916): 90; Walther Arndt, *In Kampf und Sieg durch Belgien* (Berlin: Meidinger, 1915), 100; Paul Grebein, "Unter des Reiches Sturmfahne," *Der gute Kamerad* 30 (1915/16): 19–20; Else Model, "Überall Treu!" *Deutscher Kinderfreund* 38 (December 1915): 46; K. Stauffer [Carl Felix von Schlichtegroll], *Der Fahnenträger von Verdun* (Berlin: Anton, 1916), 30–35; Schumacher, *Vater im Krieg*, 10; and Küchler, "Von der Schulbank," 352. On the revolt against parents in literature and society more generally, see Heinrich Kaulen, "Vom bürgerlichen Elternhaus zur Patchwork-Familie," in *Familienszenen: Die Darstellung familialer Kindheit in der Kinder- und Jugendliteratur,* ed. Hans-Heino Ewers and Inge Wild (Weinheim: Juventa, 1999), 113–115; Kurt Wais, *Das Vater-Sohn-Motiv in der Dichtung,* vol. 2 (Berlin: Walter de Gruyter, 1931), 47–89; and Katherine Larson Roper, "Images of German Youth in Weimar Novels," *Journal of Contemporary History* 13 (1978): 499–516.

10. Anna Heise, "Sturmtage vor Soissons," and Margarete Planert, "Englisches Schiff in Sicht," both in *Kinderaug,* ed. Karstädt, 203, 213; and Mihaly, *Girl's Diary,* 43, 77.

11. Sophie Kloerß, *Im heiligen Kampf: Eine Erzählung für junge Mädchen aus dem Weltkrieg* (Stuttgart: Union, 1915), 194 (first quotation); Wanda Gellert, *Stilles Heldentum* (Berlin: Meidinger, 1918), 187 (second quotation); Joseph von Lauff, "Es bleib mir nichts hienieden," *Krieg und Sieg* (Dresden, 1917): 89; Hedda v. Schmid, "Nach dem Sturm," *Mädchenpost* 3 (9 January 1916), 237; G. Traub, "Eine Mutter," *Gesundbrunnen* (1916), 88–89; Marie Wöhler, "Im trauten Stübchen," *Deutsche Mädchenzeitung* 47 (1915), 96; S. Freiin von Lüttwitz, "Wilko, das Kriegspflegekind," *Deutsche Mädchen-Zeitung* 49 (May 1917): 68–74; Henny Koch, "Auch eine Wunde fürs Vaterland," *Das Kränzchen* 29 (1916/17): 541; Marie von Felseneck, *Trotzkopfs Erlebnisse im Weltkriege* (Berlin: Weichert, 1916), 148, 244; "Das Heldentum einer deutschen Frau," *Kriegsblätter für unsere Jugend* 111 (19 March 1917): 882–884; Tony Schuhmacher, "Ein verlorenes Kind," *Der Jugendgarten* 41 (1916), 205–223; and Henny Koch, *Aus großer Zeit* (Berlin: Union, 1915), 30–31. See also Giesela Wilkending, "Mädchenliteratur von der Mitte des

19. Jahrhunderts bis zum Ersten Weltkrieg," in *Geschichte der deutschen Kinder- und Jugendliteratur*, ed. Reiner Wild, 220–250.

12. Eva Gaehtgens, *Dita Frohmut und ihre Geschwister: Was sie im Krieg erlebten* (Hamburg: Agentur des Rauhen Hauses, 1917), 88; E. Stramm, "Die feindlichen Schützengräben," *Für die Kinderwelt* 22 (1914/15): 172–173; Walter Schulte vom Brühl, *Der Kriegsfahrer* (Stuttgart: Bonz, 1915), 26; Marga Rayle, *Majors Einzige im Kriegsjahr* (Berlin: Meidinger's, 1915), 59–60; Felicitas Leo, "Das Kriegskränzchen oder die Tatendurftigen," *Scherls Jungmädchenbuch* (1915): 210; Thea von Harbou, "Das Licht im Nebel," *Scherls Jungmädchenbuch* (1916): 28; and Bertha Clement, *Morgenrot: Eine Erzählung aus dem großen Krieg für Mädchen* (Stuttgart: Loewe, 1916), 10. British girls' fiction also developed the same themes during the war. See Sally Mitchell, *The New Girl: Girl's Culture in England, 1880–1915* (New York: Columbia University Press, 1995), 127–130, 185. On Rosa Zenoch and female youths' sacrifice in Vienna, see Healy, *Vienna*, 166, 229–232.

13. Thomas Nipperdey, *Religion im Umbruch: Deutschland 1870–1918* (Munich: C. H. Beck, 1988), 118–123; Willfried Spohn, "Religion and Working-Class Formation in Imperial Germany 1871–1914," *Politics & Society* 19 (1991), 108–132; Daniel, *Working-Class Women*, 148; and Ziemann, *War Experiences*, 124–137.

14. Martin Greschat, "Krieg und Kriegsbereitschaft im deutschen Protestantismus," in *Bereit zum Krieg: Kriegsmentalität im wilhelmischen Deutschland, 1890–1914*, ed. Jost Düffler und Karl Holl (Göttingen: Vandenhoeck & Ruprecht, 1986); Pressel, *Die Kriegspredigt;* Missalla, *Die deutsche katholische Kriegspredigt;* Hammer, *Deutsche Kriegstheologie*, 54–59; and Wolfgang Mommsen, "Die nationalgeschichtliche Umdeutung der christlichen Botschaft im Ersten Weltkrieg," in *"Gott mit uns:" Nation, Religion und Gewalt im 19. und frühen 20. Jahrhundert*, ed. Gerd Krumreich und Hartmut Lehmann (Göttingen: Vandenhoeck & Ruprecht, 2000).

15. Franz Költzsch, "Ist Gott für Uns," *Krieg und Sieg* (Dresden, 1915), 12 (quotation); M. Engler, "Werdet wie die Kinder . . . ," *Mädchenpost* 3 (31 October 1915), 76; "Des Kreuzes Kraft," *Jugendfreund* (Stuttgart) 32 (September 1918), n.p.; "In Stunden des Leids," *Kriegsblätter für unsere Jugend* 107 (19 February 1917), 855–856; Bertha Clement, *Sturmgebraus: Erzählung für junge Mädchen aus dem Kriegsjahr, 1915* (Leipzig: Interim, 1915), 33; "Heimwärts bei Kriegsausbruch," *Gesundbrunnen* (1916): 53; "Kriegsdienst der Mädchen und Frauen," *Deutsche Mädchenzeitung* 47 (1915): 11; Franz Költzsch, "Ist Gott für Uns?" *Krieg und Sieg* (Dresden, 1915), 10–12; Clement, *Morgenrot*, 36; Stauffer, *Fahnenträger*, 32; and [Henny] Koch, "Die Bettelsuse," *Der Jugendgarten* 40 (1915): 257.

16. Georg Gellert, *Granatfeuer der Schlachtfelder: Erzählung aus dem Völkerkriege, 1914/16* (Berlin: W. Bloch, 1916), 41–45; Rheinhold Bachmann, *Aus der Schule in die Schlacht* (Leipzig: Abel & Müller, 1917), 168–179; Arthur Zapp,

Marschall von Hindenburg und sein Rekrut (Leipzig: G. Wigand, 1916), 141–158; Hans Willig, *Jungens! Frisch drauf!* (Berlin: Weichert, 1915), 230; and Sternbeck, *Weltkrieg in Frankreich*, 183. See also Samuel Hynes, *A War Imagined* (London: Bodley Head, 1990), 115–116 (quotations).

17. Hans Walter Schmidt, *Herz und Hand fürs Vaterland* (Stuttgart: Loewe, 1916); Ludwig Schroeder, *Haltet aus im Sturmgebraus* (Nürnberg: Nister, 1915); Wilhelm Kotzde, *Die Musik kommt!* (Mainz: Scholz, 1916); Sternbeck, *Weltkrieg in Frankreich*, 72, 78–79; *Viel Feind—viel Ehr* (Duisburg: Steinkamp, 1916); Mosse, *Fallen Soldiers*, 7 (first quotation); Fr. Hornig, "Kriegspfingsten: Ein Stimmungsbild," *Neuer deutscher Jugendfreund* 70 (1915): 568; Gellert, *Granatfeuer der Schlachtfelder*, 99 (last quotation). See also Kevin McAleer, *The Cult of Honor in Fin-de-Siècle Germany* (Princeton, NJ: Princeton University Press, 1994), 43–44; and Ute Frevert, *Men of Honor: A Social and Cultural History of the Duel* (Cambridge, MA: Polity, 1995), 124–134.

18. Stauffer, *Fahnenträger*, 74 (first quotation), 127–128; Paul Bliss, *Unser Hindenburg* (Berlin: Weichert, 1915), 174; Georg Gellert, *Kampf in Feindesland: Erzählungen aus dem Völkerkrieg, 1914/15* (Berlin: W. Bloch, 1916), 140–143; and Schmidt, *Herz und Hand*, 52 (last quotation).

19. *Neue deutsche Bilderbögen* 2 (1916), plate no. 41; and Alfons Krämer, "Die Gefangenen kommen!" *Für die Kinderwelt* 8 (1915/16): 58–59.

20. Otto Riebicke, "Sturmnacht," *Jung-Siegfried* 18 (1 September 1918): 194–195; "Aus einem Feldpostbrief," *Für die Kinderwelt* 21 (1914/15): 163–165; "Ein Angriff," *Der gute Kamerad* 29 (1914/15): 277–278 (first and second quotation); Ernst Georgy, "Drei von Rodenfels," in *Im Kriegsgewitter: Erzählungen und Schilderungen aus dem Weltkrieg*, ed. Paul Burg (Reutlingen: Enßlin & Laiblin, 1915), 108; Heinrich Werdenfels, "Joachim Bernbach," *Unsere Feldgrauen in Feindesland* (Berlin: Weichert, 1915), 16; "Ein Bajonettangriff," *Für die Kinderwelt* 12 (1915/16): 12–15 (third quotation); Richard Sexan, "Der dicke Förster," in *Im Kriegsgewitter*, ed. Burg, 52 (fourth quotation); Ostfrid von Hanstein, "Die Eroberung von Bailly," *In Feindesland*, ed. Burg, 94 (last quotation); Carl Diem, "Aus meinem Kriegstagebuch," *Scherls Jungdeutschlandbuch* 2 (1915): 266; and Clara Fritzsche, "Lieb Vaterland, magst ruhig sein," *Für die Kinderwelt* 12 (1914/15): 92.

21. Fullerton, "Pamphlet Fiction;" Schenda, *Lesestoff der kleinen Leute*, 87; and Ernst Schultze, *Kulturfragen der Gegenwart* (Berlin: Kohlhammer, 1913), 107.

22. "Kriegsschundliteratur," *Pädagogische Zeitung* 45 (20 April 1916): 218; Hans Fischer, *Ein gefährlicher Patrouillenritt* (Berlin: Volksliteratur und Kunst, 1915), 32; and Arnold Tell, *An der Hallue: Der Tambour von Le Bourget*, in the series, *Unter deutscher Flagge* (Berlin: Volksliteratur und Kunst, 1915), 32. Because libraries did not collect penny dreadfuls during the war, there are only a handful of extant copies today, and historians have to rely on secondary accounts.

23. "Die Bekämpfung der Kriegsschundliteratur," *Schulblatt der Provinz Sachsen* 55 (13 December 1916): 498 (first quotation); "Neue Schundliteratur," *Jugendschriften-Warte* 23 (June 1916): 20 (second quotation); "Was sollen unsere Kinder jetzt lesen?" *Hannoversche Schulzeitung* 50 (15 December 1914): 791 (third quotation); Samuleit, *Unsere Jugend*, 16 (last quotation); "Bericht über die Kriegstagung des Deutschen Lehrervereins," *Der Volksschullehrer* 10 (29 June 1916): 207; and "Verkappter Schund," *Jugendschriften-Warte* 24 (June 1917): 22–24. On the Law of Siege, see Gerald Feldman, *Army, Industry, and Labor in Germany 1914–1918* (Providence, RI: Berg, 1992), 31–33.

24. Papierfabrik Hermes & Co, 16 June 1916, StdDüss III 1705, Bl. 26; "Schund-literatur in Magdeburger Schulen," *Schulblatt der Provinz Sachsen* 56 (21 February 1917): 74–75; Walter Thielemann, "Mittel und Wege zur Bekämp-fung der Kriegsschundliteratur," *Katholische Zeitschrift für Erziehung und Unterricht* 67 (1918): 55; letters from October 1916 in ADW EEA 23; and "Jugendpfleger und Jugendpflegerinnen vom 8. bis 10. November 1917 in Berlin," 93–94, GStA I HA Rep. 169C 36D, Bl. 25b.

25. Bendick, *Kriegserwartung*, 205 (first quotation); Walder Heichen, *Unter den Fahnen Hindenburgs* (Berlin: Phönix-Verlag, 1914), 7, 9, 45–46 (second quotation); Michael Paris, "Boys' Books and the Great War," *History Today* 50 (2000): 44–49; Audoin-Rouzeau, *Guerre des enfants*, 46–58, 84–89, 105; Healy, *Vienna*, 232–235; Henry Newbolt, *Tales of the Great War* (London: Longmans, Green, and Co., 1916); Donald Mackenzie, *Heroes and Heroic Deeds of the Great War* (London: Blackie and Son, 1915), 55–56; and Herbert Strang, *Great Britain and the War: A Book for Boys and Girls* (London: Hodder & Stoughton, 1916).

5. Organized Leisure and Patriotic Voluntary Labor

1. Marie Elisabeth Lüders, *Das unbekannte Heer: Frauen kämpfen für Deutsch-land, 1914–1918* (Berlin: Mittler, 1936), 18–24; Ursula von Gersdorff, *Frauen im Kriegsdienst 1914–1945* (Stuttgart: Deutsche, 1969), 15–20; Ursula von Gersdorff, "Frauenarbeit und Frauenemanzipation im Ersten Weltkrieg," *Francia* 2 (1974): 510–512; C. E. Boyd, "Nationaler Frauendienst: The German Middle-Class Women in Service to the Fatherland, 1914–1918" (Ph.D. diss., University of Georgia, 1979), 56–67; Barbara Guttmann, *Weibliche Heimarmee: Frauen in Deutschland, 1914–1918* (Weinheim: Deutscher Studien, 1989), 131–136, 164–166; Sabine Hering, *Die Kriegsge-winnlerinnen: Praxis und Ideologie der deutschen Frauenbewegung im Ersten Weltkrieg* (Pfaffenweiler: Centaurus, 1990), 48–49, 110–117; Matthew Stibbe, "Anti-Feminism, Nationalism and the German Right, 1914–1920: A Reappraisal," *German History* 20 (2002): 193; Reagin, *German Women's Movement*, 192–200; and Verhey, *Spirit of 1914*, 97.

2. Min. Ed., Berlin, 5 August 1914, KPSK-Berichte Bd. 1, Bl. 1a (first quotation); "Die Kriegshilfsarbeiten der preußischen Schuljugend im Jahre 1917," *Pädagogische Zeitung* 47 (2 March 1918), 108 (last quotation); and Min. Ed., Berlin, 13 October 1917, KPSK-Berichte Bd. 2, Bl. 8

3. "Der Dank an die Schule," *Deutsche Tageszeitung,* 25 September 1915, BA-Li 8034 II 6939, Bl. 13; H. Bohnstedt, "Kriegswirtschaft und Schule," *Kreuz Zeitung,* 6 February 1917, BA-Li 8034 II 6940, Bl. 61; [Paul] Hildebrandt, "Kriegsschulanleihe," *Vossische Zeitung,* 2 September 1915; "Die Düsseldorfer erwerbstätige Jugend zur 7. Kriegsanleihe," *Düsseldorfer Tageblatt,* 1 October 1917, StdDüss III 1707, Bl. 224; and Richard Erfurth, "Schule und Kriegsanleihe," *Schulblatt der Provinz Sachsen* 55 (26 April 1916): 171.

4. Pol., Hanover, 5 December 1916, NHAH Hann. 180 Nr. 650, Bl. 297–298; M. Ohmann, "Eine Statistik der Schulkriegshilfe im Jahre 1917," *Pädagogische Zeitung* 47 (2 May 1918): 164; "Die Kriegshilfsarbeiten der preußischen Schuljugend im Jahre 1917," *Pädagogische Zeitung* 47 (21 March 1918): 108; Min. Ed., Berlin, "Beteiligung der Schuljugend bei kriegswirtschaftlichen Arbeiten im Jahre 1917," 17 February 1918, GStA I. HA Rep. 76. VI Sec. I. Gen. z: 242 Bd. I, Bl. 383ff; and Reissig, "Lehrerseminare," 242.

5. Min. Int. to Min. Ed., 10 March 1917; Robert Neuß to Min. Int., 15 March 1917; and "Die Kriegshilfe der Schulen," *Deutsche Tageszeitung,* 5 April 1917, all in GStA I. HA Rep. 76. VI Sec. I. Gen. z: 242 Bd. I, Bl. 310a, 314, 318. Only in March 1916 during the fourth war bonds drive were teachers first required to organize their pupils. See Reissig, "Lehrerseminare," 229.

6. For praise of teachers, see "Kriegssammlung," *Vossische Zeitung,* 30 January 1915; and report on debate in the Prussian *Landtag,* "Beteiligung der Schulen an der Kartoffelernte," 17 February 1918, GStA I. HA Rep. 169C 36D, Bl. 177ff. On the war bond drives, see "Düsseldorfer erwerbstätige Jugend"; Hildebrandt, "Kriegsschulanleihe;" Johanneson, Andreas Realgym., Berlin, 28 March 1916, LABe STA Rep. 20–01 Nr. 421; "Dank für die Opferfreudigkeit der Schuljugend," *Norddeutsche Allgemeine Zeitung,* 6 November 1915, BA-Li 8034 II 6939, Bl. 23; "Schulaufgabe," *Magdeburgische Zeitung,* 23 April 1915, and "Ein pädagogischer Mißgriff," *Berliner Tageblatt,* 24 April 1915, both in GStA I. HA Rep. 76. VI Sec. I Gen. z: 242 Bd. I, Bl. 60, 70.

7. On victory holidays, see Reissig, *Lehrerseminare,* 217.

8. "Schuljungen als Kartoffelgräber," *Deutsche Tageszeitung,* 9 November 1916, BA-Li 8034 II 6940, Bl. 27; Pol., Hanover, 5 December 1916, NHAH Hann 180 Nr. 650, Bl. 297–298; "Die Kinder und der Krieg," *Düsseldorfer Volkszeitung,* 6 July 1917, StdDüss III 1708, Bl 11; "Wie für unsere verwundeten Krieger gesorgt wird," in *Schülerkriegsaufsätze,* ed. Reiniger, 16; Min. Ed., Berlin, 5 March 1915 and 16 September 1915, GStA I. HA Rep. 76. VI Sec. I. Gen z: 242a Bd I, Bl. 37, 183; "Feldbestellung und Schule," *München-Augsburger Abendzeitung,* 17 March 1915, BHStA Mk, Nr. 20583; "Zur

Sammeltätigkeit in den Berliner Gemeindeschulen," *Pädagogische Zeitung* 47 (1 October 1918): 402; "Ein pädagogischer Unfug," *Vorwärts*, 9 March 1915; Mayor, Cologne, 18 December 1916, GStA I. HA Rep. 76 VI Sec. I. Gen. z: 3 Bd. 13, Bl. 122; and "Milliardensiege—Schulfrei!" *Vossische Zeitung*, 25 September 1915.

9. W. Masche, "Die deutsche Schule und die Kriegsanleihe," *Die Post*, 4 March 1917, GStA I. HA Rep. 76 VI Sec. I Gen. z: 242 Bd I, Bl. 303 (quotation); and "Ein pädagogischer Unfug."

10. See the reports of the youth workers in LABr Pr. Br. Rep. 2a Reg. Potsdam II Gen. Nr. 1577; HessHA 405 Nr. 3838/39 (on Frankfurt a.M., memo from 3 May 1916, Nr. 3838, Bl. 291); NWHSA Reg. Düss. 33120 and 33097a; GStA I. HA Rep. 120 E I Spez. Fach I Nr. 42 Bd. 4; and Linton, "Between School and Marriage," 399–402.

11. Malita v. Rundstedt, *Der Schützengraben des deutschen Mädchens* (Berlin: Altmärkische, 1916), 6 (quotation); "Mobilmachung der Schuljugend für landwirtschaftliche Arbeiten," *Tägliche Rundschau*, 26 January 1917, BA-Li 8034 II 6940, Bl. 55; Hoche, "Wandlungen in der häuslichen Erziehung," *Hamburger Fremdenblatt*, 18 April 1917, StHam 111–2 C II 1 13; and Samuleit, *Unsere Jugend*, 5.

12. "Ergänzung der Wanderbüchereien," *Mitteilung der Landeszentralstelle für Jugendpflege im Herzogtum Anhalt* 10 (1917): 282–284; Steitz, Kjp., Biedendorf, 10 January 1918, HessHA 405 Nr. 3839, Bl. 62–64; "Verzeichnis der Lichtbilder der Landeszentralstelle für Jugendpflege," *Mitteilung der Landeszentralstelle für Jugendpflege im Herzogtum Anhalt* 7 (December 1914): 118–119; Theodor Ebert, *Deutscher Geist für deutsche Heldentage: Beiträge aus der Jugendpflege-Arbeit* (Eisleben: Kögel in Komm., 1917), 10, 13; and "Aus den Berichten der Kreisjugendpfleger," *Mitteilung der Landeszentralstelle für Jugendpflege im Herzogtum Anhalt* 11 (March 1918): 45.

13. Landrat, Usingen, 6 April 1915, HessHA 405 Nr. 2822, Bl. 233; "Vaterländischer Abend, Jugendkompanie Bleidenstadt" (poster), 5 May 1918, HessHA 405 Nr. 3839, Bl. 28; Blume, Kjp., Neukölln, 22 February 1916, LABr Pr. Br. Rep. 2a Reg. Potsdam II Gen. Nr. 1577; Willy Lohmann, *Jugendpflegearbeit in der Kriegszeit* (Bernberg: Schwarzenberger, 1917), 30–32; Koch, "Die städtische Jugendpflege in Weimar: Jahresbericht für 1916," *Fortbildungsschulpraxis* 11 (June 1917): 82–87; and Hermann Dieckmann, "Wie gestalten wir wirkungsvoll einen Familienabend in Stadt und Land auch mit den einfachsten Mitteln?" in *Familien- und Volksabende in der Kriegszeit*, ed. Hermann Dieckmann and Hans Wilke (Cöthen-Anhalt: Both, 1917), 21 (quotation).

14. "Die militärische Vorbereitung für den Heeresdienst," Düsseldorf, 30 September 1914, StdDüss III 2177, Bl. 226–228; enrollment figures for 1912/13 in *Statistisches Jahrbuch der deutschen Städte* 21 (1916), 710, 734; Reg.

Präs., Aurich, 20 February 1915, and Reg. Präs., Hanover, 5 March 1915, NHAH Hann. 122a Nr. 4490, Bl. 163, 172; Opfergelt, "Die militärische Jugendvorbereitung," *Jugendpflege im Regierungsbezirk Cöln* 2 (21 September 1915): 25–31; "Jugendfürsorge während des Krieges," *Berliner Tageblatt,* 19 September 1915, LABe STA Rep. 20–01 Nr. 402, Bl. 210; *Junge Garde: Arbeiterjugendbewegung in Frankfurt am Main, 1904–1945,* ed. Franz Neuland and Albrecht Werner-Cordt (Gießen: Anabas, 1980), 40; and "Jugend im Schatten," 98–100.

15. Saul, "Jugend im Schatten des Krieges," 93 (first quotation), 96; Linton, *Young Workers,* 191; Schubert-Weller, *Männlichen Jugend,* 341 (second quotation); "Mittelbarer Zwang zum Beitritt zur Jugendwehr," *Vorwärts,* 15 August 1915, GStA I. HA Rep. 77 Tit. 924 Nr. 8 Bd. 2 Bl. 145; Reg. Präs., Hanover, 5 March 1915, NHAH Hann. 122a Nr. 4490, Bl. 163; Brettschneiter, 8 June 1915, GStA I. HA Rep. 120 E I Spez. Fach I Nr. 42 Bd. 4; "Teilnahme an den Jugendwehrübungen als Teil des Fortbildungsunterricht," *Volkswacht* (Breslau), 7 August 1917, GStA I. HA Rep. 77 CB Reihe S Nr. 878 Bd. 3; Mayor, Essen, 24 January 1916, NWHSA Reg. Düss. 33120; KPSK, Hanover, 9 December 1916, StHan HR 16 Nr. 550; and DCG, Altona, 15 September 1916, StHam 111–2 A II q 5 Bd. 2, Bl. 136.

16. Schubert-Weller, *Männlichen Jugend,* 340–341 (quotations); "Aenderung des Fortbildungsschulunterrichts?" *Vorwärts,* 17 December 1914, and "Teilnahme der Fortbildungschüler an militärischen Uebungen," *Vorwärts,* 27 April 1915, both in GStA I. HA Rep 120 E I Spez. Fach I Nr. 42 Bd. 4; Reg. Präs., Potsdam, 26 February 1916, and advertisement, *Intelligenz-Blatt des Teltower und Beeskow-Storkower Kreises,* 13 January 1916, both in GStA I. HA Rep. 77 Tit. 924 Nr. 8 Bd. 2, Bl. 246–248; Min. Int., Berlin, 4 September 1914, HessHA 405 Nr. 12999, Bl. 69; and "Der freiwillige Schülerhilfsdienst," War Min., 13 February 1918, LABr Pr. Br. Rep. 34 I Nr. 1297. On the Auxiliary Service Law, see Feldman, *Army, Industry and Labor,* 535–541.

17. "Zwang und Freiheit in der Jugendpflege," *Ratgeber für Jugendvereinigungen* 10 (December 1916): 178–180; Schubert-Weller, *Männlichen Jugend,* 288–312; and Saul, "Jugend im Schatten," 104–108.

18. "Militärische Vorbildung der Jugend," *Kölnische Zeitung,* 11 June 1916, LABr Pr. Br. Rep. 34 I Nr. 921; "Die militärische Vorbildung der Jugend im Herzogtum Anhalt vom August 1915 bis Februar 1917," *Mitteilung der Landeszentralstelle für Jugendpflege im Herzogtum Anhalt* 10 (February 1917): 232; Mayor, Duisberg, 19 December 1916, NWHSA Reg. Düss. 33104; Auskunftsstelle über Kriegs- und wirtschaftliche Fragen für die Jugendkompagnien, War Min., Berlin, 29 December 1916, StHam 111–2 A II p 80; and Kjp., Montabaur, 31 December 1916, HessHA 405 Nr. 3838, Bl. 416ff.

19. Landrat, Teltow, 11 February 1915, LABr Pr. Br. Rep. 2a Reg Potsdam II Gen. Nr. 1592 (quotation); "Pfälzische Jungmannschaftspost Nr. 2: Zielen

und Schießen!" *Der Rheinpfälzer,* 2 January 1915, GStA I. HA Rep. 77 Tit.
924 Nr. 8 Bd. 2; "Soll die deutsche Jugend schießen lernen?" *Kölnische
Zeitung,* 1 April 1916, StHam 111–2 A II q 6; and War Min., Berlin, 15 June
1915, NHAH Hann 122a Nr. 4490, Bl. 263.

20. KPSK, Danzig, 7 December 1919, KPSK-Berichte Bd. II, Bl. 110–14; R. R.,
"Rowdies in Jugendwehr-Uniform," *Volkswacht* (Breslau), 18 March 1918,
GStA I. HA Rep. 77 CB Reihe S Nr. 878, Bd. 3; and the following in
StaaMünch Pol. Dir. München Nr. 4554: Bayerischer Wehrkraftverein e.V.,
Orstgruppe München, 22 May 1915 (first quotation); no title, *Münchener
Post,* 21 June 1916 (second quotation); and no title, *Münchener Neueste
Nachrichten,* 19 August 1916.

21. "Die Parade der Jugendlichen," *Hannoversches Tagesblatt,* 13 September 1915,
StHan HR 16 Nr. 550; "Militärische Jugendvorbereitung," *Vossische Zeitung,*
16 November 1914; "Wer bezahlt die Kosten?" *Volksstimme* (Magdeburg), 31
October 1916, GStA I. HA Rep. 77 CB Reihe S Nr. 878 Bd. 3; "Die
Schlacht der Pfadfinder," *Vossische Zeitung,* 25 January 1915 (quotations); and
Saul, "Jugend im Schatten," 100, 104. On formations in these war games, see
Albert Huth, *Vom Kriegsspiel der Jugend* (Leipzig: Wunderlich, 1916).

22. *Lieder für die Frankfurter Jungmannschaften* (Frankfurt a.M: Voigt &
Gleibner, 1915), 6–7, 9.

23. Stéphane Audoin-Rouzeau, "Children and the Primary Schools of France,"
in *Mobilization,* ed. Horne, 50; Goebel, "Schools," 218–222; Healy, *Vienna,*
247; Becker, *Great War,* 159–160; *Kindheit,* ed. Hämmerle, 271–272; Ostler,
"'Soldatenspiererei?'" 169–170; Audoin-Rouzeau, "Die mobilisierten Kinder,"
195 (quotation); minutes, Elementary Education Subcommittee, vol. 31
(1918/19), London Metropolitan Archives LCC MIN 3289, 127; and annual
report, Lycée Janson-de-Sailly, May 1915, Archives Nationales de France
AJ16 2699. For the last two sources, I am grateful to Stefan Goebel.

24. Bendick, *Kriegswerwartung,* 128; *Kindheit,* ed. Hämmerle, 282–283; and
Hämmerle, "Wir strickten," 104.

6. Deprivation and the Collapse of Schooling

1. Belinda Davis, *Home Fires Burning: Food, Politics, and Everyday Life in World
War I Berlin* (Chapel Hill: University of North Carolina Press, 2000), 117;
Peter Loewenberg, "The Psychohistorical Origins of the Nazi Youth Cohort,"
American Historical Review 76 (1971): 1473; Avner Offer, *The First World War:
An Agrarian Interpretation* (Oxford: Clarendon, 1989), 52; Anne Roerkohl,
*Hungerblockade und Heimatfront: Die kommunale Lebensmittelversorgung in
Westfalen während des Ersten Weltkrieges* (Stuttgart: Steiner, 1991), 252,
297–299; Daniel, *Working-Class Women,* 134–138, 188–198; Akhter Ahmed,
Ruth Vargas Hill, Lisa Smith, Doris Wiesmann, and Tim Frankenberger,

The World's Most Deprived: Characteristics and Causes of Extreme Poverty and Hunger (Washington, DC: International Food Policy Research Institute, 2007), xii; and "Die Kälte," *Berliner Tageblatt*, 6 February 1917, BA-Li 8034 II 6940, Bl. 67.

2. Kröhnke, 18 December 1916, KPSK-Berichte Bd. I, Bl. 238.

3. Martin Schumacher, *Land und Politik: Eine Untersuchung über politische Parteien und agrarische Interessen, 1914–1923* (Düsseldorf: Droste Verlag, 1978), 39–69, 62 (quotation); and Lothar Burchardt, "The Impact of the War Economy on the Civilian Population of Germany during the First and the Second World Wars," in *The German Military in the Age of Total War*, ed. Wilhelm Deist (Leamington Spa: Berg, 1985), 42, 57. In Vienna, where the food crisis was as severe as in German cities, the mortality rate of schoolchildren in 1918 increased by a third over prewar levels. Healy, *Vienna*, 249.

4. "Gewichtszunahme und Längenwachstum der großstädtischen Volksschulkinder im ersten Kriegsjahr," *Pädagogische Zeitung* 45 (13 January 1916): 23 (first quotation); "Wie wirkt der Aushungerungskrieg auf die Schuljugend," *Pädagogische Zeitung* 45 (3 February 1916): 65 (second quotation); "Über den Einfluß der Kriegskost auf die Schulkinder," *Pädagogische Zeitung* 45 (5 October 1916): 559 (third quotation); and "Amtsärztlicher Bericht auf Grund der schulärztlichen Berichte," Schulamt Nr. 2233–2234.

5. "Die diesjährigen Kultusdebatten im preußischen Abegeordnetenhaus: Schule und Krieg," *Der Volksschullehrer* 11 (19 April 1917): 125 (quotation); "Krieg und Gesundheitszustand der Schuljugend," *Pädagogische Zeitung* 45 (8 June 1916): 311–312; "Schulaufsätze im Kriege," *Freie Bayerische Schulzeitung* 18 (12 April 1917): 35–36; and "Die Ernährung im dritten Kriegsjahr und unsere Jugend," *Badische Schulzeitung* 55 (10 December 1917): 284.

6. Telegrams, Magistrat, Frankfurt a.M., 27 September 1917, GStA I. HA Rep. 76 VI Sec. I Gen. z: 3 Bd. XIII, Bl. 178a–g; and "Ein unmöglicher Vorschlag," *Berliner Volkszeitung*, 8 September 1917, and "Die Zusammenlegung der Ferien," *Frankfurter Zeitung*, 15 September 1917, both in BA-Li 8034 II 6940, Bl. 162 (quotation), 164.

7. "Niederschriften über die Verhandlungen der Kreisschulkommissionen für Oberfranken," 12 December 1916, StaaMünch RA Nr. 53902, Bl. 12 (quotation); H. Dittmar, "Welche Schwierigkeiten bietet die Gegenwart unserer Schularbeit auf dem Lande?" *Die Praxis der Landschule* 25 (December 1916): 401–405; and curriculum vitae of Max Keller, StdKöln Best. 569 Nr. 3, Bl. 11, and the description of conflicts with his pupils, StdKöln Best. 569 Nr. 342, Bl. 284–285. On shortages of teachers, see report, no title, December 1915 ca., KPSK-Berichte Bd. I, Bl. 25; Paul Hildebrandt, "Kriegswirkungen in der Schule," *Vossische Zeitung*, 23 January 1918, BA-Li 8034 II, 6941, Bl. 6; KPSK, Coblenz, 6 December 1918, KPSK-Berichte Bd. II, Bl. 158–160; "Die Not der Volksschule," *Leipziger Lehrerzeitung* 24

(12 December 1917): 589; and Chickering, *The Great War and Urban Life in Germany*, 501.

8. "Verzeichnis der mit Militär belegten Gemeindeschule," LABe STA Rep. 20–01 Nr. 402, Bl. 103; Helma Riefenstahl, "Vier Jahre Kriegsarbeit im Verein kath. deutscher Lehrerinnen," *Monatsschrift für katholische Lehrerinnen* 32 (July 1918): 227–231; the reports in StdMünch Schulamt Nr. 911; and "Zusammenlegung von Schulen im Winter," *Leipziger Lehrerzeitung* 24 (26 September 1917): 496

9. "Vertretungschwierigkeiten," *Pädagogische Zeitung* 20 (20 May 1915), LABe STA Rep. 20–01 Nr. 402, Bl. 79 (quotation); Min. Ed. to KPSK, Berlin, 7 August 1914, KPSK-Berichte Bd. I, Bl. 1a; and "Bericht über den Stand der Volksschulen und der Fortbildungsschule der Stadt Mainz für das Schuljahr 1916/17," StdMainz 14 B 7, Bl. 13.

10. Riefenstahl, "Vier Jahre Kriegsarbeit," 227–231; "Coblenz: 'Ueberlastung' der Rektoren," *Der Volksschullehrer* 11 (4 January 1917): 6; and "Krieg und Schulunterricht," *Hannoversche Schulzeitung* 54 (22 January 1918): 21.

11. "Die Beurlaubung der Kinder, ein notwendiges Recht des Lehrers," *Der Volksschullehrer* 10 (14 September 1916): 291–292; "Schulschluß ohne Schüler," *Vossische Zeitung*, 4 July 1918, BA-Li 8034 II 6941, Bl. 88; *Kriegs-Gedenkschrift des Andreas-Realgymnasiums*, 11; KPSK, Schleswig, 9 December 1918, KPSK-Berichte Bd. II, Bl. 148–149; Schapler and Groeteken, *Kriegser-lasse*, 32–33; and Reissig, *Lehrerseminare*, 239, 248.

12. Ernst Liese, *Die Volksschule nach dem Krieg* (Halle: Schroedel, 1917), 11; "Eine ernste Kriegserfahrung," *Haus und Schule* 38 (December 1916): 106; "Vom Volkselend," *Leipziger Volkszeitung*, 25 September 1917, BA-Li 8034 II 6940, Bl. 176; Berta Frauendörfer, "Unsere Stadtkinder auf dem Lande," 17 October 1917, StdMünch Schulamt Nr. 2713 (quotation); Geschäftsstelle zur Verbringung von Schulkindern auf das Land, "Nürnburger Schulkinder auf dem Lande im Kriegsjahr 1917," BKrA MKr Nr. 12883, Bl. 16–17; and "Landaufenthalt und Schule," *Pädagogische Zeitung* 46 (13 June 1918): 229.

13. G. Menzel, "Lehrerinnen-Erlaß und seine Wirkung," *Pädagogische Zeitung* 45 (3 August 1916): 426–427; and Franziska Ohnesorge, "Die Lehrerinnenfrage nach dem Krieg," *Die Lehrerin* 33 (13 May 1916): 37–40.

14. KPSK, Königsberg, 7 January 1917, KPSK-Berichte Bd. I, Bl. 251 (quota-tion); "Die Durchsetzung der Volksschullehrerschaft mit Lehrerinnen," *Pädagogische Zeitung* 46 (8 February 1917): 90–91; and "Verheiratete Lehrerinnen," *Schulblatt der Provinz Sachsen* 56 (20 June 1917): 241–242.

15. "Eine Schulgeschichte," *Schulblatt der Provinz Sachsen* 55 (14 June 1916): 242.

16. "Versetzung der Schüler in der Kriegszeit," *Hannoversche Schulzeitung* 51 (23 February 1915): 91; Min. Ed., Berlin, 7 February 1917, copy, StHam 361–2 I B 11 Nr. 3, Bl. 8; "Weniger Lehrstoff oder Sonderlehrgänge," *Vossische Zeitung*, 7 September 1917, BA-Li, 8034 II 6940, Bl. 164; R. Timm,

"Versetzung der Schüler," *Hamburger Fremdenblatt,* 8 September 1915, StHam 361–2 I B 15, Nr. 6, Bl. 2 (first quotation); Flitner, *Krieg und die Jugend,* 256, 262; and Praktisch-theologische Schule, Bethel bei Bielefeld, 16 September 1918, and KPSK, Hanover, 15 December 1918, both in KPSK-Berichte Bd. II, Bl. 76–77, 151 (second quotation).

17. "Oeffentliche Sicherheit," [13 September 1918], StdMünch Schulamt Nr. 911; "Barfußgehen der Schulkinder," *Katholische Schulzeitung für Norddeutschland* 34 (28 June 1918): 259; "Das Tragen von Holzschuhen durch die gesamte Düsseldorfer Schuljugend," *Düsseldorfer Zeitung,* 5 December 1917, StdDüss III 1708, Bl. 57; and "Späterer Schulbeginn?" *Vossische Zeitung,* 13 January 1917, and "Rücksichtslosigkeit in der Schule," *Leipziger Volkszeitung,* 9 February 1917, both in BA-Li 8034 II 6940, Bl. 49, 69.

18. "Niederschriften über die Verhandlungen der Kreisschulkommissionen für Oberfranken," 12 December 1916, StaaMünch RA Nr. 53902, Bl. 12 (first quotation); "Die Straßenpolonaisen und der Schulbetrieb," *Pädagogische Zeitung* 46 (5 January 1917): 14; and "Schulschwänzer," *Vorwärts,* 8 October 1918, BA-Li 8034 II 6941, Bl. 130 (second quotation).

19. "Auf daß es uns nicht zu wohl werde!" *Leipziger Lehrerzeitung* 24 (9 May 1917): 265 (quotation); "Die sittliche Gefährdung der schulpflichtigen Jugend durch die Kriegsverhältnisse," *Pädagogische Zeitung* 45 (17 August 1916): 455–456; Nationaler Frauendienst, 1 January 1915, LABe STA Rep. 20–01 Nr. 402, Bl. 102; "Ein Erlebnis und einige Gedanken über Zucht im vierten Kriegsjahre," *Hamburgische Schulzeitung* 26 (26 January 1918): 19–20; "Die 'Verrohung der Jugend,'" *Pädagogische Zeitung* 45 (30 March 1916): 183; "Verwahrlosung der Jugend?" *Pädagogische Zeitung* 46 (1 February 1917): 82; and KPSK-Berichte.

20. "Die Ernährung der Berliner Gemeindeschulkinder," *Pädagogische Zeitung* 46 (8 February 1917): 99–100; "Kinderhorte," *Schulblatt der Provinz Sachsen* 55 (28 June 1916): 262; "Verzeichnis der Gemeindeschule, in denen Kinderhorte untergebracht sind," n.d., LABe STA Rep. 20–01 Nr. 402, Bl. 104; and Stenographische Bericht über die Sitzung der Stadtverordneten-Versammlung, 1 February 1917, LABe STA Rep. 00–02/1 Nr. 2530, Bl. 1–2; Min. Ed., Berlin, 12 November 1917, KPSK-Berichte Bd. II, Bl. 16; Min. Ed., Berlin, 7 April 1916, and responses, GStA I. HA Rep. 76 VI Sec. I Gen. z: 259, Bl. 7, 13–72; "An schweren Tagen," *Pädagogische Zeitung* 47 (10 October 1918): 400; "Die Einwirkung des Krieges auf die Schule," *Allgemeines Schulblatt* 67 (25 April 1916): 104 (first quotation); and Flitner, *Krieg und die Jugend,* 262 (second quotation).

21. Deborah Dwork, *War Is Good for Babies and Other Young Children: A History of the Infant and Child Welfare Movement in England, 1898–1918* (London: Tavistock, 1987), 208–220; Thierry Bonzon and Belinda Davis, "Feeding the Cities," in *Capital Cities,* ed. Winter and Robert, vol. 1; Becker, *The Great*

War, 325; J. M. Winter, "Military Fitness and Civilian Health in Britain during the First World War," *Journal of Contemporary History* 15 (1980): 211–244; and Jay Winter, *The Great War and the British People* (Cambridge, MA: Harvard University Press, 1986), 153, 244–245.

7. The Upheaval of Families

1. "Gesamtbericht der Tagung in Frankfurt a.M. am 7., 8. und 9. Oktober 1915," *Schriften des Ausschusses für Jugendgerichte und Jugendgerichtshilfen,* ed. Deutsche Zentrale für Jugendfürsorge (Berlin: Heymann, 1918), 103–105; "Jahresbericht für die Kriegsjahre, 1914–1918," Hartmann, Regierungs- und Gewerberats, Pol. Berlin, LABr Pr. Br. Rep. 30 Berlin C. Tit. 47, Nr. 1958; and Daniel, *Working Class Women,* 176–178. Absent working fathers were a major reason for the expulsion of secondary school boys. See BHStA Mk Nr. 20891–93.

2. Daniel, *Working-Class Women,* 173–190.

3. Gertrud Moses, *Zum Problem der sozialen Familienverwahrlosung unter besonderer Berücksichtigung der Verhältnisse im Krieg* (Langensalza: Herman Beyer & Söhne, 1920), 14; articles and summaries of rulings, StHam 354–5 I Nr. 227; KPSK-Berichte; and Dietrich, *Marlene,* 22 (quotation). See also Healy, *Vienna,* 259, 262, 267–268; and Paul Weindling, "The Medical Profession, Social Hygiene and the Birth Rate in Germany 1914–18," in *Upheaval of War,* ed. Wall and Winter, 422.

4. "Ideale von Knaben und Mädchen," 22–23 (first quotations); Lottchen Beyer, "Der Krieg," in *Kinderaufsatz,* ed. Karstädt, 31 (second-to-last quotation); Maria Bromen, "Wenn Vater im Krieg ist . . . ," *Monatsschrift für katholische Lehrerinnen* 28 (May 1915): 271 (last quotation); and "Hemmungen im Unterricht während des Krieges und die Versetzungen der Schüler," *Lehrer-Zeitung für Ost- und Westpreußen* 48 (17 February 1917): 75–76. On returning fathers, see also Reinhard Sieder, "Working-Class Family Life in Wartime Vienna," in *Upheaval of War,* ed. Wall and Winter, 129–130.

5. "Der schwerste Gang" and "Kommt denn mein Vater noch heim?" in *Freie Kriegsaufsätze,* ed. Fröhlich, 67–70; the essays all titled "In den Ferien," StdDarm, Stadtknabenschule III St 63 18/1, 1915–1916; Ernst Gläser, *Class of 1902* (New York: Viking, 1929), 269–270 (quotation); "Achtet auf die Jugend! Ein Kapitel Strafgerichtsbarkeit im Kriege," *Kölnische Zeitung,* 30 November 1915, StdMainz 70/860; KPSK-Berichte; "Fragebogen über die Wirkung von Krieg" (1920), StdMünch, Schulamt Nr. 17; and reports of Kjp., LABr, Pr. Br. Rep. 2a Regierung Potsdam II Gen. Nr., 1577, and HessHA 405, Nr. 3839.

6. Davis, *Home Fires Burning,* 32–44. See also Healy, *Vienna,* 163–210.

7. Ludwig Preller, *Sozialpolitik in der Weimarer Republik* (Stuttgart: Droste, 1949), 37–38; Stefan Bajohr, *Die Hälfte der Fabrik: Geschichte der Frauenarbeit*

in Deutschland, 1914–1945 (Marburg: Arbeiterbewegung und Gesell-
schaftswissenschaft, 1979), 149; Bernhard Adam, *Arbeitsbeziehung in der
bayerischen Großstadtmetallindustrie von 1914 bis 1932* (Munich: Uni-Druck,
1983), 155; Aneliese Seidel, *Frauenarbeit im Ersten Weltkrieg als Problem der
staatlichen Sozialpolitik: Dargestellt am Beispeil Bayerns* (Frankfurt a.M.: Rita
G. Fischer, 1979), 171; Daniel, *Working-Class Women*, 286–287; and Richard
Wall, "English and German Families and the War," and Ute Daniel,
"Women's Work in Industry and Family: Germany, 1914–1918," both in
Upheaval of War, ed. Wall and Winter, 61–62, 277–279.

8. Buchner, *Kriegstagebuch*, 185, 209–210; Davis, *Home Fires Burning*, 165; Budde,
Bürgerleben, 166–192; and Ann Taylor Allen, *Feminism and Motherhood in
Germany, 1800–1914* (New Brunswick, NJ: Rutgers University Press, 1991),
171–172. On the impoverishment of the lower middle classes, see Andreas
Kunz, *Civil Servants and the Politics of Inflation in Germany, 1914–1924* (New
York: De Gruyter, 1986), 132–142; Gunther Mai, *Kriegswirtschaft und Arbeiter-
bewegung in Württemberg, 1914–1918* (Stuttgart: Ernst Klett, 1983), 419–420;
and Jürgen Kocka, *Facing Total War: German Society, 1914–1918* (Lemington
Spa: Berg, 1984), 77–111.

9. Benninghaus, *Arbeitermädchen*, 63–65; Budde, *Bürgerleben*, 254; Michael
Mitterauer and Reinhard Sieder, *The European Family: Patriarchy to Partner-
ship from the Middle Ages to the Present* (Chicago: University of Chicago Press,
1982), 24–47.

10. Kalkle, Danzig, 13 January 1916, KPSK-Berichte Bd. I, Bl. 159ff; Spuken,
Cologne, 9 May 1916, StdKöln Best. 569 Nr. 342, Bl. 155; Sieder, "Working-
Class Family," 116; Mihaly, *Girl's Diary*; and Dietrich, *Marlene*.

11. Gertrud Meyer, *Die Frau mit grünen Haaren: Erinnerungen* (Hamburg: VSA,
1978), 33–34, 37 (first quotation); Bajohr, *Frauenarbeit*, 117; Daniel,
Working-Class Women, 192; Young Sun Hong, "The Contradictions of
Modernization in the German Welfare State: Gender and the Politics of
Welfare Reform in First World War Germany," *Social History* 17 (1992):
251–270; reports by the Hauptstelle für Kinderfürsorge in 1915 and 1917 in
Mainz, StdMainz 70/885; "Die Frankfurter Jugendherberge," *Volkstimme*
(Frankfurt a.M.), 9 October 1916, GStA I. HA Rep. 77 CB Reihe S Nr.
631, Bl. 28 (second quotation); "Jugendherbergen in Frankfurt a.M.,"
Jugendführung 5 (March–April 1918): 82–83; and Münchener Jugendheim
e.V., 1 May 1917, BHStA MJu Nr. 16049.

12. Davis, *Home Fires Burning*, 137–158; Roerkohl, *Hungerblockade*, 230–260;
Buchner, *Kriegstagebuch*, 161; and Budde, *Bürgerleben*, 82–84.

13. "Der preußische Unterrichtsminister zur Jugendheimfrage," *Vorwärts*, 28
January 1918, GStA I. HA Rep. 77 CB Reihe S Nr. 631, Bl. 42; and
"Kinderhorte unter Mitwirkung von Schülern höherer Lehranstalten,"
Pädagogische Zeitung 45 (15 June 1916): 329.

14. "Niederschrift über . . . im Abgeordnetenhause in Berlin stattgehabte Frühjahrsausschussitzung," Landaufenthalt for Stadtkinder e.V., Berlin, 5 April 1918, copy, HessHA 405 Nr. 12633, Bl. 6–16; Flitner, *Krieg und die Jugend,* 273; and Katholischer Jugendfürsorgeverein der Erzdiözese München und Freising, e.V., *Ein Jahr Arbeit in der Jugendfürsorge: Bericht über das Jahr 1917* (Munich), 23–25, 33. Little evidence supports contrary claims in Hans-Joachim Bieber, *Gewerkschaften in Krieg und Revolution: Arbeiterbewegung, Industrie, Staat und Militär in Deutschland, 1914–1920* (Hamburg: Christians, 1981), 211.

15. "Landaufenthalt der Berliner Gemeindeschüler," *Deutsche Tageszeitung,* 10 May 1917, BA-Li 8034 II 6940, Bl. 116; Elisabeth von Oertzen, *Unsere Stadtkinder* (Berlin: Verein Landaufenthalt für Stadtkinder, 1918), 5, 7, 10–11; "Die Erfahrung unserer Landbevölkerung mit den Stadtkindern," *Pädagogische Zeitung* 46 (16 August 1917): 456–457; "Stadtkinder aufs Land!" *Pädagogische Zeitung* 46 (17 May and 7 June 1917): 318–319, 367–368; Stiemke, "Erfahrungen und Vorschläge zum Landaufenthalt unserer Kinder," *Pädagogische Zeitung* 46 (31 May 1917): 350–51; Heinrich Houben, *Als die Stadtkinder kamen: Bilder aus dem Feriendorf im Kriegsjahr 1916* (Dresden: Globus, 1917), 7, 14–15, 17, 35; Geschäftsstelle zur Verbringung von Schulkindern auf das Land, *Nürnburger Schulkinder auf dem Lande im Kriegsjahr 1917* (Nürnberg, 1918), 19–22, 27–28; "Ferienkinder 1917," *Zeitschrift für Jugendhilfe* 5 (September 1917): 110–112; and survey documents dated 6 December 1917 and Berta Frauendörfer, "Unsere Stadtkinder auf dem Lande," 17 October 1917, all in StdMünch Schulamt Nr. 2713.

16. Emmy Geß, "Unsere Berliner Kinder in Pommern," *Die Jugendfürsorge* 11 (August 1916): 6 (first quotation); "Schule und Stadtkinder auf dem Lande," *Der Volksschullehrer* 11 (26 July 1917): 234 (second quotation); "Stadtkinder aufs Land," *Pädagogische Zeitung* 46 (25 April 1917): 219–220; Heinemann, "Die jugendlichen Landarbeiter im Kreise Zeven," Hamburg, 23 June 1917, StHam 361–2 I B 19, Nr 14; Schule am Winthirplatz, Munich, 11 December 1917, StdMünch Schulamt Nr. 2713 (third and fourth quotations); and Landaufenthalt für Stadtkinder, "Behandlung nicht organisationsgemäß untergebrachter Kinder," 25 April 1918, HessHA 405 Nr. 12633, Bl. 30 (last quotations).

17. "Vom deutschen Jugendfürsorgetag in Berlin," *Der Volksschullehrer* 12 (10 October 1918): 223; Bernhard Seiffert, *Landes-Jugendämter* (Halle: Marhold, 1918); Hasenclever, *Jugendgesetzgebung,* 41–47; Dickinson, *German Child Welfare,* 118, 124–138; and "Jugendämter," *Volkswacht* (Breslau), 24 July 1918, GStA I. HA Rep. 77 CB Reihe S Nr. 631, Bl. 56.

18. Günther Dehn, "Volksjugend in der Heimat," *Jugend,* ed. Müller, 8–15; Dehn, *Großstadtjugend,* 66–72; and Elfriede, *Sprechzimmer,* 12.

19. Zimmermann, *Bevölkerungsbewegung,* 359; Dönhoff, Landegewerbeamt, Berlin, 22 October 1917, copy, BHStA Mk Nr. 22816; Magistrate, Breslau, to

Mayor, Düsseldorf, 26 April 1915, StdDüss III 3606, Bl. 98–99; "Die
ländliche Fortbildungsschule in Preußen im dritten Kriegswinter 1916/17,"
Fortbildungsschulpraxis 12 (March 1918): 21–23; "Ergänzung zum Bericht
über die Gewerblichen Fortbildungschule zu Düsseldorf über das Schuljahr
1915/1916," 25 July 1917, StdDüss. III 3629, Bl. 156–58; Linton, *Young
Workers*, 188–189; Direktor, Baugewerkschule, Hildesheim, 4 May 1919,
NHAH, Hann. 180 Hildesheim, Nr. 4362; and the statistical reports on
releases for 1916/17 and 1917/19 in Munich, StdMünch Schulamt Nr. 2366.

20. "Verwaltungsbericht für das Landesgewerbeamt über die Handwerker und
    Kunstgewerbeschule zu Hildesheim während der Kriegszeit," 1919, NHAH,
    Hann. 180 Hildesheim, Nr. 4362; Report, Städtische Gewerbliche Fortbil-
    dungsschulen, Hanover, 6 November 1915, NHAH Hann. 180 Hannover
    Nr. 657, Bl. 11–12; Bezirksfortbildungsschule an der Kirchenstraße, Munich,
    21 October 1918, StdMünch Schulamt Nr. 2782; and Min. Ed., Munich, 14
    December 1915, and "Der Kampf der Fachschulen und der Arbeitgeber um
    die Lehrlinge," *Münchener Post*, 12 November 1915, both in StdMünch,
    Schulamt Nr. 2366.

21. Bezirksfortbildungsschule am Mariahilfsplatz, Munich, 23 October 1918,
    and other reports from various continuation schools in October 1918 in
    StdMünch Schulamt Nr. 2782; and "Eine recht bedenkliche Erscheinung,"
    Badische Schulzeitung 55 (10 February 1917): 13 (quotation).

22. "Oeffentlichen Arbeitsnachweises Abt. für Männer und jugendliche
    Arbeiter," Hamburg, [6 March 1916], StHam 111–2 C II 1 13, Bl. 10;
    Verband der Arbeitgeber des Baugewerbes für München und Umgebung,
    Munich, 28 December 1917, BKrA Stv.Gen.Kdo.I.b.A.K. Nr. 1002; Preller,
    Sozialpolitik, 9, 15–17; Dehn, *Großstadtjugend*, 76; Karl Korn, *Die Arbeiterju-
    gendbewegung: Eine Einführung in ihre Geschichte* (Berlin: Arbeiterjugend,
    1922), 271–272; Waldemar Zimmermann, "Die Erwerbsarbeit der Kinder
    und Jugendlichen," in *Jugendpflege*, ed. Duensing, 203; Zimmermann,
    Bevölkerungsbewegungen, 372, 376, 382–383, 386–388, 392–393, 397, 401;
    Seidel, *Frauenarbeit*, 261–262; "Jahresbericht für die Kriegsjahre 1914–1918,"
    LABr Pr. Br. Rep. 30 Berlin C. Tit. 47 Nr. 1958, Bl. 50, 86; and K. Heepe,
    "Deutsche Erziehungsaufgaben," *Deutsches Lehrerblatt*, 1 August 1917, BA-Li
    8034 II 6940, Bl. 150. See also see Detlev Peukert, *Jugend zwischen Krieg und
    Krise: Lebenswelten von Arbeiterjungen in der Weimarer Republik* (Köln: Bund,
    1987), 155.

23. "Die Straffälligkeit der Jugend während des Krieges," *Münchner Neuste
    Nachrichten*, 18 May 1917; "Der Sparzwang in den Marken," *Ratgeber für
    Jugendvereinigungen* 10 (May 1916): 75 (quotation); and "Die Wirkungen des
    Sparzwangs," *Pädagogische Zeitung* 46 (16 August 1917): 459–460. On the
    compulsory savings plans, see also the following chapter.

24. Christina Benninghaus and Deborah Cohen, "Mothers' Toil and Daughters'
    Leisure: Working-Class Girls and Time in 1920s Germany," *History*

Workshop Journal 50 (2000): 38–39, 52; Benninghaus, *Arbeitermädchen*, 78, 85; Rosa Kempf, "Das Großstadtmädchen der unteren Klassen," in *Jugendpflege*, ed. Duensing; Wegs, *Viennese Youth*, 105, 118–121, 120 (quotation); and Eric Johnson and Vincent McHale, "Socioeconomic Aspects of Delinquency Rate in Imperial Germany," *Journal of Social History* 13 (Spring 1980): 387. This interpretation relies heavily on the theory of patriarchy proposed by John Hagen, John Simpson, and A. R. Gillis, "Class in the Household: A Power-Control Theory of Gender and Delinquency," *American Journal of Sociology* 92 (1987): 788–816.

25. On crime and prostitution, see "Die Verwaltungsaufgabe im Kriege," 10 August 1915, StaaMünch Pol. Dir. München, Nr. 4543; Moritz Liepmann, *Krieg und Kriminalität in Deutschland* (New Haven, CT: Yale University Press, 1930), 106; Reagin, *German Women's Movement*, 53–54, 83–85, 147–156; Magnus Hirschfeld, *Sittengeschichte des Ersten Weltkrieges* (Hanau a.M.: Schustek, 1929), 306–307; Daniel, *Working-Class Women*, 139; and Robert Wegs, "Youth Delinquency and 'Crime:' The Perception and the Reality," *Journal of Social History* 32 (1999): 606. On wages, see Zimmermann, *Bevölkerungsbewegung*, 372; Pol. Report 1917, LAB Pr. Br. Rep. 30 Berlin C. Tit. 47 Nr. 1958; "Lohneinbehaltung," Kgl. Lokalschulkommission, Nürnberg, 3 June 1916, BKrA MKr Nr. 12649; and "Sparzwang in den Marken." On employment in and outside the home, see "Die Kriegshilfsarbeiten der preußischen Schuljugend im Jahre 1917," *Pädagogische Zeitung* 47 (21 March 1918): 108; Linton, "Young Working Women," 399; H. Bohnstedt, "Kriegswirtschaft und Schule," *Kreuz Zeitung*, 6 February 1917, BA-Li 8034 II 6940, Bl. 61; "Säuglingspflege in Kasseler Mädchenschulen," *Vorwärts*, 28 May 1918, GStA I. HA Rep. 120 E VIII Fach 1 Nr. 1 Bd. 10. For evidence of the same trends in Vienna, see Wegs, *Growing Up Working Class*, 105–111; and Hans Safrian and Reinhard Sieder, "Gassenkinder—Strassenkämpfer: Zur politischen Sozialisation einer Arbeitergeneration in Wien 1900–1938," in *"Wir Kriegen jetzt andere Zeiten": Auf der Suche nach der Erfahrung des Volkes in Nachfaschistischen Ländern*, ed. Lutz Niethammer und Alexander von Plato (Berlin: Dietz, 1985), 124.

26. Linton, "Young Working Women," 399; Meyer, *Erinnerungen*, 27–28; Arbeitsnachweis der Patriotischen Gesellschaft, Hamburg, 21 March 1916, StHam 331–1 I Polizeibehörde I Nr. 343, Bl. 8; Kjp., Biedenkopf, 13 January 1918, HessHA 405 Nr. 3839, Bl. 146f; and Zimmermann, *Bevölkerungsbewegung*, 372.

8. The Dwindling Controls over Sex, Crime, and Play

1. Peukert, *Grenzen der Sozialdisziplinierung*, 152–161; and Linton, *Young Workers*, 62–67, are the classic accounts of this phenomenon in the German context.

2. Dehn, "Volksjugend in der Heimat," 10; and Wilhelm Backhausen, "Unsere Fürsorgezöglinge und der Krieg," *Zentralblatt für Vormundschaftswesen, Jugendgericht und Fürsorgeerziehung* 6 (10 March 1915): 221–225.

3. On state authority more generally, see Sean Dobson, *Authority and Upheaval in Leipzig, 1910–1920* (New York: Columbia University Press, 2000), 131–188.

4. See LABr Pr. Br. Rep. 2a Reg. Potsdam II Gen. Nr. 1577: Wegener, Kjp., Charlottenburg, 25 January 1917; Bauer, Kjp., Spandau, 5 January 1917; and Blume, Kjp., Neukölln, 22 February 1916 and 18 January 1917.

5. See the reports of the youth workers in HessHA 405 Nr. 3838 and Nr. 3839 and in LABr Pr. Br. Rep. 2a Reg. Potsdam II Gen. Nr. 1577, including Blume, Neukölln, 21 January 1918. See also "Anstaltsbericht," *Der Gemeindehelfer* 7 (January 1919): 1–4; "Großherzogtum Hessen: Jugendfürsorge im Kriege," *Pädagogische Zeitung* 45 (27 January 1916): 52–53; and Min. Ed., Berlin, to Reg. Präs., Wiesbaden, 28 April 1916, HessHA 405 Nr. 3838, Bl. 296 (quotation).

6. Günther, "Welche Vortragstoffe eignen sich in der Jetztzeit für Jugend- und Elternabende?" in *Jugendpflege*, ed. Dieckmann, 30 (first quotation); Fritz Luckau, Kjp., Teltow, [January 1917], LABr Pr. Br. Rep. 2a Reg. Potsdam II Gen. Nr. 1577 (second quotation); Min. Ed., Berlin, 5 October 1916, copy, StdKöln Best. 569 Nr. 4, Bl. 81; Reg. Präs., Düsseldorf, 8 February 1917, NWHSA Reg. Düss. 33097; and Edmund Schopen, "Kriegsbürgerkunde," *Ratgeber für Jugendvereinigungen* 11 (February–March 1917): 24–25.

7. Koch, "Die städtische Jugendpflege in Weimar: Jahresbericht für 1916," *Fortbildungsschulpraxis* 11 (June 1917): 86; *Jahresbericht der Jugendeutschland-Ortsgruppe "Groß-Berlin" E.B. 5. Geschäftsjahr, 1916–17*, LAB, Pr. Br. Rep. 2a Reg. Potsdam II Gen. Nr. 1502, 11–13; "Jugendwohnung," *Jugendführung* 4 (August–September 1917): 252 (first quotation); Geschäftsführer, "Jungdeutschland," 14 May 1918, GStA I. HA Rep. 77 Tit. 924 Nr. 7, Bl. 199 (second quotation); Naudascher, *Freizeit in öffentlicher Hand*, 172; and Von Bailer, "Jungdeutschlandbund," 48–49.

8. Abrams, *Workers' Culture*, 104–107.

9. Daniel J. Leab, "Screen Images of the 'Other' in Wilhelmine Germany and the United States, 1890–1918," *Film History* 9 (1997): 59–64, 59 (first quotation); Hans Wollenberg, *Fifty Years of German Film* (London: Falcon, 1948), 11–12; Helmut Korte, "Krieg und das Kino," in *Fischer Filmgeschichte*, vol. 1, *Von den Anfängen bis zum etablierten Medium, 1895–1924*, ed. Werner Faulstich and Helmut Korte (Frankfurt a.M.: Fischer Taschenbuch, 1994), 308, 311, 313; Sabine Hake, *The Cinema's Third Machine: Writing on Film in Germany, 1907–1933* (Lincoln: University of Nebraska Press, 1993), 17; Friedrich Terveen, "Die Anfänge der deutschen Film-Kriegsberichterstattung in den Jahren, 1914–1916" (1946), in *Film und Gesellschaft in Deutschland*, ed. Wilfried von Bredow and Rolf Zurek (Hamburg: Hoffmann und Campe, 1975), 89–93; Siegfried Kracauer, *From Caligari to Hitler: A Psychological History of the*

German Film (Princeton, NJ: Princeton University Press, 1947), 21–23; and Ludwig Gurlitt, *Die deutsche Jugend und der Krieg* (Greiz: Hennig, 1915), 39 (last quotation).

10. Dehn, "Volksjugend in der Heimat," 25; Liepmann, *Krieg und Kriminalität in Deutschland* (New Haven: Yale University Press, 1930), 95; and Korn, *Arbeiterjugendbewegung*, 270–271.

11. "Das Kino auf dem Lande," *Donau Zeitung*, 7 July 1917, BKrA, Stv.Gen. Kdo.I.b.A.K. Nr. 999 (first quotation); "Die Jugend von heute!" *Katholische Zeitschrift für Erziehung und Unterricht* 67 (1918): 85 (second quotation); Karl Ettlinger, "Unsere Fortbildungsschuljugend im Krieg," *Fortbildungsschulpraxis* 12 (March 1918): 24, as a reprinted from *Jugend* (poem); and "Grober Unfug," *Berliner Volks-Zeitung*, 9 June 1916 (last quotation), and adjacent letters to and from the police, all in LABr Pr. Br. Rep. 30 Berlin C Tit. 133 Nr. 18713. See also Oberlehrer, Schule an der Oberhöringerstr. 15/16, 10 August 1917, StdMünch Schulamt Nr. 2782; Bayerischer Wehrkraftverein e.V., 24 September 1915, StdMünch Schulamt Nr. 2711; and Min. Int., Berlin, 21 August 1917, LABr Pr. Br. Rep. 30 Berlin C Tit. 162 Nr. 20265, Bl. 6–7.

12. DCG Cassel, 1 October 1915, KPSK-Berichte Bd. I, Bl. 152–5; and letters of support and opposition, BKrA, Stv.Gen.Kdo.I.b.A.K. Nr. 999–1003. For a chronology of the bans, see untitled, *Die Innere Mission im evangelischen Deutschland* 2 (February 1916): 62–67. On bans in Vienna, see Healy, *Vienna*, 250–254.

13. Gerhard Siebers, "Militärkontrolle und Jugendpflege," *Allgemeine Rundschau*, 31 March 1916, StaaMünch Pol. Dir. München, Nr. 4554; Sch. Dep., Munich, 17 March 1916, BKrA Stv.Gen.Kdo.I.b.A.K. Nr. 999; Opfergelt, "Die militärischen Erlasse gegen die Verwahrlosung der Jugend auf der Kriegstagung der deutschen Gerichtshilfen in Berlin, 14 April 1917," *Jugendführung* 4 (June 1917): 182–184; Min. Int., Berlin, 16 March 1916, GStA I. HA Rep. 77 Titel 421 No. 45, Bl. 14; and Verein der Tabak- und Zigarren-Ladeninhaber zu Hamburg, 26 January 1916, and "Bekanntmachung," Hamburg, 18 February 1916, both in StHam 111–2 A II p Nr. 22 b, Bl. 7, 10.

14. High Command, Berlin, 19 August 1916, copy, NHAH Hann. 122a Nr. 7020, Bl. 449 (first quotation); "Württemberg: Eine lebendlahme Verteidigung," *Schwäbische Tagewacht*, 24 November 1916, GStA I. HA Rep. 77 CB Reihe S Nr. 878 Bd. 3; "Der Sparzwang und wir: Nachschrift der Redaktion," *Zentralblatt der christlichen Gewerkschaften Detuschlands* 16 (6 November 1916): 190–191; M. Hg., "Der Sparzwang der Jugendlichen," *Zentralblatt der christlichen Gewerkschaften Deutschlands* 16 (4 December 1916): 205; and Eve Rosenhaft, "Restoring Moral Order on the Home Front: Compulsory Savings Plans for Young Workers in Germany, 1916–1919," in *Authority, Identity and the Social History of the Great War*, ed. Frans Coetzee and Marilyn Shevin-Coetze (Oxford: Berghahn, 1995).

15. "Sieg der Jugend in Braunschweig," *Jugend-Internationale* 5 (September 1916): 12; Wilhelm Münzenberg, *Die sozialistischen Jugendorganisationen vor und während des Krieges* (Berlin: Junge Garde, 1919), 122–123; Düsseldorf police report from 20 June 1916, NWHSA Reg. Düss. 16005, Bl. 420–22; and Boll, *Massenbewegungen*, 217–253, 229 (quotation).

16. Report DCG Altona, 12 May 1916, StHam 111–2 C II 1 Nr. 13, Bl. 31, 63; Min. Int., Munich, 14 December 1916, BKrA MKr Nr. 12650; "Leipzig: Die hiesige Gewerbekammer," *Die Deutsche Fortbildungsschule* 26 (1 February 1917): 92–93; C. Noppel, "Der Sparzwang für Jugendliche in Berlin," *Jugendführung* 4 (January 1917): 18; and "Sparzwang für Jugendliche," *Die deutsche Arbeitgeber-Zeitung*, 7 January 1917, GStA I. HA Rep. 77 CB Reihe S Nr. 878 Bd. 3.

17. Linton, *Young Workers*, 62–67; Peukert, *Grenzen der Sozialdisziplinierung*, 68–96; and Johnson and McHale, "Delinquency Rate."

18. Dehn, "Volksjugend in der Heimat," 10; Backhausen, "Fürsorgezöglinge"; and Kurt Wittig, *Der Einfluß des Krieges und der Revolution auf die Kriminalität der Jugendlichen* (Langensalza: Hermann Beyer & Söhne, 1921), 6–7.

19. See reports from 10 August 1915 and 13 August 1915, StaaMünch Pol. Dir. Munich Nr. 4543; Wittig, *Kriminalität* (1921), 9; Deutsche Zentrale für Jugendfürsorge, *Bericht über ihre Tätigkeit im Jahre 1915* (Berlin, 1916), 9; and Chickering, *Great War and Urban Life*, 506–509.

20. "Die näheren Ursachen für die Kriminalität der Jugendlichen in Hannover," *Hannoversche Courier*, 26 July 1916, NHAH Hann. 180 Hannover, Nr. 657, Bl. 92 (quotation); Der Bayerische Landesausschuß für Jugendfürsorge, Munich, 18 December 1915, BKrA MKr Nr. 12649; Wittig, *Kriminalität* (1921), 16–22; Kronecker, "Strafvorschriften gegen die Verwahrlosung Jugendlicher," *Leipziger Zeitschrift für deutsches Recht* 10 (15 April 1916): 576–584; Hertz, Oberamtsrichter, Hamburg, 23 August 1918, StHam 111–2 C II 1 Nr. 13, Bl. 142ff; Franz von Liszt, "Der Krieg und die Kriminalität der Jugendlichen" *Zeitschrift für die gesamte Strafrechtswissenschaft* 37 (1916): 496–516; and Liepmann, *Krieg und Kriminalität*, 100.

21. Liepmann, *Krieg und Kriminalität*, 100.

22. Elaine Spencer, *Police and the Social Order in German Cities: The Düsseldorf District, 1848–1914* (DeKalb: Northern Illinois University Press, 1992), 151; "Verwahrlosung und Verrohung der Jugend," *Hamburgischer Correspondent*, 5 April 1918, StHam 361–2 I B 28, Nr. 5; "Protokoll über die kommissarische Beratung, betreffend Maßnahmen gegen die Verwahrlosung und Verrohung der Jugend," 17 August 1918, StHam 111–2 C II 1 Nr. 13, Bl. 139; Pol., Berlin, 5 November 1917, LABr Pr. Br. Rep. 30 Berlin C Tit. 162 Nr. 20265, Bl. 25–26; Oberlehrer, Schule an der Kirchenstraße, Munich, 14 July 1917, StdMünch Schulamt Nr. 2782 (quotation); Fuhrmann, Chairman, Grundbesitzerverein, Berlin, 10 April 1916, LABr Pr. Br. Rep. 30 Berlin C Tit. 133

Nr. 18713; and *Statistik des deutschen Reichs,* vol. 304 (1921), 29, and vol. 297 (1923), 52.

23. *Wilde Cliquen: Szenen einer anderen Arbeiterjugendbewegung,* ed. Hellmut Lessing and Manfred Liebel (Bensheim: pädex, 1981), 18; Liepmann, *Kriminalität,* 112; and the following in StHam 361–2 I B 28 Nr. 5: "Kohlendiebstähle," newspaper unknown, [22 March 1917]; Hamburgisches Kriegsversorgungsamt, Gemüsestelle, 30 October 1917; and Pol., Hamburg, 11 April 1917. See also Healy, *Vienna,* 80.

24. Stefan Bajohr, "PartnerInnenwahl im Braunschweiger Arbeitermilieu 1900 bis 1933," *Jahrbuch für Forschungen zur Geschichte der Arbeiterbewegung* 3 (2003): 83–98; Bailey, *Courtship;* and Detlev Peukert, "Das Mädchen mit dem 'wahrlich metaphysikfreien Bubikopf': Jugend und Freizeit im Berlin der zwanziger Jahre," in *Im Banne der Metropolen: Berlin und London in den 20er Jahren,* ed. Peter Alter (Göttingen: Vandenhoeck & Ruprecht, 1993)

25. *Kindheit im Kaiserreich,* ed. Pörtner, 130.

26. See LABr Pr. Br. Rep. 34 Berlin I. Nr. 921: Greif, Körner Realschule, Berlin, 27 February 1917 and 30 May 1918; "Die bunten Mützen," *Berliner Tageblatt,* 6 June 1918; Lüdtke, KPSK, Berlin, 19 October 1917; KPSK, Berlin, 12 April 1918; and Director, Kirschner-Oberrealschule, Berlin, 5 February 1918 (quotations).

27. Pol., Munich, 16 February 1918, StdMünch Schulamt Nr. 2782 (first quotations); and Direktion der Stadt-Strassenbahnen, Munich, 21 February 1918, StdMünch Schulamt Nr. 2782 (last quotation).

28. Königliches Amtsgericht, Verden, 29 February 1916, StHam 111–2 C II 1 Nr. 13, Bl. 10; "Polizeiliche Massnahmen über die Verwilderung und Verrohung der Jugend," 14 December 1915, StdMainz 70/860; and Angela Woollacott, "'Khaki Fever' and its Control: Gender, Class, Age and Sexual Morality on the British Homefront in the First World War," *Journal of Contemporary History* 29 (1994): 325–347.

29. Gemeinde-Kirchenrat von St. Nicolai, Berlin, 19 February 1918, LABr Pr. Br. Rep. 34 Berlin I. Nr. 921; and the following in GStA I. HA Rep. 77 Titel 924 Nr. 7, Bl. 201–208: Schmidt, Berlin, 7 June 1918; Pol., Berlin, 17 August 1918; Meister, Berlin, 3 August 1918; and Güth, Pol., Berlin, 8 May 1918.

30. "Ein Bewohner der Roonstrase," Cologne, 15 November 1917, StdKöln Friedrich-Wilhelm Gym. Best. 561 Nr. 311, Bl. 108; Berner, Charlottenburg, 6 March 1918, GStA I. HA Rep. 76 VI Sec. XIV Berlin z: 63, Bl. 107–108; Walther Classen, "Wanderunfug," *Ratgeber für Jugendvereinigungen* 9 (October 1915): 156–158; Köhne, "Die Jugendlichen und der Krieg," *Deutsche Strafrechts-Zeitung* 3 (1916): 14–15; Mayor, Essen, 29 December 1916, NWHSA Reg. Düss. 33104; and Bremer, "Einfluß des Krieges auf die Lebensführung der Jugendlichen," *Jugendführung* 4 (January 1917): 3–4.

31. Direction, Realsch. Geisenheim, 4 May 1918 and Konferenz-Protokoll der Klinger-Oberrealsch. in Frankfurt a.M. 13 November 1917, both in GStA I.

HA I. Rep. 76 VI Sec. 35 Kassel, z: 29, Bl. 43, 53–56; Vogel, KPSK, 9
December 1916, and Marie Treise, Halle, 6 March 1917, both in GStA I.
HA I. Rep. 76 VI Sec. XI Magdeburg, z: 42, Bl. 45ff, 60ff; Hellwig, criminal
commissar, Berlin, 25 September 1917, LABr Pr. Br. Rep. 34 Berlin I. Nr.
921 (quotation); Budde, *Bürgerleben*, 214–216; Wegs, *Viennese Youth*,
121–128; and Detlev Peukert, *The Weimar Republic: The Crisis of Classical
Modernity* (New York: Hill and Wang, 1993), 176.

32. "Kriegsartikel für ein neuerrichtetes Damen Frei-Corps," 7 May 1915,
    confiscated by Apostelgym., StdKöln Best. 569 Nr. 342, Bl. 146.

33. Samuleit, *Unsere Jugend*, 34 (quotation); Mann, "Aufsätze," 61, 64, 68; Dehn,
    "Volksjugend in der Heimat," 16; Golias, *Kinder und der Krieg*, 14; and Rothe,
    Kinder und der Krieg, 9, 18.

34. Köhne, "Jugendlichen," 14"; Die Kinder und der Krieg," *Düsseldorfer
    Volkszeitung*, 6 July 1917, StdDüss III 1708, Bl. 111; Pol., Munich, 13 January
    1915, StdMünch Schulamt Nr. 2782; "Kinderhandgranaten,"
    8-Uhr-Abendblatt, 22 October 1915, LABr Pr. Br. Rep. 30 Berlin C Tit. 133,
    18713; Pol., Cologne, 1 September 1915, StdKöln Friedrich-Wilhelm Gym.
    Best. 561 Nr. 311, 106; and "Grober Unfug."

35. Wallner, Munich, 15 December 1914 (first and second quotations), and
    "Gefährlicher Unfug," clipping, newspaper unknown, [January 1915], both
    in StdMünch Schulamt Nr. 2782; War Min. to Min. Int., Munich, 20
    January 1916, BKrA MKr Nr. 12649 (third quotation); "Grober Unfug"
    (fourth and fifth quotations); Goldberg, *Schulgeschichte*, 72; "Schüler-
    schlachten als Nachspiel vor dem Jugendgericht," *Vorwärts*, 17 March 1915;
    Kjp., Dillkreis, 29 December 1918, HessHA 405 Nr. 3839, Bl. 241–242; and
    Hans Wilke, "Welche besondere Aufgabe erwachsen der Jugendpflegearbeit
    in der Kriegszeit," in *Über Jugendpflege*, ed. Dieckmann and Wilke, 6 (last
    quotation).

36. Bryan Ganaway, "Toys, Consumption, and Middle Class Childhood in
    Imperial Germany, 1871–1918" (Ph.D. diss., University of Illinois at
    Urbana-Champagne, 2003), 254–302; Heike Hoffmann, "'Schwarzer Peter
    im Weltkrieg:' Die deutsche Spielwarenindustrie, 1914–1918," in *Kriegserfah-
    rungen*, ed. Hirschfeld et al.; Budde, *Bürgerleben*, 198–201; and Ute Frevert, *A
    Nation in Barracks: Modern Germany, Military Conscription, and Civil Society*
    (New York: Berg, 2004), 218.

37. Pol., Berlin, 5 June 1915, and Doren, Neukölln, 11 June 1916 (quotation),
    both in LABr. Rep. 34 Berlin I. Nr. 921.

38. KPSK, Berlin, 8 September 1915, GStA I. HA Rep. 76 VI Sec. XIV Berlin
    z: 63, Bl. 70ff.

39. "Die Langfuhrer Einbrücke," *Danziger Neueste Nachrichten*, 10 May 1918
    (first quotation), and "Gerichtszeitung: Zum Schülerprozeß in Danzig,"
    Memeler Dampfboot, 8 June 1918 (second and last quotation), both in GStA I.
    HA Rep. 76 VI Sec. IV Danzig l: Nr. 38.

40. Klau, Breslau, 20 January 1917, KPSK-Berichte Bd. I, Bl. 272 (quotation); and the following in GStA I. HA Rep. 76 VI Sec. IV. Danzig l: Nr. 38: "Nachrichten aus der Provinz," *Westpreußisches Volksblatt*, 17 April 1915; untitled, *Schlesische Volkszeitung*, 22 April 1915; and Kahler, KPSK, Danzig, 30 October 1915.

41. See, for example, "Ausschnitt aus dem Bericht des Bürgerschaften Ausschusses zur Prüfung des Staatshaushaltsplan für das Jahr 1918," StHam 111–2 C II 1 Nr. 13, Bl. 118.

42. Peukert, *Arbeiterjungen*, 251–266; Detlev Peukert, "Die 'Wilden Cliquen' der Zwanziger Jahre," in *Autonomie und Widerstand: Zur Theorie und Geschichte des Jugendprotest*, ed. Wilfried Breyvogel (Essen: Rigodon, 1983); Eve Rosenhaft, "Organising the 'Lumpenproletariat': Cliques and Communists in Berlin during the Weimar Republic," in *German Working Class*, ed. Evans, 186–187; and Peter Stachura, *The Weimar Republic and the Younger Proletariat: An Economic and Social Analysis* (London: Macmillan, 1989), 145–156.

9. Propaganda and the Limits on Dissent

1. On deaths, see "Die diesjährigen Kultusdebatten" (1917), 124–126.

2. See Clausewitz's definition of overcoming the enemy in his classic 1832 treatise, *On War*, 4.3. The interpretation by the Prussian generals was a misreading. In categorically refusing to accept a political solution through negotiations with the Allies until defeat was imminent, Hindenburg and Ludendorff contradicted Clausewitz's overriding principle that "war is the continuation of politics by other means" (1.25).

3. Ernst Rudolf Huber, *Weltkrieg, Revolution, und Reichserneuerung, 1914–1919*, vol. 5, *Deutsche Verfassungsgeschichte seit 1789* (Stuttgart: W. Kolhhammer, 1978), 164–166, 174–177, 218–257, 225 (quotation), 270–311; Ludwig Quidde, *Der deutsche Pazifismus während des Weltkrieges, 1914–1918* (Boppard am Rhein: Harald Boldt, 1979), 95–112; Jürgen Oelkers, *Reformpädagogik: Eine kritische Dogmengeschichte* (Weinheim: Juventa, 1989), 159–160; and Weber, *Pädagogik und Politik*, 87, 113, 116. Friedrich Wilhelm Foerster had marveled at the *Burgfrieden* and the delirious optimism in August 1914, but he found almost no supporters when, few months later, he challenged the idea that war was great. In one case, when he reproached Bismarck for his legacy of militarism in a lecture to a class of secondary school children, the disgusted teacher marched his pupils out before Foerster could finish. Friedrich Wilhelm Foerster, *Erlebte Weltgeschichte, 1869–1953: Memoiren* (Nürnberg: Glock und Lutz, 1953), 171–172, 187. Although teachers supported Heinrich Wolgast in his crusade against the war penny dreadfuls, they did not share his implicit attack on the militarism and nationalism in these lurid stories. Gustav Wyneken's ideas were too controversial before the war to merit respect from most teachers.

4. Wolfgang Wittwer, "Zur Entstehung und Entwicklung sozialdemokratischer Schulpolitik vor 1918," *Archiv für Sozialgeschichte* 20 (1980): 406–407, 411 (first quotation); Anna Blos, *Krieg und Schule* (Berlin: Internationale Korrespondenz, 1915), 13 (second quotation); "Kriegsbrief an die Jugend," *Vorwärts*, 11 April 1915; and Jahnke et al., *Arbeiterjugendbewegung,* 117.

5. "Wie stellen wir uns in der Schule zum Feindeshaß?" *Preußische Volksschullehrerinnen-Zeitung* 8 (15 March 1915): 179 (quotation); B. Hochke, "Jungdeutschland und der Krieg," *Katholische Schulzeitung für Norddeutschland* 32 (22 April 1915): 171; and Treutler, *Krieg und Schule,* 16.

6. Welch, *Germany, Propaganda,* 142; Quidde, *Deutsche Pazifismus,* 90 (first quotation); and "Aufruf an Eltern, Lehrer, und Erzieher," *Hamburgische Schulzeitung* 24 (1 January 1916): 1–2, as reprinted in Saul, "Jugend im Schatten," 136–137 (second quotation). The signers were variously members of the Center, Progressive, and Social Democratic parties that eighteen months later passed the Reichstag Peace Resolution.

7. "Schule und Völkerverbrüderung," *Pädagogische Zeitung* 45 (2 March 1916): 119–120, 119 (first quotation); "In einem bemerkenswerten Erlaß," *Hamburgische Schulzeitung* 24 (26 February 1916): 38 (second quotation); Chickering, *Peace Movement,* 172; "Ein höchst unangebrachter Aufruf," *Der Volksschullehrer* 10 (20 January 1916): 19–21; KPSK, Berlin, 15 March 1916, KPSK-Berichte Bd. I, Bl. 222; and DCG Hanover, 25 March 1916, NHAH Hann. 122a Nr. 7035.

8. Max Romanowski, "Die Kriegsschule," *Deutsches Lehrerblatt,* 7 June 1916, BA-Li, 8034 II 6939, Bl. 125 (first quotation); Fr[iedrich] W[ilhelm] Foerster, *Die deutsche Jugend und der Weltkrieg: Kriegs- und Friedensaufsätze* (Leipzig: Naturwissenschaft, 1916); Quidde, *Der deutsche Pazifismus,* 148; "Ein Friedensfest in der Kriegszeit," *Badische Schulzeitung* 54 (11 November 1916): 372; "Die 'Kriegsstunden,'" *Schulblatt der Provinz Sachsen* 56 (18 July 1917): 283; and L. Eicke, "Latein," *Jahresberichte über das höhere Schulwesen* 30 (1915): vi.4 (second quotation). This last article was in a yearbook devoted to 1915 but published in 1916.

9. Min. Ed., Munich, 3 October 1917 and 10 November 1917, StaaMünch RA Nr. 57867; Oberschulbehörde to directors of all schools, 25 June 1917, 2 February 1918, and 17 January 1918, StHam 361–2 III Nr. 148, Bl. 56, 80a, 82; "Schul-Lichttheater," *Pädagogische Zeitung* 45 (13 July 1916): 386; Healy, *Vienna,* 97–106; and David Welch, "Cinema and Society in Imperial Germany, 1905–1918," *German History* 8 (1990): 28–45.

10. Asta Nielsen-Lichtspiele, 19 May 1917, StdDüss III 1706, Bl. 427; and Asta Nielsen-Lichtspiele, 12 November 1917, StdDüss III 1707, Bl. 166 (quotations).

11. Kriegspresseamt, Berlin, 26 May 1917; Oberschulbehörde, Hamburg, 2 April 1917; Landherrenschaft, Hamburg, 20 April 1917; and "Die Schuldigen," brochure, all in StHam 361–2 I B 12 Nr. 2, Bl. 15, 23, 24 (quotation).

12. Koszyk, *Pressepolitik,* 137; Mosse, *Fallen Soldiers,* 132–134, 166, 186; and Reissig, "Lehrerseminare," 229–231.

13. Min. Ed., Berlin, 30 December 1916, StdDüss III 1706, Bl. 2; Schapler and Groeteken, *Kriegserlasse,* 46; Min. Ed., Berlin, 12 September 1917, and Reg. Präs., Düsseldorf, 16 October 1917, both in StdDüss III 1707, Bl. 346; "Die Lichtspielbühne im Dienst der Schul- und Volksbildung," *Hannoverscher Anzeiger,* 11 April 1917, NHAH, Hann. 87 Hannover Nr. 250; Pallat, "Zentralinstitut," 78; G. Gille, "Durchhalten und siegen!" *Deutsche Blätter für erziehenden Unterricht* 44 (12 Janaury 1917): 124–126; and "Gebot der Stunde," *Katholische Schulzeitung für Norddeutschland* 33 (23 November 1916): 469–470.

14. Erich Meyer, "Schule und Friedensziele: Eine nationale Gefahr," *Tägliche Rundschau,* 2 June 1916, BA-Li 8034 II 6939, Bl. 115; "Alldeutsche Agitation in den Schulen," *Berliner Tageblatt,* 8 July 1917, BA-Li 8034 II 6940, Bl. 141; Goldberg, "Wo stehen wir?" *Leipziger Lehrerzeitung* 25 (9 January 1918): 3; "Krieg und Schulunterricht," *Hannoversche Schulzeitung* 54 (22 January 1918): 21; Emil Hauptmann, *Kriegsziele: Methodische Handreichungen für den Gegenwartsunterricht* (Langensalza: Beltz, 1917), 21; and "Die Schule für die Vaterlandspartei," *Die Welt am Montag,* 20 April 1918, BA-Li, 8034 II 6938, Bl. 160 (quotation). On Ziegler, see Verband der deutschen Akademien, *Deutsches biographisches Jahrbuch,* vol. 2, *1917–1920* (Berlin: Deutsche, 1928), 346–349. See also Heinz Hagenlücke, *Deutsche Vaterlandspartei: Die nationale Rechte am Ende des Kaiserreiches* (Düsseldorf: Droste, 1997), 185; and Alastair Thompson, *Left Liberals, the State, and Popular Politics in Wilhelmine Germany* (Oxford: Oxford University Press, 2000), 377–378, 388.

15. See LABr Pr. Br. Rep. 34 Berlin I Nr. 921: "Politische Brunnenvergiftung in der Schule: Eine nette Pädagogik," *Berliner Morgenpost,* 28 August 1918 (first quotation); "Alldeutsche Propaganda in der Schule," [*Vorwärts*], 27 August 1918 (second quotation); "Die Schule und das Friedensangebot: 'Die fluchwürdige Demokratie,'" *Vorwärts,* 21 October 1918; Min. Ed., Berlin, 11 September 1918; and Rosenplenter, König Friedrich-Schule, Friedrichshagen, 3 September 1918.

16. Goldberg, "Was die Stunde fordert," *Leipziger Lehrerzeitung* 25 (6 November 1918): 383–384; "Zwei Eingaben des Leipziger Lehrervereins und ihre Ergebnisse," *Leipziger Lehrerzeitung* 24 (14 February 1917): 103 (quotation); and Dobson, *Authority and Upheaval in Leipzig, 1910-1920,* 122.

17. "Saarbrücken: Kleine Bilder aus großer Zeit," *Der Volksschullehrer* 11 (8 February 1917): 45 (first and second quotations); "Richtlinien für den Gegenwartsunterricht," *Erziehung und Unterricht* 23 (27 May 1916): 91; Krug, "Zur Nagelung eines eisernen Tores durch Schulkinder," *Archiv für Volksschullehrer* 21 (September 1917): 179; "Kriegsausstellung Frankfurt am Main," [October 1916], HessHA 405 Nr. 17757, Bl. 68; Peter Hoops, "Fremdwörterei

im deutschen Unterricht," *Hamburgische Schulzeitung* 23 (25 December 1916): 237–238; "Neuorientierung auf dem Gebiete des Schulwesens," *Schulblatt der Provinz Sachsen* 56 (4 January 1917): 1–2; "Kriegsweihestunde in der Schule," *Schulblatt der Provinz Sachsen* 55 (16 August 1916): 328 (last quotation); "Deutschkunde—ein neues Lehrfach," *Berliner Neueste Nachrichten*, 8 May 1917, BA-Li 8034 II 6940, Bl. 115; and Liese, *Volksschule*, 9, 13.

18. Franziska Ohnesorge, "Kriegsbücher," *Die Lehrerin* 34 (7 July 1917): 106; Margarete Treuge, "Kriegsaufsätze und Kriegsnovellen," *Die Lehrerin* 34 (18 August 1917): 153–154; Helma Riefenstahl, "Vier Jahre Kriegsarbeit im Verein kath. deutscher Lehrerinnen," *Monatsschrift für katholische Lehrerinnen* 32 (July 1918): 228 (first and second quotations); and Gertrud Mück, "Der Krieg im Unterricht," *Monatsschrift für katholische Lehrerinnen* 31 (June 1917): 258 (last quotation).

19. Korsch, *Kriegsstunden;* and "Aus dem Schul- und Lehrerleben," *Deutsches Lehrerblatt*, 4 November 1915, BA-Li 8034 II 6939, Bl. 22–23.

20. Karl Hessel, *Gedichte aus der Zeit des Weltkrieges: Ein Anhang zu deutschen Lesebüchern* (Bonn: Marcus & Weber, 1918), 70; and Alwin Wuensche, *Kriegslesebuch über den Krieg: Sammlung der besten Kriegserzählungen: Als Vorlesebuch für den Schulgebrauch* (Leipzig: Brandstetter, 1915–1917), 174–175.

21. On soldier automatons and cynical language, see Wilhelm Arminius, *Der Spion von Tannenberg* (Stuttgart: Levy & Müller, 1918); *U-Boot-Fahrten* (Berlin: Herman Hilger, 1918); "Deutsche Weihnachtsfeier vom französischen Schützengraben aus gesehen," *Gesundbrunnen* (1917): 47–49; and M. Trott, "Der Glocke letzte Fahrt," *Das Kränzchen* 30 (1918): 22–24. On heroism, adventure, and Hindenburg, see "Opfermut," *Der gute Kamerad* 32 (1917/18): 336; "Eine kühne Tat," *Der gute Kamerad* 32 (1917/18): 112; and "Ein mutiger Retter," *Das Kränzchen* 30 (1918): 321; Else Ury, "Hänschens Ritt zu Hindenburg," *Meidinger's Kinder-Kalender* 20 (1917): 18–28; "Hindenburgworte," *Jung-Siegfried* 16 (2 September 1917): 289 (quotation). On celebrated warships, see Woldemar Urban, *Die Kriegsfahrten der Emden: Erzählung für die Jugend* (Berlin: Union, 1917); Kühlwetter, "U Boot-Krieg und U Boot-Helden," *Scherls Jungdeutschlandbuch* 5 (1918): 93–96; Heinrich Liersemann, *Wir von der "Möwe"! Husarenstreiche zur See* (Leipzig: Fock, 1916); Karl August Nerger, *S.M.S Wolf* (Berlin: Scherf, 1918); "Wie sich die Engländer vor unseren Zeppelinen warnen lassen," *Der gute Kamerad* 32 (1917/18): 253–254; and Kurt Küchler, "Zur Heimat," *Die Helden von S 90 und andere Erzählungen aus dem Weltkrieg* (Cologne: Schaffstein, 1916).

22. "Herrgott in deine Hände," *Scherls Mädchenbuch* (1917): 312; Trude Bruns, "Luiserl," *Scherls Mädchenbuch* (1917): 229–267; Luise von Brandt, "Drei Augenblicksbilder," *Gesundbrunnen* (1917), 33–36; "Fürs Vaterland," *Kriegsblätter für unsere Jugend* 101 (8 January 1917): 808; M. Feesche, "Durchhalten," *Deutsche Mädchen-Zeitung* 49 (February 1917): 17; Else

Model, "Stundenschlag," *Deutscher Kinderfreund* 40 (August 1918): 121; and Hans Reinlein, "Kriegsruf," *Jugendblätter* (Munich) 63 (1916/17): 152.

23. "Die Papierknappheit," *Pädagogische Zeitung* 46 (29 November 1917): 609; and Martin Travers, *German Novels on the First World War and Their Ideological Implications, 1918–1933* (Stuttgart: H.-D. Heinz, 1982), 239–247.

24. Niederschriften über die Verhandlungen der Kreisschulkommissionen für Oberfranken," 12 December 1916, StaaMünch RA Nr. 53902, Bl. 4, 10–12; "Lichtbildvorträge für Schulen im Schumanntheater," *Frankfurter Schulzeitung* 34 (1 October 1917): 175–176; and the following in KPSK-Berichte Bd. II: "Das Schweigen in der Schule," *Deutsche Tageszeitung*, 9 October 1917, Bl. 7 (first quotation); Min. Ed., Berlin, 13 October 1917, Bl. 8; KPSK, Schleswig-Holstein, 6 January 1917, Bl. 116 (second quotation); and KPSK, Berlin, 15 February 1919, Bl. 283ff.

25. Schapler and Groeteken, *Kriegserlasse*, 48–49; and "Die Lehr- und Lernmittel für die Volksschulen," StdDüss III 2039.

26. On the mood of pupils, see KPSK, Coblenz, 6 December 1918, KPSK-Berichte Bd. II, Bl. 158 (first quotation); Köllnisches Gymnasium zu Berlin, *Zur Geschichte des köllnischen Gymnasiums während der Kriegsjähre Ostern, 1915 bis Ostern 1919: Jahresberichte*, 9 (second quotation), LABe STA Rep. 20–09 Nr. 29; and KPSK, Magdeburg, 30 January 1919, KPSK-Berichte Bd. II, Bl. 144ff (last quotation). For examples of final exams, see Sophien-Real-Gymnasium, LABe Außenstelle STA Rep. 20–10 Nr. 105; Städtisches Gymnasium in der Kreuzgasse, StdKöln Best. 562 Nr. 264; and *Kriegsreifeprüfung: Kriegsalltag, Kriegswirklichkeit und Kriegsende im Urteil Wiesbadener Schüler, 1914–1918*, ed. Markus Müller-Henning (Wiesbaden: Hessisches Hauptstaatsarchiv, 1996).

27. "Anerkennung für Lehrer und Schüler," *Schulblatt der Provinz Sachsen* 57 (25 October 1918): 343; and Meyer-Otto, "Berthold Otto-Schule," 77–78 (quotation).

10. Politicization and Repression

1. Schwarz, *Revolution in Nürnberg*, 131, 156; Dobson, *Upheaval in Leipzig*, 148–177; and Gerald Feldman, Eberhard Kolb, and Reinhard Rürup, "Die Massenbewegung der Arbeiterschaft in Deutschland am Ende des Ersten Weltkrieges (1917–1920)," *Politische Vierteljahresschrift* 13 (1972): 84–10.

2. "Um Leben, Ehre und Freiheit," *Düsseldorfer Tageblatt*, 12 October 1918, GStA I. HA Rep. 77 CB Reihe S Nr. 631, Bl. 73; Daniel, *Working-Class Women*, 127–129; and Reissig, "Lehrerseminare," 232.

3. Schepp, "Militärische Jugendorganization," *Vossische Zeitung*, 2 March 1915; War Min., Berlin, 5 August 1915, GStA I. HA Rep. 120 E I Spez. Fach I

Nr. 42 Bd. 4; and "Zersplitterung in der militärischen Jugendorganization," *Vossische Zeitung,* 5 October 1914.

4. Wermuth, Magistrat, Berlin, 3 March 1915, GStA I. HA Rep. 120 E I Spez. Fach I Nr. 42 Bd. 4; Report, DCG, Hanover, 22 December 1916, NHAH Hann. 122a Nr. 4490, Bl. 345; "Militärische Vorbereitung der Jugend," *Hamburger Nachrichten,* 8 February 1917, StHam 111–2 A II q 6; *Kriegs-Gedenkschrift des Andreas-Realgymnasiums,* 26; and Saul, "Jugend im Schatten," 103. A figure of comparison: There were fifty-seven thousand boys in municipal vocational schools in Berlin in 1914/15, and roughly half of these were age 16, 17. or 18. *Statistisches Jahrbuch der Stadt Berlin* 34 (1915–1919): 751–752.

5. "Aus dem Regierungsbezirke Düsseldorf für die Kriegsernte 1916 entsandten Erntekommandos," GStA I. HA Rep. 76. VI Sec. I. Gen. z: 242a Bd. I; and Broßmer, "Die fürsorglichen Grundlagen des freiwilligen Schülerhilfsdienstes," *Hamburgischer Correspondent,* 27 August 1918, in StHam 361–2 III Nr. 234, Bl. 78.

6. "Jungmannen in der Landwirtschaft," Min. Ed., Munich, 2 February 1918, BHStA Mk, Nr. 20585; "Landwirtschaftlicher Hilfsdienst der Schüler," Kaiser-Friedrich-Realgym., Neukölln, 10 August 1918, LABr Pr. Br. Rep. 34 Berlin I Nr. 1297; and the following in GStA I. HA Rep. 76. VI Sec. I. Gen. z: 242a Bd. I: "Bericht über . . . die Organisation der Jungmannen für die Landwirtschaft," War Office, Berlin, 26 September 1917; directives, KPSK, Berlin, 2 April 1917 and 3 July 1917; and reports by Platte, 20 April 1917 and 14 May 1917. See also in LABr Pr. Br. Rep. 34 Berlin I Nr. 1296: "Getäuschte Hoffnungen," *Tägliche Rundschau,* 14 October 1917; report of the War Office, Berlin, 10 November 1917; and internal memo, Kaiser-Friedrich-Realgym., Neukölln, 28 April 1918.

7. Johannes Zobel, *Schüler freiwillig in Grenzschutz und Freikorps* (Berlin: Fr. Grundel, 1932), 17, 19, and 24.

8. Ostler, "Soldatenspielerei?" 104–110, 168–177, 188–239.

9. Dobson, *Upheaval in Leipzig,* 172.

10. Kruse, *Burgfriedensschluss,* 224; Dieter Groh, *Negative Integration und revolutionärer Attentismus: Die deutsche Sozialdemokratie am Vorabend des Ersten Weltkrieges* (Frankfurt: Propyläen, 1973); Günther Roth, *The Social Democrats in Imperial Germany: A Study in Working Class Isolation and Negative Integration* (Totowa, NJ: Bedminster Press, 1963); Vernon Lidtke, *The Alternative Culture: Socialist Labor in Imperial Germany* (Oxford: Oxford University Press, 1985); Evans, "Red Wednesday"; Kinter, "Kinos," 136; Miller, *Burgfrieden,* 72; and Verhey, *Spirit of 1914,* 340–341.

11. Peter Braune, "Die verspätete Reichsschulkonferenz von 1920: Höhepunkt in der Karriere von Heinrich Schulz" (Ph.D. diss., Freie Universität Berlin, 2003), 120–121; and the following articles in *Arbeiter-Jugend:* "Jugendgenossen

und -Genossinnen!" 15 August 1914, 257; "An die Front, Kameraden," 12 September 1915, 281 (quotations); Friedrich Stampfer, "Ludwig Frank," 26 September 1914, 290–291; Heinrich Schulz, "Der Krieg als Erlebnis," 5 December 1914, 329–330; and K[arl Korn], "Der Wille zur Tapferkeit," 2 January 1915, 1–2.

12. Horst Ueberhorst, *Frisch, frei, stark und treu: Die Arbeitersportbewegung in Deutschland, 1893–1933* (Düsseldorf: Droste, 1973), 60–61, 65–69; and Schorske, *German Social Democracy*, 245.

13. Dehn, "Volksjugend," 14–15; Ullrich, *Hamburger Arbeiterbewegung*, 183–184; Sieger, *Arbeiterjugend*, 65–69; Volker Ullrich, *Kriegsalltag: Hamburg im Ersten Weltkrieg* (Köln: Prometh, 1982), 34 (first quotation); Korn, *Arbeiterjugendbewegung*, 289–292, 289 (second quotation); Schulz, "Proletarische Jugendbewegung," 437 (last quotations); Braune, "Reichsschulkonferenz," 123; Jahnke et al., *Arbeiterjugendbewegung*, 118; and von Jagow, Pol., Berlin, 9 February 1915, GStA I. HA Rep. 120 E I Spez. Fach I Nr. 42 Bd. 4.

14. Ludwig Turek, *Ein Prolet erzählt: Lebensschilderung eines deutschen Arbeiters* (Berlin: Dietz, 1947), 47–48; Korn, *Arbeiterjugendbewegung*, 273–274; and Miller, *Burgfrieden*, 95, 109, 191–195.

15. Korn, *Arbeiterjugendbewegung*, 280–286, 357, 375 (quotation); Zentralstelle für die arbeitende Jugend Deutschlands, *Proletarische Jugendbewegung in der Kriegszeit: Jahresbericht für die Zeit vom 1. April 1914 bis 31. März 1915* (Berlin: Ebert, 1915), 6–7; "In anderer Richtung?" *Jugend-Echo* 13 (August 1917): 97; and "Der Wille zur Organisation," *Jugend-Echo* 20 (March 1918), 154–155.

16. Eildermann, *Tagebücher*, 303; and "Die Magdeburger Jugendbewegung," *Jugend-Echo* 10 (May 1917): 74–75.

17. Neuland and Werner-Cordt, *Junge Garde*, 51–53 (first and second quotation); "Die Opposition," *Jugend-Echo* 3 (October 1916): 18–19 (last quotations); and "Aufbauen," *Jugend-Echo* 15 (October 1917): 113–114.

18. Zentralstelle für die arbeitende Jugend Deutschlands, *Proletarische Jugendbewegung in der Kriegszeit: Jahresbericht für die Zeit vom 1. April 1915 bis 31. März 1916* (Berlin: Ebert, 1916), 25; Schulz, "Proletarische Jugendbewegung," 534; "Der preußische Kultusminister und die Freie Jugendbewegung," *Fortbildungsschulpraxis* 11 (March 1917): 48–49; and the following copies of letters and reports in BHStA Mk Nr. 13963: Delbrück, Reichskanzlei, Berlin, 7 August 1914; Würrtemburgian Department of Transportation, Stuttgart, 5 December 1916; and Min. Transportation, Munich, 27 September 1916, 29 September 1917, and 13 November 1917.

19. Zentralstelle, *Jahresbericht*, (1915), 5–7, 16, 22; "Über die sozialdemokratische Jugendbewegung im Kriege," *Jugendführung* 4 (March 1917): 92–93; "Die deutsche Jugendbewegung zur Kriegszeit," *Jugend-Internationale* 3 (March 1916): 19–20; and Korn, *Arbeiterjugendbewegung*, 268–274, 264–265.

20. "Die 'Trennung,'" *Jugend-Echo* 27 (October 1918): 210–211; Neuland and Werner-Cordt, *Junge Garde*, 37; Magdalena Musial, "Jugendbewegung und Emanzipation der Frau: Ein Beitrag zur Rolle der weiblichen Jugend in der Jugendbewegung bis 1933" (Ph.D. diss., Universität Essen, 1982), 167–168; Korn, *Arbeiterjugendbewegung*, 277–278; and Eberts, *Arbeiterjugend*, 46, 135.

21. Linton, *Young Workers*, 119–120; and Fritz Globig, *Aber verbunden sind wir mächtig: Aus der Geschichte der Arbeiterjugendbewegung* ([East] Berlin: Neues Leben, 1958), 127.

22. McMeekin, *Münzenberg*, 12–27.

23. Willi Münzenberg, *Die dritte Front: Aufzeichnungen aus 15 Jahren proletarischer Jugendbewegung* (Frankfurt a.M.: LitPol, 1978), 150, 153 (quotations), 161–162, 195–196, 205–206; Manfred Stadelmaier, *Zwischen Langemarck und Liebknecht: Arbeiterjugend und Politik im I. Weltkrieg* (Bonn: Archiv der Arbeiterjugendbewegung, 1986), 69–72; McMeekin, *Münzenberg*, 28–32; and Jahnke et al., *Arbeiterjugendbewegung*, 113. Two standard works on the antiwar movements overlook the International Socialist Youth conference and the key role of youth more generally: F. L. Carsten, *War against War: British and German Radical Movements in the First World War* (Berkeley: University of California, 1982); and David Kirby, *War, Peace, and Revolution: International Socialism at the Crossroads, 1914–1918* (New York: St. Martin's, 1986).

24. Richard Schüller, *Von den Anfängen der proletarischen Jugendbewegung bis zur Gründung der KJI* (Berlin: Jugendinternationale, 1931), 101 (quotation); "Die proletarische Jugendbewegung in Deutschland," *Jugend-Internationale* 2 (December 1915): 12–13; *Jugend-Internationale: Die elf historischen Nummern der Kriegsausgabe* (Berlin: Internationaler Jugendverlag, 1921); McMeekin, *Münzenberg*, 38; Münzenberg, *Dritte Front*, 150, 154, 158, 200–202; and Sieger, *Arbeiterjugend*, 95–97.

25. "Die proletarische Jugendbewegung in Deutschland," *Jugend-Internationale* 2 (December 1915): 12–13; Globig, *Arbeiterjugendbewegung*, 133, 154–155, 172–174; Jahnke et al., *Arbeiterjugendbewegung*, 96; Eildermann, *Tagebücher*, 315; Korn, *Arbeiterjugendbewegung*, 365; Volker Ullrich, "Der Konflikt um den Hamburger Jugendbund 1916," *Jahrbuch des Archivs der deutschen Jugendbewegung* 14 (1982/83): 32–42, 35 (quotation); Ullrich, *Hamburger Arbeiterbewegung*, 179, 315–349; and "Der Skandal mit der Hamburger Arbeiterjugend," Pol., Düsseldorf, 7 April 1916, copy, NWHSA Reg. Düss. 16005, Bl. 362–369.

26. "Hamburger Arbeiterjugend;" and Alfred Nußbaum, "Die Erziehung der proletarischen Jugend," December 1915, NWHSA Reg. Düss. 16005, Bl. 392 (quotation).

27. Ottokar Luban, "Die Auswirkungen der Jenaer Jugendkonferenz 1916 und die Beziehung der Zentrale der revolutionären Arbeiterjugend zur Führung

der Spartakus-Gruppe," *Archiv für Sozialgeschichte* 11 (1971): 191–197, 202; Neuland and Werner-Cordt, *Junge Garde*, 43–48, 46–47 (first quotation); Korn, *Arbeiterjugendbewegung*, 351 (last quotation); Jahnke et al., *Arbeiterjugendbewegung*, 125–129; Münzenberg, *Jugendorganisation*, 123–126; Stadelmaier, *Arbeiterjugend*, 36; and Pol. and Oberbürgermeister to Reg. Präs., Düsseldorf, 11 August 1916, NWHSA Reg. Düss. 16005, Bl. 450.

28. Boll, *Massenbewegungen*, 217–235; Friedhelm Boll, "Spontaneität der Basis und politische Funktion des Streiks 1914–1918," *Archiv für Sozialgeschichte* 17 (1977): 353–358; and the manuscript, *Angriff gegen die Zentralstelle der arbeitenden Jugend* (n.p., 1916), 4–5, Staatsbibliothek Berlin Krieg 1914–24384.

29. Münzenberg, *Jugendorganisation*, 115–118, 123, 127; *Angriff gegen die Zentralstelle*, 2–3 (quotation); and Wolfgang Breithaupt, *Volksvergiftung 1914–1918* (Leipzig: K. F. Koehler, 1925), 62, 65.

30. DCG Altona, 28 August 1918, StHam 111–2 A II p Nr. 197, Bl. 6; and Ullrich, *Hamburger Arbeiterbewegung*, 326–349, 341 (quotation).

31. Pol., Essen, 10 February 1917, NWHSA Reg. Düss. 16005, Bl. 458–60.

32. Anonym., "Der 1. Mai in der Heimat," *Proletarische Lebensläufe: Autobiographische Dokumente zur Entstehung der Zweiten Kultur in Deutschland*, Vol. 2, ed. Wolfgang Emmerich (Hamburg: Rowolt, 1975), 149 (first quotation); "Eine Maidemonstration der Dresdener sozialistischen Jugend im dritten Kriegsjahr," *Jugend-Internationale* 10 (1 October 1917): 14 (middle quotations); Globig, *Arbeiterjugendbewegung*, 197–199; Stadelmaier, *Arbeiterjugend*, 87–89; Eildermann, *Tagebücher*, 327; Sieger, *Arbeiterjugend*, 140; Jahnke et al., *Arbeiterjugendbewegung*, 144; and Ullrich, *Hamburger Arbeiterbewegung*, 479–481, 479 (last quotation).

33. Luban, "Jenaer Jugendkonferenz," 205; "Kriegserlebnisse in Deutschland," *Jugend-Internationale* 6 (1 December 1916): 2–4; Pol., Düsseldorf, 10 February 1917, NWHSA Reg. Düss. 16005, Bl. 458–460; High Command, Berlin, 1 May 1917, copy, and War Min., Munich, 24 September 1917, both in BHStA Mk Nr. 13963; and Ullrich, *Hamburger Arbeiterbewegung*, 564 (quotation).

34. Heinrich Scheel, "Der Aprilstreik 1917 in Berlin," in *Revolutionäre Ereignisse und Probleme in Deutschland während der Periode der Großen Sozialistischen Oktoberrevolution, 1917–18*, ed. Albert Schreiner ([East] Berlin: Akademie, 1957); Dirk Müller, "Gewerkschaften, Arbeiterausschüße und Arbeiterrräte in der Berliner Kriegsindustrie, 1914–1918," in *Arbeiterschaft, 1914–1918 in Deutschland*, ed. Günther Mai (Düsseldorf: Droste, 1985), 174; Stadelmaier, *Arbeiterjugend*, 96; Henning to Min. Int., Berlin, 6 February 1918, and "Der Streik in Berlin," *Abendblatt Germania*, 30 January 1918, both in LABr, Pr. Br. Rep. 30 Berlin C. Tit. 95 Nr. 15840; and Globig, *Arbeiterjugendbewegung*, 232 (quotation).

35. Neuland and Werner-Cordt, *Junge Garde,* 48; Bezirksamt, Wunsiedel, 7 November 1917, BHStA Mk Nr. 13963; Schwarz, 14 January 1917, GStA I. HA Rep. 77 Titel 421, No. 45, Bl. 33–35; and Molenaar, Darmstadt, 2 September 1917, BHStA MKr Nr. 12650.

36. Gudrun Fiedler, *Jugend im Krieg: Bürgerliche Jugendbewegung, Erster Weltkrieg und sozialer Wandel, 1914–1923* (Köln: Wissenschaft und Politik, 1989), 35–43, 71–76; Rudolf Kneip, *Wandervogel ohne Legende: Die Geschichte eines pädagogischen Phänomens* (Heidenhim a.d. Brenz: Südmarkverlag Fritz KG, 1984), 129; Laqueur, *German Youth Movement,* 87–88; Willibald, *Jugend,* 130–135, 130 (first quotation); contributions to *Wandervogel* (July 1915): 24, 27, 28, 110, 197–198, 275; Pross, *Jugend, Eros, Politik,* 75–86, 184; Otto Neuloh and Wilhelm Zilius, *Die Wandervögel: Eine empirisch-soziologische Untersuchung der frühen deutschen Jugendbewegung* (Göttingen: Vandenhoeck & Ruprecht, 1982), 154–155; Arnold Bergstraesser, "Ruf der Gefallenen," in *Die Wandervogelzeit: Quellenschriften zur deutschen Jugendbewegung, 1896–1919,* ed. Werner Kindt (Düsseldorf: Eugen Diederichs, 1968), 810–812; and Gerhard Ille, "Wandervogel-Ideale und Kriegsrealität—die Steglitzer Wandervögel im Ersten Weltkrieg," in *Wandervogel,* ed. Ille and Köhler, 152–156, 157 (last quotation), 174. On students more generally, see Konrad Jarausch, "German Students in the First World War," *Central European History* 17 (1984): 310–329.

37. Willibald, *Jugend,* 136–139; Laqueur, *German Youth Movement,* 94–95; Kneip, *Wandervögel,* 129–130, 133; Willibald, *Jugend:* 138; Fritz Kruse, "Zur Frage der Verjüngerung," *Wandervogel* (October 1915) in *Wandervogelzeit,* ed. Kindt, 818 (quotation); Hedwig Rokicki, "Bericht des Bundeszählamtes, 1917," *Wandervogel* (March 1918): 71; and contributions to the "Girl's Issue" of *Wandervogel* (January–February 1918).

38. Kneip, *Wandervogel,* 136 (first quotation); Ille, "Wandervogel-Ideale," 175–177; Fiedler, *Jugend im Krieg,* 32; Borinski and Werner, *Jugendbewegung,* 14; and the following in *Wandervogelzeit,* ed. Kindt: Gerhard Weisser, "Zukunftsland," 808 (second quotation); Heinz Villeneuve, "Zur Frage der Verjüngerung," 816–817; Erich Mohr, "Zur Frage der Verjüngerung," 819–823; "Wir fordern," 829–830; and Otto Schaaf, "Zur Älteren-Frage," 836.

39. Fiedler, *Jugend im Krieg,* 76–95, 85 (quotation); Willibald, *Jugend,* 140–141; and "Leitsätze über die Stellung des Wandervogels zur Jugendwehr," in *Wandervogelzeit,* ed. Kindt, 141–142.

40. Laqueur, *German Youth Movement,* 90–92, 94, 104–107; Fiedler, *Jugend im Krieg,* 116–125, 149, 166–167; Pross, *Jugend, Eros, Politik,* 191–193; "Ein Flugblatt zur Nationalversammlung" in *Wandervogelzeit,* ed. Kindt, 848–851; and Otger Gräf, "Stimmen aus Österreich," *Wandervogel* (March–April 1917): 79.

41. Breithaupt, *Volksvergiftung*, 51–57; and Globig, *Arbieterjugendbewegung*, 137.
42. Pross, *Jugend, Eros, Politik*, 193–194; Fiedler, *Jugend im Krieg*, 95–100, 127–130, 140–142, 148–149; August Messer, *Die freideutsche Jugendbewegung: Ihr Verlauf von 1913 bis 1918* (Langensalza: H. Beyer, 1919), 37, 47–49; Willibald, *Jugend*, 138; Schenk, *Freideutsche Jugend*, 87–90; and the following in *Freideutsche Jugend* (January–February, 1917): Gerhard Fils, "Politische Erziehung der Jugend," 1–7; Gehrad Weißer, "Über die Notwendigkeit und das Wesen der Konsumgenossenschaften," 21–29; and Max Hodann, "Freideutsche Jugend und Politik," 35–39.
43. Messer, Freideutsche Jugendbewegung, 56; Laqueur, *German Youth Movement*, 96, 101–103; Ernst Joël, "Der soziale Bourgeois," *Der Aufbruch: Monatsblätter aus der Jugendbewegung* (October 1915): 73–86; Borinski and Werner, *Jugendbewegung*, 14; Knud Ahlborn, "Erwiderung," *Freideutsche Jugend* (January–February 1917), 40 (first and second quotations); Pross, *Jugend, Eros, Politik*, 195–196; Ille, "Wandervogel-Ideale," 190 (third quotation); Schenk, *Freideutsche Jugend*, 102 (second- and third-to-last quotations); and Fiedler, *Jugend im Krieg*, 101–116, 139 (last quotation), 144.

Conclusion

1. Karl Mannheim, "The Problem of Generations," in *Essays on the Sociology of Knowledge* (New York: Oxford University Press, 1952); Roper, "Youth in Weimar Novels"; Vondung, "Jugendrevolte"; and Elizabeth Harvey, "The Failure of Feminism? Young Women and the Bourgeois Feminist Movement in Weimar Germany, 1918–1933," *Central European History* 28 (1995): 1–28. On the alienation and radicalism of the war youth generation after 1918 more generally, see Leopold Dingräve, *Wo steht die junge Generation?* (Jena: Diederichs, 1931), 17–21, 30–31; Gründel, *Generation*, 31–43, 81–83, 219–230, 267–269; Elizabeth Domansky, "Politische Dimensionen von Jugendprotest und Generationskonflikt in der Zwischenkriegszeit in Deutschland," in *Jugendprotest und Generationskonflikt in Europa im 20. Jahrhundert*, ed. Dieter Dowe (Bonn: Neue Gesellschaft, 1986); Irmtraud Götz von Olenhusen, "Die Krise der jungen Generation und der Aufstieg des Nationalsozialismus: Eine Analyse der Jugendorganisationen der Weimarer Zeit," in *"Neue Erziehung"—"Neue Menschen": Ansätze zur Erziehungs- und Bildungsreform in Deutschland zwischen Kaiserreich und Diktatur*, ed. Ulrich Hermann (Weinheim: Beltz, 1987); and the contributions by Hans Mommsen, Joachim Schmitt-Sasse, Joachim Radkau, Karl Prümm, in *Mythos Jugend*, ed. Koebner, Janz, and Trommler.
2. Bölling, *Volksschullehrer*, 126–129, 227–228; Lamberti, *School Reform in Weimar Germany*, 60–61, 106–122, 133–143, 245–246; Flitner, *Krieg und die Jugend*, 316–320; and Becker and Kluchert, *Bildung der Nation*, 206–262.

3. Christoph Fuhr, "Die Schulpolitik," in *Bildungsreform,* ed. Hermann; Lamberti, *School Reform in Weimar Germany,* 115–116, 143, 196–209; Flitner, *Krieg und die Jugend,* 320–326; Franz Führen, *Lehrer im Krieg: Ein Ehrenbuch deutscher Volksschullehrer* (Leipzig: Georg Kummer, 1936); and Kater, *Hitler Youth,* 40–43.

4. Martin Geyer, *Verkehrte Welt: Revolution, Inflation und Moderne: München, 1914–1924* (Göttingen: Vandenhoeck & Ruprecht, 1998), 70; Reissig, "Lehrerseminare," 338; Schumann, *Politische Gewalt,* 67–68; Eve Rosenhaft, "Organising the 'Lumpenproletariate:' Cliques and Communists in Berlin during the Weimar Republic," in *German Working Class,* ed. Evans; Eve Rosenhaft, "Compulsory Savings Plans," 101; Peukert, "Wilde Cliquen"; Elizabeth Harvey, "Weg von der Straße? Die Hamburger Volks- und Berufschulen und die Jugendarbeitslosigkeit, 1918–1933," in *Der Traum von der freien Schule: Schule und Schulpolitik in Hamburg während der Weimarer Republik,* ed. Hans-Peter de Lorent and Volker Ullrich (Hamburg: Ergebnisse, 1988), 179–180; and Larry Eugene Jones, "German Liberalism and the Alienation of the Younger Generation," in *In Search of a Liberal Germany: Studies in the History of German Liberalism from 1789 to the Present,* ed. Konrad Jarausch and Larry Eugene Jones (New York: Berg, 1990).

5. Felix Raabe, *Die bündische Jugend: Ein Beitrag zur Geschichte der Weimarer Republik* (Stuttgart: Brentano, 1961); Reulecke, "Männerbund"; Michael Kater, "Jugendbewegung und Hitlerjugend in der Weimarer Republik," in *Bildungsreform,* ed. Hermann; and James Diehl, *Paramilitary Politics in Weimar Germany* (Bloomington: Indiana University Press, 1977), 63–64, 171–173.

6. Ute Frevert, *"Mann und Weib, und Weib und Mann": Geschlechter-Differenzen in der Moderne* (Munich: C. H. Beck, 1995), 144–150; Thomas Rohkrämer, "Das Militär als Männerbund? Kult der soldatischen Männlichkeit im Deutschen Kaiserreich," *Westfälische Forschung* 45 (1995): 180, 187; Frevert, *Nation in Barracks,* 178; Frevert, *Duel,* 216, 223–224; McAleer, *Cult of Honor,* 157; Peter Gay, *The Cultivation of Hatred,* vol. 3, *The Bourgeois Experience: Victoria to Freud* (New York: W. W. Norton, 1993), 103 (quotation); Evans, "'Red Wednesday'"; and Linse, "'Animierkneipen.'" See also Sonya Rose, *Limited Livelihoods: Gender and Class in Nineteenth Century Britain* (Berkeley: University of California Press, 1993), 127–153.

7. Ute Frevert, "Nation, Krieg und Geschlecht im 19. Jahrhundert," in *Nation und Gesellschaft in Deutschland,* ed. Manfred Hettling and Paul Nolte (Munich: Beck, 1996), 158, 161; Geyer, *Verkehrte Welt,* 75; and Mosse, *Fallen Soldiers,* 132–134, 166, 186.

8. "Weibliches Dienstjahr," *Frauenbildung* 15 (1916): 115–117; and Charlotte Stein-Pick, *Meine verlorene Heimat* (Bamberg: Bayerische, 1992), 17–18.

9. Dietrich, *Marlene,* 22.

10. "Die 'Trennung,'" *Jugend-Echo* 27 (1 October 1918): 210–211; "Farbrikpflegerinnen und Jungfrauenvereine," *Arbeiter-Jugend,* 20 April 1918; *Proletarische Jugendbewegung in der Kriegszeit,* 6–7; Korn, *Arbeiterjugendbewegung,* 277–278; Münzenberg, *Jugendorganisation,* 115–117, 128–130; Willi Bohn, *Einer von vielen: Ein Leben für Frieden und Freiheit* (Frankfurt am Main: Verlag Marxistische Blätter, 1981), 22; Pol., Düsseldorf, 13 June 1916, NWHSA Reg. Düss. 16005, Bl. 407–412; and Hermann Weber and Andreas Herbest, *Deutsche Kommunisten: Biographisches Handbuch, 1918 bis 1945* (Berlin: Dietz, 2004), 249, 645

11. Ernst Glaeser, *Frieden* (Berlin: Gustav Kiepenheuer, 1930), 166–167; Hans Ostwald, *Sittengeschichte der Inflation: Ein Kulturdokument aus den Jahren des Marktsturzes* (Berlin: Neufeld und Henius, 1931), 147–149, 195–196; Reissig, "Lehrerseminare," 335; Frevert, *Women in German History,* 186; Harvey, "Failure of Feminism"; Elizabeth Harvey, "Serving the Volk, Saving the Nation: Women in the Youth Movement and the Public Sphere in Weimar Germany," in *Elections, Mass Politics, and Social Change in Modern Germany,* ed. Larry Eugene Jones and James Retallack (New York: Cambridge University Press, 1992); Helen Boak, "Women in Weimar Germany: The 'Frauenfrage' and the Female Vote," in *Social Change and Political Development in Weimar Germany,* ed. Richard Bessel and E. J. Feuchtwanger (Totowa, NJ: Barnes and Noble, 1981); and Julia Sneeringer, *Winning Women's Votes: Propaganda and Politics in Weimar Germany* (Chapel Hill: University of North Carolina Press, 2002).

12. Bohn, *Ein Leben,* 20–26; Oskar Hippe, *And Red Is the Colour of Our Flag: Memories of Sixty Years in the Workers' Movement,* trans. Andrew Drummond (London: Index, 1991), 1–24; and "Die Spartakus-Jugend auf der Straße," *Der Tag,* 16 December 1918.

13. Schumann, *Politische Gewalt,* 139–142, quotation on 142; Weber, *Stalinisierung,* 26–27, 68, 76–77, 86, 144, 213, 291, 311; Wienand Kaasch, "Die soziale Struktur der Kommunistischen Partei Deutschlands," *Die Kommunistische Internationale* 19 (1928): 1051; and Eve Rosenhaft, *Beating the Fascists? The German Communists and Political Violence, 1929–1933* (New York: Cambridge University Press, 1983), 158, 166, 193–196.

14. Fiedler, *Jugend im Krieg,* 153–155, 161–164; Schenk, *Freideutsche Jugend,* 110–111; and Laqueur, *German Youth Movement,* 111–113.

15. Laqueur, *German Youth Movement,* 108–110; Fiedler, *Jugend im Krieg,* 167–170; Ille, "Wandervogel-Ideale," 182; Else Frobenius, *Mit uns zieht die neue Zeit: Eine Geschichte der deutschen Jugendbewegung* (Berlin: Deutsche, 1927), 204–205; Michael Kater, "Die Artamanen: Völkische Jugendbewegung in der Weimarer Republik," *Historische Zeitschrift* 213 (1971): 577–638; and Neuloh and Zilius, *Die Wandervögel,* 157.

16. On the non-Nazi paramilitaries, see Schulze, *Freikorps,* 48, 51; Diehl, *Paramilitary Politics,* 63–64, 171–173; and Hertha Siemering, *Die Deutschen*

Jugendverbände: Ihre Ziele, ihre Organisation sowie ihre neuere Entwicklung und Tätigkeit (Berlin: C. Heymann, 1931), 32–50. On the Nazi Party, see Gerth, "Nazi Party"; Michael Kater, *The Nazi Party: A Social Profile of Members and Leaders, 1919–1945* (Cambridge, MA: Harvard University Press, 1983), 140–146; Michael Kater, "Generationskonflikt als Entwicklungsfaktor in der NS-Bewegung vor 1933," *Geschichte und Gesellschaft* 11 (1985), 232–233; and Jürgen Falter, "The Young Membership of the NSDAP between 1925 and 1933: A Demographic and Social Profile," in *The Rise of National Socialism and the Working Classes in Weimar Germany,* ed. Conan Fischer (Providence, RI: Berghahn, 1996), 83. On the SA, see Richard Bessel, *Political Violence and the Rise of Nazism: The Storm Troopers in Eastern Germany, 1925–1934* (New Haven, CT: Yale University Press, 1984), 33–45; and Conan Fischer, *Stormtroopers: A Social, Economic, and Ideological Analysis, 1929–1935* (Boston: George Allen & Unwin, 1983), 48–50. On Italy, see Jens Petersen, "Jugend und Jugendprotest im faschistischen Italien," in *Generationskonflikt,* ed. Dowe, 199–200; and Sven Reichardt, *Faschistische Kampfbünde: Gewalt und Gemeinschaft im italienischen Squadrismus und in der deutschen SA* (Cologne: Böhlau, 2002), 346–348.

17. Frevert, *Nation in Barracks,* 180; Laqueur, *German Youth Movement,* 101–109; Fiedler, *Jugend im Krieg,* 116–126; Bernd Rusinick, "Krieg als Sehnsucht: Militärischer Stil und 'junge Generation' in der Weimarer Republik," in *Generationalität und Lebensgeschichte im 20. Jahrhundert,* ed. Jürgen Reulecke (Munich: Oldenbourg, 2003); Ulrich Herbert, "Ideological legitimization and Political Practice of the Leadership of the National Socialist Secret Police," in *The Third Reich between Vision and Reality: New Perspectives on German History, 1918–1945,* ed. Hans Mommsen (Oxford: Berg, 2000), 98–100; and Richard Bessel, *Germany after the First World War* (New York: Clarendon, 1995), 259, 273. A widely cited but methodologically problematic argument is in Loewenberg, "Nazi Youth Cohort." Of the ten school compositions by boys mentioning peace that I located, only one called for a negotiated peace; the other nine wanted an end to the war by military force. See, for example, "Wie wir Lembergs Eroberung in der Klasse feierten," *Jugendliches Seelenleben,* ed. Stern, 177–178. On the doctrine of the *Siegfriede,* see Isabel Hull, *Absolute Destruction: Military Culture and the Practices of War in Imperial Germany* (Ithaca, NY: Cornell University Press, 2005), 160–161, 291.

18. Ziemann, *War Experiences,* 91, 216; Jochen von Lang, *The Secretary: Martin Bormann, the Man Who Manipulated Hitler* (New York: Random House, 1979), 20; Rudolph Höss, *Death Dealer: The Memoirs of the SS Kommandant of Auschwitz,* ed. Steven Paskuly (Buffalo, NY: Prometheus, 1992), 54–55; *Kindheit im Kaiserreich,* ed. Pörtner, 109, 134; and Brecht, *Erinnerungen,* 280.

19. Director, Helmholtz-Realgymnasium, Berlin-Schöneberg, 1 November 1918, LABr Pr. Br. Rep. 34 Berlin I Nr. 921 (first quotation); Ulrich Herbert, *Best: Biographische Studien über Radikalismus, Weltanschauung und Vernunft, 1903–1989* (Bonn: J.H.W. Dietz, 1996), 45–48; Werner Angress and Bradley Smith, "Diaries of Heinrich Himmler's Early Years," *Journal of Modern History* 31 (1959): 207; Richard Breitman, *The Architect of Genocide: Himmler and the Final Solution* (New York: Knopf, 1991), 12; Peter Padfield, *Himmler: Reichsführer-SS* (London: Macmillan, 1990), 27–31; Martin Matthiessen, *Erinnerungen* (Meldorf: Evers, 1980), 37 (second quotation); Ernst von Salomon, *The Captive,* trans. James Kirkump (London: Weidenfeld and Nicolson, 1961), 10, 17 (block quotation); and Markus Josef Klein, *Ernst von Salomon: Eine politische Biographie* (Limburg a.d. Lahn: San Casciano, 1994), 38 (last quotation).

20. See in HIA-TAC nos. 48 (first quotation) in box 1; nos. 62, 101 (second quotation), 103, and 120 in box 2; and nos. 183, 197, and 211 in box 3. For how Theodore Abel got the autobiographies, see his *Why Hitler Came into Power* (New York: Prentice Hall, 1938), 2–4; and his diary entries from 28 June 1934, 3 July 1934, and 17 December 1935, boxes 13 and 14, HIA-TAC. On the autobiographies of those born 1900 to 1908, see also Merkl, *Political Violence,* 28, 149–153, 238–239, 270–282, 302–304.

21. Michael Wildt and Karin Orth argue that an age-specific war experience partly explains why 60 percent of the SS leadership after 1939 was born between 1900 and 1910. Wildt, *Generation des Unbedingten: Das Führungs-korps des Reichssicherheitshauptamtes* (Hamburg: Hamburger Edition, 2002), 848–849; and Orth, *Die Konzentrationslager-SS: Sozialstrukturelle Analysen und biographische Studien* (Göttingen: Wallstein, 2000), 74–76, 103, 105–107, 165.

Bibliography

Archives

Archiv des Diakonischen Werkes des evangelischen Kirchenbund Deutschlands (ADW)
Bayerisches Hauptstaatsarchiv Munich (BHStA)
Bayerisches Kriegsarchiv Munich (BKrA)
Bayerisches Staatsarchiv Munich (StaaMünch)
Bildarchiv Preussischer Kulturbesitz (BApKb)
Bundesarchiv, Berlin-Lichterfelde (BA-Li)
Hessisches Hauptstaatsarchiv Wiesbaden (HessHA)
Hoover Institution Archives, Theodore Abel Collection (HIA-TAC)
Landesarchiv Berlin (LABe)
Landesarchiv Brandenburg Potsdam (LABr)
Niedersächsisches Hauptstaatsarchiv Hanover (NHAH)
Nordrhein-Westfalen Hauptstaatsarchiv Düsseldorf (NWHSA)
Preußisches Geheimes Staatsarchiv Berlin (GStA)
Staatsarchiv Hamburg (StHam)
Stadtarchiv Darmstadt (StdDarm)
Stadtarchiv Düsseldorf (StdDüss)
Stadtarchiv Hanover (StHan)
Stadtarchiv Köln (StdKöln)
Stadtarchiv Mainz (StdMainz)
Stadtarchiv Munich (StdMünch)

Periodicals Published before 1919

Allgemeines Schulblatt
Arbeiter-Jugend

Archiv für Volksschullehrer

Badische Schulzeitung

Das humanistische Gymnasium

Das Kränzchen

Der Aufbruch: Monatsblätter aus der Jugendbewegung

Der Gemeindehelfer

Der gute Kamerad

Der Jugendgarten

Der Volksschullehrer

Deutsche Blätter für erziehenden Unterricht

Deutsche Mädchen-Zeitung

Deutsche Strafrechts-Zeitung

Deutscher Kinderfreund

Deutsches Philologen Blatt

Die deutsche Fortbildungsschule

Die höhere Mädchenschule

Die Innere Mission im evangelischen Deutschland

Die Jugendfürsorge

Die Lehrerin

Die ostdeutsche Fortbildungsschule

Die Praxis der Landschule

Erziehung und Unterricht

Fortbildungsschulpraxis

Frankfurter Schulzeitung

Frauenbildung

Freideutsche Jugend

Freie Bayerische Schulzeitung

Für die Kinderwelt

Gesundbrunnen

Hamburgische Schulzeitung

Hannoversche Schulzeitung

Haus und Schule

Jahresberichte über das höhere Schulwesen

Jugendblätter

Jugend-Echo

Jugendführung

Jugend-Internationale

Jugendpflege im Regierungsbezirk Cöln

Jugendschriften-Warte

Jung-Siegfried

Katholische Schulzeitung für Norddeutschland

Katholische Zeitschrift für Erziehung und Unterricht

Krieg und Sieg

Kriegsblätter für unsere Jugend

Lehrer-Zeitung für Ost- und Westpreußen

Leipziger Lehrerzeitung

Leipziger Zeitschrift für deutsches Recht

Mädchenpost

Meidinger's Kinder-Kalender

Mitteilung der Landeszentralstelle für Jugendpflege im Herzogtum Anhalt

Monatsschrift für höhere Schulen

Monatsschrift für katholische Lehrerinnen

Naussische Schulzeitung

Neue deutsche Bilderbögen

Neuer deutscher Jugendfreund

Pädagogische Zeitung

Preußische Volksschullehrerinnen-Zeitung

Ratgeber für Jugendvereinigungen

Scherls Jungdeutschlandbuch

Scherls Jungmädchenbuch

Schulblatt der Provinz Sachsen

Statistisches Jahrbuch der deutschen Städte

Statistisches Jahrbuch der Stadt Berlin

Statistisches Jahrbuch für den preußischen Staat

Vorwärts

Vossische Zeitung

Wandervogel

Zeitschrift für die gesamte Strafrechtswissenschaft

Zeitschrift für Jugendhilfe

Zentralblatt der christlichen Gewerkschaften Deutschlands

Zentralblatt für die gesamte Unterrichtsverwaltung in Preußen

Zentralblatt für Vormundschaftswesen, Jugendgericht und Fürsorgeerziehung

Selected Books and Articles

Albisetti, James. *Schooling German Girls and Women: Secondary and Higher Education in the Nineteenth Century.* Princeton, NJ: Princeton University Press, 1988.

Albisetti, James. *Secondary School Reform in Imperial Germany.* Princeton, NJ: Princeton University Press, 1983.

Alexander, Thomas *The Prussian Elementary Schools.* New York: Macmillan, 1918.

Arbeitsgruppe "Lehrer und Krieg," ed. *Lehrer helfen siegen: Kriegspädagogik im Kaiserreich.* Berlin: Diesterweg, 1987.

Audoin-Rouzeau, Stéphane. *La guerre des enfants, 1914–1918.* Paris: Armand, 1993.

Audoin-Rouzeau, Stéphane, and Dominque Congar, eds. *L'enfant Yves Congar: Journal de la Guerre, 1914–1918.* Paris: Cerf, 1997.

Aufmuth, Ulrich. *Die deutsche Wandervogelbewegung unter soziologischem Aspekt.* Göttingen: Vandenhoeck & Ruprecht, 1979.

Becker, Helmut, and Gerhard Kluchert. *Die Bildung der Nation. Schule, Gesellschaft und Politik vom Kaiserreich zur Weimarer Republik.* Stuttgart: Klett-Cotta Verlag, 1993.

Bendele, Ulrich. *Krieg, Kopf und Körper: Lernen für das Leben—Erziehung zum Tod.* Frankfurt, a.M.: Ullstein, 1984.

Bendick, Rainer. *Kriegserwartung und Kriegserfahrung: Der Erste Weltkrieg in deutschen und französischen Schulgeschichtsbüchern 1900–1939 / 45).* Paffenweiler: Centaurus, 1999.

Benninghaus, Christina. *Die anderen Jugendlichen: Arbeitermädchen in der Weimarer Republik.* Frankfurt a.M.: Campus, 1999.

Berg, Christa, ed. *Handbuch der deutschen Bildungsgeschichte.* Vol. 4. *1870–1918.* Munich: C. H. Beck, 1991.

Boll, Friedhelm. *Massenbewegungen in Niedersachsen, 1906–1920.* Bonn: Neue Gesellschaft, 1981.

Bölling, Rainer. *Sozialgeschichte der deutschen Lehrer.* Göttingen: Vandenhoeck & Ruprecht, 1983.

Bölling, Rainer. *Volksschullehrer und Politik: Der Deutsche Lehrerverein 1918–1933.* Göttingen: Vandenhoeck & Ruprecht, 1978.

Braune, Peter. "Die verspätete Reichsschulkonferenz von 1920: Höhepunkt in der Karriere von Heinrich Schulz." Ph.D. diss., Freie Universität Berlin, 2003.

Breithaupt, Wolfgang. *Volksvergiftung, 1914–1918.* Leipzig: K. F. Koehler, 1925.

Buchner, Ernst [Eduard Mayer]. *1914–1918: Wie es damals daheim war: Das Kriegstagebuch eines Knaben.* Leipzig: Die neue Zeit, 1930.

Budde, Gunilla-Friederike. *Auf dem Weg ins Bürgerleben: Kindheit und Erziehung in deutschen und englischen Bürgerfamilien, 1840–1914.* Göttingen: Vandenhoeck & Ruprecht, 1994.

Chickering, Roger. *The Great War and Urban Life in Germany.* New York: Cambridge University Press, 2007.

Childs, Michael. *Labour's Apprentices: Working-Class Lads in Late Victorian and Edwardian England.* Montreal: McGill-Queen's University Press, 1992.

Christadler, Marieluise. *Kriegserziehung im Jugendbuch: Literarische Mobilmachung in Deutschland und Frankreich vor 1914.* Frankfurt: Haag-Herchen, 1979.

Conrad, Claus. *Krieg und Aufsatzunterricht: Eine Untersuchung von Abituraufsätzen vor und während des Ersten Weltkrieges.* Frankfurt a.M.: Peter Lang, 1986.

Crubellier, Maurice. *L'Enfance et la jeunesse dans la société française, 1800–1950.* Paris: Armand Colin, 1979.

Daniel, Ute. *The War from Within: German Working-Class Women in the First World War.* New York: Berg, 1997.

Davis, Belinda. *Home Fires Burning: Food, Politics, and Everyday Life in World War I Berlin.* Chapel Hill: University of North Carolina, 2000.

Dehn, Günther. *Großstadtjugend: Beobachtungen und Erfahrungen aus der Welt der großstädtischen Arbeiterjugend.* Berlin: Carl Heymann, 1922.

Demm, Eberhard. "Deutschlands Kinder im Ersten Weltkrieg: Zwischen Propaganda und Sozialfürsorge." *Militärgeschichtliche Zeitschrift* 60 (2001): 51–98.

Dickinson, Edward Ross. "Citizenship, Vocational Training, and Recreation: Continuation Schooling and the Prussian 'Youth Cultivation' Decree of 1911." *European History Quarterly* 29 (1999): 109–147.

Dickinson, Edward Ross. *The Politics of German Child Welfare from the Empire to the Federal Republic.* Cambridge, MA: Harvard University Press, 1996.

Dobson, Sean. *Authority and Upheaval in Leipzig, 1910–1920.* New York: Columbia University Press, 2000.

Dowe, Dieter, ed. *Jugendprotest und Generationskonflikt in Europa im 20. Jahrhundert.* Bonn: Neue Gesellschaft, 1986.

Dudek, Peter. *Jugend als Objekt der Wissenschaft: Geschichte der Jugendforschung in Deutschland und Österreich, 1890–1933.* Opladen: Westdeutscher, 1990.

Duensing, Frieda, ed. *Handbuch für Jugendpflege.* Langensalza: Hermann Beyer & Söhne, 1913.

Eberts, Erich. *Arbeiterjugend, 1904–1945: Sozialistische Erziehungsgemeinschaft— Politische Organisation.* Frankfurt a.M.: dipa, 1979.

Eildermann, Wilhelm. *Jugend im ersten Weltkrieg: Tagebücher, Briefe, Erinnerungen.* [East] Berlin: Dietz, 1972.

Emmerich, Wolfgang, ed. *Proletarische Lebensläufe: Autobiographische Dokumente zur Entstehung der Zweiten Kultur in Deutschland.* Vol. 2. Hamburg: Rowolt, 1975.

Emminger, Eckhard. "'Und der ganze Unterricht muss auf die große Uhr des Weltkrieges eingestellt werden!' Die Auswirkungen des Ersten Weltkrieges auf die Volksschule im Königreich Bayern 1914 bis 1918." Ph.D. diss., Augsburg University, 1988.

Engel, Max. *Leipzigs Volksschulen im Zeichen des Welkrieges: Auf Grund von Einzel- berichten und unter Mitarbeit von Lehrern und Direktoren.* Leipzig: Dürr, 1915.

Fahn, Karolina. *Der Wandel des Aufsatzbegriffes in der deutschen Volksschule von 1900 bis zur Gegenwart.* Munich: Oldenbourg, 1971.

Fiedler, Gudrun. *Jugend im Krieg: Bürgerliche Jugendbewegung, Erster Weltkrieg und sozialer Wandel, 1914–1923.* Köln: Wissenschaft und Politik, 1989.

Flitner, Wilhelm. *Der Krieg und die Jugend.* New Haven, CT: Deutsche Verlags- Anstalt, 1927.

Floerke, Hans, ed. *Die Kinder und der Krieg: Aussprüche, Taten, Opfer und Bilder.* Munich: G. Müller, 1915.

Foerster, Friedrich Wilhelm. *Die deutsche Jugend und der Weltkrieg: Kriegs- und Friedensaufsätze.* Leipzig: Naturwissenschaft, 1916.

Frank, Horst Joachim. *Geschichte des Deutschunterrichts: Von den Anfängen bis 1945.* Munich: C. Hanser, 1973.

Fröhlich, Arthur, ed. *Aus eiserner Zeit: Freie Kriegsaufsätze von Meeraner Kindern.* Leipzig: Wunderlich, 1915.

Ganaway, Bryan. *Toys, Consumption, and Middle-Class Childhood in Imperial Germany, 1871–1918.* New York: Peter Lang, 2009.

Geyer, Martin. *Verkehrte Welt: Revolution, Inflation und Moderne: München, 1914–1924.* Göttingen: Vandenhoeck & Ruprecht, 1998.

Gillis, John. *Youth and History: Tradition and Change in European Age Relations, 1770 to the Present.* New York: Academic, 1974.

Gläser, Ernst. *Class of 1902.* New York: Viking, 1929.

Globig, Fritz. *Aber verbunden sind wir mächtig: Aus der Geschichte der Arbeiterjugendbewegung.* [East] Berlin: Neues Leben, 1958.

Hämmerle, Christa, ed. *Kindheit im Ersten Weltkrieg.* Wien: Böhlau, 1993.

Harp, Stephen. *Learning to Be Loyal: Primary Schooling as Nation Building in Alsace and Lorraine, 1850–1940.* Dekalb: Northern Illinois University Press, 1998.

Harvey, Elizabeth. *Youth and the Welfare State in Weimar Germany.* Oxford: Clarendon Press, 1993.

Hasenclever, Christa. *Jugendhilfe und Jugendgesetzgebung seit 1900.* Göttingen: Vandenhoeck und Ruprecht, 1978.

Häußner, Josef. *Der Weltkrieg und die höheren Schulen Badens im Schuljahr, 1914–1915.* Karlruhe: Gutsch, 1915.

Healy, Maureen. *Vienna and the Fall of the Habsburg Empire: Total War and Everyday Life in World War I.* New York: Cambridge University Press, 2004.

Hendrick, Harry. *Images of Youth, Age and Class and the Male Youth Problem.* New York: Oxford University Press, 1990.

Hermann, Ulrich, ed. *"Neue Erziehung"—"Neue Menschen": Ansätze zur Erziehungs- und Bildungsreform in Deutschland zwischen Kaiserreich und Diktatur.* Weinheim: Beltz, 1987.

Humphries, Stephen. *Hooligans or Rebels? An Oral History of Working-Class Childhood and Youth, 1889–1939.* Oxford: Basil Blackwell, 1981.

Ille, Gerhard, and Günter Köhler, eds. *Der Wandervogel.* Berlin: Stapp, 1987.

Jahnke, Karl Heinz, Rudolf Falkenberg, Bernd Ferchland, Werner Lamprecht, Horst Pietschmann, and Siegfried Scholze. *Geschichte der deutschen Arbeiterjugendbewegung, 1904–1945.* [East] Berlin: Neues Leben, 1973.

Jannel, Walther. *Kriegspädagogik: Berichte und Vorschläge.* Leipzig: Akademische Verlagsgesellschaft, 1916.

Karstädt, Otto, ed. *Kinderaug' und Kinderaufsatz im Weltkrieg.* Osterwieck: Zickfeldt, 1916.

Kett, Joseph. *Rites of Passage: Adolescence in America 1790 to the Present.* New York: Basic Books, 1977.

Kift, Dagmar, ed. *Kirmes-Kneipe-Kino: Arbeiterkultur im Ruhrgebiet zwischen Kommerz und Kontrolle (1850–1914).* Paderborn: Ferdinand Schönigh, 1992.

Kindt, Werner, ed. *Die Wandervogelzeit: Quellenschriften zur deutschen Jugendbewegung, 1896–1919.* Düsseldorf: Eugen Diederichs, 1968.

Kneip, Rudolf. *Wandervogel ohne Legende: Die Geschichte eines pädagogischen Phänomens.* Heidenhim a.d. Brenz: Südmarkverlag Fritz KG, 1984.

Koebner, Thomas, Rolf-Peter Janz, and Frank Trommler, eds. *"Mit uns zieht die neue Zeit": Der Mythos Jugend.* Frankfurt a.M.: Suhrkamp, 1985.

Korn, Karl. *Die Arbeiterjugendbewegung: Eine Einführung in ihre Geschichte.* Berlin: Arbeiterjugend, 1922.

Kruse, Wolfgang. *Krieg und nationale Integration: Eine Neuinterpretation des sozialdemokratischen Burgfriedensschlusses 1914/15.* Essen: Klartext, 1994.

Lamberti, Marjorie. "Elementary School Teachers and the Struggle against Social Democracy in Wilhelmine Germany." *History of Education Quarterly* 32 (1992): 73–97.

Lamberti, Marjorie. "Radical Schoolteachers and the Origins of the Progressive Education Movement in Germany, 1900–1914." *History of Education Quarterly* 40 (2000): 22–48.

Lamberti, Marjorie. *The Politics of Education: Teachers and School Reform in Weimar Germany.* New York: Berghahn, 2002.

Langewiesche, Dieter, and Heinz-Elmar Tenorth, eds. *Handbuch der deutschen Bildungsgeschichte,* Vol. 5. *1918–1945.* Munich: C. H. Beck, 1989.

Laqueur, Walter. *Young Germany: A History of the German Youth Movement.* London: Routledge & Kegan Paul, 1962.

Learned, William. *An American Teacher's Year in a Prussian Gymnasium.* New York: Carnegie Foundation, 1911.

Lemmermann, Heinz. *Kriegserziehung im Kaiserreich: Studien zur politischen Funktion von Schule und Schulmusik 1890–1918.* Lilienthal: Eres Edition, 1984.

Lexis, Wilhelm, ed. *Das Unterrichtswesen im Deutschen Reich.* Vols. 1–4. Berlin A. Asher, 1904.

Linton, Derek. *"Who Has the Youth Has the Future": The Campaign to Save Young Workers in Imperial Germany.* New York: Cambridge University Press, 1991.

Linton, Derek. "Between School and Marriage, Workshop and Household: Young Working Women as a Social Problem in Late Imperial Germany." *European History Quarterly* 18 (1988): 387–408.

Lobsien, Max. *Unsre Zwölfjährigen und der Krieg.* Leipzig: Säemann-Schriften, 1916.

Loewenberg, Peter. "The Psychohistorical Origins of the Nazi Youth Cohort." *American Historical Review* 76 (1971): 1457–1502.

Luban, Ottokar. "Die Auswirkungen der Jenaer Jugendkonferenz 1916 und die Beziehung der Zentrale der revolutionären Arbeiterjugend zur Führung der Spartakus-Gruppe." *Archiv für Sozialgeschichte* 11 (1971): 185–223.

Ludwig, Otto. *Der Schulaufsatz: Seine Geschichte in Deutschland.* Berlin: Walter de Gruyter, 1988.

Maynes, Mary Jo. *Taking the Hard Road: Life Course in the French and German Workers' Autobiographies in the Era of Industrialization.* Chapel Hill: University of North Carolina Press, 1995.

McMeekin, Sean. *The Red Millionaire: A Political Biography of Willi Münzenberg, Moscow's Secret Propaganda Tsar in the West.* New Haven, CT: Yale University Press, 2003.

Merkl, Peter. *Political Violence under the Swastika: 581 Early Nazis.* Princeton, NJ: Princeton University Press, 1975.

Mihaly, Jo [Piete Kuhr]. *Da gibt's ein Wiedersehen! Kriegstagebuch eines Mädchens, 1914–1918.* Freiburg: Kerle, 1982. Translated as *There We'll Meet Again: A Young German Girl's Diary of the First World War.* Gloucester: Walter Wright, 1998.

Miller, Susanne. *Burgfrieden und Klassenkampf: Die deutsche Sozialdemokratie im Ersten Weltkrieg.* Düsseldorf: Droste, 1974.

Mitterauer, Michael. *A History of Youth.* Oxford: Blackwell, 1992.

Müller, Wilhelm, ed. *Wie Deutschlands Jugend den Weltkrieg erlebt.* Berlin: Mitteldeutsche, 1918.

Müller-Henning, Markus, ed. *Kriegsreifeprüfung: Kriegsalltag, Kriegswirklichkeit und Kriegsende im Urteil Wiesbadener Schüler, 1914–1918.* Wiesbaden: Hessisches Hauptstaatsarchiv, 1996.

Münzenberg, Willi [Wilhelm]. *Die dritte Front: Aufzeichnungen aus 15 Jahren proletarischer Jugendbewegung.* Frankfurt a.M.: LitPol, 1978.

Münzenberg, Wilhelm. *Die sozialistischen Jugendorganisationen vor und während des Krieges.* Berlin: Junge Garde, 1919.

Muth, Heinrich. "Jugendpflege und Politik: Zur Jugend- und Innenpolitik des Kaiserreichs." *Geschichte in Wissenschaft und Unterricht* 12 (1961): 597–619.

Neubauer, John. *The Fin-De-Siècle Culture of Adolescence.* New Haven, CT: Yale University, 1992.

Neuland, Franz, and Albrecht Werner-Cordt, ed. *Junge Garde: Arbeiterjugendbewegung in Frankfurt am Main 1904–1945.* Gießen: Anabas, 1980.

Neuloh, Otto, and Wilhelm Zilius. *Die Wandervögel: Eine empirisch-soziologische Untersuchung der frühen deutschen Jugendbewegung.* Göttingen: Vandenhoeck & Ruprecht, 1982.

Oelkers, Jürgen. *Reformpädagogik: Eine kritische Dogmengeschichte.* Weinheim: Juventa Verlag, 1989.

Olson, James. "The Prussian Volksschule: A Study of the Social Implications of the Extension of Elementary Education." Ph.D. diss., New York University, 1971.

Ostler, Hans Jürgen. "'Soldatenspielerei?' Vormilitärische Ausbildung bei Jugendlichen in der österreichischen Reichshälfte der Donaumonarchie, 1914–1918." M.A. thesis, Hamburg University, 1990.

Ozouf, Jacques and Mona Ozouf. "Le thème due patriotisme dans les manuels primaires." *Le mouvement social* 49 (1964): 5–31.

Parker, David. "'Talent at Its Command': The First World War and the Vocational Aspect of Education, 1914–1939." *History of Education Quarterly* 35 (1995): 237–259.

Paulsen, Friedrich. *German Education: Past and Present.* London: T. Fisher Unwin, 1908.

Peukert, Detlev. *Grenzen der Sozialdisziplinierung: Aufstieg und Krise der deutschen Jugendfürsorge von 1878 bis 1932.* Köln: Bund, 1986.

Peukert, Detlev. *Jugend zwischen Krieg und Krise: Lebenswelten von Arbeiterjungen in der Weimarer Republik.* Köln: Bund, 1987.

Pörtner, Rudolf, ed. *Kindheit im Kaiserreich: Errinerungen an vergangene Zeiten.* Düsseldorf: Deutscher Taschenbuchverlag, 1987.

Pross, Harry. *Jugend, Eros, Politik: Die Geschichte der deutschen Jugendverbände.* Bern: Scherz, 1964.

Reagin, Nancy. *A German Women's Movement: Class and Gender in Hanover, 1880–1933.* Chapel Hill: University of North Carolina Press, 1995.

Reich, Hermann, ed. *Das Buch Michael: Mit Kriegsaufsätzen, Tagebuchblättern, Gedichten, Zeichnungen aus Deutschlands Schulen.* Berlin: Weidmann, 1918.

Reiniger, Max, ed. *Der Weltkrieg im persönlichen Ausdruck der Kinder: 150 Schüler-kriegsaufsätze.* Langensalza: Beltz, 1915.

Reissig, Harald. "Die Lehrerseminare in Preußen im Ersten Weltkrieg." Ph.D. diss., Freie Universität, Berlin, 1987.

Reulecke, Jürgen. "Bürgerliche Sozialreformer und Arbeiterjugend im Kaiserreich." *Archiv für Sozialgeschichte* 22 (1982): 299–329.

Rosenbaum, Heidi. *Formen der Familie: Untersuchungen zum Zusammenhang von Familienverhältnissen, Sozialstruktur und sozialem Wandel in der deutschen Gesellschaft des 19. Jahrhunderts.* Frankfurt a.M.: Suhrkamp, 1982.

Rosenbaum, Heidi. *Proletarische Familien: Arbeiterfamilien und Arbeiterväter im frühen 20. Jahrhundert zwischen traditioneller, sozialdemokratischer und klein-bürgerlicher Orientierung.* Frankfurt a.M.: Suhrkamp, 1992.

Samuleit, Paul. *Wie unsere Jugend den Krieg erlebt.* Berlin: Sigismund, 1917.

Saul, Klaus. "Der Kampf um die Jugend zwischen Volksschule und Kaserne: Ein Beitrag zur 'Jugendpflege' im Wilhelminischen Reich, 1890–1914." *Militärge-schichtliche Mitteilung* 9 (1971): 97–160.

Saul, Klaus. "Jugend im Schatten des Krieges: Dokumentation." *Militärgeschichtliche Mitteilung* 34 (1983): 91–184.

Saupe, Emil. *Deutsche Pädagogen der Neuzeit.* Osterwieck am Harz: Zickfeldt, 1927.

Schach, Max, ed. *Das Kind und der Krieg: Kinderaussprüche, Aufsätze und Zeichnungen.* Berlin: G. Müller, 1916.

Schapler, Julius, and Friedrich Groeteken, ed. *Kriegserlasse für die preußische Volksschule.* Arnsberg: Stahl, 1918.

Scheibe, Wolfgang. *Die reformpädagogische Bewegung (1900–1932).* Weinheim: Beltz, 1974.

Schenk, Dietmar. *Die Freideutsche Jugend, 1913–1919/20: Eine Jugendbewegung in Krieg, Revolution und Krise.* Münster: Lit, 1991.

Scholze, Siegfried. "Karl Liebknecht und die Jenaer Jugendkonferenz Ostern 1916." *Zeitschrift für Geschichtswissenschaft* 19 (1971): 1016–1033.

Schorske, Carl. *German Social Democracy, 1905–1917: The Development of the Great Schism.* New York: Russel & Russel, 1955.

Schubert-Weller, Christoph. *"Kein schönerer Tod . . .": Die Militarisierung der männlichen Jugend und ihr Einsatz im Ersten Weltkrieg, 1890–1918.* Munich: Juventa, 1998.

Schwabe, Klaus. *Wissenschaft und Kriegsmoral: Die deutschen Hochschullehrer und die politischen Grundlagen des ersten Weltkrieges.* Göttingen: Musterschmidt, 1969.

Siegel, Mona. *The Moral Disarmament of France: Education, Pacifism, and Patriotism, 1914–1940.* New York: Cambridge University Press, 2004.

Sieger, Walter. *Junge Front: Die revolutionäre Arbeiterjugend im Kampf gegen den Ersten Weltkrieg.* [East] Berlin: Neues Leben, 1958.

Siemering, Hertha, ed. *Jugendpflegeverbände.* Berlin: Carl Heymanns, 1918.

Sienknecht, Helmut. *Der Einheitsschulegedanke.* Berlin: Beltz, 1968.

Springhall, John. *Coming of Age: Adolescence in Britain, 1860–1960.* Dublin: Gill and Macmillan, 1986.

Stachura, Peter. *The German Youth Movement, 1900–1945: An Interpretative and Documentary History.* New York: St. Martin's, 1981

Stadelmaier, Manfred. *Zwischen Langemarck und Liebknecht: Arbeiterjugend und Politik im I. Weltkrieg.* Bonn: Archiv der Arbeiterjugendbewegung, 1986.

Stern, William, ed. *Jugendliches Seelenleben und Krieg.* Leipzig: Barth, 1915.

Tirado, Isabel. *Young Guard! The Communist Youth League, Petrograd, 1917–1920.* Westport, CT: Greenwood, 1988.

Ullrich, Volker. "Der Konflikt um den Hamburger Jugendbund 1916." *Jahrbuch des Archivs der deutschen Jugendbewegung* 14 (1982/83): 29–46.

Ullrich, Volker. *Die Hamburger Arbeiterbewegung am Vorabend des Ersten Weltkrieges bis zur Revolution, 1918/19.* Hamburg: Ludke, 1976.

Verhey, Jeffrey. *The Spirit of 1914: Militarism, Myth and Mobilization in Germany.* New York: Cambridge University Press, 2000.

Wall, Richard, and Jay Winter, eds. *Upheaval of War: Family, Work and Welfare in Europe, 1914–1918.* New York: Cambridge University Press, 1988.

Weber, Bernd. *Pädagogik und Politik vom Kaiserreich zum Faschismus: Zur Analyse politischer Optionen von Pädagogikhochschullehrern von 1914–1933.* Königstein/Ts.: Scriptor, 1979.

Wegs, Robert. *Growing Up Working Class: Continuity and Change among Viennese Youth, 1890–1938.* University Park: Pennsylvania State University Press, 1989.

Wild, Reiner, ed. *Geschichte der deutschen Kinder- und Jugendliteratur.* Stuttgart: J. B. Metzler, 2002.

Willibald, Karl. *Jugend, Gesellschaft und Politik im Zeitraum des Ersten Weltkrieges.* Munich: Neue Schriftsreihe, 1973.

Winter, Jay, and Jean-Louis Robert, eds. *Capital Cities at War: Paris, London, Berlin, 1914–1919.* 2 vols. New York: Cambridge University Press, 1997, 2007.

Wittig, Kurt. *Der Einfluß des Krieges und der Revolution auf die Kriminalität der Jugendlichen.* Langensalza: Hermann Beyer & Söhne, 1921.

Zahra, Tara. *Kidnapped Souls: National Indifference and the Battle for Children in the Bohemian Lands, 1900–1948.* Ithaca, NY: Cornell University Press, 2008.

Zentralinstitut für Erziehung und Unterricht. *Schule und Krieg: Sonderausstellung.* Berlin: Weidmann, 1915.

Ziemann, Benjamin. *War Experiences in Rural Germany, 1914–1923.* New York: Berg, 2007.

Index